ANTHOLOGY OF WORLD SCRIPTURES: EASTERN RELIGIONS

ANTHOLOGY OF WORLD SCRIPTURES: EASTERN RELIGIONS

Robert E. Van Voorst

Western Theological Seminary

WADSWORTH
CENGAGE Learning™

Australia • Brazil • Japan • Korea • Mexico • Singapore • Spain • United Kingdom • United States

Anthology of World Scriptures: Eastern Religions
Robert E. Van Voorst

Publisher: Holly J. Allen

Acquisitions Editor: Steve Wainwright

Assistant Editor: Barbara Hillaker

Editorial Assistant: Gina Kessler

Technology Project Manager: Julie Aguilar

Marketing Manager: Worth Hawes

Marketing Assistant: Alexandra Tran

Marketing Communications Manager: Stacey
   Purviance

Project Manager, Editorial Production:
   Megan E. Hansen

Creative Director: Rob Hugel

Executive Art Director: Maria Epes

Print Buyer: Doreen Suruki

Permissions Editor: Roberta Broyer

Production Service: Aaron Downey, Matrix
   Productions, Inc.

Copy Editor: Patricia Herbst

Cover Designer: Hatty Lee

Cover Image: © Getty Images. LAMAYURU
   MONASTERY, LADAKH, INDIA by Andrea
   Pistolesi

Compositor: International Typesetting
   and Composition

For product information and technology assistance, contact us at
Cengage Learning Customer & Sales Support, 1-800-354-9706

For permission to use material from this text or product,
submit all requests online at **www.cengage.com/permissions**
Further permissions questions can be emailed to
permissionrequest@cengage.com

Library of Congress Control Number: 2005933304

ISBN-13: 978-0-495-17060-0

ISBN-10: 0-495-17060-7

Wadsworth
10 Davis Drive
Belmont, CA 94002
USA

Cengage Learning is a leading provider of customized learning solutions with
office locations around the globe, including Singapore, the United Kingdom,
Australia, Mexico, Brazil, and Japan. Locate your local office at
www.cengage.com/global

Cengage Learning products are represented in Canada by
Nelson Education, Ltd.

To learn more about Wadsworth, visit **www.cengage.com/wadsworth**

Purchase any of our products at your local college store or at our preferred
online store **www.ichapters.com**

Printed in the United States of America
2 3 4 5 6   22 21 20 19 18

To My Students, Past and Present,
in New York, Pennsylvania, Oxford, and Holland

Contents

CHAPTER FOUR
Jainism   129

CHAPTER FIVE
Sikhism   147

CHAPTER SIX
Confucianism   165

CHAPTER SEVEN
Taoism   195

CHAPTER EIGHT
Shinto   221

Preface

The major living religions of Asia have expressed their teachings and practices in writing. Over the course of time, some of these writings gained unique standing and became scriptures. As scriptures, they continue to influence the course of their religions. To read them is to encounter Eastern religions in a direct and meaningful way.

My *Anthology of World Scriptures: Eastern Religions* is intended to facilitate that encounter for the general reader and especially for the student of Eastern religion. Its pages contain the most notable and instructive holy writings of Hinduism, Buddhism, Jainism, Sikhism, Confucianism, Taoism, and Shinto. The collection began with my efforts to gather the most important passages of world scripture for my students, organize them in a way helpful for teaching and learning, and include the pedagogical aids that students have come to expect. This anthology not only presents scripture readings but also sets them in the context of their application in the religions themselves, taking into account recent scholarship on the role of scriptures in religion. Moreover, it does this in one volume and in one format. Designed to be used as a secondary textbook, the anthology has an organization that is easily adaptable to a range of primary textbooks and to most of the current methods of teaching comparative religion.

In the first chapter I examine the phenomenon of scripture in the world's religions, its nature, use, and place in modern scholarship, with a particular focus on Eastern religions. Each subsequent chapter presents the scripture of a single religion and is organized as follows: vignettes about scripture and its usage, intended to stir readers' interest and imagination, open each chapter. An introduction establishes the context in an overview of the use, structure, origin, and development of the scripture in its religion. Scripture passages in the first grouping concern the history of the religion, especially the founder (if any) and early history of the religion. The second grouping covers main doctrinal teachings, including divine or ultimate reality, creation and the environment, human nature, and human fulfillment. The third grouping deals with ethical systems, both personal and social; topics such as war and peace, justice, and the role of women are anthologized as fully as possible here. Passages in the fourth grouping focus on organization—the ways in which the religion orders itself and seeks to order its wider culture. The fifth grouping includes worship, devotion, ritual, and meditation. (Because Shinto recognizes no book as officially authoritative and has no canon, I use a different format to deal with its holy books.) In most chapters a final section, "Later Developments of Scriptural Themes," shows some of the subsequent understanding and use of scriptures. For each chapter I provide many pedagogical aids, such as headnotes for every passage, annotations (placed at the bottom of the page) to explain difficult terms and concepts in the readings, a brief treatment of how scriptures of most religions are treated in Hollywood films, questions for study and discussion, a glossary with pronunciations, and suggestions for further reading.

The scriptures presented in this anthology come from the religions commonly understood to be the major living world religions in Asia. By "world religion," scholars generally mean those religions that have had an impact on the world's leading cultures, not necessarily religions that are spread throughout the world. By "Asia" or "Eastern," scholars typically mean the "Far East," not the Asian continent as a whole, which includes the "Near East" in which Judaism, Christianity, and Islam were born and still have a strong presence.

I am very grateful for the strong reception that the fifth edition of my *Anthology of World Scriptures* has received. I trust that this volume on Eastern scriptures will also stimulate readers to explore the world of religion. Finally, once again this book gives me the happy opportunity to express my deep gratitude to my wife, Mary, and our two sons, Richard and Nicholas, for all their love and support.

Acknowledgments

The editorial staff at Wadsworth have been fine partners in developing and producing this book. I especially want to thank religion editor Steve Wainwright and assistant editor Barbara Hillaker. Aaron Downey of Matrix Productions and my copyeditor Pat Herbst also did excellent work for this book.

Scholars at numerous institutions offered detailed, insightful critiques at many points along the way. I thank those who reviewed the content of these chapters as it appears in *Anthology of World Scriptures* and in *Anthology of Asian Scriptures:* David W. Aiken, Ferris State University; Vivodh J. Z. Anand, Montclair State University; Paul Bernadicou, University of San Francisco; Anne Birdwhistell, Richard Stockton College of New Jersey; James Cook, Oakland Community College, Orchard Ridge; Dell deChant, University of South Florida; Marianne Ferguson, Buffalo State College; Roger Keller, Brigham Young University; Richard Mahon, Riverside Community College; William K. Mahony, Davidson College; Michael McKale, Saint Francis College; Anne Monius, University of Virginia; Vivian-Lee Nyitray, University of California at Riverside; Patrick S. O'Donnell, Santa Barbara City College; Richard Penaskovic, Auburn University; Christopher Queen, Harvard University; Stephen J. Reno, Southern Oregon State College; Philip Riley, Santa Clara University; Roger L. Schmidt, San Bernardino Valley College; Philip Schmitz, Eastern Michigan University; Daniel Sheridan, Loyola University of New Orleans; Robert Smith, Trenton State College; Gail Hinich Sutherland, Louisiana State University; Donald Swearer, Swarthmore College; James Whitehill, Stephens College; Boyd Wilson, Hope College; and Glenn Yocum, Whittier College. For their helpful review of the current book, I thank Guy L. Beck, Tulane University; Thomas Burns, University of Oklahoma; Jennifer G. Jesse, Truman State University; Bryan Polk, Pennsylvania State University, Abington; and Joseph Schaller, Nazareth College.

All those people made this a better book, and any errors that remain are mine alone. I would be most grateful if users of this book and its Wadsworth website resources would send me comments and suggestions for improvements. You can reach me at my postal address (Western Theological Seminary, 101 East 13th Street, Holland, MI 49423-3622) or by e-mail (bob.vanvoorst@westernsem.edu).

CHAPTER ONE

Eastern Scripture among the World's Religions

❖ In an Indian city, Hindu priests and Sanskrit-language scholars call a news conference to criticize a song, "Shanti," in an album by the American pop singer Madonna. Unlike most religious critiques of rock music, which focus on a supposed lack of moral values, the Hindus' criticisms focus on Madonna's pronunciation of that ancient divine name. Reflecting Hindu spoken use of scripture, the priests and scholars state that the spiritual power of this name is not effective unless it is pronounced correctly.

❖ In New York City, the government of Taiwan takes out a large, expensive advertisement in the *New York Times*. It argues that Taiwan is an orderly, virtuous, and industrious society because it is founded on the principles of Confucius' *Analects* and *Great Learning,* the key texts of Confucian scripture. Therefore, the advertisement says, Taiwan is an excellent partner in international trade. The value of Confucian morals is not lost on mainland China, either. As communist social values lose their grip on society, Confucian ethics are being reintroduced in schools and civic organizations.

❖ In London, a Sikh family gathers at the dining room table for devotional reading of the *Adi Granth*. Because the *Adi Granth* itself is an enormous book, they read from an anthology called the *Gutka*. The adults take turns reading, and everyone pays reverent attention to the words. This daily event is one of the main building blocks of faith and family solidarity among observant Sikhs.

The influence of Eastern scripture is felt throughout the world in ways both extraordinary and commonplace. Not all contemporary examples of scripture usage are as dramatic or controversial as these sketches suggest. They do indicate, though, that the scriptures of Asia's religions have a continuing profound impact on life and culture. This anthology introduces these scriptures and encourages a deep encounter with them in all their variety. Scriptures of Asia are so vast in number— Max Müller's *Sacred Books of the East*[1] series had fifty volumes when it was finished in 1910, and its coverage of Asian scripture was still far from complete—that some sort of sampling is necessary for all but the most expert specialist. This anthology thus offers excerpts from each tradition that faithfully reflect the history and continuing life of the tradition.

---

[1] F. Max Müller, gen. ed., *The Sacred Books of the East,* 50 vols. (Oxford: Oxford University Press, 1879–1910; reprinted in 1969 in India, with some volumes still in print).

A BRIEF HISTORY OF SCRIPTURE SCHOLARSHIP

In the last 150 years, the scholarly study of world scriptures has passed through three distinct stages that have strongly influenced how we read Asian scriptures.[2] In the first stage, at the middle of the nineteenth century, European scholars began a vast enterprise of making critically reliable translations. They focused on the little-translated sacred literature of Asia. Their concern was to translate individual texts, not to examine the general religious features of scripture. They treated scripture as a mine out of which to dig the history and doctrine of religions, with little regard for the ways scripture functioned in religious communities. Müller's *Sacred Books of the East* series is the most prominent result of this first stage.[3]

The academic movement known as the "History of Religions school" dominated the second stage in the study of scriptures. This school, which continues to exert a strong influence today, analyzes the historical development of each religion. Perhaps in reaction to the earlier methodological reliance on world scriptures, scholars like Joachim Wach and Mircea Eliade relied on the study of ritual, myth, symbols, and other nontextual elements of religion. Scripture, both Eastern and Western, was largely neglected at this stage. Such a respected treatment of comparative religion as Gerardus van der Leeuw's *Religion in Essence and Manifestation* contains only a brief discussion of scripture as a feature of religion.[4] Also, as social science methods increasingly entered the field of religious scholarship, researchers turned away from studying literary sources from the past in favor of the study of present-day living communities of faith.[5]

Although this second stage is still very influential, a third stage is emerging in which scholars are rediscovering the value of scripture. The overreliance on scripture characteristic of the first stage and the neglect of scripture in the second stage are being balanced as scholars increasingly view scripture as an important feature among the religions of the world. Now scripture is correctly seen as one religious facet

---

[2] For an excellent comprehensive discussion of the history of the academic study of world religions, with some detailed comments on scripture study, see E. Sharpe, *Comparative Religion: A History,* 2d ed. (LaSalle, IL: Open Court Press, 1987). Perhaps the best succinct presentation of this topic is by S. Cain, "History of the Study of Religion," in M. Eliade, ed., *Encyclopedia of Religion* (New York: Macmillan, 1987), vol. 14, pp. 64–83.

[3] A continuing feature of this first stage is a number of popular anthologies of scriptures that use Asian scriptures as a mine for enlightenment and pay little attention to how scripture functions in world religious communities. For example, Robert Ballou's *The Bible of the World* (New York: Viking, 1939) and its abridgment in *World Bible* (New York: Viking, 1944) have remained in print continually, although never revised. The Unification Church has published *World Scripture: A Comparative Anthology of Sacred Texts,* ed. Andrew Wilson (New York: Paragon House, 1991). Philip Novak has edited *The World's Wisdom: Sacred Texts of the World's Religions* (San Francisco: HarperSanFrancisco, 1994).

[4] Gerardus van der Leeuw, *Religion in Essence and Manifestation* (London: Allen & Unwin, 1938; German original, 1933). One short chapter, 64, deals almost exclusively with Western scripture.

[5] For example, the widely used *Reader in Comparative Religion: An Anthropological Approach,* ed. W. A. Lessa and E. Z. Vogt, 4th ed. (New York: Harper & Row, 1997), has excellent readings in all the basic topics in the cultural-anthropological study of religion—symbol, myth, ritual, shamanism, magic—but not one essay on scripture and its uses.

among many and therefore not to be isolated from the others. Another new element is an emphasis on the particular ways in which scripture is viewed and used in Asian religions. To understand scripture, according to this view, we must know not just the scriptural text but also how it comes alive in the total life of the religion.

Recent research gives evidence of this emerging third stage. Large-scale studies such as Geo Widengren's *Phenomenology of Religion* and Friedrich Heiler's *Manifestations and Essence of Religion* deal extensively with the nature and use of scripture among the world's religions.[6] Ninian Smart's *Sacred Texts of the World* uses scripture to approach several different religious phenomena in each world religion.[7] Five recent books deal with scripture and its role in religion, including Asian religions: *The Holy Book in Comparative Perspective,* by Frederick Denny and Roderick Taylor; *Sacred Word and Sacred Text,* by Harold Coward; *Rethinking Scripture: Essays from a Comparative Perspective,* by Miriam Levering; *Sacred Texts and Authority,* by Jacob Neusner; and *What Is Scripture? A Comparative Approach,* by Wilfred Cantwell Smith.[8] As a result of this research, the comparative study of scripture is today one of the leading features in the study of world religions. Smith, of Harvard University, and some of his students have had a strong influence on current scripture study. They argue for scripture study centered on the actual reception and use of scriptures. The work of William Graham on the oral dimensions of scripture has been especially influential.[9] A measure of the strength of this stage is that it is now appearing in textbooks, where several works are notable.[10] As a representative of this third stage of scripture study, the present work offers a wide range of scripture selections from the religions of Asia, with introductions and annotations to set the readings in the context of their actual usage.

THE NATURE AND DEFINITION OF SCRIPTURE

At first glance, defining scripture seems easy enough. We think of scripture as the holy writing, the sacred text of a religion. All religions of the world seem to have scriptures, and all appear to use them in the same way. As a phenomenon among religions, scripture

---

[6] Geo Widengren, *Religionsphänomenologie* (Berlin: de Gruyter, 1969); Friedrich Heiler, *Erscheinungsformen und Wesen der Religion,* 2d ed. (Stuttgart: Kohlhammer, 1979).

[7] Ninian Smart, *Sacred Texts of the World* (London: Macmillan, 1982).

[8] F. M. Denny and R. L. Taylor, eds., *The Holy Book in Comparative Perspective* (Columbia: University of South Carolina Press, 1985); Harold Coward, *Sacred Word and Sacred Text* (Maryknoll, NY: Orbis, 1988); Miriam Levering, ed., *Rethinking Scripture* (Albany: State University of New York Press, 1989); Jacob Neusner, ed., *Sacred Texts and Authority* (Cleveland: Pilgrim, 1998); Wilfred Cantwell Smith, *What Is Scripture? A Comparative Approach* (Philadelphia: Augsburg Fortress, 1993).

[9] See especially William Graham's *Beyond the Written Word: Oral Aspects of Scripture in the History of Religion* (Cambridge: Cambridge University Press, 1983).

[10] T. W. Hall, R. B. Pilgrim, and R. R. Cavanagh, *Religion: An Introduction* (San Francisco: Harper & Row, 1985); Kenneth Kramer, *World Scriptures: An Introduction to Comparative Religion* (New York: Paulist, 1986); Roger Schmidt, *Exploring Religion,* 2d ed. (Belmont, CA: Wadsworth, 1988); Jean Holm and John Bower, *Sacred Writings* (London: Pinter, 1994); Richard Viladesau and Mark Massa, *World Religions: A Sourcebook for the Student of Christian Theology* (New York: Paulist, 1994); Ian S. Markham, ed., *A World Religions Reader,* 2d ed. (Oxford: Blackwell, 2000).

seems on the surface to be a constant. On closer examination, however, these simple notions vanish.

Books that are traditionally regarded as scriptures vary in several important aspects. The first variation among scriptures is in *literary form*. People who come from religious traditions that include scriptures naturally tend to assume that the sacred texts of other religions look more or less like theirs. Scriptures, however, are as varied as the religions and cultures from which they come:

❖ Some scriptures feature **narratives,** the telling of an event in story form.

❖ Some scriptures enshrine their religion's vision of a moral life in law codes, some feature more loosely bound moral precepts, and still others do not seem concerned about ethics.

❖ Poetry is the leading literary form of some scriptures; others feature prose.

❖ Some scriptural books have metaphysical philosophy (for example, the Hindu *Upanishads*), others have moral philosophy (the Confucian *Analects*), but many have no explicit philosophy at all.

❖ Some scriptures contain directions and songs for sacrifice (the Hindu *Vedas*), whereas others have no prescriptions for rites and ceremonies (the *Analects*).

❖ Also present in scriptures are myth, legend, prophecy, sermons, love poems, divination, and magic, among many other **genres,** or literary forms.

Even this brief overview shows that scriptures do not take a fixed literary form. Therefore, we cannot open any Asian book, browse through it, and pronounce it scriptural. Scripturalness is primarily a relational, not a literary, quality. As William Graham has written, the holiness of a book is not automatically accepted when the text is first written, but it is "realized historically in the life of communities who respond to it as something sacred or holy."[11] Communities shape and receive scripture, and scripture shapes the life of faith. The relation between scripture and religion is reciprocal and dynamic.

The second variation among scriptures has to do with their *number*. In Asian religions, they range in number from one book (the *Adi Granth* of Sikhism, albeit a huge book!), to the dozen or so texts of Confucianism, to the hundred or more texts of Hinduism, to the more than a thousand texts of Taoism and some forms of Buddhism. In general, Asian scripture canons have a much larger number of books than do Western scripture canons.

The third variation in scriptures lies in *function*. In some religions, scripture is so central—or seems so to outsiders—that the lives of all devout believers seem almost dictated by scripture. Among all world religions, Zoroastrianism, Judaism, Christianity, Islam, and Sikhism are all properly called "religions of the book" because of the high place and powerful function of their scriptures. In contrast, *lay* devotees of most Asian religions are likely to have a less formal relationship with their scriptures, consulting them mainly for general guidance and inspiration. However, *professional* users of scriptures in Asia—priests, monks, and nuns—have a strong attachment to scriptural texts.

---

[11] W. A. Graham, "Scripture," *Encyclopedia of Religion*, vol. 13, p. 134.

The varying oral and textual dimensions of scripture also lead to differences in function. Some religions view the spoken word of scripture as primary. Hindus, for example, regard their *Vedas* essentially as speech rather than as printed word, and they see the written text as inferior to its oral form. In other religions, the power and function of the book seem to depend on its written, textual nature. Sikhs view their scripture as the written incarnation of the one soul of the gurus who founded their faith. A later section of this chapter deals more fully with the uses of Asian scriptures, but enough has been said here to suggest that they function in significantly different ways.

Given all this variety, is it possible to define the word *scripture* in a way that takes variety into account yet applies to all religions? Although some scholars answer in the negative,[12] most argue that a comprehensive definition is possible and necessary. The definition we use here is this: **Scripture** *is writing that is accepted and used in a religious community as especially sacred and authoritative.* By looking closely at the key words and implications of this definition, we can discuss formal and functional aspects of scriptures—what they are and how people use them.

First, every scripture is a *writing*. Scriptures exercise much of their authority as books, and we encounter them as books. Some scholars argue that **oral tradition,** the passing down of material by word of mouth only, can be "scriptural."[13] Although oral and written traditions do have some similar characteristics and functions, strictly speaking "oral scripture" is a contradiction in terms—scripture is by definition written. (The word *scripture* comes from the Latin *scriptura,* or "writing.") The scriptures of all religions, however, do have continuing, significant oral (spoken) and aural (heard) dimensions.[14] Most scriptures originated in oral tradition and stayed in oral tradition for several generations before being put in writing. Although the writing of scripture obscures its oral dimensions, the orality of the text is still embedded in the writing, waiting to be drawn out by faithful vocalizing of the words. Scripture comes most fully alive when believers read it aloud and hear it in worship. Most believers, even those in highly literate cultures, hear scripture in worship more often and more meaningfully than they read it privately. In this book, as in any book, we encounter scriptures as texts, but these texts are meant to be spoken and heard.

According to our definition, scriptures are *especially sacred*. They have special religious significance in pointing to ultimate reality and truth. Sacredness should not be seen simply as being of divine origin or even as the "wholly other," Rudolf Otto's influential conception of sacredness that suits Western religions but not many Eastern faiths. For example, the sacred Tao ("Way") witnessed by the *Tao Te Ching* is not wholly other but is hidden in the universe and the self, waiting to be discovered and "tuned in to." Moreover, only a few books among Asian scriptures explicitly claim

[12] In their essays in Levering, *Rethinking Scripture,* for example, Coburn and Folkert reject the term *scripture* in favor of *the Word* and *canon,* respectively. The other authors in that book keep "scripture" as a conceptual category, and it is the dominant category in the volume as a whole, as the title implies.

[13] See, for example, Schmidt, *Exploring Religion,* p. 208: "Broadly conceived, *scripture* refers to oral as well as written traditions that a people regard as sacred. Each religious community has a scripture, a body of sacred oral or written traditions."

[14] See especially Graham, *Beyond the Written Word.* For a general treatment of orality, see W. Ong, *Orality and Literacy* (New York: Routledge, Chapman and Hall, 1982), and J. Goody, *The Interface between the Written and the Oral* (Cambridge: Cambridge University Press, 1982).

sacredness for themselves; the *Adi Granth* is the most notable example. Most scriptures receive their sacred status only after they have been written, circulated, and widely accepted as reflecting the faith in some special sense. The relational aspect of all scripture comes to the fore in a religious community.

Notice that scriptures are books held to be *especially* sacred. Most religions, including those from Asia, have a secondary religious literature that is also viewed as holy, instructive, or authoritative. This may seem to complicate the matter of defining the idea of scripture. On what basis can we say that a certain holy book in a religious tradition is scripture but another holy book is not? The answer lies in the special reception and usage that believers give to works that they see as *especially* sacred. Most religions explicitly or implicitly hold some works to be secondary to scripture. Almost every religion has commentarial, devotional, or legal literature that follows up on scripture, and believers typically make a careful distinction between scripture and these works.

Another mark of special holiness is use in ritual. When believers read books aloud in worship, when they speak their words to carry out sacrifice, and especially when they venerate (pay formal respect to) books during worship, we have a sure indication that these books are especially sacred. Secondary religious literature rarely makes its way into worship. Different types of veneration are practiced in Buddhism, Taoism, and Sikhism. Even in everyday life, scriptures enjoy special respect; for example, Buddhist scriptures for monastic use are still handwritten on specially treated palm leaves. In the new religious movements, the key writings of the founders that function as scriptures are often printed and bound to resemble more traditional holy books.

The third element of our definition of *scripture* is the authority of the text. Just as sacredness is an aspect of every scripture, scriptures are also *especially authoritative* in their communities. Among all written texts in a community, a scripture is always the most authoritative and is often the court of final appeal in religious matters. The range of this authority and the way it is exercised vary depending on the nature of the religion and the content of its scriptures. In the Western "religions of the book," scriptures are comprehensive in content and regulate much of life. In the Eastern religions, scriptures are often not authoritative in the same way as in the Western traditions. Yet Asian scriptures often express the heart of their faith, the way of salvation. The *Lotus Sutra* in Japanese Nichiren Buddhism is a prominent example of a book with a limited theme and purpose that has great standing in the sect because it addresses what is perceived as the heart of the religion. Moreover, "at least four of the six South Asian or Far Eastern fundamentalist-like movements . . . do in fact privilege a sacred text and presume to draw certain fundamentals—beliefs and behaviors—from it."[15] The authority of scripture for most followers of a given religion is paradoxically acknowledged even when some occasionally reject it. For example, some Hindu Brahmins burn their *Veda* books when they become homeless holy men. For the sake of greater enlightenment, some Zen Buddhist monks make disparaging comments about the Buddha (for example, "That old degenerate!") and his scriptural teachings; sometimes they have ripped up their scripture books.

---

[15] M. E. Marty and R. S. Appleby, eds., *Fundamentalisms Observed* (Chicago: University of Chicago Press, 1991), p. 820.

Scriptures are generally authoritative for their believers alone, who accept them as expressing the heart of the religion. One prominent exception to this rule is in Chinese religion, where some older Classics like the *I Ching* are used to some degree as scripture by both Confucians and Taoists. More typically among religions, to receive one religion's texts as scripture is automatically to exclude the texts of other religions. For example, Confucian scriptures like the *Analects* are generally not given scriptural authority by Taoists, even though Confucian texts form the basis of education for all Chinese, including Taoists. As Chapter 18 of the *Tao Te Ching* cuttingly remarks against two Confucian virtues in the *Analects*, "When the great way [Tao] falls into disuse, there are benevolence and rectitude."

The authority of scripture is established by a special class of scholars who are the guardians of scripture and recognized experts in its interpretation. In Buddhism, monks with special training and ability teach the sacred writings to other monks and inquiring laypeople. The Confucian scholar is the master of the Classics and teaches them to others. The authority of scripture in nearly every faith, therefore, is mediated largely by individuals considered to be its official interpreters. **Commentary,** a book written to explain another book, has a large role in the history of many religions and regulates how scriptures are received and used, especially at the official level. As John Henderson states, "Commentaries and commentarial modes of thinking dominated the intellectual history of most premodern civilizations. . . . Until the seventeenth century in Europe, and even later in China, India, and the Near East, thought, especially within high intellectual traditions, was primarily exegetical [text-interpretive] in character and expression."[16] We must also remember that only quite recently in the sweep of human history have mass-produced books appeared and mass literacy become possible. This is another reason for the existence of a special class to read, comment on, and relate sacred books to a religious community. Of course, the uses of scriptures by ordinary followers of a religion are at times quite different from the official prescribed use.

Two features of scripture not directly related to our definition should be stated here. First, scriptures of every religion are often heterogeneous but are nonetheless *seen as a unity* by their communities. This is obvious for scriptures, such as the Sikh *Adi Granth,* that comprise sections written by several different authors—many books bound as a single book, diverse yet one. Some religions recognize different levels of authority and originality in their scriptures, as in Hinduism's distinction between Vedic scripture, which is called *Shruti* ("what is heard" from the beginning), and the post-Vedic *Smirti* ("what is remembered"). All of it is the scripture of Hinduism, and believers see it as speaking essentially the same message. In China, the principle holds even in reverse: The secondary scriptures are the earlier Classics, and Confucians see their later *Analects* and Taoists their *Tao Te Ching* as one with earlier tradition.

A second important feature of scripture is that it has *a degree of closure*. This closure is often called a **canon,** a list or collection of books recognized as scriptural. The canon is absolutely fixed in Sikhism, as it is in all major Western religions (Judaism, Christianity, and Islam). All the scriptures of these religions were long ago

---

[16] J. B. Henderson, *Scripture, Canon, Commentary: A Comparison of Confucian and Western Exegesis* (Princeton: Princeton University Press, 1991), p. 3.

officially identified, and nothing can now be added or subtracted from their canons. In Hinduism, Buddhism, Jainism, Confucianism, and Taoism, however, the situation is quite different, for two reasons. First, their sacred literature is vast. The problems in defining a canon for a religion like Taoism, for example, which has 1,200 sacred texts, are enormous. Second, the process of producing scripture has not officially ended. Where new books can be added—as Taoists added one at the beginning of the twentieth century—a closed canon cannot exist.

How can believers relate to their religion's scriptures when they are so vast that no one person or group can know them all, let alone be expert in them all? In traditions with large canons, certain books, such as the *Tao Te Ching,* are basic for almost everyone. Also, different groups in a religion attach themselves to a few select scriptures that reflect their particular interests. In Taoism, as L. G. Thompson explains, "the practitioner or priest would usually be an adherent to one of the several major 'schools' or traditions of Taoism, and would specialize in those texts relevant to his school's interests."[17] This tendency to choose specific books from among the total corpus of scripture results in a "canon within the canon." Most commonly it occurs in religions with very large numbers of books, but it also can be found in religions with smaller canons.

THE USES OF SCRIPTURE

When scripture is set in the full context of the everyday life of believers, its uses become plain. How believers use scripture shows its status and role in a religion. The following chapters of this book outline the varied uses of scripture in each Asian religion. In this section, we discuss some basic dimensions of the comparative study of scripture usage, with special attention to Asian religions.

We begin with three uses that are primarily *cognitive,* understanding and thinking in some way about the words and their meaning. First, scripture is a source for establishing and defending key doctrines. Scriptures can be used doctrinally because they typically contain the key teachings of the faith and because believers usually see them as continuing the voice of the founders. They have primary importance as statements of the deep truths of the universe and the right way to live in it. These teachings can assume different forms: God(s) and humanity; human imperfections and release from them; beginnings and ends of the individual and the cosmos; the moral life and how to achieve it. When scripture is used to establish doctrine, its official interpreters—monks, priests, scholars, and the like—most often do this. Sometimes formal debate in councils or assemblies sets down doctrines, often within the confines of a monastery or temple. Defending doctrine occurs less often at the popular level, but even here scripture can function authoritatively. An appeal to a passage of holy writ is often the final word in any argument about religion.

Second, scripture is also prominently used in public worship. Worshippers often display and read it aloud. Although this is characteristic especially of the "religions of the book," it is also significant in religions such as Hinduism and Buddhism that are not so book oriented. The worship that goes on in a Buddhist monastery, for example,

---

[17] L. G. Thompson, "Taoism: Classic and Canon," in Denny and Taylor, *Holy Book,* p. 205.

prominently features scriptures. Monks read them, chant them, meditate on them, and walk around them in solemn procession. Even when the book is not prominent in worship, its content often permeates the ceremonies of most scripturalizing religions. Prayers, sacrifices, and hymns come from and echo the language of scripture. Many lyrics of the music of worship are drawn from the scriptural text. Hymns and chants, with their emotional power, are significant vehicles for use of scripture in most religious traditions in both East and West.

Perhaps the place and function of scripture are never so prominent as when worshippers formally venerate it. Almost every religion with scripture pays it ritual respect in some way. Hindus speak the words of a *Veda* with great care. These words are the center of holiness in worship, though the *Veda* book is usually not to be seen. In certain Taoist and Confucian temples, the location of the scripture collection is itself holy. **Bibliolatry** [bib-lee-AHL-ah-tree] results when believers give excessive veneration to their scriptures or become absolutely dependent on them. Of course, the line between ordinary veneration and bibliolatry is not always easy to discern.

A third typical cognitive use of scripture is in meditation and devotion. This is usually private and individual, but it can also occur in group settings, as when Buddhist monks meditate in session on sutra passages or on mantras drawn from scripture. Sometimes they meditate on the words and at other times "look through" the words to find the truth believed to lie "behind" them. The conclusions of many Hindu scriptures specify a blessing on people who listen or read faithfully. The scripture books are often marked into sections for devotional reading; it is the duty of believers to read, ponder, and often memorize the words. In meditation and devotion, the scriptures teach the truth of the religion and promote the growth of the reader into the fullness of the faith.

Another important dimension of scripture use—one often overlooked—is *noncognitive*, using the words in a variety of ways without any mental attempt to understand their meaning. One noncognitive use occurs when scriptures are written in a language that followers of the faith cannot understand. This is especially the case when a religion like Hinduism holds that its scriptures are so essentially bound to their original language that they cannot be translated and retain their sacred nature. The words of the Vedic rituals have power to transform the life of believers whether they understand the words or not.

A second noncognitive use of scripture is decorative and iconic. Many Hindus cannot read their sacred literature, but images and pictures of the gods—**icons**—and their stories are all around them. These decorations are not meant to be read so much as to be felt, or revered as holy objects, thereby exercising their holy presence for the blessing of the community. In these and other iconic usages of scripture, the appeal is typically more to the imagination and emotion than to the mind.

A third noncognitive application mixes religion and magic. The power of scripture is such that it can bring blessing and keep away evil; it has an objective supernatural power quite by itself. Scripture can be used in charms or talismans, manifestations of the supernatural power of scripture. Perhaps this was the function of the oldest surviving fragment of the scripture of a modern religion, a tiny Israelite silver scroll from the seventh century B.C.E. with a priestly blessing from what was becoming Israelite/Jewish scripture written on the inside, probably worn on a necklace. The mere possession of a holy book also has power to bless and ward off evil. For example, putting a certain Taoist text in the hands of a woman undergoing a perilous child-birth is said to cause the immediate safe birth of her child. In many religions, individuals who can afford to do so often buy a holy book for possession in the home. Available for Sikhs, for example, is the *Gutka,* an anthology of the most important passages in the massive *Adi Granth.*

Perhaps the most striking noncognitive use of scripture is **bibliomancy** [BIB-lee-oh-man-see], the use of holy books to foresee the future and guide one's response to it. Many religions feature the informal practice of opening a scripture book at random and reading the first passage that meets the eye. This passage, it is thought, has special power to direct the believer through an uncertain or difficult situation in life or through the difficulties of the new day. Sikhism has formalized bibliomancy in its "taking the word" ceremony in which Sikh scripture is opened at random and read for a special meaning. Some Taoists read the *I Ching* philosophically, but more use it in divination. Its many hexagrams and their fortune-telling interpretations are selected by a special procedure with sticks. All these forms of bibliomancy assume that supernatural guidance is exercised in and through the book for the blessing of the believer.

Scholars of religion have categorized scripture uses in other ways beyond cognitive and noncognitive. Perhaps the most helpful is that of Sam D. Gill, who proposed that uses of scripture are informative or performative. *Informative* means imparting information in various ways, such as in doctrine and history. *Performative,* in contrast, means doing something, as for example when scripture is used to make sacrifice, to make the laws of a religious or civil community, or to bless and curse.[18] In both its informative and its performative aspects, scripture is also used for transformation. This transformative power is a result of its sacredness and authority. Scriptures come from a sacred source and are themselves sacred. This sacred quality generally entails some power to make holy those who read or listen to them.

The transformative power of scripture occurs in both individual and communal ways—for example, to gain insight about personal or group problems and find the resources to solve them. Not all religions consider their scriptures to be divinely inspired, but all hold them to be inspiring and transformative in some way. This transformative power can be based on cognition, in which believers directly encounter the scriptures and experience their life-changing meaning. It can also happen just as often in noncognitive ways, as described earlier.

ADVANTAGES AND DISADVANTAGES OF STUDYING EASTERN RELIGIONS THROUGH THEIR SCRIPTURES

The study of Eastern religions through their sacred scriptures has both advantages and disadvantages. We need to be aware of the limitations of this method and work from strengths to overcome the weaknesses as much as possible.

---

[18] Sam D. Gill, "Nonliterate Traditions and Holy Books: Toward a New Model," in Denny and Taylor, *Holy Book,* p. 234.

The first disadvantage is that scriptures are *not universal*. Some religions do not have them. If a culture has no writing, it obviously can have no scripture. This is the case with most of the traditional indigenous religions of Asia, the so-called folk religions. Of course, not having a scripture does not invalidate a religion. The religions and cultures of nonliterate peoples do have oral traditions that function prominently in storytelling and in rituals that enact myths. A religion based on oral traditions is every bit as living and real for its followers as a religion that produces and uses scripture.

Second, as we saw earlier, the reception and use of scripture is *not uniform* across religions. Believers regard their scriptures in different ways, and scriptures function differently in each religion. As a student of Eastern religions you must take note of these variations and learn to look at each religion's scriptures in a fresh way. Readers of scripture who come from a "religion of the book" must especially try to lay aside their preconceptions. Protestant Christians, for example, must beware of assuming that certain qualities of scripture and its function to which they are accustomed (for example, the belief that scripture is best absorbed by individual silent reading and meditation) are true of every religion's scripture. Moreover, the use of new scriptures in new religious movements such as the Church of Jesus Christ of Latter-day Saints (the "Mormons") and the Unification Church often differs from usage in older, classical religious movements. The more we genuinely encounter world scriptures in their full range of reception and use, the less likely we will be to inject our own biases into the scriptures of others. Then "scripture" itself will become a fuller, more useful category.

A third disadvantage is that we must *read translations,* which cannot fully capture the literary characteristics or meaning of the original. We can lay out four aspects of this disadvantage.

❖ Some of the original meaning and resonance of the words is lost or distorted in translation. For example, among Brahmanic Hindus, the oral power of the *Vedas* in their Sanskrit language is such that it would be unthinkable to translate them into another language for use in worship.

❖ Some languages and styles are hard to translate into English. For example, the formal Chinese style used by many Confucian and Taoist scriptures is often elusive or even cryptic. Moreover, to cross the borders of language families in translation (for example, to go from Semitic languages or Asian languages into English) is more difficult than staying inside a language family (to go from the Greek *New Testament* of the Christian *Bible* into English). These difficulties result in translations that vary widely.

❖ Bias creeps in. Translators inevitably cannot be fully objective and sometimes distort meaning.

❖ Updating is needed because languages change. Some scripture translations are updated regularly; others are not, for a variety of reasons, and become more and more outmoded as time goes on.

A fourth disadvantage is that scriptures tend to *reflect only the patriarchal and elite perspectives* of their traditions. They come from times and cultures that are patriarchal, where the voices of women—if they come through at all—are muted and filtered.[19] Scriptures strongly tend to embody official and elite ideas, the mainstream that feminist scholars call "malestream." Comparatively little of popular religion can be found in them. Although the contents of scripture are patriarchal and elitist, feminist scholars today in many religions are working to make contemporary understanding and use of these scriptures more equalitarian. This book offers some coverage of social justice and the role of women, but the perspective through which these scriptures are filtered is necessarily that of the elite male.[20]

Finally, and perhaps most seriously, we *lack the living context* of scripture when we encounter only its textual form. Scripture, which for most traditions comes from ancient times, comes alive as it is appropriated in the life of religious communities. Despite growing religious pluralism, many North American readers of scripture do not have access to these communities. They cannot easily visit a Sikh temple, see the ritual of a Hindu home, or live for a time in a Buddhist monastery. They cannot directly see the broad ways that scripture is reflected in religious life, or the more specific ways it is used in worship, devotion, or law. What can be reproduced in a book like this is primarily the written text itself. The uses of scripture can be outlined here, but a printed book inevitably emphasizes the written, textual aspects of scripture over the oral and living.

These disadvantages might seem strong enough to cause you to give up the encounter with Asian scriptures. The advantages of studying religions through their scriptures are compelling, however. By working from the strengths of this approach, you can overcome the weaknesses to some extent and use scripture appropriately to enter the world of other religions.

The first advantage of this approach is that scripture is *widespread* among religions. Even though it is not fully universal, each "major" (to use a traditional but rather prejudicial term) living religion has a scripture. Scriptures naturally vary in form, content, and usage, but they are usually present in a religion. As we have seen, recent researchers emphasize that they constitute a distinct and important element in the life of most religions. The tendency to *scripturalize,* to make and use scriptures, is strong among Asian religions. Indeed, almost every contemporary religion that is based in a literate culture produces and uses scriptures of some sort.[21]

Second, scriptures tend to be *comprehensive* for their faiths. Matters that a religion considers of great importance for its life are generally written down for the continuing community. "The sacred writings provide not only the essence of each particular religious tradition, but also the archetypal experiences which stir in the depths of all human lives: death, trust, anxiety, wonder, loyalty to a cause greater than oneself, fascination, healing, fulfillment, peace." [22] Of course, what religions view as important

---

[19] See the introductory section of Serinity Young, ed., *An Anthology of Sacred Texts by and about Women* (New York: Crossroad, 1993), for good treatment of this issue.

[20] An excellent current series of books edited by Donald S. Lopez Jr., "Princeton Readings in Religions," seeks to rectify this male-elite perspective with anthologies drawing from popular writings and anthropological field reports on nearly all religions of the world.

[21] Only Shinto does not treat its holy books as scripture in the full sense. Thus Shinto is the exception that proves the rule that religions based in literate cultures produce and use scriptures.

[22] Leonard J. Biallas, "Teaching World Religions through Their Scriptures," *Horizons* 17 (1990): 80.

does vary, and scriptures reflect this variety. For example, the Confucian *Analects* deals almost exclusively with the moral virtues that can make one "superior." What each religion considers of supreme importance is strongly reflected in its scriptures. Scriptures offer broad insight into the key characteristics of their faiths.

Third, scriptures are *authoritative* for their religions. Because they are believed to come from God or the gods, an enlightened teacher, or a wise sage, and because they bear witness to an ultimate cosmic reality, the truth contained in scriptures is recognized and lived out by believers. To read a scripture is to discover what is of primary value in a religion. And because scriptures are authoritative, they typically reflect the distinctive main aspects of each tradition. "Despite the variety of attitudes to scriptural works [in religions], there is a continuing tendency to find in a sacred text . . . the primary source for true doctrine, correct ritual, [and] appropriate conduct."[23]

The fourth advantage of studying scriptures lies in their *ancient or foundational* character. They or the oral traditions on which they are based arise soon after the beginning of a religion and often signal important stages in its early development. Chinese religions call their oldest scriptures "Classics," and in a sense all world scriptures are classic treatments of their religious tradition. Where a religion has a founder or founders, scriptures usually give deep insight into the life of the founder(s) from the perspective of later followers. The foundational character of scriptures thus makes them valuable as a primary source for the history of religions.

Furthermore, because the traditional religions of Asia have so richly influenced and been influenced by their cultures, scriptures are among the most important literary sources for the understanding of Asian cultures. Even though scriptures are indeed ancient and important, it is usually erroneous to argue, as does Charles Braden, that religion is somehow "founded on" scriptures.[24] This is a common misconception, especially in "religions of the book." Rather, as T. W. Hall puts it so well, "Historical investigations show that the religious communities existed prior to the writing of their scripture . . . religions produced scripture and scripture did not produce religion."[25]

Fifth, scriptures are *accessible* in translation to English-language readers. Most of the important religious books of Asia have been translated into English, and many of those that have not are now being translated. Sometimes the translations of a certain scripture are few, but others can boast a near riot of English versions. The *Tao Te Ching*, for example, had more than twenty English versions in print in 2005. Although no translation can convey the full meaning and feeling of the original, a good translation can suggest it. Students of world scripture who want a closer, more accurate look at a given passage should consult at least two or three different contemporary translations of it, comparing them closely.

Finally, scriptures as literary texts are *open to critical analysis*. Both the specialist scholar and the beginning reader can analyze them directly or, better yet, enter a

---

[23] Richard C. Bush et al., *The Religious World: Communities of Faith,* 2d ed. (New York: Macmillan, 1988), p. 3.

[24] Charles Braden, *The Scriptures of Mankind: An Introduction* (New York: Macmillan, 1952), p. 8.

[25] Hall, Pilgrim, and Cavanagh, *Religion,* p. 109.

conversation with them. Although most religious texts range from mildly strange to completely baffling for those who come from other cultures and religious traditions, the same intellectual and scholarly skills that you use to read any other text can be put to use on Eastern scriptures. With some effort, you can understand scriptures and use them as a pathway into other faiths.

EASTERN SCRIPTURES AND MODERN SCHOLARSHIP

The earlier discussion of critical analysis of scripture leads us to an important but often neglected topic. How does the modern academic study of scripture influence how Eastern religions use their scriptures and how we read them?

Historical and critical literary scholarship is largely Western and European in origin, stemming from various methods of interpreting literature developed in the Renaissance, the Enlightenment, and more recent times. Textual criticism methodically judges manuscripts to find the likely original reading; grammatical criticism analyzes the content and style of the wording of a work in its original language; literary criticism studies genres. Most important is historical criticism, which probes the developmental genesis of works from the past, their original meaning and authenticity. In the early nineteenth century this approach began to be applied to the *Bible*. Critical study of the Christian scripture has uncovered development, diversity, and even some disagreement within it. Christianity's effort to understand the *Bible* critically has suffered reversals from time to time. Yet most Protestant groups accept this critical study, perceiving that it offers a fuller understanding of scripture that is compatible with faith.

In the early twentieth century, biblical criticism spread to Judaism, and today Conservative and Reform Jews widely accept it; only Orthodox Jews still oppose it. Since the Second Vatican Council (1962–1965), Roman Catholics have also embraced the **historical-critical method** of biblical study, which derives meaning from the earliest phases of the *Bible*'s literature.[26] Today the basic methods of literary study still are largely European academic methods. Scholars and students most often read Asian sacred texts through Western eyes and by Western methods.

The effort to collect, edit, and publish the literature of world religions is also a Western academic enterprise. It had its roots in the eighteenth century, when the first copies of Chinese and Indian scripture made their way to Europe and were greeted with great interest, even enthusiasm, in some circles. One reason for this enthusiasm was an Enlightenment hope that these scriptures might be a religious or philosophical alternative to what some saw as the hidebound clericalism of Christianity. The *Vedas*, for example, were at first viewed as religious expressions from near the dawn of time, pristine and unspoiled by priestcraft. Gradually Europeans realized that the *Vedas* reflect a priestly system as traditional as that of Christianity. By the middle of the nineteenth century, a more mature scholarly interest in scriptures blossomed into a systematic effort to publish

---

[26] See G. P. Fogarty, *American Catholic Biblical Scholarship* (San Francisco: HarperCollins, 1989), and R. B. Robinson, *Roman Catholic Exegesis since* Divino Afflante Spiritu (Atlanta: Scholars Press, 1988).

reliable translations. The editing and publishing of sacred texts continue today, especially in religions that have large canons. The methods used to edit, translate, publish, and interpret these scriptures draw generally from the Western tradition.

As we have seen, scholarship in comparative religion came from a background that was largely Protestant in orientation. Thus, over the last century, an inevitable "Protestant bias" has crept into the way scholarship has looked at the scriptures of Asian faiths. Certain mainstream Protestant ideas about the nature of scripture colored the study of the scriptures of other religions and only today are being identified and corrected. These include

❖ An emphasis on textuality that excludes orality, from the Protestant emphasis on the scripture as *written*.

❖ An orientation that assumes that scriptures are to be read mainly by the individual, from Protestant ideas of the "priesthood of all believers" and universal literacy.

❖ The notion that scriptures are widely authoritative over every aspect of religious life, from the Protestant assertion that the scriptures are the sole authority in the Christian faith.

❖ The assumption that scriptures are best understood by objective, academically recognized methods of study, from mainstream Protestant attachment to sound academic procedures.[27]

Of course, believers of the other religions of the world do not share this bias, as we can see when we reflect comparatively on each of these assumptions. In some religions, such as Hinduism, the oral dimension dominates the written. In others, such as Islam, written and oral traditions are more in balance. Next, most religions do not share the Protestant notion that scriptures should be read by the individual; rather, their adherents speak and hear their scriptures in groups, usually in worship and ritual. Indeed, it comes as a striking realization for modern North Americans that most followers of most religions throughout history (and even today!) cannot read and therefore cannot read their sacred texts. For the typical follower of most faiths, texts must be *spoken* (often from memory) and *heard*.

We examined earlier the next Protestant assumption, that scriptures seek to regulate every aspect of religious life, and we concluded that they seek to regulate the center of religious life as their religion conceives that center. For many religions of the world, the Western academic approach to scripture goes against the grain of faith and is consequently viewed as alien. To study scripture historically and objectively is to question its sacredness because such study employs the same methods used to study other, nonsacred literature. Each religion has some systematic study of its sacred texts, but such study usually remains devotional, meditative, and interpretive. Noncritical and unthreatening, it does not question the received beliefs about the origin and standing of the text.

When we read scriptures, then, we must always remember that the way we read is fully conditioned by our cultural backgrounds and academic enterprises. Those who

---

[27] See Levering, *Rethinking Scripture,* pp. 3–5, for more on this Protestant bias.

read from a religious background must always try to keep their own viewpoints identified and in check. Those with no religious commitments must try to suspend any doubts they may have about religion and scriptures. We read scriptures as *outsiders*, in an objective, scholarly, noncommittal way. This is altogether necessary as a first step in coming to grips with Eastern scriptures. A second step, more difficult than the first but equally necessary, is to read them as much as possible as *insiders*, with the eyes, minds, and hearts of those for whom these texts are much more than the object of scholarship.[28]

EASTERN SCRIPTURES AND THE WORLD WIDE WEB

The last ten years have seen the explosive growth of the World Wide Web. Much information about religion can be found on the web; it seems to be one of the leading topics of discussion and inquiry. As a part of this interest in religion, many websites feature Eastern scriptures in translation or sometimes in the original.

Many positive features of this new opportunity to encounter the scriptures of Eastern religions are obvious. The access is almost always free. The amount of scripture on the web is growing rapidly and may someday encompass most world scriptures. The Internet is an appealing way for most young, computer-oriented students (but not always their professors!) to encounter scriptures. It presents different ways of studying and learning—for example, the ability to search a text electronically. The Internet by its structure encourages exploration. Some sites are fully interactive, allowing students to ask questions and participate in online discussion groups. Finally, but not least, when students explore a religion site sponsored by its followers, the perspective provided there is likely to be more that of an "insider" than classroom or textbook descriptions.

The drawbacks of studying scriptures on the web are also obvious. Some sites are not well constructed; they may have poor layout, little eye appeal, out-of-date links, or other technical deficiencies. Although Internet coverage of world scripture is growing, it is still largely incomplete. Eastern scriptures do not have as much coverage on the Internet as do Western scriptures, largely because the Internet came later to Asia. The translations used are usually public domain works that are out-of-date. When representatives of a religion post that religion's writings for missionary or public relations purposes, the interpretations they provide may not agree with the current academic consensus about that religion. Most significantly, these electronic publications are subject to little or no scholarly control, such as editorial or peer review before publication, so their quality varies greatly. Some sites are excellent, some average, and some poor.

This mixed situation means that many students need help in finding, using, and especially analyzing critically these web-based scripture sites. Readers of this anthology may access a special website to further their use of the web in religious studies. The address is: http://religion.wadsworth.com.

---

[28] See the excellent remarks by Eric Sharpe in *Encyclopedia of Religion,* vol. 14, p. 85, on "imaginative sympathy" in reading scripture as "insiders." See also Ross N. Reat, "Insiders and Outsiders in the Study of Religious Traditions," *Journal of the American Academy of Religion* 51 (1983): 459–475.

THE PLAN OF THIS BOOK

This book contains excerpts of Eastern scriptures in the following order of religions: Hinduism, Buddhism, Jainism, Sikhism, Confucianism, Taoism, and Shinto. (Although Islam and, to a lesser degree, Christianity, have numerous followers in Asia, they are not indigenous to the Far East and so are not treated here.) This progression keeps the religions of India (Hinduism, Buddhism, Jainism, and Sikhism), and China (Confucianism and Taoism) together, usually in their family groups. Moreover, the reader can see the relationships among religions and scriptures more easily when related bodies of texts are dealt with in succession. This is true to a significant degree with Hinduism, Buddhism, and Jainism, and to a lesser degree with Confucianism and Taoism.

Each chapter is structured as follows: An introduction outlines the scriptures included, setting them in the context of the whole religion by examining briefly their name(s), overall structure, use, origin, and growth. The first grouping of scripture passages deals with the history of the religion. If the faith has a founder, special attention is given to him or her; any subsequent history of the religion that scripture reflects is also excerpted. Second are passages covering the main doctrinal teaching of the religion. These topics include divine or ultimate reality, creation and the environment, the nature of humanity, and achieving human fulfillment (salvation, release, harmony, etc.). Third are passages about the moral/ethical structure of the scriptures: good, evil, and the authentic human life. Personal morality is probably more widely treated in Eastern scriptures, but social ethics are also prominent. Such topics as war and peace, violence and nonviolence, tolerance and intolerance of people of other faiths, the status of women, and a just society are represented as fully as possible. Fourth are passages about the organization of the religion, either in its internal organization (for example, monks and laity in Buddhism) or in its attempts to organize its wider culture (such as the Hindu caste system in India). Last are passages about religious worship, ritual, devotion, and meditation. Of course, some religions have more in some of these categories than in others, but most religions do fit into them without significant distortion. Where they do not fully fit, this format is adapted to do justice to the particular nature of the texts.

The predominant rationale for this organization is pedagogical. It is meant to further the learning of students being introduced to the religions of the world. North American readers are familiar with the categories used here, and both teachers and students of Eastern religions will recognize them as a standard paradigm for research and teaching in religion. Moreover, they are categories that seem to fit world scriptures themselves. Why not discard any attempt to use categories of organization and simply provide one or two longer excerpts from each religion's body of scripture? A rather uniform scripture like the *Adi Granth* of Sikhism may be possible to encompass in a few long readings. However, what Paul Muller-Ortega says about Hinduism is true of most Eastern religions: "It is not possible to put a single sacred text in the hands of students and expect the reading of that one text to allow students to encompass the tradition. . . . Thus, the preferred method of exposing students to the enormity of the Hindu sacred literature has been by means of anthologies."[29]

---

[29] Paul Muller-Ortega, "Exploring Textbooks: Introductions to Hinduism," in B. R. Gaventa, ed., *Critical Review of Books in Religion, 1988* (Atlanta: Scholars Press, 1989), p. 71.

SUGGESTIONS ON HOW TO READ EASTERN SCRIPTURES

Individuals reading Eastern scriptures for the first time often feel they are entering a strange new world. Sometimes preconceived notions of what reading a given scripture will be like turn out to be quite wrong. Students of Eastern religions are especially susceptible to the difficulties of reading scripture. Their textbooks usually try to make scriptures easier to encounter by simplifying and summarizing the content. To encounter scriptures more directly and in their original form is a harder process. As Mortimer Adler and Charles Van Doren once wrote, "The problem of reading the Holy Book . . . is the most difficult problem in the field of reading."[30] In the end, however, it is more profitable for readers to wrestle as directly as possible with the texts. Of course, an anthology such as this does not present Eastern scriptures in their totality but serves as a bridge to the full scripture text.

Each reader must ultimately find an individually suitable method for reading Eastern scriptures. But these ten suggestions drawn from my experience and the experience of others may be helpful:

1. *Use your knowledge of religion to set these readings in a fuller context.* Try to relate scriptures as fully as possible to the life of the religions from which they come. For example, when you are reading a passage about ritual, visualize how the ritual is carried out.

2. *Read the introductions to each chapter before you turn to the passages.* They will provide an important background for understanding the passages.

3. *Take a few moments to skim the selections.* Having a general feel for the "lay of the land" will help you when you begin to read in detail.

4. *Read the scripture passages academically.* Use the same intellectual skills that you bring to any other text, religious or nonreligious. Remember their holy status in their religions, but don't be intimidated by it.

5. *Mark the text as you read.* Research into reading shows that readers who mark the text, underlining or highlighting as few as three or four items per page, understand and remember more than readers who do not mark the text. Marking helps to make the text your own.

6. *Pay attention to literary genre.* The form and content of any literary passage reflects its genre. Read with a feeling for the differences among myth, poetry, narrative, law, and other literary forms.

7. *Make a personal glossary of unfamiliar terms and names as you go along.* You can do this easily by circling them in the text and writing them in the bottom margin. Then you can go back later to make a short note of their meaning, also in the margin. The unfamiliarity and difficulty of so many words is an obstacle for many students of Eastern religions. With a little extra effort, you can minimize this difficulty.

---

[30] Mortimer Adler and Charles Van Doren, *How to Read a Book* (New York: Simon & Schuster, 1940), p. 288.

8.   *Read each selection repeatedly.* Read until you are familiar with it and can identify any problems you have in understanding it. View these problems as opportunities for achieving greater understanding, not as roadblocks.

9.   *Read the selections aloud as much as possible.* Reading aloud may feel embarrassing at first because you are not accustomed to it. Listen to the sounds of the words, and try to get a sense of the oral dimensions of the text. You cannot reproduce the feeling of the original language, but reading aloud will at least remind you that the text does have an oral dimension.

10.   *Put yourself, as well as you can, inside the faith of the scripture.* What could this text mean to you today if you were a typical follower of that faith? By using your knowledge and imagination, you can participate in the unique use of scripture in each religion and become—partially and temporarily—an insider.[31]

GLOSSARY

bibliolatry [bib-lee-AHL-ah-tree]   Excessive veneration of a scripture book.

bibliomancy [BIB-lee-oh-man-see]   The use of scripture to foresee future events and guide one's response to them.

canon   A more or less fixed collection of books regarded as scriptural.

commentary   A book written to explain another book, often passage by passage. Many religions possess commentaries on their scriptures.

genre   A literary form, such as poetry, myth, proverb, narrative history, and philosophical meditation.

historical-critical method   The scholarly study of a text that derives meaning from the text's earliest phases and traces the text's historical development.

icon   A holy picture. Metaphorically, scripture is an icon when it is revered as a sacred object apart from its content.

narrative   The telling of an event or series of events in story form.

oral tradition   The passing down, usually through many generations, of myths, narratives, poems, and the like by word of mouth.

scripture   Text that a religious community holds to be especially sacred and authoritative.

QUESTIONS FOR STUDY AND DISCUSSION

1.   What does the word *scripture* mean to you?

2.   "Scripture is more a Western concept than an Eastern concept." To what extent do you agree or disagree with this common statement?

---

[31] "By an act of historical imagination we can actually participate up to a certain point in the aspirations and devotions of other times and places. Yet this truly is only up to a certain point, for the curtain is suddenly lowered and we realize with a shock just how far away those places and times really are. That experience has been called 'the paradox of understanding.'" Jaroslav Pelikan, *On Searching the Scriptures— Your Own or Someone Else's* (New York: Quality Paperback Book Club, 1992), p. 7.

3.   What special problems and opportunities are posed by a very large scripture canon such as in Taoism or Buddhism?

4.   Suppose that a new potential scripture—a new gospel book about Jesus or a collection of new sayings from Buddha or Confucius—is discovered and shown to be authentic. Would such a potential scripture actually get into the scripture canons of these religions? Why or why not?

5.   What uses of scripture seem most important or interesting to you? Why?

6.   What disadvantages are posed by the ancient character of scriptures? Can these be overcome? If so, how?

7.   Reflect on this description of Mohandas Gandhi's teachings about studying others' scriptures: "One should read others' scriptures with respect and reverence even to be enriched in one's own religious convictions."

8.   What other advantages and disadvantages of using the Internet in religious studies occur to you, besides the ones given here?

SUGGESTIONS FOR FURTHER READING

L. J. Biallas, "Teaching World Religions through Their Scriptures." *Horizons* (Villanova University) 17 (1990): 76–91. Especially useful to teachers, but students can profit from it as well; focuses on narrative forms.

H. Coward, *Sacred Word and Sacred Text: Scripture in World Religions.* Maryknoll, NY: Orbis, 1988. Sound chapter-length treatments (especially of orality) of scripture in Hinduism, Sikhism, and Buddhism.

H. Coward, ed., *Experiencing Scripture in World Religions.* Maryknoll, NY: Orbis, 2000. Brief, lively essays by various scholars who are also believers, on the use of scripture in Hinduism, Sikhism, and Buddhism.

F. M. Denny and R. L. Taylor, eds., *The Holy Book in Comparative Perspective.* Columbia: University of South Carolina Press, 1985. After an introduction by the editors, this volume features up-to-date treatments of the scriptures of nine major religions.

W. A. Graham, "Scripture." In M. Eliade, ed., *The Encyclopedia of Religion,* vol. 13, pp. 133–145. New York: Macmillan, 1987. This lucid article is the best short survey of its topic.

P.-L. Kwok and E. Schüssler Fiorenza, eds., *Women's Sacred Scriptures.* London: SCM Press/Maryknoll, NY: Orbis, 1998. A treatment of the scriptures of several world religions with a view to a feminist reclaiming of scripture.

M. Levering, ed., *Rethinking Scripture: Essays from a Comparative Perspective.* Albany: State University of New York Press, 1989. Begins with two excellent essays by W. C. Smith, "The Study of Religion and the Study of the Bible" and "Scripture as Form and Concept: Their Emergence in the Western World." There are chapters on Buddhist scripture by Levering, on Hinduism by T. B. Coburn, and on Jainism by K. W. Folkert. W. A. Graham also has an essay, "Scripture as Spoken Word."

W. C. Smith, *What Is Scripture? A Comparative Approach.* Minneapolis: Fortress, 1993. A full survey of its topic by the most influential researcher on scripture.

S. Young, *An Anthology of Sacred Texts by and about Women.* New York: Crossroad, 1993. A comprehensive selection of scriptures and other important religious writings from, among others, Hinduism, Buddhism, Confucianism, and Taoism.

Reading Hindu Scripture
A Hindu woman in Banaras, India, reads the *Bhagavad-Gita* devotionally. *Credit:* Photo by Diana Eck, from the Image Bank of the Center for the Study of World Religions, Harvard University. Photo courtesy Diana Eck.

CHAPTER TWO

Hinduism

❧ After the monsoon season, people all over northern India gather outside their cities and villages to celebrate Rama-Lilas, a dramatic reading and reenactment of the *Ramayana,* the epic Hindu scripture. At its decisive point, wood and straw effigies of the demon Ravana are made and stuffed with fireworks. When night falls, the fireworks are set off and the demon is destroyed. Rama and the forces of good have prevailed.

❧ Just before dawn breaks in India, a householder rises and purifies himself with water. He then stirs back to life the embers of the sacred household fire while chanting sacred verses. Raising his arms to the rising sun, he recites a prayer to the sun-god from the most ancient scripture, the *Rig-Veda.* This ritual, the Agnihotra, has been performed continually in India for more than three thousand years.

❧ In Hardwar, India, people gather in the "world's largest religious festival." Ten million people came to this site on the upper Ganges River. According to Hindu scriptures, bathing during this festival is the supreme act of worship. Much of the other activity focuses on scripture: Holy men read scripture aloud, chant their mantras, and teach mantras to the pilgrims.

❧ In Bangalore, twenty-three-year-old Lakshmi works in a call center, answering inquiries from customers of a prominent American corporation. She dropped out of college to work in the center, and she is paid enough to live a middle-class life and be independent of her parents. She and thousands of others like her have provoked a growing social crisis in India. According to Indian cultural norms grounded in ancient scripture called the *Laws of Manu,* young people live with their parents and are under their direction until they get married. "I want to live on my own," Lakshmi says.

INTRODUCTION

Hinduism is one of the oldest of world religions and certainly the most internally diverse. It encompasses many gods and offers many paths to salvation. The scriptures of Hinduism mirror this diversity. Vast in size, varied in usage, and profound in influence, many scriptures have been chanted, heard, taught, and repeated for three thousand years. Generalizations about Hindu scriptures are thus especially difficult to make; almost every statement has exceptions. Still, the main lines of these scriptures can be reliably traced, and they provide good doors into the many-roomed mansion of Hinduism.

Overview of Structure

Hindus have not given any single comprehensive name to their scripture. They divide their scriptures into two classes: *Shruti* and *Smriti* (see Table 2.1). *Shruti* [SHROO-tee], "what is heard," is the primary revelation. It has no human or divine author but captures the cosmic sounds of truth first heard by **rishis** [REE-shees], ancient seers. Later seers began a process of oral transmission and practice through priestly families that continues today. *Shruti* consists of four *Vedas* (Books of Knowledge), the *Brahmanas* (Brahmin Books), the *Aranyakas* (Forest Books), and the *Upanishads* (Sittings near a Teacher). Altogether it is "Vedic" scripture. The canon of *Shruti* has been basically fixed for almost two thousand years, and all of Hinduism is in some sense based on it.

Smriti [SMRIH-tee], "what is remembered," designates all other scripture. All of it is post-Vedic. The role of *Smriti* is to bring out the meaning of *Shruti* and apply it to later ages. Hindus consider *Smriti* revelatory only to the extent that it is grounded in *Shruti*. The *Smriti* literature is vast in size and scope. It ranges from myths and legends of the *Puranas*, epics like the *Mahabharata* and the *Ramayana*, and law codes like the *Laws of Manu* and the *Institutes of Vishnu*. These scriptures have been widely translated from their original Sanskrit into the other languages of the Indian subcontinent, and the canon of *Smriti* is still open. Because of its more popular and ever-developing nature, *Smriti* scripture has had, despite its officially secondary status to *Shruti*, a strong influence on Hindu religion and Indian culture.

In the *Shruti* category, the four **Vedas** [VAY-duhs] are the foundation of Hindu scripture. They are **samhitas** [SAHM-hee-tuhs], "collections" of hymns, formulas, songs, and spells.

Table 2.1
Hindu Scriptures

Division	Name	Translation/Content	Size
Shruti *(Vedic scripture)*	*Vedas* *Rig-Veda* *Yajur-Veda* *Sama-Veda* *Atharva-Veda*	Hymn *Veda* Formula *Veda* Song *Veda* Spell *Veda*	1,028 hymns in 10 books 1,549 mantras 731 hymns in 20 books
	Brahmanas	Brahmin Books	Correspond to each *Veda*
	Aranyakas	Forest Books	
	Upanishads	Sittings near a Teacher	123 total; 13 principal
Smriti *(Post-Vedic scripture)*	*Puranas*	Legends	18 books
	Mahabharata	Great Story of the Bharatas	18 books
	Ramayana	Story of Rama	50,000 lines in 7 books
	Manusmriti	Laws of Manu	12 books
	Vishnusmriti	Institutes of Vishnu	100 chapters
	Tantras	Weavings	Uncertain number of books

❖ The *Rig-Veda* samhita has 1,028 hymns divided into ten books. Each hymn (*Rig*) is addressed to a single god or goddess. When a god is extolled in a hymn, the hymn praises that god above other deities, a form of worship called *henotheism*. Each hymn of the *Rig-Veda* has a fairly common sequence: It begins with the invocation of a deity; it then makes requests of that deity and offers praises by recounting her or his deeds in myth; it finishes with a brief restatement of the worshippers' request.

❖ The *Yajur-Veda* samhita consists mostly of prose sacrificial formulas (*yajus*) used by the presiding priest in a sacrifice.

❖ The *Sama-Veda* is a collection of songs and melodies (*saman*) used in sacrifice; most of the words are taken from the *Rig-Veda*. The *Rig, Yajur,* and *Sama Vedas* together are known in Hinduism as the "threefold *Veda*."

❖ The *Atharva-Veda* differs remarkably from the other three, containing mostly spells, curses, and charms in 731 hymns divided into twenty books. It reflects the everyday religious life of ordinary people just as the threefold *Veda* reflects the religious life of the priestly group.

The next part of *Shruti* to emerge was the **Brahmanas** [BRAH-muh-nuhs], which are manuals for sacrifice. They describe ancient Vedic sacrifice in great and fascinating detail and are organized to correspond to the four *Veda* samhitas. They present sacrifice—and especially ritual utterance, the powerful sacrificial word correctly spoken—as the power that strengthens the gods, keeps the universe intact, and brings blessing to the sacrificer. Brahmin priests sacrificed meat and other offerings to all the gods. The soma sacrifice is the most prominent. The **Aranyakas** [ah-RUN-yah-kuhs], which contain philosophical thoughts on sacrifice, especially the sacrificial fire, are a development of the *Brahmanas*. Reflections on the New Year festival are also prominent. These speculations were considered unsuitable for open knowledge and so were made in the privacy of the forest. Some *Aranyakas* have been incorporated into the *Upanishads*.

The **Upanishads** [oo-PAH-nee-shahds] form the final part of *Shruti*. One hundred twenty-three *Upanishads* have survived, but only thirteen have been influential in Hindu history. The *Upanishads* are philosophical treatments on cosmic reality and sometimes feature debates between opposing teachers. Their emphasis is on self-denial as a way to find religious truth, the way of asceticism. The ritualism of the four *Vedas* and especially of the *Brahmanas* is downplayed and even attacked in the *Upanishads*. The *Upanishads* are concerned to find the One, the absolute spiritual reality that lies in and behind all the visible elements and beings of this physical world. As the conclusion of *Shruti* and the Vedic scripture collection, the *Upanishads* are also known as the *Vedanta* (End of the *Veda*).

We begin describing the *Smriti* with the two main epics, the *Mahabharata* and the *Ramayana*. The *Ramayana* (Story of Rama) is traditionally attributed to the poet Valkimi. It was written in the third century B.C.E. Prince Rama was exiled from his kingdom and his wife Sita was kidnapped by the demon Ravana, but Rama was restored to his kingdom and his wife with the help of the monkey-god. The *Mahabharata* (Great Story of the Bharatas) is the longest epic in the world—four times longer than the Christian *Bible*. Its basic story involves the feud and eventual war between two sides of King Bharata's family. The *Mahabharata* is a vast repository of Indian myths and legends, and the **Bhagavad-Gita** (Song of the Lord) is a small part of this larger epic. The *Mahabharata* and the *Ramayana* share a common body of myth and folklore.

The *Puranas,* traditionally eighteen in number, are also concerned with myth, lore, and legend. Like the epics (and like *Smriti* in general), they are addressed to the ordinary person. Emerging about 400 to 1000 C.E., they stress devotion to a specific divinity as the way to release. Thus some speak of Shiva, some of Vishnu, and some of Shakti, the three main devotional movements of Hinduism. By far the most popular, and influential for medieval and early modern Indian popular literature and painting, is the *Bhagavata-Purana.* This tenth-century work provides background on the Krishna of the *Bhagavad-Gita* [BAH-gav-vahd GEE-tuh], especially his youth among the cowherders of his village and his romantic adventures with the cowherd women.

Tantras ("looms, weavings") mirror the Hinduism of medieval India. Books of mystical teachings, spells, and rituals, they deal with beliefs and yogic meditation in a popular way. Each of the three main devotional movements—Shiva, Vishnu, and Shakti—has its own official collections of tantras, which tell the exploits of the movement's gods and bring their powers to devotees by means of ritual and yoga.

The final type of *Smriti* to be considered here are manuals of dharma, or law codes. Law here is broadly conceived in its social and personal dimensions; it encompasses caste, life stages, diet, government, and other matters. The most important dharma manual is the *Laws of Manu,* composed around 200 C.E. in twelve books. The main concern of *Manu* is the codification and operation of the four-caste system, and *Manu*'s influence on Hindu life has been profound. Indeed, the two things that are most often said to define a practicing Hindu are acceptance of the *Vedas* and following caste duty.

Use

Hindu scriptures have a wide variety of uses, some of which have already been mentioned. In what follows, we trace these uses briefly, with a special focus on orality.

The four *Vedas* were orally composed and were handed down orally for thousands of years. To put them in a book would have seemed absurd, even sacrilegious, because they were in essence a spoken and heard revelation (*Shruti*) and their power resided in their spokenness.

Brahmin priests use the *Vedas* for ritual. The threefold *Veda* has always been the text of this religious aristocracy, never of the people as a whole. From the first, the sound of these scriptures was more important than their content. Traditionalist Hindus believe that the sounds of the *Veda* were the sounds that the sages heard reverberating from the creation of the universe and that the same sounds will be used again at the next cycle of re-creation. These sounds have been passed on orally from guru to student for thousands of years. Gurus teach their students every element of correct oral usage of the *Veda,* including correct enunciation, poetic meter, volume, and pitch. Brahmins who excel in *Veda* memorization and ritual enactment are known as **pandits** (compare with the English word *pundit*). As a student, each young

Brahmin is educated in one of the four *Vedas* and becomes an expert in the use of that *Veda* in sacrifice. Hymns in the *Rig-Veda* often end with a request to the deity that the sacrificers might "speak as men of power" during the rites.

Hindus do not study the content of the *Vedas* in, for example, meditation or doctrinal instruction. Much of the ancient Vedic form of the Sanskrit language has been lost, and much of its meaning is not recoverable. For the past two thousand years, accordingly, Brahmins often have not understood what they were saying as they chanted the *Vedas* in the rituals. This is not important; only the correct sounds matter. Today only a few Brahmin families keep up a ritually correct form of the ancient Vedic sacrifices. However, all domestic rituals are done with Vedic formulas. Speaking and concentrating on the **mantra** [MAHN-truh] allows the believer to tap into the cosmic power of creative speech.

The *Upanishads* became the texts of the philosophers, especially of the Vedanta school of Hindu philosophy. Reflecting on the meaning of this scripture in a life of strict renunciation allows the sage to be set free from desire and rebirth. In the last hundred years a neo-Vedantic school has arisen, mainly drawing on ancient Hindu themes and also influenced by Western religious ideas such as theism and inter-religious tolerance.

Law codes are used for the ordering of society. They especially reflect the Brahmin caste and its view of Hindu life. How closely these books were followed and enforced in ancient times cannot now be determined, but their broadest aspects have certainly retained much authority.

Of all Hindu scripture, the epics have been the best known and most loved. The *Bhagavad-Gita*, because of the way it affirms and integrates many main aspects of Hinduism, has been acceptable and influential among most Hindus. For its promotion of one way as the best, however, it remains the special text of the Vishnu-Krishna devotional movement.

For most of Hindu history, the primacy of these works has been in their oral, not their written, form. For example, the four *Veda* samhitas probably were composed and collected before writing was known in India. The *Upanishads* were not fully written down until 1656 C.E., and then only at the command of the non-Hindu Sultan Dara Shakoh, who ordered a translation of these oral works into Persian. Since then, the *Upanishads* have been translated by Hindus into the other main Indian languages; the original Sanskrit was written down as well. The Hindu tradition has regarded writing itself as polluting compared with the sanctity of the spoken word. Now, however, orality is fading, and it is common to see even holy men reading aloud from books instead of "reading" from memory. Still, the "sound" of the scriptures continues to be important, for sound is their very essence.

Comparing a typical Hindu attitude toward scripture with Western attitudes, Daniel Gold remarks, "The idea of Vedic authority known to traditional Hindus is much more diffuse and abstract than the idea of a closed biblical canon known to the West. Christians, for example, variously interpret a revealed text to which most people have access and of which they can make some literal sense. For Hindus, by contrast, a reverence for scriptural authority can often mean simply that they think that what they do somehow comes from the Vedas, texts which in their antiquity are very rarely used or understood anymore. . . . They exist now primarily as words of power incorporated into newer rites."[1]

To sum up: Hindus' use of scripture depends on their class and occupation and on the particular type of Hinduism (philosophical, devotional, etc.) they follow. All Hindus have a strong, if vague, reverence for the threefold *Veda*, a feeling for the structure of society as reflected in the law codes, and, in devotional Hinduism, a strong feeling for the literature of one's single chosen god or goddess.

Origin and Development

The long history of Hindu scripture parallels to a large degree the history of Hinduism as a whole. We here briefly survey how Hindu scripture began, the process of its growth, and how it took its present form. Keep in mind this general principle of Hindu scripture as we begin this section: The literature grows by association. Earlier works, no matter how sacred, invite and attract later works with related themes and styles, which in turn attract still more sacred literature.

The four *Vedas* have their origin in ritual. Sacrifice itself seems to have come first, for even the earliest *Vedas* presuppose an established sacrifice. The songs, melodies, and formal directions for their performance were drawn up later, soon after the Aryan invasion of India around 1500 B.C.E. The *Rig-Veda* contains songs for sacrifice. The oldest hymns deal with the gods of the Indo-Aryans: the sky-god Dyaus Pitar, whom the Greeks knew as Zeus, and the earth-goddess Prithivi Mater. In the next stage, these old gods receded and new gods arose: Indra the new sky-god, Agni the god of fire, Soma the god of drugged sacrifice. The final hymns written down are found in the present *Rig-Veda* Books 1 and 10, which move from polytheistic nature gods to the kind of cosmic speculations that search for the oneness of all being. The final form of the *Rig-Veda* was reached about 1200 B.C.E.

The *Sama-Veda* was composed after the *Rig-Veda* was complete. It has lines from the *Rig-Veda*, chanted to fixed melodies. The melodies are not captured in the written text but are passed on from singing priest to his disciples. The proper lyrics and music were essential to the success of the rite. The *Yajur-Veda* contains directions for sacrifice and also was written down after the *Rig-Veda* was established. The *Atharva-Veda* with its magical spells gives a glimpse into the more popular levels of ancient Hinduism. The spells are addressed not to the great gods but to the gods and spirits that control everyday life, its cycles and challenges. The first seven books are the earliest; Books 8 through 12 are more recent and contain cosmological speculations similar to Book 10 of the *Rig-Veda* and the later *Upanishads*.

The *Brahmanas* mark the high point of Hindu ritualism. The power of the priesthood steadily grew in Vedic times (2000–1000 B.C.E.), and the focus of the *Brahmanas* is on sacrifice itself, not on the gods. Sacrifice is the power that generates the cosmos and keeps it going. The main group of the *Brahmanas* deals with the

[1] D. Gold, "Organized Hinduisms," in M. E. Marty and R. S. Appleby, *Fundamentalisms Observed* (Chicago: University of Chicago Press, 1991), pp. 542–543.

Yajur-Veda and the ritual process. Sacrifices using soma are prominent, as is the horse sacrifice, which took great expense and an entire year to enact.

The *Aranyakas* mark the beginning of a departure from Vedic ritualism. Mixed and disjointed in content, these reflections may have been developed by marginalized Brahmins or by members of the warrior caste.

The *Upanishads,* the last of the Vedic scriptures, are close in style to the *Aranyakas.* Most were written from the eighth to the fourth centuries B.C.E. The so-called principal *Upanishads* number about thirteen and are the only *Upanishads* accepted by all Hindus. Some with special devotion to a particular deity date from the beginnings of the Common Era all the way to the sixteenth century C.E. and are accepted only by certain Hindu sects as interest in ritual fades and philosophy/renunciation advances. The oldest of these are the *Chandogya* and *Brihad-Aranyaka Upanishads.*

The *Upanishads,* like most *Shruti,* are not uniform or systematic; they are diverse collections of philosophical materials from different teachers over the centuries. The "world-affirming" Vedic religion that originally sought blessing in this world has also become a "world-negating" religion that seeks release from continually reincarnated existence in this world. These *Upanishads* present the way of knowledge, the search for the eternal One called **Brahman** [BRAH-muhn] as it relates to **Atman** [AHT-muhn], the eternal Self at the hidden center of every human. They are the beginnings of Hindu philosophy, which has been and remains influential, although it has been an option for only a tiny minority of Hindus of any period.

Unlike the *Shruti,* the epics of *Smriti* display very little interest in ritual and instead deal with broad religious and cultural topics. The *Mahabharata* was finished by 400 C.E., the *Ramayana* by 200 B.C.E. Evident in both are many layers of development: (1) myths of the gods, from earliest Hinduism; (2) the central plot of each epic; (3) discussions of religious duty and law. The insertion of this last layer into the epic is a typically Indian practice: to pause at key points in the narrative for a religious discussion. The most famous of these insertions, the *Bhagavad-Gita,* section 6 of the *Mahabharata,* today is reckoned a book in itself. These discussions are precursors of the law books, to which we now turn.

The law codes are called **Dharma-Shastras** [DAHR-muh SHAS-truhs], "Writings on Duty." Books on duty began to be compiled in the schools in which the *Vedas* and *Brahmanas* were studied. They developed into comprehensive and systematic books that eventually formed the basis of Hindu law. *Manu* was written perhaps about 200 C.E. as a full code for all Hindu society, for every caste, occupation, and stage of life. Like the law books of most religions and civilizations, *Manu* and the other law codes were developed by commentary as the centuries passed, and thus their influence was perpetuated. How deep this influence may have been is unknown because *Manu* (again like most law codes) gives prescriptions for an ideal society. Real Hindu life, like the life of all religions, no doubt fell short of its ideals.

Eighteen of the ancient stories of the *Puranas* are especially important. Their themes are creation, re-creation, origins of the gods and sages, eras of common history, and dynastic histories. Some, like the *Upanishads,* are sectarian, appealing to devotees of only one god. The *Puranas* fall into three main categories as they promote the gods Vishnu, Shiva, and others. The most important *Purana* is the *Bhagavata-Purana,* composed about 400–1000 C.E. It is based on and furthers the book for which it is named, the *Bhagavad-Gita.*

Tantras—books of mystical teachings, spells, and directions for rituals—arose as a popular supplement to Vedic religion. While acknowledging the truth and authority of the *Vedas*, the tantras go beyond them to provide updated rituals. They perfect the use of specific techniques for the body and the mind. Tantrism is widespread in Hindu religion, but the devotional cult of the goddess Shakti has a special attachment to it. The Shaktic tantras occasionally feature "left-handed" tantrism, which most Westerners wrongly associate with tantrism as a whole: esoteric practices, magic, and exotic sexual practices. The tantras were written in the period 500–1800 C.E.

TEACHING

Aditi and the Birth of the Gods*

This hymn presents several different and seemingly contradictory explanations of the creation of the world: It was spoken by the lord of sacred speech; it came from nonexistence; the mother-goddess gave birth to it; it was formed from the mutual births of Aditi and Daksa; it was formed from Martanda. These and other explanations still exist among Hindus today.[2]

Let us now speak with wonder of the births of the gods, so that someone may see them when the hymns are chanted in this later age. The lord of sacred speech, like a smith, fanned them together. In the earliest age of the gods, existence was born from nonexistence. In the first age of the gods, existence was born from nonexistence. After this the quarters of the sky were born from her who crouched with legs spread. The earth was born from her who crouched with legs spread, and from the earth the quarters of the sky were born. From Aditi, Daksa was born, and from Daksa Aditi was born. [5] For

Aditi was born as your daughter, O Daksa, and after her were born the blessed gods, the kinsmen of immortality. When you gods took your places there in the water with your hands joined,[3] a thick cloud of mist arose from you like dust from dancers. When you gods like magicians caused the worlds to swell, you drew forth the sun that was hidden in the ocean. Eight sons are there of Aditi, who were born of her body. With seven she went forth among the gods, but she threw Martanda, the sun, aside. With seven sons Aditi went forth into the earliest age. But she bore Martanda so that he would in turn beget offspring[4] and then soon die.

Rig-Veda 10.72.
[2] All selections from the *Rig-Veda* are reprinted from *The Rig Veda, An Anthology,* by Wendy Doniger O'Flaherty (London: Penguin, 1981). Copyright © 1981 Wendy Doniger O'Flaherty. Used by permission.
[3] *hands joined:* the typical Indian posture of greeting and respect.
[4] *offspring:* humanity, which begets its offspring and dies.

Two Philosophical Views of Creation**

Many accounts of the origin of the universe are philosophical rather than mythological. Questioning and puzzling, they stir the listener to reflection. In the first selection, "that one" is the impersonal creator by *whom the gods themselves are created. This hymn has been most influential among Hindus. The second*

**Rig-Veda* 10.129; *Brihad-Aranyaka Upanishad* 1.4.1–7.

selection, from an important Upanishad, *presents a philosophical reflection on the origin of the world. It traces creation to Brahman, the world-soul that is the All in and behind the world. The cosmic Person* (purusha) *identified with the world-soul is neither male nor female, despite the references to the Person as "he."* [5]

[*Rig-Veda* 10.129] There was neither nonexistence nor existence then; there was neither the realm of space nor the sky which is beyond. What stirred? Where? In whose protection? Was there water, bottomlessly deep? There was neither death nor immortality then. There was no distinguishing sign of night or of day. That one breathed, windless, by its own impulse. Other than that there was nothing beyond. Darkness was hidden by darkness in the beginning; with no distinguishing sign, all this was water. The life force that was covered with emptiness arose through the power of heat. Desire came upon that one in the beginning; that was the first seed of mind. Poets seeking in their heart with wisdom found the bond of existence in nonexistence. [5] Their cord[6] was extended across. Was there below? Was there above? There were seed-placers; there were powers. There was impulse beneath; there was giving-forth above. Who really knows? Who here will proclaim it? Where was it produced? Where did this creation come from? The gods came afterwards, with the creation of this universe. Who then knows where it has arisen? Where this creation has arisen—perhaps it formed itself, or perhaps it did not—the one[7] who looks down on it, in the highest heaven, only he knows—or perhaps he does not know.

[*Brihad-Aranyaka Upanishad* 1.4.1–7] In the beginning this world was Soul alone, in the shape of a Person. He looked around and saw nothing but himself. He first said, "This is I." Therefore, he became I by name. Therefore even now, if a man is asked he first says, "This is I," and then pronounces his other name. Before [*purva*] all this he burnt down [*ush*] all evils; therefore he was a Person [*purusha*]. Truly he

who knows this burns down everyone who tries to be before him.

He feared, and therefore anyone who is lonely fears. He thought, "As there is nothing but myself, why should I fear?" Then his fear passed away. For what should he have feared? But he felt no delight. Therefore a man who is lonely feels no delight. He longed for a second person. As he was as large as a man and woman together, he made his Self to fall in two, and there came husband and wife. Therefore Yajnavalkya said: "We two are thus like half a shell." Therefore the void that was there [in the male] is filled by the wife. He had sexual intercourse with her, and humans were born.

She thought, "How can he have sexual intercourse with me, after having produced me from himself? I shall hide myself." She then became a cow. But he became a bull and had sex with her, and therefore cows were born. Then she became a mare, and he a stallion; then he a male ass, and she a female ass. He had sex with her [in both forms], and therefore one-hoofed animals were born. He became a she-goat, she a he-goat; he became a ewe, she a ram. He had sex with her, and therefore goats and sheep were born. In this way he created everything that exists in pairs, down to the ants. [5] He knew this: "I indeed am this creation, for I created all this." Therefore he became the creation, and he who knows this lives in this his creation.

Next he thus produced fire by rubbing. From the mouth, as from the fire-hole,[8] and from the hands he created fire. Therefore both the mouth and the hands are hairless inside, for the fire-hole is without hair inside.

---

[5] This and all other selections from the *Upanishads* are taken, with editing, from F. Max Müller, trans., *The Upanishads, Sacred Books of the East,* vols. 1 and 15 (Oxford: Oxford University Press, 1878, 1884).

[6] *cord:* the bond of existence, extending across the universe.

[7] *the one:* Prajapati, the high god.

[8] *fire-hole:* Sanskrit *yoni,* the circular religious image of the human vagina symbolizing the female cosmic creative power.

People say, "Sacrifice to this god or that god." But each god is his manifestation, for he is all gods.

Whatever is moist he created from semen; this is Soma. So this universe is really either food or eaters of food. Soma is food, Agni the eater. This is the highest creation of Brahman, when he created the gods from his better part, and when he who was then mortal created the immortals. Therefore it was the highest creation. He who knows this lives in this highest creation. . . .

He cannot be seen, for when breathing he is called breath. When speaking, he is called speech; when seeing, eye; when hearing, ear; when thinking, mind. All these are only the names of his acts. He who worships him as the one or the other, does not know him. . . . Let men worship him as Soul [Atman], for in the Soul all these are one. This Soul is the footprint of everything, for through it one knows everything. As one can find again by footprints what was lost, he who knows this finds glory and praise.

The God Indra*

Indra is the sky-god, the king of the gods. This hymn extols Indra's accomplishments over several opposing gods and for promoting the welfare of the people. It seeks to defend the importance of Indra against those who ignore him or even deny his existence (verse 5). This defense evidently did not succeed, because in post-Vedic Hinduism Indra has largely disappeared.

The god who had insight the moment he was born, the first who protected the gods with his power of thought, before whose hot breath the two world-halves tremble at the greatness of his manly powers—he, my people, is Indra. He who made fast the tottering earth, who made still the quaking mountains, who measured out and extended the expanse of the air, who propped up the sky—he, my people, is Indra. He who killed the serpent and loosed the seven rivers, who drove out the cows that had been pent up by Vala,[9] who gave birth to fire between two stones, the winner of booty in combats—he, my people, is Indra. He by whom all these changes were rung, who drove the race of Dasas[10] down into obscurity, who took away the flourishing wealth of the enemy as a winning gambler takes the stake—he, my people, is Indra.

[5] He about whom they ask, "Where is he?," or they say of him, the terrible one, "He does not exist," he who diminishes the flourishing wealth of the enemy as gambling does—believe in him! He, my people, is Indra. He who encourages the weary and the sick, and the poor priest who is in need, who helps the man who harnesses the stones to press Soma, he who has lips fine for drinking—he, my people, is Indra.

He under whose command are horses and cows and villages and all chariots, who gave birth to the sun and the dawn and led out the waters, he, my people, is Indra. He who is invoked by both of two armies, enemies locked in combat, on this side and that side, he who is even invoked separately by each of two men standing on the very same chariot, he, my people, is Indra. He without whom people do not conquer, he whom they call on for help when they are fighting, who became the image of everything, who shakes the unshakable—he, my people, is Indra.

[10] He who killed with his weapon all those who had committed a great sin, even when they did not know it, he who does not pardon the arrogant man for his arrogance, who is the slayer of the Dasas, he, my people, is Indra. He who in the fortieth autumn discovered Sambara living

---

*Rig-Veda 2.12.
[9] *Vala:* Indra's demonic enemy, who penned up the cows.
[10] *Dasas:* literally, "slaves," enemies of the Aryans whom they subjugated.

in the mountains, who killed the violent serpent, the Danu, as he lay there, he, my people, is Indra. He, the mighty bull who with his seven reins let loose the seven rivers to flow, who with his thunderbolt in his hand hurled down Rauhina as he was climbing up to the sky, he, my people, is Indra. Even the sky and the earth bow low before him, and the mountains are terrified of his hot breath.

He who is known as the Soma-drinker, with the thunderbolt in his hand, with the thunderbolt in his palm, he, my people, is Indra. He who helps with his favor the one who presses and the one who cooks,[11] the praiser and the preparer, he for whom prayer is nourishment, for whom Soma is the special gift, he, my people, is Indra. [15] You who furiously grasp the prize for the one who presses and the one who cooks, you are truly real. Let us be dear to you, Indra, all our days, and let us speak as men of power in the sacrificial gathering.

---

[11] *presses . . . cooks:* in preparation of the soma.

Rudra and Shiva*

Although one of the main branches of devotional Hinduism is Shaivism, Shiva does not have a well-known text to celebrate him as Krishna does in the Bhagavad-Gita. This late Upanishadic hymn identifies the Vedic god Rudra and the Cosmic Person with Shiva. It is used today by the worshippers of Shiva to express his praise. This hymn shows how the worship of one god characteristic of devotional Hinduism is related to the wider Hindu traditions with many gods.

The snarer rules alone by his powers, rules all the worlds by his powers. He is the same, while things arise and exist. They who know this are immortal. There is only one Rudra. They do not allow a second; he rules all the worlds by his powers. He stands behind all persons. Having created all worlds, he, the protector, rolls it up at the end of time. This god has his eyes, his face, his arms, and his feet in every place. When producing heaven and earth, he forges them together with his arms and his wings. He is the creator and supporter of the gods. Rudra is the great seer, the lord of all, who formerly gave birth to Hiranyagarbha. May he endow us with good thoughts.

[5] O Rudra, dweller in the mountains, look upon us with your most blessed form that is auspicious, not terrible, and reveals no evil! O lord of the mountains, make lucky that arrow that you hold in your hand to shoot. Do not hurt man or beast! Beyond this is the High Brahman, the vast, hidden in the bodies of all creatures. He alone envelops everything, as the Lord. Those who know this become immortal. I know that great Person [*purusha*] of sunlike luster beyond the darkness. A man who truly knows him passes over death; there is no other path to go.

This whole universe is filled by this Person, to whom there is nothing superior, from whom there is nothing different, than whom there is nothing smaller or larger. This Person stands alone, fixed like a tree in the sky. [10] That which is beyond this world is without form and without suffering. They who know this become immortal, but others suffer pain.

The Blessed One exists in the faces, the heads, the necks of all. He dwells in the cave of the heart of all beings. He is all-pervading, and therefore he is the omnipresent Shiva. That Person is the great lord. He is the mover of existence.

Shvetashvatara Upanishad 3.1–13.

He possesses the purest power reaching everything. He is light; he is undecaying. The Person, not larger than a thumb, always dwelling in the heart of man, is perceived by the heart, the thought, and the mind. Those who know this become immortal.

"That You Are"*

In this reading, the Oneness that exists in and beyond the world is developed in a dialogue between a son and his father. Popularly known as "The Education of Svetaketu," this story points to the cosmic Self as the inner essence of all that is.

Om.[12] There lived once Svetaketu Aruneya, the grandson of Aruna. To him his father, Uddalaka, the son of Aruna, said: "Svetaketu, go to school. For there is none belonging to our race, who, not having studied the *Veda*, is, so to speak, a Brahmana by birth only."

Having begun his apprenticeship with a teacher when he was twelve years of age, Svetaketu returned to his father when he was twenty-four, having then studied all the *Vedas*. But he was conceited, considering himself well read and stern. His father said to him: "Svetaketu, as you are so conceited, considering yourself so well read, and so stern; my dear, have you ever asked for that instruction by which we hear what cannot be heard? Have you asked for that by which we perceive what cannot be perceived, by which we know what cannot be known?"

"What is that instruction, sir?" he asked.

The father replied: "My dear, as by one clod of clay all that is made of clay is known, the difference being only a name, arising from speech, but the truth being that all is clay. As, my dear, by one nugget of gold all that is made of gold is known, the difference being only a name, arising from speech, but the truth being that all is gold. As, my dear, by one pair of nail scissors all that is made of iron is known, the difference being only a name, arising from speech, but the truth being that all is iron—thus, my dear, is that instruction."

The son said: "Surely those venerable men, my teachers, did not know that. For if they had known it, why should they not have told it me? Sir, tell me that."

"In the beginning, my dear, there was one thing only, without a second. It thought, May I be many, may I grow forth. It sent forth fire. That fire thought, May I be many, may I grow forth. It sent forth water. Therefore whenever anybody anywhere is hot and perspires, water is produced on him from fire alone. Water thought, May I be many, may I grow forth. It sent forth earth (food). Therefore whenever it rains anywhere, most food is then produced. From water alone is eatable food produced. . . .

[9] "As the bees, my son, make honey by collecting the juices of distant trees, and reduce the juice into one form, and as these juices have no discrimination, so that they might say, I am the juice of this tree or that, in the same manner, my son, all these creatures, when they have become merged in the True (either in deep sleep or in death), know not that they are merged in the True. Whatever these creatures are here, whether a lion, or a wolf, or a boar, or a worm, or a midge, or a gnat, or a mosquito, that they become again and again. Now that which is that subtle essence, in it all that exists has its self. It is the True. It is the Self, and that, Svetaketu, you are."

"Please, Sir, inform me still more," said the son.

Chandogya Upanishad 6.1–2, 9–11.
[12] *Om:* A lesson is often begun with this cosmic sound [OHM].

"These rivers, my son, run, the eastern like the Ganges, toward the east, the western like the Sindhu, toward the west. They go from sea to sea, that is, the clouds lift up the water from the sea to the sky, and send it back as rain to the sea. They become indeed sea. And as those rivers, when they are in the sea, do not know I am this or that river, in the same manner, my son, all these creatures, when they have come back from the True, know not that they have come back from the True. Whatever these creatures are here, whether a lion, or a wolf, or a boar, or a worm, or a midge, or a gnat, or a mosquito, that they become again and again.

"That which is that subtle essence, in it all that exists has its self. It is the True. It is the Self, and that, Svetaketu, you are."

"Please, Sir, inform me still more," said the son.

"If someone were to strike at the root of this large tree here, it would bleed, but live. If he were to strike at its stem, it would bleed, but live. If he were to strike at its top, it would bleed, but live. Pervaded by the living Self that tree stands firm, drinking in its nourishment and rejoicing; but if the life (the living Self) leaves one of its branches, that branch withers; if it leaves a second, that branch withers; if it leaves a third, that branch withers. If it leaves the whole tree, the whole tree withers.

"In exactly the same manner, my son, know this. This body indeed withers and dies when the living Self has left it; the living Self dies not.

"That subtle essence is the self of all that exists. It is the True. It is the Self, and that, Svetaketu, you are."

The Goddess as Kali*

The Devi-Mahatmya, *or "The Greatness of the Goddess," is a leading medieval* Purana. *Popular since its oral origins among goddess devotees, it is now the best-known and most often recited goddess text in modern India. The goddess has many names and forms; here she fights a fearsome battle in her form as Kali, the goddess of destruction.*[13]

Directed in this fashion . . . the demons,
　　arranged as a fourfold army
With Canda and Munda at their head, went
　　forth with upraised weapons.
Then they saw the Goddess, smiling slightly,
　　mounted
On her lion on the great golden peak of the
　　highest mountain.
Having seen her, they made ready in their
　　efforts to abduct her,
While others approached her with swords
　　drawn and bows bent.
Ambika then uttered a great wrathful cry
　　against them,

And her face became black as ink in anger.
[5] From the knitted brows of her forehead's
　　surface immediately
Came forth Kali, with her dreadful face,
　　carrying sword and noose.
She carried a strange skull-topped staff, and
　　wore a garland of human heads.
She was shrouded in a tiger skin, and looked
　　utterly gruesome with her emaciated skin,
Her widely gaping mouth, terrifying with its
　　lolling tongue,
With sunken, reddened eyes and a mouth that
　　filled the directions with roars.
She fell upon the great Asuras in that army,
　　slaying them immediately.

Markandeya Purana, Devi-Mahatmya 7.1–25.

[13] From Thomas B. Coburn, *Encountering the Goddess: A Translation of the* Devi-Mahatmya *and a Study of Its Interpretation* (Albany, NY: State University of New York Press, 1991), pp. 60–62. Copyright © 1991 State University of New York Press. Used by permission.

She then devoured the forces of the enemies of the gods.

Attacking both the front and rear guard, having seized the elephants
Together with their riders and bells, she hurled them into her mouth with a single hand.
[10] Likewise having flung the cavalry with its horses and the chariots with their charioteers
Into her mouth, she brutally pulverized them with her teeth.
She seized one by the hair, and another by the throat.
Having attacked one with her foot, she crushed another against her breast.
The weapons and missiles that were hurled by the demons
She seized with her mouth, and crunched them to bits with her teeth.
The army of all those mighty and distinguished demons
She destroyed: she devoured some, and thrashed the others.
Some were sliced by her sword, others pounded with her skull-topped staff.
Just in this way the Asuras met their destruction, ground up by the edges of her fangs.
[15] Immediately upon seeing the entire army of the Asuras slain,
Canda rushed at the incredibly fearsome Kali.
The great Asura enveloped the dread-eyed female with a horrendous great shower of arrows,

And Munda did the same with discuses hurled by the thousand.
This stream of discuses entering her mouth
Resembled a multitude of suns entering into the middle of a black cloud.
Then Kali, her ugly teeth gleaming within her dreadful mouth,
Angrily cackled with terrible sounds.
Mounting her great lion, the Goddess ran at Canda,
And having seized him by the hair, she cut off his head with her sword.
[20] On seeing Canda slain, Munda rushed at her.
She caused him to fall to the ground, wrathfully smitten with her sword.
On seeing Canda slain, and also Munda,
What was left of the assaulted army was overcome with fear, and fled in all directions.
Picking up the heads of Canda and Munda,
Kali approached Candika and spoke words mixed with loud and cruel laughter:
"Here, as a present from me to you, are Canda and Munda, two beasts
Slain in the sacrifice of battle.
Now you yourself can slay Shumbha and Nishumbha!" . . .

Seeing the two great Asuras brought there,
The beautiful Candika spoke these playful words to Kali:
"Because you have seized Canda and Munda and brought them here,
You will henceforth be known in the world as the Goddess 'Camundi.'"

ETHICS

Sin and Forgiveness*

The god Varuna protects the cosmic order and punishes those humans who violate it by misdeeds. This passage presents the heartfelt pleas of the worshipper to Varuna to reveal his unknown sin to him and pardon it.

The generations have become wise by the power of [Varuna], who has propped apart the two world-halves even though they are so vast.

*Rig-Veda 7.86.

He has pushed away the dome of the sky to make it high and wide; he has set the sun on its double journey and spread out the earth. I ask my own heart, "When shall I be close to Varuna? Will he enjoy my offering and not be provoked to anger? When shall I see his mercy and rejoice?" I ask myself what that transgression was, Varuna, for I wish to understand. I turn to the wise to ask them. The poets have told me the very same thing: "Varuna has been provoked to anger against you."

O Varuna, what was the terrible crime for which you wish to destroy your friend who praises you? Proclaim it to me so that I may hasten to prostrate myself before you and be free from sin, for you are hard to deceive and are ruled by yourself alone. [5] Free us from the harmful deeds of our fathers, and from those that we have committed with our own bodies. O king, free

Vasistha[14] like a thief who has stolen cattle, like a calf set free from a rope. The mischief was not done by my own free will, Varuna; wine, anger, dice, or carelessness led me astray. The older shares in the mistake of the younger. Even sleep does not avert evil. As a slave serves a generous master, so would I serve the furious god and be free from sin. The noble god[15] gave understanding to those who did not understand; being yet wiser, he speeds the clever man to wealth. O Varuna, you who are ruled by yourself alone, let this praise lodge in your very heart. Let it go well for us always with your blessings.

---

[14] *Vasistha:* a wise man who, according to myth, broke into Varuna's house; he was tied up but then freed when he praised Varuna.

[15] *the noble god:* Varuna.

The Three *Da*'s*

The main virtues of Hinduism are often put in their most elemental form as the three da's: damyata, *restraint and self-control;* datta, *generosity; and* dayadhvam, *compassion. These are said to be commanded from the beginning.*

The threefold offspring of Prajapati—gods, men, and demons—lived as students of sacred knowledge with their father Prajapati. Having lived the life of a student of sacred knowledge, the gods said: "Speak to us, sir." Prajapati spoke to them this syllable, "*Da.* Do you understand this?" They said to him, "We did understand. You said to us, 'Control yourselves (*damyata*).'" "*Om!*" he replied. "You did understand."

Then they said to him again, "Speak to us, sir." He spoke to them this syllable, "*Da.* Do

you understand this?" They said to him: "We do understand. You said to us, 'Give (*datta*).'" "*Om!*" he said. "You did understand."

So then the spiritual beings said to him, "Speak to us, sir." He said this syllable to them, "*Da.* Do you understand?" They said, "We understand. You said to us, 'Be compassionate (*dayadhvam*).'" "*Om!*" he said. "You did understand."

The divine voice of the thunder repeats, "*Da! Da! Da!* Control yourself, give, be compassionate." One should practice this same triad: self-control, giving, compassion.

Brihadaranyaka Upanishad 5.2.

The Way of Asceticism*

This reading presents all the ancient practices of Hinduism as necessary. But they are "unsafe boats," and those who trust in them to accomplish release are "fools" and "ignorant." The only effective way of release is the way of knowledge based on renunciation and asceticism. This belief has been a guiding principle for ascetics and holy men from Upanishadic times until today.

This is the truth: the sacrificial works that the poets saw in the hymns [of the *Veda*] have been performed in many ways in the Vedic age. Practice them diligently, you lovers of truth! This is your path that leads to the world of good works!

When the fire is lighted and the flame flickers, let a man offer his oblations between the two portions of melted butter, as an offering with faith. A man's Agnihotra sacrifice destroys his seven worlds if it is not followed by the new-moon and full-moon sacrifices, by the four-months' sacrifices, and by the harvest sacrifice. It destroys his seven worlds if it is unattended by guests, not offered at all, done without the ceremony to all the gods, or not offered according to the rules. . . .

[5] If a man performs his sacred works when these flames are shining, and the sacrificial offerings follow at the right time, they lead him as sunrays to where the one Lord of the gods dwells. "Come here, come here!," the brilliant offerings say to him. They carry the sacrificer on the rays of the sun, while they utter pleasant speech and praise him: "This is your holy Brahma-world, gained by your good works."

But those boats, the eighteen sacrifices,[16] are truly frail. Fools who praise this as the highest good are subjected again and again to old age and death. Fools dwelling in darkness, wise in their own conceit and puffed up with vain knowledge, go round and round, staggering back and forth; they are like blind men led by the blind. . . . [10] Considering sacrifice and good works as the best, these fools know no higher good. Having enjoyed their reward in the height of heaven, gained by good works, they come back again to this world or a lower one. But those who practice penance and faith in the forest, who are tranquil, wise and live on alms, depart free from passion through the sun to where that immortal Person dwells, whose nature is imperishable.

Let a Brahmin, after he has examined all these worlds that are gained by works, acquire freedom from all desires. Nothing that is eternal can be gained by what is not eternal. To understand this, let him take fuel in his hand[17] and approach a guru who is learned and dwells entirely in Brahman. The wise teacher truly tells that knowledge of Brahman through which he knows the eternal and true Person. He tells a pupil who has approached him respectfully, whose thoughts are not troubled by any desires and who has obtained perfect peace.

Mundaka Upanishad 2.1–3, 5–8, 10–13.
[16] *eighteen sacrifices:* Vedic rituals.
[17] *fuel in his hand:* a sign of studentship.

Stages of Life for a Twice-Born Man**

The first stage of Hindu life is that of the student, who lives and studies with his guru (private teacher). The first passage gives the rules for the student's relationship with his teacher, especially the respect

owed to one's teacher. The second stage is that of the householder, when the young man, his studies

---

**Laws of Manu* 2.69–74, 191–201; 3.1–19; 6.1–9, 33–49.

complete, must marry and father children. Here the rules for whom to marry are presented. The third stage is that of retirement into the forest, and Manu sets forth the style of life and religious aims of this stage. The fourth stage is that of the ascetic who renounces all typical life to find release from rebirth. These laws on the stages of life reflect the situation of about 200 C.E., when Manu was written. Some differ from present practice. Asceticism, for example, no longer requires a prior retirement stage but can be entered by an adult male at any time. The system presented here is idealized—only a minority of Hindus in the past and present have experienced it fully. Nonetheless, it continues to be influential.[18]

[2.69, The Stage of Studentship] Having performed the rite of initiation,[19] the teacher must first instruct the pupil in the rules of personal purification, conduct, fire-worship, and twilight devotions. [70] A student who is about to begin the study of the *Veda* shall receive instruction after he has sipped water according to the sacred law, has made the Brahmangali,[20] has put on clean clothing, and has brought his sexual organs under due control. At the beginning and at the end of a lesson in the *Veda* he must always clasp both the feet of his teacher. He must study by joining hands; that is called the Brahmangali [joining the palms for the sake of the *Veda*]. With crossed hands he must clasp the feet of the teacher, and touch the left foot with his left hand, the right foot with his right hand. The teacher, always unwearied, must say to him who is about to begin studying, "Recite!" He shall stop when the teacher says: "Let a stoppage take place!" Let him always pronounce the syllable "Om" at the beginning and at the end of a lesson in the *Veda*. Unless the syllable "Om" precedes, the lesson will slip away from him, and unless it follows it will fade away. . . .

[191] Both when ordered by his teacher, and without a command, a student shall always exert himself in studying [the *Veda*], and in doing what is serviceable to his teacher. Controlling

his body, his speech, his organs of sense, and his mind, let him stand with joined hands, looking at the face of his teacher. Let him always keep his right arm uncovered, behave decently, and keep the rest of his body well covered. When he is addressed with the words, "Be seated," he shall sit down, facing his teacher. In the presence of his teacher let him always eat less [than the teacher], and wear less valuable clothing and ornaments. Let him rise earlier and go to bed later. [195] Let him not answer or talk with his teacher while reclining on a bed, or while sitting, or eating, or standing, or with an averted face. Let him talk standing up, if his teacher is seated, advancing toward him when he stands, going to meet him if he advances, and running after him when he runs. . . .

When his teacher is near, let his bed or seat be low; but within sight of his teacher he shall not sit carelessly at ease. Let him not pronounce the name of his teacher without adding an honorific title, even when talking about him behind his back. Let him not mimic his gait, speech, or conduct. [200] Wherever people justly criticize or falsely defame his teacher, he must cover his ears or depart to another place. By criticizing his teacher, even though justly, he will become in his next birth an ass. By falsely defaming him, he will become a dog. He who lives on his teacher's belongings will become a worm, and he who is envious of his merit will become a larger insect.

[3.1, The Stage of the Householder] The vow of studying the three *Vedas* under a teacher must be kept for thirty-six years, or for half that time, or for a quarter, or until the student has

---

[18] Selections from *Manu* are taken, with editing, from G. Buhler, trans., *The Laws of Manu, Sacred Books of the East,* vol. 25 (Oxford: Oxford University Press, 1886).
[19] *rite of initiation:* the acceptance of a male into full membership in the Hindu community.
[20] *Brahmangali:* the traditional Indian gesture of greeting and respect, explained more fully in the next verse.

perfectly learned them. A student who has studied in due order the three *Vedas,* or two, or even only one, without breaking the rules of studentship, shall enter the order of householders. He who is famous for the strict performance of his duties and has received his heritage, the *Veda,* from his father, shall be honored. He will sit on a couch and be adorned with a garland, with the present of a cow and honey-mixture. With the permission of his teacher, having bathed and performed according to the rule the ritual for returning home, a twice-born man shall marry a wife of equal caste who is endowed with auspicious bodily marks. [5] A young woman who is neither a Sapinda[21] on the mother's side nor belongs to the same family on the father's side is recommended to twice-born men for marriage and conjugal union.

In connecting himself with a wife, let him carefully avoid the ten following types of families, even if they are great, or rich in cattle, horses, sheep, grain, or other property. He must avoid a family that neglects the sacred rites, one in which no male children are born, one in which the *Veda* is not studied, one that has thick hair on the body, those that are subject to hemorrhoids, tuberculosis, weakness of digestion, epilepsy, or white and black leprosy. Let him not marry a young woman with reddish hair, nor one who has a redundant body part, nor one who is sickly, nor one either with no hair on the body or too much hair. Let him not marry one who is too talkative or has red eyes. Let him not marry one named after a constellation, a tree, or a river, nor one bearing the name of a low caste, or of a mountain, nor one named after a bird, a snake, or a slave, nor one whose name inspires terror. [10] Let him wed a female free from bodily defects and who has an agreeable name. She must have the graceful gait of a swan or of an elephant, moderate hair on the body and on the head, small teeth, and soft limbs.

For the first marriage of twice-born men, wives of equal caste are recommended. But for those who because of desire take a second wife,

the following females are approved. They are chosen according to the order of the castes. It is declared that a Shudra woman alone can be the wife of a Shudra, she and one of his own caste the wives of a Vaisya, those two and one of his own caste the wives of a Kshatriya, those three and one of his own caste the wives of a Brahmin. A Shudra woman is not mentioned even in any ancient story as the first wife of a Brahmin or of a Kshatriya, though they lived in the greatest distress. [15] Twice-born men who foolishly marry first wives of the low caste degrade their families and their children to the state of Shudras. According to Atri and to Gautama the son of Utathya,[22] he who weds a Shudra woman becomes an outcast. According to Saunaka, he becomes an outcaste on the birth of a son, and according to Bhrigu when he has a male child from a Shudra female. A Brahmin who takes a Shudra wife to his bed will sink into hell. If he begets a child by her, he will lose the rank of a Brahmin. The spirits of deceased ancestors and the gods will not eat the offerings of a man who performs the rites in honor of the gods, of the manes, and of guests with a Shudra wife's assistance. Such a man will not go to heaven. No way of forgiveness is prescribed for him who drinks the moisture of a Shudra's lips, who is tainted by her breath, and who begets a son on her.

[6.1, The Stage of Retirement] A twice-born Snataka,[23] who has lived according to the law of householders, taking a firm resolution and keeping his organs in subjection, may dwell in the forest. He must duly observe the rules given below. When a householder sees his skin wrinkled, and his hair white, and the sons of his sons, then he may depart to the forest. Abandoning all food raised by cultivation, and all his belongings, he may depart into the forest. He may either commit his wife to his sons or be accompanied

---

[21] *Sapinda:* a relative; literally, "a sharer in the funeral feast," an obligation usually considered to go back six generations.
[22] *Gautama:* not Gautama Buddha.
[23] *Snataka:* a Brahmin who has completed his studentship.

by her.[24] Taking with him the sacred fire and the implements required for domestic sacrifices, he may go forth from the village into the forest and reside there, controlling his senses.

[5] Let him offer those five great sacrifices according to the rule, with various kinds of pure food fit for ascetics, or with herbs, roots, and fruit. Let him wear a skin or a tattered garment; let him bathe in the evening or in the morning. Let him always wear his hair in braids, with the hair on his body, his beard, and his nails uncut. Let him perform the Bali-offering with the kind of food he eats, and give alms according to his ability. Let him honor those who come to his hermitage to give him alms of water, roots, and fruit. Let him always be industrious in privately reciting the *Veda*. Let him be patient in hardships, friendly toward all, collected in mind, always liberal and never a receiver of gifts, and compassionate toward all living creatures. Let him offer, according to the law, the Agnihotra with three sacred fires, and never omit the new-moon and full-moon sacrifices at the proper time. . . .

[6.33, The Stage of Asceticism] Having passed the third part of his natural term of life in the forest, a man may live as an ascetic during the fourth part of his existence. First he must abandon all attachment to worldly objects. He who . . . offers sacrifices and subdues his senses, busies himself with giving alms and offerings of food, and becomes an ascetic gains bliss after death. [35] When he has paid the three debts,[25] let him apply his mind to the attainment of final liberation. He who seeks it without having paid his debts sinks downwards. Having studied the *Vedas* according to the rule, having fathered sons according to the sacred law, and having offered sacrifices according to his ability, he may direct his mind to the attainment of final liberation. A twice-born man who seeks final liberation sinks downward if he has not studied the *Vedas*, fathered sons, and offered sacrifices. Having performed the Ishti, sacred to the Lord of creatures, in which he gives all his property as the sacrificial fee, having reposited the sacred fires in himself, a Brahmin may depart from his

house as an ascetic. Worlds, radiant in brilliancy, become his who recites the texts regarding Brahman and departs from his house as an ascetic, after giving a promise of safety to all created beings.[26] [40] For that twice-born man who causes not even the smallest danger to created beings, there will be no danger from anything after he is freed from his body.

Departing from his house fully provided with the means of purification, let him wander about absolutely silent. He must care nothing for enjoyments that may be offered to him. Let him always wander about alone to attain final liberation. The solitary man, who neither forsakes nor is forsaken, gains his desired result. He shall possess neither a fire nor a dwelling. He may go to a village for his food. He shall be indifferent to everything, firm of purpose, meditating and concentrating his mind on Brahman. The marks of one who has attained liberation are a broken pot instead of an alms-bowl, the roots of trees for a dwelling, coarse wornout garments, life in solitude, and indifference toward everything. [45] Let him not desire to die; let him not desire to live. Let him wait for his appointed time as a servant waits for the payment of his wages. Let him put down his foot purified by his sight,[27] let him drink water purified by straining with a cloth, let him utter speech purified by truth, let him keep his heart pure. Let him

---

[24] *accompanied by her:* Note in the next passage that if the husband chooses the way of ascetic renunciation, the wife cannot accompany him. She is in a difficult situation: Having renounced his old life, her husband no longer belongs to her, but she still belongs to him.

[25] *the three debts:* the three obligations discussed in the next verses: study, having sons, sacrifice. These are similar to the modern Hindu expression "the three debts": to the gods, to the guru, to be a father.

[26] *promise of safety to all created beings:* the vow of ahimsa, nonviolence to all creatures.

[27] *put down his foot purified by his sight:* i.e., in a place on the ground with no visible living beings on it; so too he must *drink water purified* of living creatures. This requirement, which follows up on the ascetic's "promise of safety to all created beings" (verse 39), will become more important in Jainism.

patiently bear hard words, let him not insult anybody. Let him not become anybody's enemy for the sake of this perishable body. Against an angry man let him not show anger, let him bless when he is cursed, and let him not utter false speech. . . .

The Life of Women*

The first passage is often quoted as an example of a positive Hindu attitude toward women. It gives some indication of the respected place of Hindu women in the home (in the context of a strongly patriarchal society, of course). Much of this passage has as its background the participation of the wife in all the sacred rites of the home. The second passage contains rules for the whole life of women, emphasizing respect and obedience to husbands during their life. After her husband's death, a woman must not remarry and must live an ascetic life.

[3.55] Women must be honored and adorned by their fathers, brothers, husbands, and brothers-in-law, who desire their own welfare. Where women are honored, there the gods are pleased. Where they are not honored, no sacred rite yields rewards. Where the female relations live in grief, the family soon perishes completely. But the family where they are not unhappy always prospers. Female relatives pronounce a curse on houses where women are not honored; these houses perish completely, as if destroyed by magic. Men who seek their own welfare should always honor women on holidays and festivals with gifts of jewelry, clothes, and dainty food. [60] In a family where the husband is pleased with his wife and the wife with her husband, happiness will certainly be lasting.

[5.147] Nothing must be done independently by a girl, by a young woman, or by an old woman, even in her own house. In childhood a female must be subject to her father, in youth to her husband, and when her husband is dead to

He shall delight in matters of the Soul, sit in the postures prescribed by the Yoga, be independent of external help, entirely abstain from sensual enjoyments, and have himself for his only companion. He shall live in this world, but desire only the bliss of final liberation.

her sons. A woman must never be independent. She must not seek to separate herself from her father, husband, or sons. By leaving them she would make both her own and her husband's families contemptible.

[150] She must always be cheerful, clever in household affairs, careful in cleaning her utensils, and economical in expenditure. She shall obey the man to whom her father may give her . . . as long as he lives. When he is dead, she must not insult his memory. For the sake of getting good fortune for brides, the recitation of benedictory texts and the sacrifice to the Lord of creatures are used at weddings; but the betrothal by the father or guardian is the cause of the husband's dominion over his wife. The husband who wedded her with sacred texts always gives happiness to his wife, both in season and out of season, in this world and in the next. Although he may be destitute of virtue, or seek pleasure elsewhere, or be lacking good qualities, yet a husband must be constantly worshipped as a god by a faithful wife. [155] No sacrifice, no vow, no fast must be performed by women apart from their husbands. If a wife obeys her husband, she will for that reason alone be exalted in heaven.[28]

A faithful wife who desires to dwell after death with her husband must never do anything that might displease him, whether he is alive or dead. She may emaciate her body by living on pure

---

*Laws of Manu 3.55–60; 5.147–165.
[28] *heaven:* as elsewhere in Hinduism, usually a temporary reward before reincarnation.

flowers, roots, and fruit; but she must never even mention the name of another man after her husband has died. Until death let her be patient in hardships, self-controlled, and chaste. Let her strive to fulfil that most excellent duty that is prescribed for wives who have one husband only. Many thousands of Brahmins who were chaste from their youth have gone to heaven without continuing their race. [160] A virtuous wife who constantly remains chaste after the death of her husband reaches heaven although she has no son, just like those chaste men.

But a woman who desires to have offspring violates her duty toward her [deceased] husband. She brings disgrace on herself in this world, and loses her place with her husband in heaven. Offspring begotten by another man is not considered lawful; offspring begotten on another man's wife does not belong to the begetter, nor is a second husband anywhere allowed for virtuous women.[29] She who lives with a man of higher caste, forsaking her own husband who belongs to a lower one, will become contemptible in this world, and is called a remarried woman. By violating her duty toward her husband, a wife is disgraced in this world. After death she enters the womb of a jackal, and is tormented by diseases as the punishment of her sin. [165] She who controls her thoughts, words, and deeds, and never slights her husband, will reside after death with him in heaven. She is called a virtuous wife.

---

[29] *anywhere allowed . . . women:* no ancient stories or laws permit it.

ORGANIZATION

Creation and the Caste System*

One of the many creation hymns of the Rig-Veda, *this poem presents the cosmic Man* (Purusha) *as the one through whose sacrifice the gods fashioned the universe. The making of humanity is presented in terms of the caste system, its first appearance in Hindu literature and the foundation of its later authority. Much of the caste system is undergoing a liberalizing change in modern India, especially in the cities. But it is still important and pervasive as a general social structure and cultural inheritance.*

The Man has a thousand heads, a thousand eyes, a thousand feet. He pervaded the earth on all sides and extended beyond it as far as ten fingers. It is the Man who is all this, whatever has been and whatever is to be. He is the ruler of immortality, when he grows beyond everything through food. This is his greatness, and the Man is yet more than this. All creatures are a quarter of him; three quarters are what is immortal in heaven.

With three quarters the Man rose upwards, and one quarter of him remains here.

From this he spread out in all directions, into that which eats and that which does not eat. [5] From him Viraj[30] was born, and from Viraj came the Man. When he was born, he ranged beyond the earth behind and before. When the gods spread the sacrifice with the Man as the offering, spring was the clarified butter, summer was the fuel, autumn was the oblation.[31] They anointed the Man, the sacrifice born at the beginning, upon the sacred grass. With him the gods, Sadhyas,[32] and sages sacrificed. From that sacrifice in which everything was offered, the melted fat was collected. He made it into those

---

Rig-Veda 10.90.
[30] *Viraj:* the female counterpart of the man.
[31] *oblation:* what is sacrificed.
[32] *Sadhyas:* saints, called in the last verse of this hymn "the ancient gods."

beasts who live in the air, in the forest, and in villages. From that sacrifice in which everything was offered, the verses and chants were born, the meters were born from it, and from it the formulas were born.[33] [10] Horses were born from it, and those other animals that have two rows of teeth; cows were born from it, and from it goats and sheep were born.

When they divided the Man, into how many parts did they apportion him? What do they call his mouth, his two arms and thighs and feet? His mouth became the Brahmin; his arms were made into the Warrior, his thighs the People, and from his feet the Servants were born. The moon was born from his mind; from his eye the sun was born. Indra and Agni came from his

mouth, and from his vital breath the Wind was born. From his navel the middle realm of space arose; from his head the sky evolved. From his two feet came the earth, and the quarters of the sky from his ear. Thus they set the worlds in order. [15] There were seven enclosing-sticks for him, and thrice seven fuel-sticks, when the gods, spreading the sacrifice, bound the Man as the sacrificial beast. With the sacrifice the gods sacrificed to the sacrifice. These were the first ritual laws. These very powers reached the dome of the sky where dwell the Sadhyas, the ancient gods.

---

[33] *verses, chants, meters, formulas:* the *Vedas.*

The Four Castes*

This passage contains a short description of the main structure of the caste system. The duties and means of livelihood of each caste are indicated. The end of this passage gives the moral duties binding on everyone of whatever caste, gender, or stage of life. These general rules are growing more important in contemporary Hinduism as the caste system fades.[34]

Brahmins, Kshatriyas, Vaishyas, and Shudras are the four castes. The first three of these are called twice-born. They must perform with mantras[35] the whole number of ceremonies, which begin with impregnation and end with the ceremony of burning the dead body. Their duties are as follows. [5] A Brahmin teaches the *Veda.* A Kshatriya has constant practice in arms. A Vaishya tends cattle. A Shudra serves the twice-born. All the twice-born are to sacrifice and study the *Veda.* [10] Their modes of livelihood are as follows. A Brahmin sacrifices for others and receives alms. A Kshatriya protects the world.

A Vaishya engages in farming, keeps cows, trades, lends money at interest, and grows seeds. A Shudra engages in all branches of crafts. In times of distress, each caste may follow the occupation of that below it in rank. Duties common to all castes are patience, truthfulness, restraint, purity, liberality, self-control, not to kill, obedience toward one's gurus, visiting places of pilgrimage, sympathy, straightforwardness, freedom from covetousness, reverence toward gods and Brahmins,[36] and freedom from anger.

Institutes of Vishnu 2–1.17.
[34] Taken, with editing, from Julius Jolly, trans., *The Institutes of Vishnu, Sacred Books of the East,* vol. 7 (Oxford: Oxford University Press, 1880).
[35] *mantras:* sacred words or syllables chanted to create and acquire cosmic spiritual power.
[36] *reverence towards . . . Brahmins:* As sacrificers, the Brahmins preserve the order of the universe, and other castes are to honor them. India has seen an almost continuous struggle between the priestly caste and the warrior-ruler caste.

The Outcastes*

About fifteen to twenty percent of Indians are outside the caste system—"outcastes." They are known by various names: untouchables (a designation now widely regarded as impolite), Harijans ("Children of God," Gandhi's term), the legal term "the scheduled [listed] classes," and Dalits ("the downtrodden"), the most preferred name. Hindus of the four castes regard them as non-Hindu. The so-called outcastes do the most menial and ritually polluting jobs in Indian society, such as cleaning sewers and digging graves. In India today, Dalits' challenges to their status are sources of serious conflict often resulting in violence. This selection from the Laws of Manu *gives a summary of their traditional state.*

The dwellings of Untouchables must be outside the village. They must use discarded bowls, and their only possessions are their dogs and donkeys. They take for their clothing the clothes of the dead, and eat their food in broken dishes.

Their ornaments are made of black iron only, and they should always wander from place to place. A [Hindu] man should not deal with them in any way; they must do business and marry only among themselves. Their food, for which they are dependent upon others, should be left for them in broken dishes, and they should not walk at night in cities or villages. [55] They may walk around during the day to do their work,[37] with recognizably distinctive clothing. They are to carry out the corpses of people with no relatives. By the king's command, they are to execute those condemned to death, and take for themselves the clothes, beds, and ornaments of those condemned to death.

---

*Laws of Manu *10.51–57.
[37] *They may walk around during the day:* Some "Untouchable" subgroups are considered so polluting that they must do their work only at night; hence, they are called "Unseeables."

RITUAL AND MEDITATION

The Gayatri Mantra**

The name of this short prayer means "the savior of the singer." This mantra is considered the single most important prayer-formula of Hinduism. Pious believers repeat it at least three times a day. On a literal level, this verse is a simple prayer to the sun-god Savitar for blessing. At a deeper level, it expresses and applies the power that the god himself holds. Given to a young man at his initiation with the sacred thread, it helps to produce his rebirth.

Believers in other Hindu deities have adapted it for their use from early times through today.

May we attain to the excellent glory of Savitar the god; so may he stimulate our prayers.

**Rig-Veda *3.62.10.

Devotion to Agni in Prayer and Sacrifice*

Agni is the god of fire, especially the sacrificial fire, and he is the priest among the gods (verse 1). This first hymn of the Rig-Veda *seeks to please Agni by praises and invoke his blessings. Like many other hymns of the* Rig, *it uses both the second person (e.g., "To you, Agni . . .") and the third person ("Agni earned the prayers . . ."), but all of it is addressed to Agni. The second reading is a good example of the Brahmanic exposition and development of the sacrificial rite. The ritual expounded here is the Agnihotra, the daily household sacrifice to Agni. The god Prajapati is the precursor of Brahman.*[38]

[*Rig-Veda* 1.1] I pray to Agni, the household priest who is the god of the sacrifice, the one who chants and invokes and brings most treasure. Agni earned the prayers of the ancient sages, and of those of the present, too; he will bring the gods here. Through Agni one may win wealth, and growth from day to day, glorious and most abounding in heroic sons. Agni, only the sacrificial ritual that you encompass on all sides goes to the gods. [5] Agni, the priest with the sharp sight of a poet, the true and most brilliant, the god will come with the gods. Whatever good you wish to do for the one who worships you, Agni, through you, O Angiras,[39] that comes true. To you, Agni, who shine upon darkness, we come day after day, bringing our thoughts and homage. [We come to] you, the king over sacrifices, the shining guardian of the Order, growing in your own house. Be easy for us to reach, like a father to his son. Abide with us, Agni, for our happiness.

[*Agni-Brahmana* 1.1–19] Prajapati alone existed here in the beginning. He considered, "How may I be reproduced?" He toiled and performed acts of penance. He generated Agni from his mouth. Because he generated him from his mouth, therefore Agni is a consumer of food. Truly, he who knows Agni to be a consumer of food becomes himself a consumer of food. He thus generated him first of the gods; and therefore [he is called] Agni, for *agni* [they say] is the same as *agri*. He, being generated, went forth as the first; for of him who goes first, they say that he goes at the head. Such, then, is the origin and nature of that Agni.

Prajapati then considered, "In Agni I have generated a food-eater for myself. But there is no other food here but myself, whom Agni certainly would not eat." Then this earth had been made quite bald; there were neither plants nor trees. This, then, weighed on his mind. Then Agni turned toward him with open mouth. Prajapati was terrified, and his own greatness departed from him. Now his own greatness is his speech; his speech departed from him. He desired an offering in himself and rubbed his hands; and because he rubbed his hands, palms are hairless. He then obtained either a butter-offering or a milk-offering; but they are both made of milk.

[5] But this offering did not satisfy him, because it had hairs mixed with it. He poured it away into the fire, saying, "Drink, while burning!" From it plants sprang; hence their name "plants." He rubbed his hands a second time, and by that obtained another offering, either a butter-offering or a milk-offering. This offering then satisfied him. He hesitated, thinking, "Shall I offer it up? Or shall I not offer it up?" His own greatness said to him, "Offer it up!" Prajapati was aware that it was his own [*sva*] greatness that had spoken [*aha*] to him; he offered it up with the word *svaha!* This is why offerings are made with *svaha!* Then that burning one, the sun, rose; and then that blowing

---

Rig-Veda 1.1; *Agni-Brahmana* 1.1–19.
[38] Taken, with editing, from Julius Eggeling, trans., *The Satapatha-Brahmana*, part 1, *Sacred Books of the East*, vol. 12 (Oxford: Oxford University Press, 1882).
[39] *Angiras:* messenger to the gods and the father of an ancient family of priests.

one, the wind, sprang up. Then Agni turned away.

Prajapati, having performed offering, reproduced himself, and saved himself from Agni as he was about to devour him. Truly whoever, knowing this, offers the Agnihotra reproduces himself by offspring even as Prajapati reproduced himself. He saves himself from Agni,

death, when he is about to devour him. And when he dies, and when they place him on the fire, then he is born again out of the fire, and the fire only consumes his body. Even as he is born from his father and mother, so is he born from the fire. But he who does not offer the Agnihotra does not come into life at all. Therefore the Agnihotra must be offered.

The Puja of a Yogin*

*Puja is the worship of a god, including ritual actions such as invoking and praising the god, caring for the image of the deity, and offering the image food. This reading describes puja offered by a **yogin** (a practitioner of yoga); ritual actions by ordinary worshippers also are included.*

I will now describe the mode of puja by performing which the sages attain all objects of life. After washing his head, rinsing his mouth and controlling his speech, one should sit well-protected in a *svastika* posture, *padma* posture or any other sitting position, with his face directed towards the east. He should then meditate in the middle of his navel on the mantra Yam, smoke colored and identical with the terrific wind, and purify all the impurities of the body. Then meditating on the mantra Kshoum, the ocean of light situated in the lotus heart, he should, with flames going up, down and in contrary directions, burn down all impurities. He should then meditate with the mantra Van on the shape of the moon in the sky. And then the intelligent worshipper should sprinkle his own body extending from the lotus heart with nectarine drops passing through the generative organ and other tubes.

Having purified the ingredients of worship he should assign them. He should then purify his hand and the implements. First, he should assign, beginning with the thumb of the right hand, the fingers of the two hands to the principal limbs.

Then with the sixty-two mantras he should assign the twelve limbs to the body namely heart, head, tuft of hair on head, skin, two eyes, belly, back, arms, thighs, knee-joints and feet. Then having offered hand postures and recited his name one hundred and eight times he should meditate on and adore Vishnu. Having placed a water-jar on his left and articles of worship on his right he should wash them with implements and then place flowers and scents. Having recited eight times the adorable light of Omnipresence and consciousness he should take up water in his palm with the mantra Phat and then meditate on Hari. With his face directed towards the south-east direction presided over by Agni he should pray for virtue, knowledge, disassociation from worldly objects and lordly powers. He should cast off his sins and physical impurities in the Yoga postures beginning with the East. In the tortoise posture he should adore Ananta [Vishnu], Yama, the sun and other luminous bodies. Having first meditated on them in his heart, invoked them and adored them in the circle he should again place offerings, water for washing the feet and for rinsing the mouth. Then by means of the knowledge of the art of worshipping the lotus-eyed deity [Vishnu] he should place water for bathing, ornaments, scents, flowers, incense, lamps and edibles.

---

*Agni Purana.

He should first adore the limbs at the gate in the east and then Brahma. He should then assign the discus and club to the southern quarter and the conch-shell and bow to the corner presided over by the moon. He should then assign arrows and the quiver to the left and right side of the deity. He should assign leathern fence and prosperity to the left and nourishment to the right. With mantras he should worship the garland of wild-flowers, the mystic mark *Srivasta* [Vishnu]

and the *kaustava* gem and all the deities of the quarters in the outside—all these paraphernalia and attendants of Vishnu. Either partially or wholly he should recite the mantras for adoring limbs, and adore them, circumambulate them and then offer offerings. He should meditate in his mind "I am Brahma, Hari" and should utter the world "come" and the words "forgive me." Those who seek salvation should thus perform *puja*.

Soma*

Soma is here, as elsewhere in the Vedas, *at once a plant, a drink, and a god. To judge from this hymn, soma had an effect that was hallucinogenic. The term* soma *is still used today, but it refers not to a hallucinogenic drug but to a fruit drink made of wild rhubarb. Other religions have words spoken during ritual intoxication. Few, however, are as evocative as this hymn's "We have drunk the Soma; we have become immortal; we have gone to the light; we have found the gods."*

I have tasted the sweet drink of life, knowing that it inspires good thoughts and joyous expansiveness to the extreme, that all the gods and mortals seek it together, calling it honey. When you penetrate inside, you will know no limits, and you will avert the wrath of the gods. Enjoying Indra's friendship, O drop of Soma, bring riches as a docile cow brings the yoke. We have drunk the Soma; we have become immortal; we have gone to the light; we have found the gods. What can hatred and the malice of a mortal do to us now, O immortal one? When we have drunk you, O drop of Soma, be good to our heart, kind as a father to his son, thoughtful as a friend to a friend. Far-famed Soma, stretch out our lifespan so that we may live.

[5] The glorious drops that I have drunk set me free in wide space. You have bound me together in my limbs as thongs bind a chariot.

Let the drops protect me from the foot that stumbles and keep lameness away from me. Inflame me like a fire kindled by friction; make us see far; make us richer, better. For when I am intoxicated with you, Soma, I think myself rich. Draw near and make us thrive. We would enjoy you, pressed with a fervent heart, like riches from a father. King Soma, stretch out our lifespans as the sun stretches the spring days. King Soma, have mercy on us for our well-being. Know that we are devoted to your laws. Passion and fury are stirred up. O drop of Soma, do not hand us over to the pleasure of the enemy. For you, Soma, are the guardian of our body; watching over men, you have settled down in every limb.

If we break your laws, O god, have mercy on us like a good friend, to make us better. [10] Let me join closely with my compassionate friend so that he will not injure me when I have drunk him. O lord of bay horses, for the Soma that is lodged in us I approach Indra to stretch out our lifespan. Weaknesses and diseases have gone; the forces of darkness have fled in terror. Soma has climbed up in us, expanding. We have come to the place where they stretch out lifespans. The drop that we have drunk has entered our hearts, an immortal inside mortals.

---

*Rig-Veda 8.48.

O fathers, let us serve that Soma with the oblations and abide in his mercy and kindness. Uniting in agreement with the fathers, O drop of Soma, you have extended yourself through sky and earth. Let us serve him with an oblation; let us be masters of riches. You protecting gods, speak out for us. Do not let sleep or harmful speech seize us. Let us, always dear to Soma, speak as men of power in the sacrificial gathering. [15] Soma, you give us the force of life on every side. Enter into us, finding the sunlight, watching over men. O drop of Soma, summon your helpers and protect us before and after.

Marriage*

The first part of this hymn, not given here, recounts the myth of the marriage of Surya the goddess. The part printed here contains the incantations and blessings still spoken at weddings to bring good and repel evil. The bride is compared to Surya, and the wedding of the humans is set in parallel with divine marriage. The words are designed to bring good fortune: that the wife continues to have beauty and passion, and so be loved by her husband; that both have a long life together; that the marriage produce many sons. The careful reader can discern several different ritual actions of the marriage. First comes leaving the site of the wedding, then traveling to the couple's home, then consummation of marriage, and finally the anointing of the couple. Verses from this hymn are still a part of traditional Hindu weddings.

Mount the world of immortality, O Surya, that is adorned with red flowers and made of fragrant wood, carved with many forms and painted with gold, rolling smoothly on its fine wheels. Prepare an exquisite wedding voyage for your husband. "Go away from here! For this woman has a husband." Thus I implore Visvavasu[40] with words of praise as I bow to him. "Look for another girl who is ripe and still lives in her father's house." That is your birthright; find it. "Go away from here, Visvavasu, we implore you as we bow. Look for another girl, willing and ready. Leave the wife to unite with her husband." May the roads be straight and thornless on which our friends go courting. May Aryaman and Bhaga united lead us together. O Gods, may the united household be easy to manage.

I free you from Varuna's snare, with which the gentle Savitr bound you. In the seat of the Law, in the world of good action, I place you unharmed with your husband. [25] I free her from here, but not from there.[41] I have bound her firmly there, so that through the grace of Indra she will have fine sons and be fortunate in her husband's love. Let Pusan lead you from here, taking you by the hand; let the Asvins carry you in their chariot. Go home to be mistress of the house with the right to speak commands to the gathered people. May happiness be fated for you here through your progeny. Watch over this house as mistress of the house.

Mingle your body with that of your husband, and even when you are gray with age you will have the right to speak to the gathered people. The purple and red appears, a magic spirit; the stain is imprinted.[42] Her family prospers, and her husband is bound in the bonds. Throw away

---

*Rig-Veda 10.85.20–47.

[40] *Visvavasu:* a demigod who possesses virgins.

[41] *here:* her father's house; *there:* her new house with her husband.

[42] *The purple and red appears . . . imprinted:* In the consummation of the marriage, the bride bleeds on her wedding robe as her hymen is ruptured. The resulting stain becomes a magic spirit with power to curse and destroy the marriage. The procedure for dealing with the robe is given at the end of this paragraph.

the gown, and distribute wealth to the priests. It becomes a magic spirit walking on feet, and like the wife it draws near the husband. [30] The body becomes ugly and sinisterly pale if the husband with evil desire covers his sexual limb with his wife's robe. The diseases that come from her own people and follow the glorious bridal procession, may the gods who receive sacrifices lead them back whence they have come. Let no highwaymen, lying in ambush, fall upon the wedding couple. Let the two of them on good paths avoid the dangerous path. Let all demonic powers run away. This bride has auspicious signs; come and look at her. Wish her the good fortune of her husband's love, and depart, each to your own house. It burns, it bites, it has claws, it is as dangerous as poison to eat.[43] Only the priest who knows the Surya hymn is able to receive the bridal gown. [35] Cutting, carving, and chopping into pieces—see the colors of Surya, which the priest alone purifies.

I [the husband] take your hand for good fortune, so that with me as your husband you will attain a ripe old age. Bhaga, Aryaman, Savitr, Purandhi—the gods have given you to me to be mistress of the house. Pusan, rouse her to be most eager to please, the woman in whom men sow their seed, so that she will spread her thighs in her desire for us and we,[44] in our desire, will plant our penis in her. To you first of all they led Surya, circling with the bridal procession. Give her back to her husbands, Agni, now as a wife with progeny. Agni has given the wife back again, together with long life and beauty. Let her have a long lifespan, and let her husband live for a hundred autumns. [40] Soma first possessed her,

and the Gandharva possessed her second. Agni was your third husband, and the fourth was the son of a man. Soma gave her to the Gandharva, and the Gandharva gave her to Agni. Agni gave me wealth and sons—and her.

Stay here and do not separate. Enjoy your whole lifespan playing with sons and grandsons and rejoicing in your own home. Let Prajapati create progeny for us; let Aryaman anoint us into old age. Free from evil signs, enter the world of your husband. Be good luck for our two-legged creatures and good luck for our four-legged creatures. Have no evil eye; do not be a husband-killer. Be friendly to animals, good-tempered and glowing with beauty. Bringing forth strong sons, prosper as one beloved of the gods and eager to please. Be good luck for our two-legged creatures and good luck for our four-legged creatures. [45] Generous Indra, give this woman fine sons and the good fortune of her husband's love. Place ten sons in her and make her husband the eleventh.[45] Be an empress over your husband's father, an empress over your husband's mother; be an empress over your husband's sister and an empress over your husband's brothers. Let all the gods and the waters together anoint our two hearts together. Let Matarisvan[46] together with the Creator and together with her who shows the way join the two of us together.

---

[43] *it:* the spirit arising from the stained robe.
[44] *us, we:* the husband, and the gods who are said to have spiritually possessed the wife before her marriage.
[45] *her husband the eleventh:* A common Hindu idea is that the husband is the last son of the wife, perhaps signifying the care given to the husband by his wife.
[46] *Matarisvan:* an assistant of Agni.

Cremation*

Agni is petitioned here to bring a good burning to the body of the dead, strikingly called in sacrificial imagery "a good cooking." The proper funeral ritual enables the dead man to go to his fathers. No explicit mention is made here of heaven or hell, *transmigration, or reincarnation, important in later Hinduism and today.*

---

*Rig-Veda 10.16.

[To Agni:] Do not burn him entirely, Agni, or engulf him in your flames. Do not consume his skin or his flesh. When you have cooked him perfectly, O knower of creatures, only then send him forth to the fathers. When you cook him perfectly, O knower of creatures, then give him over to the fathers. When he goes on the path that leads away the breath of life, then he will be led by the will of the gods.

[To the dead man:] May your eye go to the sun, your life's breath to the wind. Go to the sky or to earth, as is your nature; or go to the waters, if that is your fate. Take root in the plants with your limbs.

[To Agni:] The goat is your share; burn him with your heat. Let your brilliant light and flame burn him. With your gentle forms, O knower of creatures, carry this man to the world of those who have done good deeds. [5] Set him free again to go to the fathers, Agni, when he has been offered as an oblation in you and wanders with the sacrificial drink. Let him reach his own descendants, dressing himself in a lifespan. O knower of creatures, let him join with a body.

[To the dead man:] Whatever the black bird has pecked out of you, or the ant, the snake, or even a beast of prey, may Agni who eats all things make it whole, and Soma who has entered the Brahmins. Gird yourself with the limbs of the cow as an armor against Agni, and cover yourself with fat and suet, so that he will not embrace you with his impetuous heat in his passionate desire to burn you up.

[To Agni:] O Agni, do not overturn this cup that is dear to the gods and to those who love Soma, fit for the gods to drink from, a cup in which the immortal gods carouse. I send the flesh-eating fire far away. Let him go to those whose king is Yama, carrying away all impurities. But let that other, the knower of creatures, come here and carry the oblation to the gods, since he knows the way in advance. [10] The flesh-eating fire has entered your house, though he sees there the other, the knower of creatures; I take that god away to the sacrifice of the fathers. Let him carry the heated drink to the farthest dwelling-place. Agni carries away the corpse and gives sacrifice to the fathers who are strengthened by truth. Let him proclaim the oblation to the gods and to the fathers.

[To the new fire:] Joyously would we put you in place, joyously would we kindle you. Joyously carry the joyous fathers here to eat the oblation. Now, Agni, quench and revive the very one you have burnt up. Let Kiyamba, Pakadurva, and Vyalkasa plants grow in this place. O cool one, bringer of coolness; O fresh one, bringer of freshness; unite with the female frog.[47] Delight and inspire this, O Agni.

---

[47] *unite with the female frog:* In this last section, the ritual action implied in the text calls for water to be thrown on the fire, dousing it. This produces, at least poetically, a marsh where water-plants and frogs live. The female frog symbolizes fertility, the new life that comes at the end of the funeral.

Charms and Spells*

The first of these incantations is a charm against fever, the second a spell to frustrate the sacrifice of an enemy, the third a charm to induce the sexual passion of a woman (perhaps a wife who comes by an arranged marriage), the fourth a spell for success in business. Note that the main point of the charm is often repeated to increase its power.

Ritual actions that accompany the saying of these spells are occasionally suggested in the words.[48]

---

*Atharva-Veda 6.20; 7.70; 6.9; 3.16.
[48] Taken, with editing, from Maurice Bloomfield, trans., *Hymns of the Atharva-Veda, Sacred Books of the East,* vol. 42 (Oxford: Oxford University Press, 1897).

[6.20, against fever] As if from this Agni [fire], that burns and flashes, the fever comes. Let him pass away like a babbling drunkard! Let him, the impious one, search out another person, not ourselves! Reverence be to the fever with the burning weapon![49] Reverence be to Rudra, reverence to the fever, reverence to the luminous king Varuna! Reverence to heaven, reverence to earth, reverence to the plants! To you that burns through, and turns all bodies yellow . . . to the fever produced by the forest, I render honor.

[7.70, for frustration of sacrifice] Whenever that person over there in his thought and with his speech offers sacrifice accompanied by offerings and benedictions, may Nirriti the goddess of destruction ally herself with death and strike his offering before it takes effect! May the sorcerers Nirriti and Rakshas mar his true work with error![50] May the gods, despatched by Indra, churn up his sacrificial butter! May that which he offers not succeed! . . . I tie back both your arms, I shut your mouth. With the fury of Agni, I have destroyed your sacrifice.

[6.9, for love] Desire my body, my feet, my eyes, my thighs! As you lust after me, your eyes and your hair shall be hot with love! I make you cling to my arm, cling to my heart, so that you shall be in my power and shall come to my wish! The cows, the mothers of the sacrificial butter who lick their young, in whose heart love is planted, shall make this woman love me!

[3.16, for success in business] I urge Indra the merchant, come to us and be our forerunner. Ward off the unpaying one, the cutting beast, and let masterful Indra be a bringer of wealth to me. O Gods! That money with which, desiring more money, I conduct my business, let that multiply and never decrease. O Agni, with this sacrifice frustrate those who would ruin my profit.

---

[49] *Reverence:* The spell uses flattering praise, as well as insults, to drive the fever away.
[50] *mar . . . with error:* If an error of word or deed is made in the sacrificial ceremony, it is not effective. Such a belief is common to many religions with well-developed sacrificial systems.

Chanting of *Om**

The udgitha, *or "loud chant," is the important* Om *in the Vedic ritual. Members of the various Hindu schools differ on whether* Om *is Brahman itself or a near verbal expression of Brahman. But for all Hindus it is the most sacred of sounds, the mantra that contains all other mantras, all the* Vedas, *all the meaning of the universe. Those who chant it with full knowledge will be freed from* karma.

Let a man meditate on the syllable *Om*, called the *udgitha;* for the *udgitha* is sung, beginning with *Om*. The full account of *Om* is this.

The essence of all beings is the earth, the essence of the earth is water, the essence of water the plants, the essence of plants man, the essence of man speech, the essence of speech the

Rig-Veda, the essence of the *Rig-Veda* the *Sama-Veda*, the essence of the *Sama-Veda* the *udgitha*, Om. The *udgitha* is the best of all essences, the highest, deserving the highest place, the eighth.

What then is the *Rig*? What is the *Sama*? What is the *udgitha*? This is the question. [5] The *Rig* is speech, *Sama* is breath, the *udgitha* is the syllable *Om*. Now speech and breath, or *Rig* and *Sama*, form one couple. That couple is joined in the syllable *Om*. When two people come together, they fulfill each other's desire. Thus he who knowing this meditates on the syllable *Om*, the *udgitha*, becomes a fulfiller of desires.

**Chandogya Upanishad* 1.1.1–10.

That syllable is a syllable of permission, for whenever we permit anything, we say *Om*, yes. Now permission is gratification. He who knows this and meditates on the syllable *Om* becomes a gratifier of desires.

By that syllable proceeds the threefold knowledge (of the three *Vedas*). When the Adhvaryu priest gives an order, he says *Om*. When the Hotri priest recites, he says *Om*. When the Udgatri priest sings, he says *Om*, all for the glory of that syllable. The threefold knowledge and threefold sacrifice proceed by the greatness of that syllable and by its essence. [10] Therefore it seems that both he who knows this [the true meaning of *Om*], and he who does not, perform the same sacrifice. But this is not so, for knowledge and ignorance are different. The sacrifice that a man performs with knowledge, faith, and the *Upanishad* is more powerful. This is the full account of the syllable *Om*.

The Practice of Yoga*

Yoga is a spiritual and mental discipline to promote knowledge that the individual-soul and the world-soul are one. It does so by harnessing the power of the body to this end, but it is not (as often thought and practiced in the West) primarily a method of exercise with some meditation thrown in. This passage relates some of the main components of yogic meditation.[51]

Holding his body steady with the three [upper
    parts][52] erect,
And causing the senses with the mind to enter
    the heart,
A wise man with the Brahma-boat will cross
All the fear-bringing streams.

Compressing his breathings here in the body,
    and having his movements checked,
One should breathe through his nostrils with
    diminished breath.
Like that chariot yoked with vicious horses,
His mind the wise man should restrain undis-
    tractedly.

[10] In a clean level spot, free from pebbles,
    fire, and gravel,
By the sound of water and similar things
Favorable to thought, not offensive to the eye,
In a hidden retreat protected from the wind,
    one should practice Yoga.

Fog, smoke, sun, fire, wind,
Fire-flies, lightning, a crystal, a moon—
These are the preliminary appearances,
Producing the manifestation of Brahma in Yoga.

When the fivefold quality of Yoga is produced,
Arising from earth, water, fire, air, and space,
No sickness, no old age, no death has he
Who has obtained a body made out of the fire
    of Yoga.

Lightness, healthiness, steadiness,
Clearness of countenance and pleasantness of
    voice,
Sweetness of odor, and scanty excretions—
These, they say, are the first stage in the
    progress of Yoga.

Even as a mirror stained by dust
Shines brilliantly when it has been cleansed,
So the embodied one, on seeing the nature of
    the Soul,
Becomes unitary, his end attained, from sorrow
    freed.

[15] When with the nature of the self, as with
    a lamp,
One who practices Yoga beholds here the
    nature of Brahma,
Unborn, steadfast, from every nature free—
By knowing God one is released from all
    fetters!

Shvetashvatara Upanishad 2.8–15.
[51] F. Max Müller, trans., *The Upanishads,* part 2, *Sacred Books of the East,* vol. 15 (Oxford: Oxford University Press, 1884), pp. 241–243.
[52] *the three [upper parts]:* head, neck, and torso.

SELECTIONS FROM THE *BHAGAVAD-GITA*

The most famous and influential text of Hinduism is section 6 of the *Mahabharata* epic known as the *Bhagavad-Gita* (Song of the Lord). The *Gita* is especially important for an understanding of the devotional Hinduism that has flourished from about 400 C.E. until today. The background of the *Gita* is the rivalry between the Kaurava brothers and the Pandava brothers for the rule of India. In a game of dice, the leader of the Pandavas loses their claim to the throne. For thirteen years the Pandavas are forced into exile. Civil war results when the Pandavas return to seize rule. As preparation for war begins, the god Krishna becomes a charioteer for Arjuna, a Pandava prince.

As the battle is about to begin, Arjuna is appalled by thoughts of the fratricide that will surely result. Moreover, he is afraid that this great evil will harm his own soul now and, by implication, in its later incarnations. His charioteer Krishna teaches Arjuna divine truths that enable him to overcome his doubts. This teaching forms the content of the *Gita*. First, and most immediately for the plot of the *Mahabharata*, Krishna teaches Arjuna that he must do his caste duty and fight. Arjuna acknowledges that his warfare will not harm the souls of the slain. Second, Krishna explains that the several ways to salvation offered by Hinduism—sacrifice (the Vedic path), meditation (the Upanishadic and ascetic path), and action (the way of caste duty)—are effective only if approached in a spirit of complete detachment. The *Gita* teaches full involvement in life coupled with inner restraint and indifference. Third, the best way to salvation is devotion to Krishna, whom the *Gita* portrays as both the "base of Brahman, the impersonal world-soul," and a god filled with personal love for his devotees. In typically Hindu fashion, the *Gita* acknowledges and affirms all Hindu ways to the truth but affirms its own way as the best.

The *Gita* contains 7,000 verses grouped into eighteen chapters. It has no plot, only the setting just outlined that poses the religious problem. Most chapters begin with Arjuna's question, which typically deals with the meaning of previous teachings in the *Gita*; a lengthy answer from Krishna follows. Many chapters end with a call for devotion to Krishna. Much of the content of the *Gita* is repetitious; the key teachings are returned to again and again and examined from different perspectives. The following excerpts attempt to reduce this repetition and present the essence of the *Gita*'s argument. A short paragraph introduces and summarizes the content of each of the selections given here.[53]

[1.20–47] Chapter 1 provides the narrative setting and the religious problem of the Gita. King Dhritarashtra's charioteer, Sanjaya, tells the king, a Kaurava, what happened before the battle that took place to decide the fate of his kingdom. As Prince Arjuna came onto the battlefield, he was overcome by the horrors of the impending fratricidal war. He expressed his misgivings to his charioteer, Krishna, saying that war would lead to ruin and that he preferred death to fighting such a war. Then he dropped his weapons, waiting for his death at the hands of the enemy.

Sanjaya:
Arjuna, his war flag a rampant monkey,
saw Dhritarashtra's sons assembled as
weapons were ready to clash, and he lifted his
    bow.

He told his charioteer: "Krishna,
halt my chariot between the armies!
Far enough to see these men who lust for war,
ready to fight with me in the strain of battle.

---

[53] From *Bhagavad-Gita*, translation by Barbara Stoler Miller, copyright © 1986 by Barbara Stoler Miller. Used by permission of Bantam Books, a division of Random House, Inc.

I see men gathered here, eager to fight,
bent on serving the folly of Dhritarashtra's son."

When Arjuna had spoken, Krishna halted
their splendid chariot between the armies.

[25] Facing Bhishma and Drona
and all the great kings, he said,
"Arjuna, see the Kuru men assembled here!"

Arjuna saw them standing there:
fathers, grandfathers, teachers, uncles, brothers,
sons, grandsons, and friends.
He surveyed his companions in both armies,
all his kinsmen assembled together.

Dejected, filled with strange pity, he said this:
"Krishna, I see kinsmen gathered here, wanting
    war.
My limbs sink, my mouth is parched,
my body trembles, the hair bristles on my flesh.

[30] The magic bow slips
from my hand, my skin burns,
I cannot stand still, my mind reels.

I see omens of chaos, Krishna;
I see no good in killing my kinsmen in battle.
Krishna, I seek no victory, kingship or plea-
    sures.
What use are kingship, delights, or life itself?

We sought kingship, delights,
and pleasures for the sake of those
assembled to abandon their lives
and fortunes in battle.

They are teachers, fathers, sons,
and grandfathers, uncles, grandsons,
fathers and brothers of wives,
and other men of our family.

[35] I do not want to kill them
even if I am killed, Krishna;
not for kingship of all three worlds,
much less for the earth!

What joy is there for us, Krishna,
in killing Dhritarashtra's sons?
Evil will haunt us if we kill them,
though their bows are drawn to kill.

Honor forbids us to kill
our cousins, Dhritarashtra's sons;

how can we know happiness
if we kill our own kinsmen?

The greed that distorts their reason
blinds them to the sin they commit
in ruining the family, blinds them
to the crime of betraying friends.

How can we ignore the wisdom
of turning from this evil when we see
the sin of family destruction, Krishna?

[40] When the family is ruined, the timeless
    laws
of family duty perish; and when duty is lost,
chaos overwhelms the family.

In overwhelming chaos, Krishna,
women of the family are corrupted;
and when women are corrupted,
disorder is born in society.

This discord drags the violators
and the family itself to hell;
for ancestors fall when rites
of offering rice and water lapse.

The sins of men who violate
the family create disorder in society
that undermines the constant laws
of caste and family duty.

Krishna, we have heard that a place in hell
is reserved for men who undermine family
    duties.

[45] I lament the great sin
we commit when our greed
for kingship and pleasures
drives us to kill our kinsmen.

If Dhritarashtra's armed sons
kill me in battle when I am unarmed
and offer no resistance,
it will be my reward."

Saying this in the time of war,
Arjuna slumped into the chariot
and laid down his bow and arrows,
his mind tormented by grief.

*[2:1–7, 11–27, 31–38, 47–48] In Chapter 2,
Krishna rebukes Arjuna and urges him to fight.
Krishna advances several arguments: (1) The soul*

is immortal, and all else is impermanent; there-
fore the battle has no real eternal significance. (2)
Arjuna, a Kshatriya (warrior), must do his caste
duty and fight. (3) He must fight in a contempla-
tive, detached manner. (4) Yoga (discipline) is the
way to such detachment. Verse 38 is the key:
"Impartial to joy and suffering, gain and loss,
victory and defeat, arm yourself for the battle, lest
you fall into evil."

Sanjaya:
Arjuna sat dejected, filled with pity, his sad eyes
    blurred by tears.
Krishna gave him counsel.

Lord Krishna:
Why this cowardice in time of crisis, Arjuna?
The coward is ignoble, shameful, foreign to the
    ways of heaven.
Don't yield to impotence!

It is unnatural in you!
Banish this petty weakness from your heart.
Rise to the fight, Arjuna!

Arjuna:
Krishna, how can I fight Bhishma and Drona
    with arrows when they deserve my worship?

[5] Better in this world to beg for scraps
of food than to eat meals smeared with the
    blood of elders
I killed at the height of their power,
while their goals were still desires.

We don't know which weight is worse to
    bear—
our conquering them or their conquering us.
We will not want to live if we kill the sons of
    Dhritarashtra assembled before us.

The flaw of pity blights my very being; conflict-
    ing sacred duties confound my reason.
I ask you to tell me decisively—Which is better?
I am your pupil. Teach me what I seek! . . .

Lord Krishna:
[11] You grieve for those beyond grief,
and you speak words of insight;
but learned men do not grieve
for the dead or the living.

Never have I not existed,
nor you, nor these kings;
and never in the future
shall we cease to exist.

Just as the embodied self
enters childhood, youth, and old age,
so does it enter another body;
this does not confound a steadfast man.

Contacts with matter make us feel
heat and cold, pleasure and pain.
Arjuna, you must learn to endure
fleeting things—they come and go!

[15] When these cannot torment a man,
when suffering and joy are equal
for him and he has courage,
he is fit for immortality.

Nothing of nonbeing comes to be,
nor does being cease to exist;
the boundary between these two
is seen by men who see reality.

Indestructible is the presence
that pervades all this;
no one can destroy
this unchanging reality.

Our bodies are known to end,
but the embodied self is enduring,
indestructible, and immeasurable;
therefore, Arjuna, fight the battle!

He who thinks this self a killer
and he who thinks it killed,
both fail to understand;
it does not kill, nor is it killed.

[20] It is not born, it does not die;
having been, it will never not be;
unborn, enduring, constant, primordial,
it is not killed when the body is killed.

Arjuna, when a man knows the self
to be indestructible, enduring, unborn,
unchanging, how does he kill
or cause anyone to kill?

As a man discards worn-out clothes
to put on new and different ones,
so the embodied self discards

its worn-out bodies to take on new ones.

Weapons do not cut it, fire does not burn it,
waters do not wet it, wind does not wither it.
It cannot be cut or burned, wet or withered;
it is enduring, all-pervasive, fixed,
immovable, and timeless.

[25] It is called unmanifest,
inconceivable, and immutable;
since you know that to be so,
you should not grieve!

If you think of its birth
and death as ever-recurring,
then too, Great Warrior,
you have no cause to grieve!

Death is certain for anyone born,
and birth is certain for the dead;
since the cycle is inevitable,
you have no cause to grieve! . . .

[31] Look to your own duty;
do not tremble before it;
nothing is better for a warrior
than a battle of sacred duty.

The doors of heaven open for warriors who
    rejoice
to have a battle like this thrust on them by
    chance.

If you fail to wage this war of sacred duty,
you will abandon your own duty
and fame only to gain evil.

People will tell of your undying shame,
and for a man of honor shame is worse than
    death.

[35] The great chariot warriors will think
you deserted in fear of battle;
you will be despised
by those who held you in esteem.

Your enemies will slander you,
scorning your skill
in so many unspeakable ways—
could any suffering be worse?

If you are killed, you win heaven;
if you triumph, you enjoy the earth;
Arjuna, stand up and resolve to fight the battle!

Impartial to joy and suffering,
gain and loss, victory and defeat,
arm yourself for the battle, lest you fall into
    evil. . . .

[47] Be intent on action, not the fruits of
    action;
avoid attraction to the fruits
and attachment to inaction!

Perform actions, firm in discipline,
relinquishing attachment;
be impartial to failure and success—
this equanimity is called discipline.

*[4:1–15] In Chapter 4 Krishna tells Arjuna of
his many incarnations. The* Gita *itself does not
explicitly state that Krishna is an incarnation of
Vishnu, but the Vaishnavites of later devotional
Hinduism saw this relationship and developed it
fully.*

Lord Krishna:
I taught this undying discipline
to the shining sun, first of mortals, who
told it to Manu, the progenitor of man;
Manu told it to the solar king Ikshvaku.

Royal sages knew this discipline,
which the tradition handed down;
but over the course of time
it has decayed, Arjuna.

This is the ancient discipline
that I have taught to you today;
you are my devotee and my friend,
and this is the deepest mystery.

Arjuna:
Your birth followed the birth of the sun;
how can I comprehend that you taught it
in the beginning?

Lord Krishna:
[5] I have passed through many births
and so have you;
I know them all, but you do not, Arjuna.

Though myself unborn, undying,
the lord of creatures, I fashion nature,
which is mine, and I come into being
through my own magic.

When sacred duty decays, chaos prevails;
then I create myself, Arjuna. To protect men
of virtue and destroy evil men, to set the
standard of sacred duty, I appear in every age.

He who really knows my divine
birth and my action, escapes rebirth
when he abandons the body—
and he comes to me, Arjuna.

[10] Free from attraction, fear, and anger,
filled with me, dependent on me,
purified by the fire of knowledge,
many come into my presence.

As they seek refuge in me,
I devote myself to them;
Arjuna, men retrace
my path in every way.

Desiring success in their actions,
men sacrifice here to the gods;
in the world of man success
comes quickly from action.

I created mankind in four classes,
different in their qualities and actions;
though unchanging, I am the agent of this,
the actor who never acts!

I desire no fruit of actions,
and actions do not defile me;
one who knows this about me
is not bound by actions.

[15] Knowing this, even ancient seekers
of freedom performed action—
do as these seers did in ancient times.

*[9:16–28] Chapter 9 tells how the universe was
spun out of Krishna's body. Next come the attributes of God (Krishna), service of different
(Hindu) gods, and a critique of Vedic religion.
At the end, devotion to Krishna is emphasized as
the part that, in contrast to the Vedic cult, is open
to all.*

Lord Krishna:
I am the rite, the sacrifice,
the libation for the dead, the healing herb,
the sacred hymn, the clarified butter,
the fire, the oblation.

I am the universal father,
mother, granter of all, grandfather,
object of knowledge, purifier,
holy syllable *Om,* threefold sacred lore.

I am the way, sustainer, lord,
witness, shelter, refuge, friend,
source, dissolution, stability,
treasure, and unchanging seed.

I am heat that withholds
and sends down the rains;
I am immortality and death;
both being and nonbeing am I.

[20] Men learned in sacred lore,
Soma drinkers, their sins absolved,
worship me with sacrifices,
seeking to win heaven.

Reaching the holy world of Indra,
king of the gods,
they savor the heavenly delights
of the gods in the celestial sphere.

When they have long enjoyed the world of
heaven and their merit is exhausted,
they enter the mortal world; following
the duties ordained in sacred lore,
desiring desires, they obtain what is transient.

Men who worship me, thinking solely of me,
always disciplined, win the reward I secure.

When devoted men sacrifice
to other deities with faith,
they sacrifice to me, Arjuna,
however aberrant the rites.
I am the enjoyer and the lord of sacrifices;
they do not know me in reality, so they fail.

[25] Votaries of the gods go to the gods,
ancestor-worshippers go to the ancestors,
those who propitiate ghosts go to them,
and my worshippers go to me.

The leaf or flower or fruit or water
that he offers with devotion,
I take from the man of self-restraint
in response to his devotion.

Whatever you do—what you take,
what you offer, what you give,

what penances you perform—
do as an offering to me, Arjuna!

You will be freed from bonds of action,
from the fruit of fortune and misfortune;
armed with the discipline of renunciation,
your self liberated, you will join me.

*[11:1–20, 50–55] In Chapter 11, after Arjuna
asks to see Krishna's divine form, Krishna shows
him all his divine forms at once. Arjuna is filled
with awe and praises Krishna. Krishna then
returns to his human form. The praise of Krishna
expresses the kind of attachment to one god that is
characteristic of devotional Hinduism.*

Arjuna:
To favor me you revealed
the deepest mystery of the self,
and by your words
my delusion is dispelled.

I heard from you in detail
how creatures come to be and die,
Krishna, and about the self
in its immutable greatness.

Just as you have described yourself,
I wish to see your form in all its majesty,
Krishna, Supreme among Men.

If you think I can see it, reveal to me your
immutable self, Krishna, Lord of Discipline.

Lord Krishna:
[5] Arjuna, see my forms
in hundreds and thousands;
diverse, divine, of many colors and shapes.

See the sun gods, gods of light,
howling storm gods, twin gods of dawn,
and gods of wind, Arjuna,
wondrous forms not seen before.

Arjuna, see all the universe,
animate and inanimate,
and whatever else you wish to see;
all stands here as one in my body.

But you cannot see me with your own eye;
I will give you a divine eye to see
the majesty of my discipline.

Sanjaya:
O King, saying this, Krishna, the lord
of discipline, revealed to Arjuna
the true majesty of his form.

[10] It was a multiform, wondrous vision,
with countless mouths and eyes
and celestial ornaments,
brandishing many divine weapons.

Everywhere was boundless divinity
containing all astonishing things,
wearing divine garlands and garments,
anointed with divine perfume.

If the light of a thousand suns
were to rise in the sky at once, it would
be like the light of that great spirit.

Arjuna saw all the universe
in its many ways and parts, standing
as one in the body of the god of gods.

Then filled with amazement,
his hair bristling on his flesh,
Arjuna bowed his head to the god,
joined his hands in homage, and spoke.

Arjuna:
[15] I see the gods in your body, O God,
and hordes of varied creatures:
Brahma, the cosmic creator,
on his lotus throne, all the seers
and celestial serpents.

I see your boundless form everywhere,
the countless arms, bellies, mouths, eyes;
Lord of All, I see no end,
or middle or beginning to your totality.

I see you blazing through the fiery rays
of your crown, mace, and discus,
hard to behold in the burning light
of fire and sun that surrounds
your measureless presence.

You are to be known as supreme eternity,
the deepest treasure of all that is,
the immutable guardian of enduring duty;
I think you are man's timeless spirit.

I see no beginning, middle or end to you;
only boundless strength in your arms,

the moon and sun in your eyes,
your mouths of consuming flames,
your own brilliance scorching the universe.

[20] You alone fill the space between heaven
and earth and all the directions;
seeing this awesome, terrible form of yours,
Great Soul, the three worlds tremble. . . .

Sanjaya:
[50] Saying this to Arjuna, Krishna again
revealed his intimate form;
resuming his gentle body, the great spirit
let the terrified hero regain his breath.

Arjuna:
Seeing your gentle human form, Krishna,
I recover my nature, my reason is restored.

Lord Krishna:
This form you have seen is rarely revealed;
the gods are constantly craving
for a vision of this form.

Not through sacred lore, penances, charity,
or sacrificial rites can I be seen in the form
that you saw me. By devotion alone can I, as
I really am, be seen and entered into, Arjuna.

[55] Acting only for me, intent on me,
free from attachment, hostile to no creature,
Arjuna, a man of devotion comes to me.

*[16:1–11, 21–24] Chapter 16 is a summary of
general morality suitable for all twice-born
Hindus. It first describes the person "born to
inherit a godly destiny," who quickly escapes the
process of rebirth. Then it tells of "human devils,"
who are eternally recycling through rebirth.*

Lord Krishna:
Fearlessness, purity, determination
in the discipline of knowledge,
charity, self-control, sacrifice,
study of sacred lore, penance, honesty;

Nonviolence, truth, absence of anger,
disengagement, peace, loyalty,
compassion for creatures, lack of greed,
gentleness, modesty, reliability;

Brilliance, patience, resolve,
clarity, absence of envy and of pride;

these characterize a man
born with divine traits.

Hypocrisy, arrogance, vanity,
anger, harshness, ignorance;
these characterize a man
born with demonic traits.

[5] The divine traits lead to freedom,
the demonic lead to bondage;
do not despair, Arjuna;
you were born with the divine.

All creatures in the world
are either divine or demonic;
I described the divine at length;
hear what I say of the demonic.

Demonic men cannot comprehend
activity and rest; there exists no clarity,
no morality, no truth in them.

They say that the world
has no truth, no basis, no god,
that no power of mutual dependence
is its cause, but only desire.

Mired in this view, lost to themselves
with their meager understanding,
these fiends contrive terrible acts
to destroy the world.

[10] Subject to insatiable desire,
drunk with hypocrisy and pride,
holding false notions from delusion,
they act with impure vows.

In their certainty that life
consists in sating their desires,
they suffer immeasurable anxiety
that ends only with death. . . .

[21] The three gates of hell
that destroy the self
are desire, anger, and greed;
one must relinquish all three.

Released through these three gates
of darkness, Arjuna,
a man elevates the self
and ascends to the highest way.

If he rejects norms of tradition
and lives to fulfill his desires,

he does not reach perfection
or happiness or the highest way.

Let tradition be your standard
in judging what to do or avoid;
knowing the norms of tradition,
perform your action here.

*[18:1–9, 41–49, 60–73] In the eighteenth and
last chapter of the Gita, the topics of renunciation
and the three constituents of nature are treated
for the last time. Krishna summarizes the duties
of the castes and stresses the importance of doing
one's caste duty in a spirit of detachment. Then
come a short summary of the teaching of the whole
book and a description of the merits obtained by
reading it. Arjuna is convinced by Krishna and
surrenders himself in obedience.*

Arjuna:
Krishna, I want to know the real essence
of both renunciation and relinquishment.

Lord Krishna:
Giving up actions based on desire,
the poets know as "renunciation";
relinquishing all fruit of action,
learned men call "relinquishment."

Some wise men say all action
is flawed and must be relinquished;
others say action in sacrifice, charity,
and penance must not be relinquished.

Arjuna, hear my decision
about relinquishment;
it is rightly declared
to be of three kinds.

[5] Action in sacrifice, charity,
and penance is to be performed,
not relinquished—for wise men,
they are acts of sanctity.

But even these actions
should be done by relinquishing to me
attachment and the fruit of action—
this is my decisive idea.

Renunciation of prescribed action
is inappropriate; relinquished in delusion,
it becomes a way of dark inertia.

When one passionately relinquishes
difficult action from fear
of bodily harm, he cannot win
the fruit of relinquishment.

But if one performs prescribed action
because it must be done,
relinquishing attachment and the fruit,
his relinquishment is a lucid act. . . .

[41] The actions of priests, warriors,
commoners, and servants
are apportioned by qualities
born of their intrinsic being.

Tranquility, control, penance,
purity, patience and honesty,
knowledge, judgment, and piety
are intrinsic to the action of a priest.

Heroism, fiery energy, resolve,
skill, refusal to retreat in battle,
charity, and majesty in conduct
are intrinsic to the action of a warrior.

Farming, herding cattle, and commerce
are intrinsic to the action of a commoner;
action that is essentially service
is intrinsic to the servant.

[45] Each one achieves success
by focusing on his own action;
hear how one finds success
by focusing on his own action. . . .

Better to do one's own duty imperfectly
than to do another man's well;
doing action intrinsic to his being,
a man avoids guilt.

Arjuna, a man should not relinquish
action he is born to, even if it is flawed;
all undertakings are marred by a flaw,
as fire is obscured by smoke.

His understanding everywhere detached,
the self mastered, longing gone,
one finds through renunciation
the supreme success beyond action. . . .

[60] You are bound by your own action,
intrinsic to your being, Arjuna;

even against your will you must do
what delusion now makes you refuse.

Arjuna, the lord resides
in the heart of all creatures,
making them reel magically,
as if a machine moved them.

With your whole being, Arjuna,
take refuge in him alone—
from his grace you will attain
the eternal place that is peace.

This knowledge I have taught
is more arcane than any mystery—
consider it completely,
then act as you choose.

Listen to my profound words,
the deepest mystery of all,
for you are precious to me
and I tell you for your good.

[65] Keep your mind on me,
be my devotee, sacrificing, bow to me—
you will come to me, I promise,
for you are dear to me.

Relinquishing all sacred duties to me,
make me your only refuge; do not grieve,
for I shall free you from all evils.

You must not speak of this to one
who is without penance and devotion,

or who does not wish to hear,
or who finds fault with me.

When he shares this deepest mystery
with others devoted to me,
giving me his total devotion,
a man will come to me without doubt.

No mortal can perform
service for me that I value more,
and no other man on earth
will be more dear to me than he is.

[70] I judge the man who studies
our dialogue on sacred duty
to offer me sacrifice
through sacrifice in knowledge.

If he listens in faith,
finding no fault, a man is free
and will attain the cherished worlds
of those who act in virtue.

Arjuna, have you listened
with your full powers of reason?
Has the delusion of ignorance
now been destroyed?

Arjuna:
Krishna, my delusion is destroyed,
by your grace I have regained memory;
I stand here, my doubt dispelled,
ready to act on your words.

LATER DEVELOPMENTS OF SCRIPTURAL THEMES

Mohandas Gandhi on the *Bhagavad-Gita**

The Bhagavad-Gita *has inspired many generations of Hindu leaders, including Mohandas Gandhi, the twentieth-century leader of Indian independence. Gandhi called it "a dictionary for life." Here is his reflection on the meaning of the* Gita.[54]

Even in 1888–9, when I first became acquainted with the *Gita,* I felt that it was not an historical

work, but that, under the guise of physical warfare, it described the duel that perpetually went on in the hearts of mankind, and that physical warfare was brought in merely to make the description

*The Gospel of Selfless Action.
[54] From M. K. Gandhi, The Gospel of Selfless Action or The Gita according to Gandhi (Ahmedabad: Navagivan Publishing, 1946), 123–131.

of the internal duel more alluring. This preliminary intuition became more confirmed on a closer study of religion and the *Gita*. A study of the *Mahabharata* gave it added confirmation. I do not regard the *Mahabharata* as an historical work in the accepted sense. . . . The persons therein described may be historical, but the author of the *Mahabharata* has used them merely to drive home his religious theme.

The author of the *Mahabharata* has not established the necessity of physical warfare; on the contrary he has proved its futility. He has made the victors shed tears of sorrow and repentance, and has left them nothing but a legacy of miseries. In this great work the *Gita* is the crown. Its second chapter, instead of teaching the rules of physical warfare, tells us how a perfected man is to be known. In the characteristics of the perfected man of the *Gita* I do not see any to correspond to physical warfare. Its whole design is inconsistent with the rules of conduct governing the relations between warring parties.

Krishna of the *Gita* is perfection and right knowledge personified; but the picture is imaginary. That does not mean that Krishna, the adored of his people, never lived. But perfection is imagined. The idea of a perfect incarnation is an aftergrowth.

In Hinduism, incarnation is ascribed to one who has performed some extraordinary service of mankind. All embodied life is in reality an incarnation of God, but it is not usual to consider every living being an incarnation. Future generations pay this homage to one who in his own generation, has been extraordinarily religious in his conduct. I can see nothing wrong in this procedure. It takes nothing from God's greatness, and there is no violence done to Truth. There is an Urdu saying which means, "Adam is not God but he is a spark of the Divine." And therefore he who is the most religiously

behaved has most of the divine spark in him. It is in accordance with this train of thought, that Krishna enjoys, in Hinduism, the status of the most perfect incarnation.

This belief in incarnation is a testimony of man's lofty spiritual ambition. Man is not at peace with himself till he has become like God. The endeavor to reach this state is the supreme, the only ambition worth having. And this is self-realization. This self-realization is the subject of the *Gita*, as it is of all scriptures. But its author surely did not write it to establish that doctrine. The object of the *Gita* appears to me to be that of showing the most excellent way to attain self-realization. That which is to be found, more or less clearly, spread out here and there in Hindu religious books, has been brought out in the clearest possible language in the *Gita* even at the risk of repetition.

The *Gita* is not an aphoristic work; it is a great religious poem. The deeper you dive into it, the richer the meanings you get. It being meant for the people at large, there is pleasing repetition. With every age the important words will carry new and expanding meanings. But its central teaching will never vary. The seeker is at liberty to extract from this treasure any meaning he likes so as to enable him to enforce in his life the central teaching.

Nor is the *Gita* a collection of do's and don'ts. What is lawful for one may be unlawful for another. What may be permissible at one time, or in one place, may not be so at another time, and in another place. Desire for fruit is the only universal prohibition. Desirelessness is obligatory.

The *Gita* has sung the praises of Knowledge, but it is beyond the mere intellect; it is essentially addressed to the heart and capable of being understood by the heart. Therefore the *Gita* is not for those who have no faith.

Two Tamil Poets

*Much of the Sanskrit foundation of Hinduism was
creatively adapted for the myriad languages of
India. These adaptations preserved and extended
the basic ideas of the ancient scriptural sources. The
first two poems in this section sample the Tamil
(south Indian) religious poetry of Appar (seventh
century), the best known of the "Shaivite saints"
whose writings are given a scriptural function, if
not formal status.[55] The last two poems are by
Tukaram (seventeenth century), the greatest
Maharashtrian poet. These poems reflect popular*
bhakti *(devotional) tradition, and many of them
are recited in the humblest households in India.*

Confession of Sin

Evil, all evil, my race, evil my qualities all,
Great am I only in sin, evil is even my good.
Evil my innermost self, foolish, avoiding the
    pure,
Beast am I not, yet the ways of the beast I can
    never forsake.
I can exhort with strong words, telling men
    what they should hate.
Yet can I never give gifts, only to beg them
    I know.
Ah! wretched man that I am, why did I come
    to birth?

The Presence of God

No man holds sway over us,
Nor death nor hell fear we;
No trembling, grief of mind,
No pain nor cringing see.

Joy, day by day, unchanged
Is ours, for we are His,
His ever, who does reign,
Our Shankara,[56] in bliss.

Here to His feet we've come,
Feet as plucked flow'rets fair;
See how His ears divine
Ring and white conch-shell wear.

He is ever hard to find, but He lives in the
    thought of the good;
He is innermost secret of Scripture, inscrutable,
    unknowable;
He is holy and milk and the shining light.

He is the king of the Devas,
Immanent in Vishnu, in Brahma, in flame and
    in wind,
Yet in the mighty sounding sea and in the
    mountains.

He is the great One who chooses Shiva's
    paradise for his own.
If there be days when my tongue is dumb and
    speaks not of him,
Let no such days be counted in the record of
    my life.

[Tukaram:] Waiting[57]

With head on hand before my door,
I sit and wait in vain.
Along the road to Pandhari
My heart and eyes I strain.

When shall I look upon my Lord?
When shall I see him come?
Of all the passing days and hours
I count the heavy sum.

With watching long my eyelids throb,
My limbs with sore distress,
But my impatient heart forgets
My body's weariness.

Sleep is no longer sweet to me;
I care not for my bed;
Forgotten are my house and home,
All thirst and hunger fled.

[55] Taken from F. Kingsbury and G. E. Phillips, *Hymns of the Tamil Shaivite Saints* (Calcutta: Association Press, 1921), pp. 47–51.
[56] *Shankara:* Shiva.
[57] Taken from N. Macnicol, *Psalms of the Maratha Saints* (Calcutta: Association Press, 1920), p. 58.

Says Tuka,[58] Blest shall be the day—
Ah, soon may it betide!—
When one shall come from Pandhari
To summon back the bride.

The Burden of the Past[59]

I have been harassed by the world.
I have dwelled in my mother's womb and I
    must enter the gate of the womb eight
    million times.
I was born a needy beggar and my life is passed
    under a stranger's power.

I am bound fast in the meshes of my past and
    its later influence continues with me;
It puts forth its power and whirls me along.
My stomach is empty and never at rest.
I have no fixed course or home or village.

I have no power, O God, to end my wander-
    ings;
My soul dances about like rice in a frying pan.

Ages have passed in this way and I do not know
    how many more await me.
I cannot end my course, for it begins again;
Only the ending of the world can set me free.

Who will finish this suffering of mine?
Who will take my burden on himself?
Your name will carry me over the sea of this
    world,
You run to the help of the distressed.

Now run to me, Narayana,[60] to me, poor and
    wretched as I am.
Consider neither my merits or my faults.
Tukaram implores your mercy.

---

58 *Tuka:* the poet Tukaram himself. In a custom of Indian
poetry, the author includes his own name in the poem.
59 From J. N. Fraser and K. B. Marathe, *The Poems of
Tukaram* (Madras: Christian Literature Society, 1909),
pp. 114–115.
60 *Narayana:* Vishnu.

The Poems of Mira, a Hindi Female Saint

*Here are two Hindi-language poems by the most
famous female saint, the sixteenth-century poet
Mirabai (Mira for short). The themes of her
poetry are typical of the other bhakti saints.*

[4] O Hari! You are the support of my life!
I have no other refuge but you
In all three worlds.

I have searched the whole universe for you,
Nothing pleases me but you.
Mira says, "O Lord, I am your slave.
Do not forget me."

[63] Without Hari, behold my wretched condition.
They say that you are my protector
And I your servant.

I have practiced remembrance of your name
In my heart, day and night.
Again and again I call upon you,
In grievous affliction.

This world is a threatening sea,
Surrounding me on every side.
My boat has broken;
Hoist the sail quickly
Before it sinks.

This forlorn one waits anxiously for her Lord;
Grant her your nearness.
Your servant Mira repeats, "Ram, Ram!"
I take refuge in you alone.

GLOSSARY

Aranyakas [ah-RUN-yah-kuhs] "Forest Books"; philosophical thoughts on sacrifice; part of the canon of *Shruti*.

Atman [AHT-muhn] The individual self or soul.

Bhagavad-Gita [BAH-gah-vahd GEE-tuh] "Song of the Lord"; a long poem on religious duty in the *Mahabharata*.

Brahman [BRAH-muhn] The ultimate, absolute reality of the cosmos; the world-soul.

Brahmanas [BRAH-muh-nuhs] "Brahmin Books"; Vedic expositions of sacrifice; part of the canon of *Shruti*.

Dharma-Shastras [DAHR-muh SHAS-truhs] Writings on personal and social duties.

mantra [MAHN-truh] A short sacred formula used in prayer or meditation (not, as often thought in North America, a common or personal motto).

Om (or *Aum*) [OHM] A spoken syllable symbolizing the fundamental hidden reality of the universe.

pandit A Brahmin who specializes in Vedic memorization and ritual enactment.

rishis [REE-shees] "Seers" who heard the sounds of the four *Vedas* and collected them into the *Veda*.

samhitas [SAHM-hee-tuhs] "Collections" of hymns, formulas, songs, and spells that constitute the four *Vedas*.

Shruti [SHROO-tee] "What is heard"; the primary revelation heard by the ancients; the first level of Hindu scripture, considered of cosmic, not human, authorship.

Smriti [SMRIH-tee] "What is remembered" about divine revelation; epics, myths and legends, tantras, and law codes that constitute the second level of Hindu scripture.

Upanishads [oo-PAH-nee-shahds] "Sittings near a Teacher"; philosophical collections forming the end of the *Veda*; part of the canon of *Shruti*.

Vedas [VAY-duhs] "Books of Knowledge"; the four *Vedas*—*Rig, Yajur, Sama,* and *Atharva*—are part of the canon of *Shruti*.

Yogin [YO-gin] A practitioner of yoga.

QUESTIONS FOR STUDY AND DISCUSSION

1. To what degree, if any, can the *Vedas* be described as reflecting a nature-worship religion?

2. Compare the use and effects of soma to the modern use of drugs by people who argue that drug use brings a higher consciousness. What might the similarities and differences be?

3. In what ways do the *Upanishads* differ from and agree with earlier Vedic literature? Do you agree with those scholars who argue that the differences between the earlier *Vedas* and later writings (including the *Upanishads*) justify calling the first stage "Vedic religion" and only the second stage "Hinduism"?

4. How does the variety of usages of Hindu scripture in the past and present mirror the variety of Hindu religion?

5. If you were to become a Hindu, to which caste would you like to belong? Which sex? Why?

6. How would you characterize the role of women in Hinduism? Are the texts given here reflective of what you see as women's actual conditions in India?

7.   How and why does the *Bhagavad-Gita* present the path of devotion as the best form of Hinduism?

8.   How does the *Bhagavad-Gita* present and answer the problem of war? What is your critique of its answer? How may its answer be applicable to peoples of other cultures and other religions?

9.   How do the later devotional songs carry forth and develop the traditions of devotional Hinduism?

SCRIPTURES IN FILM

The Indian film industry, popularly known as "Bollywood," is second in size only to the film industry of the United States. However, it has not produced many English-language films that deal with Hindu scriptures. *The Mahabharata* (1989, not rated), directed by Peter Brooks, is a short version of the lengthy stage play done by the Brooklyn Academy of Music and has a short section on the *Bhagavad-Gita*. For a treatment of the history and culture of modern India with indirect treatment of scriptural ideas, see *Gandhi* (1982, rated PG), directed by Richard Attenborough and starring Ben Kingsley. This excellent film won three Academy Awards. For a contemporary treatment of stages of life, marriage, and role relationships in a modern Western context, see *Monsoon Wedding* (2001, rated R), directed by Mira Nair, who also directed the Cannes prize-winning *Salaam Bombay!*, the story of children's appalling lives on the street.

SUGGESTIONS FOR FURTHER READING

Primary Readings

The most complete and accessible translations of Hindu scripture remain the several volumes in F. Max Müller, gen. ed., *Sacred Books of the East* (Oxford: Oxford University Press, 1879–1910). For more recent translations, begin with the following works.

T. B. Coburn, *Encountering the Goddess: A Translation of the Devi-Mahatmya and a Study of Its Interpretation*. Albany: State University of New York Press, 1991. A translation and study of the best-known goddess text in modern India.

W. Doniger and S. Kakar, eds., *Kamasutra*. New York: Oxford University Press, 2002. A scholarly translation designed to correct Richard Burton's famous translation. Includes samples of commentaries from the thirteenth to the twentieth centuries but no illustrations.

R. E. Hume, *The Thirteen Principal Upanishads,* 2d ed. Oxford: Oxford University Press, 1983. Perhaps the best translation of the most important *Upanishads.*

D. S. Lopez Jr., *Religions of India in Practice*. Princeton: Princeton University Press, 1995. Contains primary documents, many never translated before, of more recent Hindu literature that has scriptural use. See especially the section "Songs of Devotion and Praise," which treats devotional poetry.

B. S. Miller, *The Bhagavad-Gita: Krishna's Counsel in Time of War*. New York: Columbia University Press, 1986. The most readable recent translation of the *Gita,* and one that suggests its power and literary beauty.

W. Doniger O'Flaherty, ed., *Textual Sources for the Study of Hinduism*. Totowa, NJ: Barnes & Noble, 1988. A selection of readings from both *Shruti* and *Smriti*.

P. Olivelle, *Samnyasa Upanishads: Hindu Scriptures on Asceticism and Renunciation.* New York: Oxford University Press, 1992. Full introduction, fresh translation, and notes for those *Upanishads* that deal with the stage of renunciation. See also his *Upanishads* (World's Classics Series; Oxford: Oxford University Press, 1998).

Secondary Readings

T. B. Coburn, "'Scripture' in India: Towards a Typology of the Word in Hindu Life." In M. Levering, ed., *Rethinking Scripture: Essays from a Comparative Perspective.* Albany: State University of New York Press, 1989, pp. 102–128; also published in the *Journal of the American Academy of Religion* 52 (1984): 435–459. Argues that *scripture* is an ill-fitting term for Hinduism and proposes instead a nuanced understanding of oral use of scripture.

H. Coward, "Scripture in Hinduism." In Coward, *Sacred Word and Sacred Text: Scripture in World Religions.* Maryknoll, NY: Orbis, 1988. A survey of the Hindu scriptures with special attention to orality.

K. Kostermaier, *Hindu Writings: A Short Introduction to the Major Sources.* Oxford: Oneworld, 2000. Treats *Veda* to contemporary writings, with emphasis on scripture.

R. C. Lester, "Hinduism: Veda and Sacred Texts." In F. M. Denny and R. L. Taylor, eds., *The Holy Book in Comparative Perspective.* Columbia: University of South Carolina Press, 1985, pp. 126–147. A good treatment of the relationship of Vedic texts and other Hindu scriptures, especially the *Smriti.*

K. Sivaraman, ed., *Hindu Spirituality: Vedas through Vedanta.* New York: Crossroad, 1989. A treatment by mostly Indian scholars of the continuing significance of Vedic and Upanishadic traditions for contemporary Hinduism.

K. K. Young, "[Women in] Hinduism." In A. Sharma, ed., *Women in World Religions.* Albany: State University of New York Press, 1987, pp. 59–103. This concise but fairly comprehensive survey has good references to the content and usage of Hindu sacred writings.

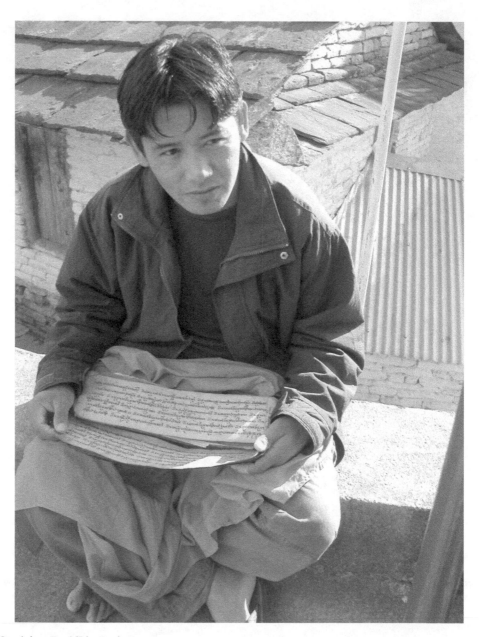

Studying Buddhist Scripture
Palden Wangchuk, a young monk in the village of Sirubari, Nepal, reads and reflects on Buddhist scripture, written here on the traditional palm-leaf material. Activity with scripture forms a good deal of the Buddhist monk's typical day. *Credit:* Photo courtesy of Chuck Conner Photography. Copyright © 2004 Chuck Conner.

CHAPTER THREE

Buddhism

✤ In a Chinese convent, Buddhist nuns gather daily to read scripture. A low hum fills the reading room as they recite in unison. They are "making merit," doing a deed that will wear away karma. This merit will enable them to be reborn after death into a better existence, eventually to achieve Nirvana and be reborn no more.

✤ In Washington, D.C., a new "Dharma Wheel Cutting Karma" has been turning since 1997 in the Asian section of the Library of Congress. The wheel contains 208 repetitions of forty-two Tibetan scriptures, which otherwise fill fifteen Tibetan volumes. The spiritual power generated by the constant electrical turning of the wheel is said to generate compassion, prevent natural disasters, and promote peace in the world.

✤ In Thailand, a leading Buddhist authority urges that country's 300,000 monks to join in the fight against AIDS. Dr. Chatsumarn Kabilsingh of the Dharma Practice Center said that monks should acquire a better understanding of Buddhist scriptures to be more effective in teaching the scriptural command against adultery. She says, "Sex springs from the love and care shown by two individuals, and they need to be responsible to each other. With true love, there is no need to change partners, and that is the best prevention against AIDS."

✤ In Maharagama, Sri Lanka, several Buddhist monks work at computer keyboards. They are keying in the complete text of the Pali canon of Buddhist scriptures. In 1994, after three years of work, the scriptures were published on the World Wide Web (only in the Pali language); later they became available in a fully searchable CD-ROM. The monks and the private patrons funding this project see it as yet another phase in the preservation of Buddhist scripture from 2,500 years ago.

INTRODUCTION

The Buddhist religion is based on the life and teaching of the Indian sage Siddhartha Gotama (ca. 536–476 B.C.E.), the Enlightened One, or **Buddha** [BUH-dah; the first syllable rhymes with "wood," not "mood"]. Buddhists believe that individuals can overcome the misery of the world and reach their own Buddha status by a process of mental and moral purification. The term *Buddha* applies to every individual who attains this state. Gotama Buddha is the Buddha par excellence.

Buddhism has spread throughout most of Asia. With this growth has come a wide diversity within Buddhism that is mirrored in its scriptures. The Buddhist canon has three main forms—*Theravadin, Mahayanan,* and *Tibetan*—hundreds of scriptural texts, and many different types of usage. This assemblage of scriptures provides a fascinating overview of the early history of the Buddhist tradition and insight into the contemporary life of Buddhists everywhere.

Overview of Structure

The scriptures of Theravada (south Asian) Buddhism are known as the *Tipitaka*[1] [tih-pee-TAH-kuh], the "Three Baskets" (see Table 3.1). Tradition says that the early disciples of Buddha wrote down his words on palm leaves and separated them into three baskets (*pitakas*): the *Vinaya Pitaka,* "Discipline Basket"; the *Sutta Pitaka,* "Discourse Basket"; and the *Abhidhamma Pitaka,* "Special Teaching Basket." In this section we first consider each basket and then survey the structure of the Chinese and Tibetan forms of the Buddhist canon.

The *Vinaya Pitaka* contains regulations for the communal life of the monks and nuns. All these rules are said to be the words of the Buddha. The *Vinaya* [vih-NIGH-yuh] has three divisions: the *Sutta-vibhanga* (Division of Rules), the *Khandhaka* (Sections), and the *Parivara* (Accessory), a short summary of the rules and how to apply them. The *Vinaya* presents 227 different rules for monks—most of them prohibitions of forbidden activities—grouped according to importance. They range from a few major offenses that result in permanent expulsion from the order to many minor offenses that a monk need only confess to his monastic leader. All the rules for monks apply in a general way to the nuns as well, but a special section of the *Sutta-vibhanga* gives specific regulations for nuns. The size of the *Vinaya Pitaka* is indicated by its most recent English translation, which runs to six substantial volumes. That the *Vinaya* is first among the three baskets of scripture attests to the leading role that monasticism has played in Buddhism as a whole and especially in its scriptures.

The second basket, the *Sutta* [SUH-tuh] *Pitaka,* contains teachings attributed to Gotama Buddha. The word **sutta** (Sanskrit: *sutra*) refers to a scriptural text. Buddhists divide the *Sutta Pitaka* into five sections: *Long Discourses, Medium-Length Discourses, Corrected Discourses, Item-More* [or *Gradual*] *Discourses,* and *Short Texts.* Each of the discourses has many subdivisions, and most follow a common structure: First comes "Thus I have heard [from the Buddha]," then a statement of the place and occasion of the hearing, next the body of the teaching, and last the listener's confession of the truth of the teaching and acknowledgment that he (the listener) is Buddha's disciple. The *Sutta Pitaka* is probably the best known of the three baskets. With its rationale for the first basket, its collections of wise sayings, its stories of former lives of the Buddha and other famous Buddhists, and its general writings on doctrines and ethics, the *Sutta Pitaka* provides for students of Buddhism the best access to the essence of the religion's tradition.

The third basket, the *Abhidhamma* [ahb-hee-DAHM-muh] *Pitaka,* contains seven scholastic treatises based on the teachings of Buddha. They deal with advanced, difficult topics and are often highly philosophical. Although the Pali and Sanskrit

---

[1] Sanskrit: *Tripitaka.* Throughout this chapter, we generally use Pali language forms of key Buddhist words; Sanskrit equivalents appear in parentheses. The titles of scripture books reflect their language of origin, which is generally Pali.

Table 3.1

The Theravadin Canon: The *Tipitaka*

Name	Translation	Content/Size
Vinaya Pitaka	Discipline Basket	
1. *Sutta-vibhanga*	Division of Rules	Monastic rules stated and expanded
a. *Mahavibhanga*	Great Division	227 rules for monks
b. *Bhikkuni-vibhanga*	Division about Nuns	Rules for nuns
2. *Khandhaka*	Sections	
a. *Mahavagga*	Great Group	Main rules
b. *Cullavagga*	Small Group	Miscellaneous rules
3. *Parivara*	Accessory	Summaries of rules
Sutta Pitaka	Discourse Basket	
1. *Digha-nikaya*	Collection of Long Discourses	34 suttas
2. *Majjhima-nikaya*	Collection of Medium-Length Discourses	152 suttas
3. *Samyutta-nikaya*	Collection of Corrected Discourses	56 groups of suttas
4. *Anguttara-nikaya*	Collection of Item-More Discourses	2308 suttas
5. *Khuddaka-nikaya*	Collection of Short Texts	
a. *Khuddaka-patha*	Little Readings	A meditation book
b. *Dhammapada*	Verses on Teaching	26 chapters
c. *Udana*	Utterances	80 utterances
d. *Itivuttaka*	Thus-saids	112 suttas
e. *Sutta-nipata*	Sutta Collection	71 suttas
f. *Vimana-vatthu*	Tales of Heavenly Mansions	85 poems
g. *Peta-vatthu*	Tales of Ghosts	Rebirth as Ghosts
h. *Thera-Gatha*	Verses of Elder Men	Poems from earliest monks
i. *Theri-Gatha*	Verses of Elder Women	Poems from early nuns
j. *Jataka*	Lives	550 past lives of Gotama
k. *Nidessa*	Exposition	2 commentaries
l. *Patisambhida-magga*	Way of Analysis	Doctrinal exposition
m. *Apadana*	Stories	Saints' past lives
n. *Buddhavamsa*	Lineage of the Buddhas	Stories of 24 pre-Gotama Buddhas
o. *Gariya-pitaka*	Basket of Perfections	35 tales from *Jataka*

Table 3.1
Continued

Name	Translation	Content/Size
Abhidhamma Pitaka	Special Teaching Basket	
1. *Dhamma-sangani*	Summary of Teaching	
2. *Vibhanga*	Divisions	
3. *Dhastu-Kadha*	Discussions of Elements	
4. *Puggala-pannatti*	Designation of Persons	
5. *Yamaka*	The Pairs	
6. *Patthama*	Activations	

Source: From *The Buddhist Religion*, 1st edition, by Richard H. Robinson. Copyright 1970. Reprinted with permission of Wadsworth, a division of Thomson Learning: www.thomsonrights.com Fax 800 730–2215.

versions of the first two baskets are similar in content, they vary quite a bit in the third basket. The Pali version, used by South Asian Theravada Buddhism, tries to adhere conservatively to the exact words of Buddha. Its six treatises are *The Summary of Teaching, Divisions, Discussion of Elements, The Designation of Person, The Pairs,* and *Activations.* The Sanskrit version, *Abhidharma,* is important for the growth of Buddhist philosophy because these Sanskrit books deal with the ideas of Buddha more than with his words. Like the Pali version, the Sanskrit has seven books, but they differ from the Pali name and content, and Chinese and Tibetan translations of them also differ. The seven most commonly recognized are *Method of Knowledge, Treatise, Overview of Consciousness, Collection on the Teaching, Treatise on Communication, Overview of the Elements,* and *Discourse on Sacred Beliefs.*

The scriptures of Mahayana (north Asian, especially China and Japan) Buddhism are known as the "Chinese canon." The Mahayana canon did not adopt the three-fold-basket division of the Pali canon. It has no main divisions (see Table 3.2), but many of the most important books of the Pali canon were incorporated in the Mahayana canon. The Theravadin and Mahayanan canons share important works such as the **Jatakas** (Lives), the *Death of the Buddha* (Pali: *Mahaparinibbana;* Sanskrit: *Mahaparinirvana*), *Vinaya* texts on monastic discipline, and various *Abhidhamma* texts. Some books from the Mahayana canon have even penetrated Theravada Buddhism and are recognized and used as scripture though not formally admitted to the historic Pali canon. In Sri Lanka, for example, the *Buddhacarita* (Acts of the Buddha) and the *Visuddhimagga* (Path of Purification) are widely received and used as scripture.

The Mahayana canon also added many other new books, all of them claiming to be the true word of the Gotama Buddha. Among the most important are *Prajna-Paramita* (Perfection of Knowledge) sutras, philosophical discussions of the denial of the reality of existence and nonexistence. Their almost constant repetitiveness contributes to their great length. Another important work is the *Description of the Happy Land*—that is, the land where the gracious Buddha Amitabha rules and invites

Table 3.2
The Mahayana or Chinese Canon

Name of Section	Translation	Size
Agama	Limbs	2 vols., 151 texts
Jatakas	Lives	2 vols., 68 texts
Prajna-Paramita	Perfect Wisdom	4 vols., 42 texts
Saddharma-Pundarika	—	1 vol., 16 texts
Avatamsaka	—	2 vols., 31 texts
Ratnakuta	—	
Mahaparinirvana	Great Decease	1 vol., 23 texts
—	Great Assembly	1 vol., 28 texts
Sutra-Pitaka	Sutra Collection	4 vols., 423 texts
Tantra	Tantra	4 vols., 572 texts
Vinaya	Discipline	3 vols., 86 texts
—	Commentary on Sutras	3 vols., 31 texts
Abhidhamma	Special Teaching	4 vols., 28 texts
Madhyamika		1 vol., 15 texts
Yogacara	Yoga Practice	2 vols., 49 texts
—	Treatises	1 vol., 65 texts
—	Commentaries on Sutras	7 vols.
—	Commentaries on *Vinaya*	1 vol.
—	Commentaries on Shastras	5 vols.
—	Chinese Sectarian Writings	5 vols.
—	History and Biography	4 vols., 95 texts
—	Encyclopedias and Dictionaries	2 vols., 16 texts
—	Non-Buddhist Writings	1 vol., 8 texts
—	Catalogues	1 vol., 40 texts

Source: From *The Buddhist Religion,* 1st edition, by Richard H. Robinson. Copyright 1970. Reprinted with permission of Wadsworth, a division of Thomson Learning: www.thomsonrights.com Fax 800 730–2215.

his followers to share eternal life with him. This text has become important in the Japanese Pure Land Buddhist sect. A third major work is the *Lotus Sutra of the True Law.* This work has become the leading text of Nichiren Buddhism. In sum, with its adoption of many older books along with an astonishing variety of new books, the literature of Mahayana Buddhism is vast and complex.

The third main Buddhist canon is the Tibetan (see Table 3.3). In the seventh century C.E., Buddhism came to Tibet, where it is known as Lamaism (from the Tibetan *bla-ma,* the "superior person"). The Tibetan king sent a delegation to India, where an alphabet was devised for the Tibetan language and the entire Buddhist literature was translated into it. The Tibetans added many books of their own, secular as well as religious, to this Indian collection. The final and official assembling of these

Table 3.3
The Tibetan Canon

Name	Translation	Size
Kanjur	Translation of the Ordinances	108 vols.
'Dul-ba	Discipline [for monastics]	13 vols.
Shes-rab-kyi-pha-rol-tu-phyin-pa	Supreme Otherworldly Knowledge	21 vols.
Phal-chen	Buddhist Cosmology	6 vols.
dKon-brtsegs	Heap of Jewels	6 vols.
mDo	Teaching Lectures	38 vols.
Mya-ngan-'das	Nirvana	2 vols.
rGyud	Texture [Tantra]	22 vols.
Tanjur	Translation of the Doctrine	225 vols.
mDo	Teaching [Sutra]	136 vols.
rGyud	Texture [Tantra]	87 vols.
	A book of Hymns	1 vol.
	An index	1 vol.

books came in the fourteenth century, when they were fixed into two sections: the *Kanjur* (Translation of the Ordinances) and the *Tanjur* (Translation of the Doctrine).

The *Kanjur* contains 689 books of various lengths in 100 or 108 volumes. It contains only those texts that the Buddha himself is said to have taught. The first main division is the *Discipline,* for monks; the second is *Supreme Otherworldly Knowledge;* the third deals with Buddhist cosmology; the fourth is *Heap of Jewels;* the fifth is *Teaching Lectures;* the sixth is *Nirvana;* the last is *Texture* (Tantra). The *Tanjur* is not, as is often stated, a commentary on the *Kanjur.* It contains 225 volumes in two main sections, *Teaching* (Sutra) and *Texture* (Tantra). The *Teaching* section includes many translations of Indian commentaries on older scriptures. The *Tanjur* deals with an even wider variety of topics than does the *Kanjur:* traditional religious teachings, magical texts drawn mainly from native Tibetan religion, and texts on alchemy and astrology. Today the preservation and further dissemination of Tibetan scriptures is a primary task of Tibetan Buddhist exiles.

Use

Buddhist use of scripture centers around monastic activity. Since early times, when the teaching of Buddha was passed along orally and then written down, the role of monks (but not nuns) in scriptural activity has been primary. The scriptures themselves bear the marks of this orientation. For example, the first and the third baskets are explicitly for monastics. Other reasons also figure in. The expense of owning such a large canon makes it accessible mainly to monastic orders. Its size demands a lifetime of study to master it; its content is challenging and specialized, calling for special teachers who can be found only among the monks. Buddhism in general demands withdrawal from the distractions of daily life in order to give the scriptures the kind of in-depth study they deserve.

What does this monastic usage entail? First, Buddhism has traditionally distinguished between study monks and meditation monks. The very term *study monk* indicates the first use of scripture—the study of the content of its teachings. A new monk studies scripture to learn the first and most important of the monastic rules that govern his life. He also studies the most easily understood texts in the *Sutta Pitaka*, such as the *Dhammapada* and the *Jataka* [JAH-tah-kuh] verses. As time progresses and he masters this material, he learns the other rules in the *Vinaya Pitaka* and the other texts of the *Sutta Pitaka*. If, at the height of his monastic career, he displays excellence in study and teaching, he may go on to master the intricacies of the *Abhidhamma Pitaka*. Because study of the scriptures is in most forms of Buddhism a prerequisite for becoming a meditation monk, all monks pass through this first phase. Throughout the history of Buddhism and even today, study monks have greatly outnumbered meditation monks. This is especially the case in modern times, when the general conviction has grown in many Buddhist circles that one cannot reach enlightenment in this life. In all this study and teaching, the goal is to realize in one's own life the teachings of the Buddha that lead toward nirvana, enlightenment. The scripture itself, as a book, is worth little or nothing. The *meaning* of the words, not the words themselves, has value in the search for purification.

Monks also pursue scriptural activity for the laity. At funerals they recite texts for the merit of the deceased. Monks often officiate at wedding ceremonies. They lecture on the scriptures to the laity, both individuals and groups. Some monks preach the scriptures to the laity, often using such popular material as the *Jataka* tales. Wealthy layfolk often sponsor long recitations of scripture in the monasteries and pay for the publication of scriptures, all for the sake of making merit for loved ones. But all these activities with the laity are mostly incidental to a monk's main activity—studying and meditating on scripture in order to travel the road to personal enlightenment.

The Tibetan form of Buddhism holds its scriptures in great ritual esteem. The books are venerated in worship; incense and prayer are offered to them. They are produced in the traditional way, either printed by hand or with woodblocks, and are preserved in the monasteries with great care. Although these books are produced and preserved in Tibet and northern India, no scholarly critical edition of them has been compiled. Modern-language translations are very incomplete, and only a few European and North American libraries possess a complete copy of the *Kanjur* and *Tanjur*.

Origin and Development

The development of Buddhist scripture begins with Gotama Buddha himself. Buddhists believe that Prince Gotama established among his monk disciples an oral transmission of his teachings on which later written scriptures are based. They trace all the varied scripture collections and their contents back to Buddha. All scriptures are his word.

Before Gotama died, he did not appoint a human successor. He taught instead that the leader of the Buddhists was to be his teaching—**dhamma** [DAH-muh]

(Sanskrit: *dharma*)—and the monastic order (Sangha) he founded. Soon after his death, his disciples gathered at the first general council of Buddhists, held at Rajagaha in 483 B.C.E., to formalize his teachings. After seven months of work collecting and examining the supposed sayings of Buddha for authenticity, they drafted an official version and committed it to memory. Ananda, his chief disciple, is said to have recited them all. The sayings were written down on palm leaves (more durable than paper or parchment in the hot, humid Indian climate) and then separated into baskets. Mahayana Buddhists believe that all three baskets were developed at this time. Theravada Buddhists believe that the last basket, *Abhidhamma Pitaka,* was formed at the third general council of Buddhists in 253 B.C.E. Most modern scholars agree that the nature of this basket seems to suggest a later origin.

Even after this initial conversion to writing, oral transmission continued and was seen as the primary mode of scripture preservation by all early Buddhists. An early *Abhidhamma* text, the *Samuccaya,* indicates reasons for this preference: Memorizing is easy, accumulates merit, aids understanding, brings mental satisfaction, and promotes one's good standing among others. In addition, early Buddhists saw transmission by an exacting oral tradition as offering a more reliable way than writing to preserve the exact words of the Buddha.

When Mahayana Buddhism arose in the first century C.E., it showed new concern for liberation through the assistance of a **bodhisattva** [bohd-hee-SAHT-vuh], a person who postpones his or her own full enlightenment in order to help others. The older idea of self-redemption characteristic of Theravada Buddhism gave way to redemption through the grace of this Buddha. The new movement required a new body of scripture, and so began the Mahayana canon (see Table 3.2). Although this collection is typically called the "Chinese canon," it is also used in Japan, usually in its Chinese-language form.

HISTORY

The Past Lives of Siddhartha Gotama*

After his enlightenment, Siddhartha knew all his past lives. In the Jatakas *(Lives), he recounts in detail 550 episodes from as many past lives, each story revealing his gradual progress to perfection in his last incarnation as Gotama. Each* Jataka *teaches one point, always to edify the reader. Only the verses at the end are considered inspired, and the stories are built from them. They come from a Mahayana setting that features the bestowal of merit from one person to another, but they are widely known in Theravada lands as well. In this story the layman transfers merit to the barber.[2]*

The Master told this story about a believing layman. This was a faithful, pious soul, and a chosen disciple. One evening, on his way to Jetavana, he came to the bank of a river. The ferrymen had already pulled up their boat on the shore in order to attend service. No boat

*Jataka 190, *Birth-Story of the Blessing of the Commandments.*
[2] Taken, with editing, from E. B. Cowell, ed., *The Jataka,* vol. 2 (Cambridge: Cambridge University Press, 1895), pp. 77–78.

could be seen at the landing, and our friend's mind was full of delightful thoughts of the Buddha, so he walked into the river. His feet did not sink below the water. He got as far as mid-river walking as though he were on dry land, but then he noticed the waves. Then his ecstasy subsided, and his feet began to sink. But he stirred himself up to high tension [by meditation], and walked on over the water. So he arrived at Jetavana, greeted the Master, and took a seat on one side. The Master entered into conversation with him pleasantly: "I hope, good layman, you had no mishap on your way."

"O Sir," he replied, "I was so absorbed in thoughts of the Buddha that when I set foot upon the river, I walked over it as though it had been dry ground!"

"Ah, friend layman," said the Master, "you are not the only one who has been kept safe by remembering the virtues of the Buddha. In older days pious laymen have been shipwrecked in mid-ocean, and saved themselves by remembering the Buddha's virtues." Then, at the man's request, he told a story from his past lives.

Once upon a time . . . a disciple who had entered on the Paths went on a ship with a barber of some considerable property. The barber's wife had given him charge of our friend, to look after him in better and in worse. A week later, the ship was wrecked in mid-ocean. These two persons clung to one plank, and were cast up on an island. There the barber killed some birds, and cooked them, offering a share of his meal to the lay brother. "No, thank you," said he, "I have had enough." He was thinking to himself, "There is no help for us here except the Three Jewels,"[3] and so he pondered upon the blessings of the Three Jewels. As he pondered, a Serpent-king who had been born in that isle changed his own body to the shape of a great ship. The ship was filled with the seven kinds of precious things. An ocean god was the helmsman. The three masts were made of sapphire, the anchor of gold, the ropes of silver, and the planks were golden. The Sea-spirit stood on board, crying, "Any passengers for India?"

The lay brother said, "Yes, that's where we are headed."

"In with you then, on board with you!" He went aboard, and wanted to call his friend the barber. "You may come," said the helmsman to the lay brother, "but he may not. He is not a man of holy life. I brought this ship for you, not for him."

The lay brother replied, "Very well; the gifts I have given, the virtues I have practiced, the powers I have developed—I give him the fruit of all of them!"

"I thank you, master!" said the barber.

"Now," said the Sea-spirit, "I can take the barber aboard." He conveyed them both over the sea, and sailed upstream to Benares. There, by his power, he created a store of wealth for both of them, and spoke this to them: "Keep company with the wise and good. If this barber had not been in company with this pious layman, he would have perished in the deep." Then he said this poem in praise of good company:
"Behold the fruit of sacrifice, virtue, and piety:
A serpent in ship-shape conveys the good man
 o'er the sea.
Make friendship only with the good, and keep
 good company;
Friends with the good, this barber could his
 home in safety see." . . .

Master Gotama, after finishing this discourse, declared the Truths and identified the [connection to his] Birth. At the conclusion of the Truths the pious layman entered on the Fruit of the Second Path.[4] "On that occasion the converted lay brother attained Nirvana; Sariputta was the Serpent-king, and I myself was the ocean-god."

---

[3] *Three Jewels:* the Buddha, the Dhamma (Teaching), and the Sangha (monastic order); also called the "Three Refuges."
[4] *the Fruit of the Second Path:* the path of those who are reborn again only once.

The Life of Siddhartha Gotama*

Scholars of Buddhism today place the Acts of the Buddha (Buddhacarita) *by Ashvaghosha, who lived in the first century* B.C.E., *between Theravada and Mahayana Buddhism. It is a favorite book in the latter. It deals in poetic form with the life and teachings of the Buddha. This selection recounts the birth of Gotama, the "Four Sights," his "Great Retirement," and his enlightenment. It portrays the life of Siddhartha as an example for all Buddhists: All his followers should reach Nirvana in this manner. It opens, as do many Buddhist scriptures, with an invocation to the Buddha. This salutes him as an* **Arhat** *[AHR-haht], a "Worthy One" who has achieved enlightenment.*[5]

That Arhat is here saluted, who has no counterpart. Giving supreme happiness, he surpasses Brahman the Creator. Driving away darkness, he vanquishes the sun. Dispelling all burning heat, he surpasses the beautiful moon.

There was a city, the dwelling-place of the great saint Kapila, that had its sides surrounded by the beauty of a lofty broad plain like a line of clouds. With its high-soaring palaces, it was immersed in the sky. . . . [9] A king by the name of Suddhodana ruled over the city. He was a relative of the sun, anointed to stand at the head of earth's monarchs. He adorned it as a bee adorns a full-blown lotus. [10] He was the very best of kings, intent on liberality but empty of pride. . . .

[15] He had a queen named Maya, who was free from all deceit. She was a brilliance proceeding from his brilliance, like the splendor of the sun when it is free from all the influence of darkness. . . . Truly the life of women is always darkness; yet when it encountered her, it shone brilliantly. . . .

[19] Falling from the host of beings in heaven, and illumining the three worlds, the most excellent of Bodhisattvas[6] suddenly entered her womb. [20] He assumed the form of a huge elephant as white as Himalaya, armed with six tusks, with his face perfumed with flowing ichor. Then he entered the womb of the queen of king Suddhodana to destroy the evils of the world. The guardians of the world hastened from heaven to watch over the world's one true ruler. . . . [23] Later, one day by the king's permission the queen, having a great longing in her mind, went with the residents of the women's apartments into Lumbini Garden. As the queen supported herself by a bough that hung with a weight of flowers, the Bodhisattva suddenly came forth, splitting open her womb. [25] Then the constellation Pushya was auspicious. From the side of the queen, her son Gotama was born for the welfare of the world. He was born without pain and without illness [for his mother]. . . . [34] He said, "I am born for supreme knowledge, for the welfare of the world. Therefore, this is my last birth. . . ."

[54] The great seer Asita learned of this birth, the birth of him who was to destroy all birth, by signs and through the power of his penances. In his thirst for the excellent Law, he came to the palace of the Sakya king. . . . [59] The sage, being invited by the king, filled with properly intense feeling, uttered his deep and solemn words [to the king] as his large eyes opened wide with wonder: . . . [62] "Hear the reason for my coming and rejoice in it. I have heard a heavenly voice saying that your son has been born for the sake of supreme knowledge. . . ."

[72] Knowing that the king was disturbed by his fear of some impending evil, the sage spoke to him. "Let not your mind, O monarch, be disturbed.

---

*Buddhacarita 1.1–2, 9–10, 15–17, 19–21, 23–25, 34, 54, 59, 62, 72–74, 83; 2.24–26, 28–32; 3.1–8, 26–33, 40–44, 53–61; 5.7–20; 12.88–104; 14.1–9, 35–37, 64–68, 79–81.

[5] Taken, with editing, from E. B. Cowell, trans., *Buddhist Mahayana Texts, Sacred Books of the East,* vol. 49 (Oxford: Oxford University Press, 1894), pp. 1–157.

[6] *Bodhisattvas:* individuals who have reached enlightenment but postpone entering Nirvana in order to help others reach it.

All that I have said is certainly true. I have no feeling of fear about his being subject to change, but I am distressed for my own disappointment. It is my time to depart, and this child is now born. He knows the mystery hard to attain, the means of destroying rebirth. When he has forsaken his kingdom, become indifferent to all worldly things, and attained the highest truth by his strenuous efforts, he will shine as a sun of knowledge to destroy the darkness of illusion in the world. . . ."

[83] When he heard these words, the king, his queen, and his friends abandoned sorrow and rejoiced. Thinking, "Such is this son of mine," he considered that his son's excellence was his own. But he let his heart be influenced by the thought, "He will travel by the noble path." He was not opposed to religion, but he was alarmed at the prospect of losing his child [to a religious life]. . . .

[2.24] When the young prince had passed the period of childhood and reached his youth, he learned in a few days the various sciences suitable to his caste, which generally took many years to master. [25] But remembering what the great seer Asita said about his embrace of transcendental happiness, the anxious care of the king . . . turned the prince to sensual pleasures. He sought for him a bride possessed of beauty, modesty, gentle bearing, and widespread honor. She was from a family of unblemished moral excellence. Yasodhara was her name, a veritable goddess of good fortune. . . .

[28] "He might see some discouraging sight that could disturb his mind." Reflecting this way, the king had a dwelling prepared for his son in the private recesses of the palace. They were furnished with the delights proper for every season, gaily decorated like heavenly chariots upon the earth, and bright like the clouds of autumn. He spent time among the splendid musical concerts of singing women. [30] With the soft tambourines beaten by the tips of the women's hands, and ornamented with golden rims, and with the dances that were like the dances of the heavenly nymphs, that palace shone like Mount Kailasa. The women delighted him with their soft voices, their beautiful pearl-garlands, their playful intoxication, their sweet laughter, and their furtive glances. Carried away in the arms of these women well skilled in the ways of love and reckless in the pursuit of pleasure, he fell from the roof of a pavilion and yet did not reach the ground. It was like a holy sage had stepped from a heavenly chariot. . . .

[3.1] On a certain day he heard about the forests carpeted with tender grass. They had been all bound up in the cold season, but now their trees resounded with birds and they were adorned with lotus ponds. When he heard of the delightful appearance of these parks beloved by the women, he resolved to go outdoors. He was like an elephant shut up in a house for a long time.

When the king learned the wish expressed by his son, he ordered an excursion to be prepared, one worthy of his own affection and his son's beauty and youth. But he prohibited any encounter with any afflicted common person on the road. He said, "Heaven forbid that the prince with his tender nature should even imagine himself to be distressed." [5] Then he removed from the road with the greatest gentleness all those who had mutilated limbs, the old, the sick, and all squalid beggars. They made the highway assume its perfect beauty. Along this road now made beautiful, the prince and his attendants came down one day at a proper time from the roof of the palace, and went to visit the king to gain his permission to leave. Then the king, with tears rising in his eyes, smelled his son's head and gazed for a long time upon him. He gave him his permission, saying, "Go." But in his heart he did not want him to depart. . . .

[26] But then the gods, dwelling in their pure abodes, saw the city rejoicing like heaven itself. They created an old man to walk along and to stir the heart of the king's son. The prince saw him overcome with weakness and different in form from other men. With his gaze intently fixed on him, he asked his driver, "Who is this man with white hair and his hand resting

on a staff, his eyes hidden beneath his brows, his limbs bent down and hanging loose? Is this a change produced in him, or his natural state, or an accident?"

The charioteer revealed to the king's son the secret that should have been kept so carefully. He thought no harm, for those same gods had bewildered his mind. He said, [30] "Old age has broken him down. It is the ravisher of beauty, the ruin of vigor, the cause of sorrow, the destruction of delights, the affliction of memories, the enemy of the senses. He too once drank milk in his childhood, and in time he learned to crawl on the ground. Step by step he became a vigorous youth, and now step by step he has reached old age."

The startled prince spoke these words to the charioteer: "What! Will this evil come to me also?" To him the charioteer spoke again, "It will certainly come in time even to my long-lived lord. All the world knows that old age will destroy their beauty, and they are content to have it so. . . ."

[40] Then the same deities created another man with his body all afflicted by disease. On seeing him the son of Suddhodana addressed the charioteer, having his gaze fixed on the man. "That man with a swollen belly, his whole frame shaking as he pants, his arms and shoulders hanging loose, his body all pale and thin, saying pathetically the word 'mother' when he embraces a stranger—what is the matter with him?"

Then his charioteer answered, "Gentle Sir, it is a very great affliction called sickness that has grown in him. It has made even this strong man no longer master of himself."

Then the prince again addressed him, looking upon the man compassionately, "Is this evil peculiar to him, or are all people threatened by sickness?" The charioteer answered, "O prince, this evil is common to all. Pressed by diseases, people try to find pleasure, even though they are racked with pain. . . ."

[53] When the royal road was especially adorned and guarded, the king let the prince go out once more. He ordered the charioteer and chariot to proceed in a direction different from the previous one. But as the king's son was going on his way, the very same deities created a dead man. Only the charioteer and the prince saw him as he was carried dead along the road. [55] Then the prince spoke to the charioteer, "Who is this carried by four men, and followed by mournful companions? He is no longer breathing!"

Then the driver, whose mind was overpowered by the gods who possess pure minds and pure dwellings, and who knew the truth, uttered to his lord this truth that he had been forbidden to tell. "This is some poor man who, deprived of his intellect, senses, vitality, and qualities, lies as if he is asleep or unconscious, like mere wood or straw. He is abandoned by both friends and enemies after they have carefully swathed and guarded him."

Hearing these words of the charioteer, he was startled. He said to him, "Is this an accident particular to him alone, or is this the end of all living creatures?" Then the charioteer replied to him, "This is the final end of all living creatures. No matter if one is a poor man, a man of middle state, or a noble, destruction will come to all in this world."

[60] Then the king's son, calm though he was, immediately sank down overwhelmed. . . . He spoke with a loud voice, "This is the end appointed to all creatures, and yet the world throws off all fear and is infatuated [with life]! The hearts of men must be hard, to be self-composed in such a situation. . . ."

[5.7] Then he wanted to become perfectly alone in his thoughts, and stopped those friends who were following him. He went to the root of a rose-apple in a solitary spot, with its beautiful leaves all quivering [in the wind]. There he sat on the ground covered with leaves, and with its young grass bright like lapis lazuli. Meditating on the origin and destruction of the world, he laid hold of the path that leads to firmness of mind. [10] Having attained firmness of mind, and being immediately set free from all sorrows such as the desire of worldly objects, he attained the first stage of contemplation.

He considered thoroughly these faults of sickness, old age, and death that belong to all living beings. Then all the joy that he had felt in the activity of his vigor, in his youth, and in his life vanished in a moment. [15] He did not rejoice; he did not feel remorse. He suffered no hesitation, indolence, nor sleep. He felt no attraction to the qualities of desire. He neither hated nor scorned another person. This pure, passionless meditation grew within the great-souled Gotama. Then, unobserved by the other men with him, a man in a beggar's clothing crept up.

The king's son asked him, "Tell me, who are you?" He replied, "O bull of men, I who am terrified at birth and death have become an ascetic for the sake of liberation. Desiring liberation in a world subject to destruction, I seek that happy indestructible abode. I am isolated from mankind. My thoughts are unlike those of others, and my sinful passions are turned away from all objects of sense. Dwelling anywhere, at the root of a tree, or in an uninhabited house, a mountain, or a forest, I wander without a family and without home. I am a beggar ready for any food, and I seek only the highest good."

[20] When he had spoken, while the prince was looking on, he suddenly flew up to the sky. This ascetic was a heavenly inhabitant who, knowing that the prince's thoughts were other than what his outward form promised, had come to him to rouse his recollection. When the other man had gone like a bird to heaven, the foremost of men rejoiced and was astonished. Having comprehended the meaning of the term *dhamma,* he set his mind on how to accomplish his deliverance. . . .

[12.88] Then the saint whose every effort was pure [Gotama] fixed his dwelling on the pure bank of the Nairangana. He wanted a lonely habitation. Five beggars who desired liberation came up to him when they saw him

there. . . . [90] He was honored by these disciples who were dwelling in that family. . . . Thinking, "This may be the means of abolishing birth and death," he at once began a series of difficult austerities by fasting. For six years, vainly trying to attain merit, he practiced self-mortification. He performed many rules of abstinence that are hard for a man to carry out. At the hours of eating, longing to cross to the world whose distant shore is so difficult to reach, he broke his vow with single jujube fruits, sesame seeds, and rice. But the emaciation that was produced in his body by that asceticism became positive fatness because of his splendor. [95] With his glory and his beauty unimpaired although he was thin, he caused gladness to other eyes, as the autumnal moon in the beginning of her bright fortnight gladdens the lotuses. He had only skin and bone remaining. His fat, flesh, and blood had faded completely. Yet, though diminished, he still shone with undiminished grandeur like the ocean.

Then the seer, having his body emaciated to no purpose in a cruel self-mortification, and dreading continued existence, reflected in his longing to become a Buddha. "This is not the way to passionlessness, nor to perfect knowledge, nor to liberation. That was certainly the true way that I found at the root of the Gambu tree. But that cannot be attained by one who has lost his strength."

So resuming his care for his body, he next pondered how best to increase his bodily vigor. [100] He said, "Wearied with hunger, thirst, and fatigue, with one's mind no longer self-possessed through fatigue, how can one who is not absolutely calm reach the purpose that is to be attained by the mind? True calm is properly obtained by the constant satisfaction of the senses. The mind's self-possession is only obtained when the senses are perfectly satisfied. True meditation is produced in one whose mind is self-possessed and at rest. In one whose thoughts are engaged in meditation, the exercise of perfect contemplation begins at once.

By contemplation are obtained those conditions through which supreme calm is eventually gained. This is the undecaying, immortal state, which is so hard to reach." Having thus resolved, "This is based on eating food," the wise seer of unbounded wisdom decided to accept the continuance of his life. . . .

[14.1] When he attained the highest mastery in all kinds of meditation, he remembered in the first watch the continuous series of all his former births. "In such a place I was so and so by name, and from there I passed and came here." Thus he remembered his thousands of births, experiencing each as it were over again. Having remembered each birth and each death in all those various transmigrations, the compassionate one then felt compassion for all living beings. [5] This world of living beings rolls on helplessly like a wheel, having willfully rejected the good guides in this life and done all kinds of actions in various [previous] lives. As he remembered, in his strong self-control this conviction came to him, "All existence is unsubstantial, like the fruit of a banana plant."

When the second watch came, he was possessed of unequaled energy. He who was the highest of all seeing beings received a preeminent divine sight. By that divine, perfectly pure sight he saw the whole world as in a spotless mirror. He saw the various transmigrations and rebirths of the various beings with their several lower or higher merits from their actions, and compassion grew up more within him. . . .

[35] Having pondered all this, in the last watch he reflected, "Alas for this whole world of living beings who are doomed to misery, all wandering astray! They do not know that all this universe, destitute of any real refuge, is born and decays through that existence which is the site of the skandhas[7] and pain. It dies and passes into a new state and then is born anew. . . ."

[64] The all-knowing Bodhisattva, the illuminated one, pondered and meditated again and came to his conclusion. [65] "This is pain; this also is the origin of pain in the world of living beings; this also is the stopping of pain; this is that course which leads to its stopping."[8] Having determined this, he knew everything as it really was. He, the holy one, sitting there on his seat of grass at the root of the tree, pondered by his own efforts and attained perfect knowledge. Then he bursted the shell of ignorance, and gained all the various kinds of perfect intuition. He attained all the partial knowledge of alternatives that is included in perfect knowledge. He became the perfectly wise, the Bhagavat, the Arhat, the king of the Law, the **Tathagata** [tah-THAH-gah-tuh],[9] the one who has attained the knowledge of all forms, the Lord of all knowledge. . . .

[79] The gods rejoiced, and paid him worship and adoration with divine flowers. All the world, when the great saint had become all-wise, was full of brightness. Then the holy one descended and stood on his throne under the tree.[10] There he passed seven days filled with the thought "I have here attained perfect wisdom." [80] When the Bodhisattva had attained perfect knowledge, all beings became full of great happiness. All the different universes were illumined by a great light. The happy earth shook in six different ways like an overjoyed woman. The Bodhisattvas, each dwelling in his own special abode, assembled and praised him.

---

[7] *skandhas:* the components that constitute the human person, physical and mental.

[8] *This is pain . . . its stopping:* The Buddhist reader would easily recognize here the Four Noble Truths.

[9] *Bhagavat:* the "Blessed One"; *Arhat:* the "Worthy One"; *Tathagata:* "One who has come [or "gone"] thus," a title of Buddha indicating his achievement of Nirvana.

[10] *the tree:* the bo tree, so called because Gotama achieved enlightenment (*Bodhi*) there.

The Death of Gotama Buddha*

In this excerpt from The Death of the Buddha Sutra, *Buddha makes provision for life in the monastic community after his death. The unity and knowledge of the community is stressed—the Buddha leaves it in an ideal state.*[11]

The Blessed One addressed the venerable Ananda and said, "It may be, Ananda, that some of you may think, 'The word of the Master is ended, we have a teacher no more!' Do not think this way. The truths and the rules of the order that I have set forth and laid down for you all, let them be your Teacher when I am gone.

"Ananda! When I am gone, do not address one another in the way in which the brothers have until now addressed each other, with the title of 'Friend.' A younger brother may be addressed by an elder with his name, or his family name, or the title 'Friend.' But an elder should be addressed by a younger brother as 'Lord' or as 'Venerable Sir.' And when I am gone, Ananda, let the order, if it should so wish, abolish all the lesser and minor precepts. . . ."[12]

[10] Then the Blessed One addressed the brothers and said, "Behold now, brothers, I exhort you, saying, 'Decay is inherent in all component things! Work out your salvation with diligence!' " This was the last word of the Tathagata. . . .

Then the Blessed One, passing out of the state in which both sensations and ideas have ceased to be, entered the state between consciousness and unconsciousness. Passing out of the state between consciousness and unconsciousness, he entered the state of mind to which nothing at all is especially present. Passing out of the consciousness of no special object, he entered the state of mind to which the infinity of thought is the only thing present. Passing out of the mere consciousness of the infinity of thought, he entered the state of mind to which the infinity of space is alone present. Passing out of the mere consciousness of the infinity of space, he entered the fourth stage of deep meditation.

Passing out of the fourth stage, he entered the third. Passing out of the third stage, he entered the second. Passing out of the second, he entered the first. Passing out of the first stage of deep meditation, he entered the second. Passing out of the second stage, he entered the third. Passing out of the third stage, he entered the fourth stage of deep meditation. Then he passed out of the last stage of deep meditation, and immediately he died.

When the Blessed One died, at the moment of his passing out of existence, a mighty earthquake arose, terrible and awe-inspiring. The thunders of heaven burst forth. . . .

[33] Then the Mallas of Kusinara said to the venerable Ananda, "What should be done, Lord, with the remains of the Tathagata?"

"As men treat the remains of a king of kings, so should they treat the remains of a Tathagata."

"And how, Lord, do they treat the remains of a king of kings?"

"They wrap the body of a king of kings in a new cloth. When that is done, they wrap it in cotton wool. When that is done, they wrap it in a new cloth, and so on till they have wrapped the body in five hundred successive layers of both kinds. Then they place the body in a vessel of iron, and cover that up with another vessel of iron. They then build a funeral pyre of all kinds of perfumes, and burn the body of the king of kings. Then at the four crossroads they build a burial mound to the king of kings. This is the way in which they treat the remains of a king of kings. As they treat the remains of a king of kings, so should they treat the remains of the Tathagata. At the four crossroads a burial mound should be built to

---

Mahaparinibbana Sutta 6.1–12, 33–35, 45–48.

[11] Taken, with editing, from T. W. Rhys Davids, trans., *Buddhist Suttas, Sacred Books of the East,* vol. 11 (Oxford: Oxford University Press, 1881), pp. 112–130.

[12] This was not done because the monastic order could not distinguish between major and minor rules.

the Tathagata. Whoever shall place garlands or perfumes or paint there, or make salutation there, or become in its presence calm in heart, shall have a profit and a joy for a long time."

Then the Mallas gave orders to their attendants, saying, "Gather all the carded cotton wool of the Mallas!" [35] Then the Mallas of Kusinara wrapped the body of the Blessed One in a new cloth. And when that was done, they wrapped it in cotton wool. And when that was done, they wrapped it in a new cloth, and so on till they had wrapped the body of the Blessed One in five hundred layers of both kinds. Then they placed the body in a vessel of iron, and covered that up with another vessel of iron. Then they built a funeral pyre of all kinds of perfumes, and they placed the body of the Blessed One on it. . . .

[45] Then the venerable Maha Kassapa went . . . to the funeral pyre of the Blessed One. When he had come up to it, he arranged his robe on one shoulder. Bowing down with clasped hands, he walked three times reverently around the pyre. Then, uncovering his feet, he bowed down in reverence at the feet of the Blessed One. Those five hundred brethren arranged their robes on one shoulder. Bowing down with clasped hands, they walked reverently around the pyre three times, and then bowed down in reverence at the feet of the Blessed One. When the homage of the venerable Maha Kassapa and of those five hundred brothers was ended, the funeral pyre of the Blessed One caught fire by itself. Now as the body of the Blessed One burned itself away, neither soot nor ash was seen from the skin and from the flesh and the nerves and the fluid of the joints. Only the bones remained behind. . . . Of his five hundred pieces of clothing only the innermost and outermost were consumed.

TEACHING

The Sermon on the Four Noble Truths*

This excerpt from the Turning the Wheel of the Law Sutra *is commonly known as the "Benares Sermon." It is an excellent short statement of the essentials of Buddhist teaching: the Four Noble Truths and the Eightfold Path.*[13]

Reverence to the Blessed One, the Holy One, the Fully Enlightened One!

Thus have I heard. The Blessed One was once staying at Benares, at the hermitage called Migadaya. The Blessed One addressed the company of the five monks, and said, "There are two extremes, O monks, which the man who has given up the world ought not to follow. The first is the habitual practice of those things whose attraction depends upon the passions. This is especially true of sensuality. It is a low and pagan way, unworthy, unprofitable, and fit only for the worldly-minded. Second is the habitual

practice of asceticism, which is painful, unworthy, and unprofitable.

"There is a middle path, O monks, avoiding these two extremes, discovered by the Tathagata. This path opens the eyes, bestows understanding, leads to peace of mind, to the higher wisdom, to full enlightenment, and to Nirvana! What is that middle path, O monks, avoiding these two extremes? Truly, it is this Noble Eightfold Path, that is to say: Right views; Right aspirations; Right speech; Right conduct; Right livelihood; Right effort; Right mindfulness; and Right contemplation. . . .

[5] "Now this, O monks, is the noble truth concerning suffering. Birth brings pain, decay is

---

Dhammacakkapparattana Sutta 1–8, 21–30.
[13] Taken, with editing, from Davids, *Buddhist Suttas,* pp. 146–155.

painful, disease is painful, and death is painful. Union with something unpleasant is painful, and separation from something pleasant is painful. Any craving that is unsatisfied is painful. In brief, the five aggregates that spring from attachment, the conditions of individuality and their cause, are painful. This, O monks, is the noble truth concerning suffering.

"Now this, O monks, is the noble truth concerning the origin of suffering. Truly, it is thirst or craving. It causes the renewal of existence, and is accompanied by sensual delight, seeking satisfaction now here, now there. It is the craving for the gratification of the passions, or the craving for a future life, or the craving for success in this present life. This, O monks, is the noble truth concerning the origin of suffering.

"Now this, O monks, is the noble truth concerning the destruction of suffering. Truly, it is the destruction of this very thirst. It is the laying aside of, the getting rid of, the being free from, the harboring no longer of this thirst. This, O monks, is the noble truth concerning the destruction of suffering.

"Now this, O monks, is the noble truth concerning the way which leads to the destruction of sorrow. Truly, it is this Noble Eightfold Path. . . .

[21] "As long, O monks, as my knowledge and insight were not quite clear regarding each of these Four Noble Truths in this triple order, in this twelvefold manner, I was uncertain whether I had attained to the full insight of that wisdom that is unsurpassed in the heavens or on earth, among the whole race of Samanas and Brahmins, or of

gods or men. But as soon as my knowledge and insight were quite clear regarding each of these four noble truths, in this triple order, in this twelvefold manner, then I became certain that I had attained to the full insight of that wisdom that is unsurpassed in the heavens or on earth, among the whole race of Samanas and Brahmins, or of gods or men. Now this knowledge and this insight has arisen within me. The emancipation of my heart is immovable. This is my last existence. Now there will be no rebirth for me!"

Thus spoke the Blessed One. The five monks praised the words of the Blessed One and were glad. When the discourse had been uttered, there arose within the venerable Kondanna the eye of truth, spotless, and without a stain. He saw that whatever has an origin also inherently must end.

[25] And when the royal chariot wheel of the truth had been set rolling by the Blessed One, the gods of the earth . . . the attendant gods of the four great kings . . . and the gods in the highest heaven gave forth a shout. They said, "In Benares, at the hermitage of the Migadaya, the supreme wheel of the empire of Truth has been set rolling by the Blessed One. That wheel can never be turned back by any Samana or Brahmin, nor by any god, nor by any Brahma or Mara, not by anyone in the universe!" In an instant, a second, a moment, this sound went up to the world of Brahma. This great ten-thousand-world-system quaked and trembled and was shaken violently. An immeasurably bright light appeared in the universe, beyond even the power of the gods!

The Noble Eightfold Path*

The "Benares Sermon" also contains a full explanation of the Noble Eightfold Path, a practical system that follows up on the more abstract Four Noble Truths. The Noble Eightfold Path offers practical guidelines to mental and moral development with the goal of freeing individuals from attachments and delusions; it leads to understanding the truth about all things. By following the eight guidelines, the monk follows the path of the Buddha to release.

---

*Dhammacakkapparattana Sutta 9–20.

The eight guidelines are often reduced to three categories: morality, wisdom, and meditation.[14]

The Blessed One then addressed the monks, saying, "Monks."

"Yes, lord," the monks responded.

The Blessed One said, "I will teach and interpret for you the Noble Eightfold Path. Listen and pay attention as I speak."

"We will do as you say, lord," the monks replied.

The Blessed One said, "What, monks, is the Noble Eightfold Path? Right view, right resolve, right speech, right action, right livelihood, right effort, right mindfulness, and right concentration.[15]

"What is right view? It is knowledge with regard to suffering, knowledge with regard to the origination of suffering, knowledge with regard to the stopping of suffering, knowledge with regard to the way of practice leading to the stopping of suffering.[16] This, monks, is called right view.

"What is right resolve? It is being resolved to practice renunciation, to be free from ill will, to be harmless. This, monks, is called right resolve.

"What is right speech? It is refraining from lying, refraining from divisive speech, refraining from abusive speech, and refraining from idle talk. This, monks, is called right speech.

"What is right action? It is not taking life, not stealing, and being chaste. This, monks, is called right action.

"What is right livelihood? This is when a disciple of the noble ones, having abandoned a dishonest livelihood, sustains his life with right livelihood. This, monks, is called right livelihood.

"What is right effort? This is when a monk desires, endeavors, persists, upholds, and exerts his intent so that evil, unhelpful qualities do not arise [in him]. He generates desire, endeavors, activates persistence, and upholds and exerts his intent to abandon evil, unhelpful qualities that have arisen. He generates desire, endeavors, activates persistence, and upholds and exerts his intent to bring about helpful qualities that have

not yet arisen. He generates desire, endeavors, activates persistence, and upholds and exerts his intent for the maintenance, increase, fullness, development, and culmination of helpful qualities that have arisen. This, monks, is called right effort.

"What is right mindfulness? This is when a monk remains focused on the body in and of itself—he is fervent, aware, and mindful—putting away the greed and distress of the world. He remains focused on feelings in and of themselves—he is fervent, aware, and mindful—putting away the greed and distress of the world. He remains focused on the mind in and of itself—he is fervent, aware, and mindful—putting away the greed and distress of the world. He remains focused on mental qualities in and of themselves—he is fervent, aware, and mindful—putting away the greed and distress of the world. This, monks, is called right mindfulness.

"What is right concentration? This is when a monk—quite withdrawn from sensuality, withdrawn from unskillful (mental) qualities—enters and remains in the first stage of concentration: rapture and pleasure born from withdrawal, accompanied by directed thought and evaluation. With the stilling of his directed thought and evaluation, he enters and remains in the second stage of concentration: rapture and pleasure born of concentration, unification of awareness free from directed thought and evaluation. This brings internal assurance. With the fading of rapture, he remains calm, mindful and alert, and physically sensitive of pleasure. He enters and remains in the third stage of concentration, of which the noble ones declare, 'Calm and mindful, he has a pleasurable abiding.' With the abandoning of pleasure

---

[14] Taken, with editing, from Davids, *Buddhist Suttas,* pp. 149–152.
[15] *concentration:* can also be translated throughout this section as "meditation."
[16] *It is knowledge . . . stopping of suffering:* This sentence is a restatement of the Four Noble Truths.

and pain, as with the earlier disappearance of rapture and distress, he enters and remains in the fourth stage of concentration: purity of calmness and mindfulness, having neither pleasure nor pain. This, monks, is called right concentration."

This is what the Blessed One said. The monks were delighted at his words.

The Skandhas and the Chain of Causation*

The skandhas *are the elements that together make up the human personality. They relate to the no-soul doctrine of Theravada Buddhism. This passage outlines these skandhas and then traces the chain of causation that leads to suffering.*[17]

The omniscient lion of the Sakyas [i.e., Buddha] then caused all the assembly, headed by those who belonged to the company of Maitriya, to turn the wheel of the Law.[18] . . . [28] "The body is composed of the five skandhas, and produced from the five elements. It is empty and without soul, and arises from the action of the chain of causation. This chain of causation is the cause of coming into existence, and the cessation of this chain is the cause of the state of cessation.

[30] "He who knows this wants to promote the good of the world. Let him hold fast the chain of causation, with his mind fixed on wisdom. Let him embrace the vow of self-denial for the sake of wisdom, and practice the four perfections, and go through existence always doing good to all beings. Then having become an Arhat and conquered all the wicked, even the hosts of Mara, and attained the threefold wisdom, he shall enter Nirvana. Whoever has his mind indifferent and is empty of all desire for any further form of existence, let him abolish one by one the several steps of the chain of causation. When these effects of the chain of causation are ended one by one, he at last, being free from all stain and substratum, will pass into a blissful Nirvana.

[35] "Listen, all of you, for your own happiness, with your minds free from stain. I will declare to you step by step this chain of causation. The idea of ignorance is what gives the root to the huge poison-tree of mundane exis-

tence with its trunk of pain. This causes the impressions, which produce [the acts of] the body, voice, and mind. Consciousness arises from these impressions, which produces the five senses and the mind. The organism that is sometimes called samgna or samdarsana springs from this; and from this arises the six organs of the senses, including the mind.

"The association of the six organs with their objects is called 'contact.' The consciousness of these different contacts is called 'sensation.' [40] Craving is produced by this, which is the desire of being troubled by worldly objects. 'Attachment to continued existence,' arising from this, sets itself in action toward pleasure and the rest. From attachment springs continued existence, which is sensual, possessing form, or formless. From existence arises birth through a returning to various wombs. On birth is dependent the series of old age, death, sorrow, and the like. By putting a stop to ignorance and what follows from it, all these cease successively. This is the chain of causation, which has many turns, whose sphere of action is created by ignorance. This is to be meditated upon by you who enjoy dwelling tranquilly in lonely woods. He who knows it thoroughly reaches at last to absolute thinness. Then he becomes blissfully extinct.

Buddhacarita 16.1, 28–50.
[17] Taken, with editing, from Cowell, *Buddhist Mahayana Texts,* pp. 174–180.
[18] *turn the wheel of the Law:* give and spread the true teaching.

"When you have learned this, to be freed from the bond of existence you must cut down ignorance with all your efforts, for it is the root of pain. [45] Then, set free from the bonds of the prison-house of existence, you will possess as Arhats natures perfectly pure. You shall attain Nirvana."

Having heard this lesson preached by the chief of saints, all the mendicants understood the course and the cessation of embodied existence. As these five ascetics listened to his words, their intellectual eye was purified for the attainment of perfect wisdom. The eye of dharma was purified in six hundred millions of gods, and the eye of wisdom in eight hundred millions of Brahmans. The eye of dharma was purified in eighty thousand men, and even in all beings an ardor for the Law was made visible. [50] Everywhere all kinds of evil became tranquillized, and everywhere an ardor for all that helps the good Law manifested itself.

The Essence of Buddhism*

This scripture—its full title is Heart of Transcendent Wisdom—*is one of the best known in Buddhism. It personifies wisdom as a woman, especially at its beginning and end. In a religion often given to verbose writings, this sutra is remarkable for its brevity.*[19]

Honor to the Omniscient. [or, Honor to the Lady, Noble Transcendent Wisdom.]

The noble bodhisattva Avalokitesvara was brooding in the flowing depths of the course of Transcendent Wisdom. Looking about, he sees the five skandhas to be empty of essence.

Here, Sariputra, form is emptiness, emptiness is form. Form is not other than emptiness, and emptiness is not other than form. That which is form equals emptiness, and that which is emptiness is also form. Precisely the same may be said of form and the other skandhas: feeling, perception, impulse, and consciousness.

Here, Sariputra, all dharmas bear the marks of emptiness, which are: not to have arisen nor to have been suppressed, neither to be corrupt nor pure, and to be neither unfinished nor complete.

Therefore, Sariputra, emptiness is not form, nor feeling, perception, impulse, nor consciousness. It is not the eye, ear, nose, tongue, body, or mind. It is not shape, sound, odor, flavor, nor object of touch or thought. It is not the experience of vision (and so on until we reach) it is not elements of mental discrimination. It is not learning or ignorance, and it is not the elimination of learning or ignorance (and so on until we reach) it is not senility and death, and it is not the elimination of senility and death. It is not suffering, beginning, ceasing, or a path. It is not knowledge, not attainment or realization, and therefore neither is it nonattainment.

[5] The bodhisattva, bound to Transcendent Wisdom, lives with nothing clouding his mind. Lacking confusion, he is intrepid, and having passed beyond error, reaches nirvana.

All Buddhas, of the past, present, or future, bound to irrefutable Transcendent Wisdom, reach completely full understanding and the highest awakening.

Therefore Transcendent Wisdom should be known as the great mantra, the great knowledge mantra, the invincible mantra, the unsurpassable

---

*The Heart Sutra.
[19] From Douglas A. Fox, trans., *The Heart of Buddhist Wisdom* (Lewiston, NY: Mellen, 1986). Copyright © 1985 Douglas A. Fox. Used by permission.

mantra, causing all suffering to cease. It is trustworthy because it is not false. It is the mantra proclaimed in the *Prajnaparamita*, and it is this: Oh, you [Lady] who are gone, gone, gone beyond, gone utterly beyond: Hail Wisdom!

With these words the *Heart of Transcendent Wisdom* is complete.

A Description of Nirvana*

The Milindapanha, *or "Questions of King Milinda," is a famous text illustrating the kind of doctrinal conversations that took place as Buddhism spread through Asia. The* Milindapanha *is the most important book of Theravada Buddhist doctrine outside the Pali* Tipitaka *and is still widely studied. A translation of it is found in the Chinese canon. King Milinda (Menander) was a king of Greek descent who ruled in the far north-west of India in the second century* B.C.E. *This passage explains basic Buddhist teaching on* Nirvana.[20]

King Milinda said: "I will grant you, Nagasena, that nothing is like nirvana. It is pure bliss. One cannot point to its form or shape, its duration or size, either by simile or explanation, by reason or by argument. But is there perhaps some quality of nirvana which it shares with other things that lends itself to a metaphorical explanation?"

"Its form, O king, cannot be elucidated by similes, but its qualities can."

"How good to hear that, Nagasena! Speak then, quickly, so that I may have an explanation of even one of the aspects of nirvana! Appease the fever of my heart! Allay it with the cool sweet breezes of your words!"

"Nirvana shares one quality with the lotus, two with water, three with medicine, ten with space, three with the wishing jewel, and five with a mountain peak. As the lotus is unstained by water, so is nirvana unstained by all the defilements. As cool water allays feverish heat, so also nirvana is cool and allays the fever of all the passions. Moreover, as water removes the thirst of men and beast who are exhausted, parched, thirsty, and overpowered by heat, so also nirvana removes the craving for sensuous enjoyments, the craving for further becoming, the craving for the cessation of becoming. As medicine protects from the torments of poison, so nirvana from the torments of the poisonous passions. Moreover, as medicine puts an end to sickness so nirvana to all sufferings. Finally, nirvana and medicine both give security. And these are the ten qualities which nirvana shares with space. Neither is born, grows old, or passes away, or is reborn; both are unconquerable, cannot be stolen, are unsupported, are roads respectively for birds and arhants to all one can desire, bring joy, and shed light. As a mountain peak is lofty and exalted, so is nirvana. As a mountain peak is unshakeable, so is nirvana. As a mountain peak is inaccessible, so is nirvana inaccessible to all the passions. As no seeds can grow on a mountain peak, so the seeds of all the passions cannot grow in nirvana. And finally, as a mountain peak is free from all desire to please or displease, so is nirvana."

"Well said, Nagasena! So it is, and as such I accept it."

---

*Milindapanha 4.8.65–66.
[20] Taken, with editing, from T. W. Rhys Davids, *The Questions of King Milinda* (Oxford: Oxford University Press, 1894), pp. 188–189.

A Mahayana View of the Buddha*

In Mahayana, the Buddha is a gracious savior who enables both monks and laity to reach Nirvana. This first selection from the Lotus Sutra *of the True Law argues that the Mahayana ("Large Vehicle") is in fact the only vehicle in Buddhism. In the second, the* Lotus Sutra *itself is the gift of the Buddha that enables those who read and venerate it to come to Nirvana. This veneration is today especially prominent in Nichiren Buddhism.*[21]

Only now and then, Sariputra, does the Tathagata preach such a discourse on the law as this. Just as only now and then is seen the blossom of the fig tree, Sariputra, so does the Tathagata only now and then preach such a discourse on the law. Believe me, Sariputra. I speak what is real, I speak what is truthful, I speak what is right. It is difficult to understand the exposition of the mystery of the Tathagata, Sariputra. For in explaining the law, Sariputra, I use hundreds of thousands of various skillful means, such as different interpretations, indications, explanations, illustrations. It is not by reasoning, Sariputra, that the law is to be found: It is beyond the pale of reasoning, and must be learned from the Tathagata. For, Sariputra, it is for a sole object, a sole aim, truly a lofty object, a lofty aim that the Buddha, the Tathagata, appears in the world. And what is that sole object, that sole aim, that lofty object, that lofty aim of the Buddha, the Tathagata, appearing in the world? To show all creatures the sight of Tathagata-knowledge, the Buddha, the Tathagata, appears in the world. To open the eyes of creatures for the sight of Tathagata-knowledge, the Buddha, the Tathagata, appears in the world. . . .

For, Sariputra, I show all creatures the sight of Tathagata-knowledge. I open the eyes of creatures for the sight of Tathagata-knowledge.

I firmly establish the teaching of Tathagata-knowledge, Sariputra. I lead the teaching of Tathagata-knowledge on the right path, Sariputra. By means of one sole vehicle, namely, the Buddha-vehicle, Sariputra, I teach creatures the law. There is no second vehicle, nor a third. This is the nature of the law, Sariputra, universally in the world, in all directions. For all the Tathagatas, who in times past existed in countless, innumerable spheres in all directions for the welfare of many, the happiness of many, out of pity to the world, for the benefit, welfare, and happiness of the great body of creatures, preached the law to gods and men with able means. These means include several directions and indications, various arguments, reasons, illustrations, fundamental ideas, interpretations. They pay regard to the dispositions of creatures whose inclinations and temperaments are so varied.

All those Buddhas and Lords have preached the law to creatures by means of only one vehicle, the Buddha-vehicle, which finally leads to omniscience. It is identical with showing all creatures the sight of Tathagata-knowledge; with opening the eyes of creatures for the sight of Tathagata-knowledge; with the awakening (or admonishing) by the display (or sight) of Tathagata-knowledge; with leading the teaching of Tathagata-knowledge on the right path. Such is the law they have preached to creatures. And those creatures who have heard the law from the past Tathagatas have all reached supreme, perfect enlightenment.

Saddharma-Pundarika Sutra 2.36; 10.1.
[21] Taken, with editing, from H. Kern, trans., *The Saddharma-Pundarika, Sacred Books of the East,* vol. 21 (Oxford: Oxford University Press, 1884), pp. 39–49, 213–214.

The Tathagatas who shall exist in the future, Sariputra, in countless, innumerable spheres in all directions for the weal of many, the happiness of many, out of pity to the world, for the benefit, weal, and happiness of the great body of creatures, shall preach the law to gods and men. . . . Such is the law they shall preach to creatures. Those creatures, Sariputra, who shall hear the law from the future Tathagatas shall all reach supreme, perfect enlightenment.

The Tathagatas who now are staying, living, existing, Sariputra, in countless, innumerable spheres in all directions preach the law to gods and men. . . . Such is the law they are preaching to creatures. Those creatures, Sariputra, who are hearing the law from the present Tathagatas shall all reach supreme, perfect enlightenment.

I myself also, Sariputra, am at the present period a Tathagata, for the weal of many. . . . I myself, also, Sariputra, am preaching the law to creatures. . . . Such is the law I preach to creatures. Those creatures, Sariputra, who now are hearing the law from me shall all reach supreme, perfect enlightenment. In this sense, Sariputra, it must be understood that nowhere in the world a second vehicle is taught, far less a third.

[10.1] The Lord then addressed the eighty thousand Bodhisattvas Mahasattvas by turning to Bhaishajyaraga as their representative. "Do you see, Bhaishajyaraga, in this assembly the many gods, Nagas, goblins, Gandharvas, demons, Garudas, Kinnaras, great serpents, men and beings not human, monks, nuns, male and female lay devotees, votaries of the vehicle of disciples, votaries of the vehicle of Pratyekabuddhas, and those of the vehicle of Bodhisattvas, who have heard this teaching from the mouth of the Tathagata?"

"I do, Lord; I do, Sugata."

The Lord proceeded: "All those Bodhisattvas Mahasattvas who in this assembly have heard well only a single stanza, a single verse [or word], or who even by a single rising thought have joyfully accepted this Sutra, to all of them, Bhaishajyaraga, among the four classes of my audience I predict their destiny to supreme and perfect enlightenment. Whoever after the complete extinction of the Tathagata shall hear this Dharmaparyaya and after hearing, if only a single stanza, joyfully accept it, even with a single rising thought, to those also, Bhaishajyaraga, be they young men or young women of good family,[22] I predict their destiny to supreme and perfect enlightenment. Those young men or women of good family, Bhaishajyaraga, shall be worshippers of many hundred thousand myriads of kotis of Buddhas. Those young men or women of good family, Bhaishajyaraga, shall make a vow under hundreds of thousands of myriads of Buddhas. They must be considered as reborn among the people of Gambudvipa, out of compassion to all creatures.

They shall be reborn who shall take, read, make known, recite, copy, and after copying always keep in memory and from time to time regard only a single stanza of this teaching. They shall be reborn who by that book shall feel veneration for the Tathagatas, treat them with the respect due to Masters, honor, revere, worship them. They shall be reborn who shall worship that book with flowers, incense, perfumed garlands, ointment, powder, clothes, umbrellas, flags, banners, music, etc., and with acts of reverence such as bowing and joining hands. In short, Bhaishajyaraga, any young men or young women of good family who shall keep or joyfully accept only a single stanza of this teaching, to all of them I predict their destiny of supreme and perfect enlightenment."

---

22 *Young men or women of good family*: layfolk can also reach Nirvana.

Poems of Early Nuns*

Buddhist scripture records many poems from the first generations of nuns. The first one given here is by Pajapati, Gotama's "nanny"; here she tells of her previous lives and liberation by the Buddha. In the second poem, Buddha and Pajapati's daughter Nanda converse prior to her entering the sangha. The final poem is by Vaddhesi, Pajapati's friend, and relates her enlightenment.[23]

A Poem by Prajapati

Homage to you Buddha, best of all creatures,
    who set me and many others free from pain.
All pain is understood, the cause, the craving is
    dried up, the Noble Eightfold Way unfolds;
I have reached the state where everything stops.
I have been mother, son, father, brother,
    grandmother; knowing nothing of the truth
    I journeyed on.
But I have seen the Blessed One; this is my last body,
    and I will not go from birth to birth again.
Look at the disciples all together, their energy,
    their sincere effort.
This is homage to the buddhas.
Maya gave birth to Gautama for the sake of us all.
She has driven back the pain of the sick and the dying.

A Poem by Nanda

[Buddha:] Nanda, look at the body, diseased,
    impure, rotten.
Focus the mind on all this foulness.
(Then the Buddha made an image of a lovely
    woman and it aged before Nanda's eyes. He
    went on:) Your body is like this, and this is like
    your body.

It stinks of decay, only a fool would love it.
[Nanda:] So day and night without letting up,
    I looked at it this way, and by my own
    wisdom, I perceived it fully, I saw.
Watching carefully, I plumbed to the very origin,
    and saw this body as it really is, inside and out.
Deep inside myself, I have lost interest in passion.
I am careful, quenched, calm, and free.

A Poem by Vaddhesi

It was twenty-five years since I left home, and
    I hadn't had a moment's peace.
Uneasy at heart, steeped in longing for pleasure,
    I held out my arms and cried out as I entered
    the monastery.
I went up to a nun I thought I could trust.
She taught me the Dharma, the elements of
    body and mind, the nature of perception,
    and earth, water, fire, and wind.
I heard her words and sat down beside her.
Now I have entered the six realms of sacred
    knowledge:
I know I have lived before, the eye of heaven is
    pure, and I know the minds of others.
I have great magic powers and have annihilated
    all the obsessions of the mind.
The Buddha's teaching has been done.

---

* *Therigatha.*
[23] From Susan Murcott, *The First Buddhist Women: Translations and Commentaries from the Therigatha* (Berkeley, CA: Parallax Press, 1991). Copyright © 1991 Parallax Press. Used by permission.

The Blessings of the Pure Land**

The "Pure Land" tradition of Buddhism teaches that a Buddha named Amitabha ("Unlimited Light") created and now rules over a "Buddha-land" called the Pure Land, a paradise so *wonderful that beings born into it will quickly proceed toward full awakening. This passage calls*

**Array of the Joyous Land Sutra.*

that place the Joyous Land. The Pure Land sect of Mahayana Buddhism has as its main belief salvation by faith in Amidabha; it is a popular form of Buddhism in China and Japan. Most Pure Land groups teach that good Buddhist character and constant repetition of the saying "Praise to Amida Buddha" are necessary to enter the Pure Land after death. Shinran and other groups teach that all that is necessary is one moment of pure belief and one pure recitation of the saying.[24]

Thus have I heard: Once the Buddha was dwelling in the Anathapindada Garden of Jetavana in the country of Shravasti. He was with a large company of monks, twelve hundred and fifty members. They were all great Arhats, well known among the people: Shariputra the elder, Mahamaudgalyayana, Mahakashyapa, Mahakatyayana, Mahakaushthila, Revata, Shuddhipanthaka, Nanda, Ananda . . .; in short, all the great disciples. He was also with many Bodhisattvas: Manjushri, the Prince of the Lord of Truth, Bodhisattva Ajita, Bodhisattva Gandhahastin, Bodhisattva Nityodyukta, and the rest, all great Bodhisattvas. He was also with a large company of innumerable deities such as Shakrodevanam-Indra and the rest.

Then the Buddha addressed Shariputra and said, "Beyond a hundred thousand Buddha-lands westward from here, there is a world named Joyous Land. In that world there is a Buddha, Amida by name, now dwelling and preaching the law. Shariputra, why is that country named the Joyous Land? The living beings in that country have no pains, but receive pleasures only. Therefore, it is called the Joyous Land.

"Again, Shariputra, in the Joyous Land there are seven rows of balustrades, seven rows of fine nets, and seven rows of arrayed trees; they are all of four gems and surround and enclose the land. For this reason the land is called the Joyous Land.

"Again, Shariputra, in the Joyous Land there are lakes of the seven gems, in which is filled water with the eight meritorious qualities. The lake-bases are strewn with golden sand, and the stairs of the four sides are made of gold, silver, beryl, and crystal. On land there are stories and

galleries adorned with gold, silver, beryl, crystal, white coral, red pearl and diamond. The lotus-flowers in the lakes, large as chariot wheels, are blue-colored with blue splendor, yellow-colored with yellow splendor, red-colored with red splendor, white-colored with white splendor, and they are all most exquisite and purely fragrant. Shariputra, the land Joyous Land is arrayed with these good qualities and adornments.

[5] "Again, Shariputra, in that Buddha-land there are heavenly musical instruments always played on. Gold is spread on the ground, and six times every day and night it showers blossoms of the Mandarava flower.[25] Usually at dawn all of those who live in that land fill their plates with those wonderful blossoms, and go to make offering to a hundred thousand Buddhas of other regions. At the time of the meal they come back to their own country, eat their meal, and take a walk. Shariputra, the Joyous Land is arrayed with these good qualities and adornments.

"And again, Shariputra, in that country there are always various wonderful birds of different colors: swan, peacock, parrot . . . and the bird with two heads. Six times every day and night all those birds sing in melodious tune, and that tune proclaims the Five Virtues, the Five Powers . . . the Noble Eightfold Path, and other laws of the kind. The living beings in that land, having heard that singing, all invoke the Buddha, invoke the Dharma, and invoke the Sangha.[26] Shariputra, you should not think that these birds are in fact born as punishment for sin. What is the reason? In that Buddha-land

---

[24] Taken, with editing, from Nishu Utsuki, *Kumarajiva* (Kyoto, Japan: Publication Bureau of Buddhist Books, 1924), pp. 2–5.

[25] *Mandarava flower:* According to Buddhist legend, the mandarava flower exists only in heaven, and blossoms only when portentous things are happening in the world. Thus, to have constant showers of these blossoms is extraordinary indeed.

[26] *Buddha . . . Dharma . . . Sangha:* the "Three Refuges" of Buddhism. Invoking them involves saying "I take refuge in the Buddha, the Dharma [teaching, religion], and the Sangha [monastic community]."

nothing evil exists. Shariputra, in that Buddha-land even the names of anything evil are not heard. How could there be the realms of evil themselves! All those birds are what Buddha Amida miraculously created with the desire to let them spread the voice of the Law. Shariputra, when in that Buddha-land a gentle breeze happens to blow, the precious trees in rows and the gemmed nets emit a delicate enrapturing tune, and it is just as if a hundred thousand musical instruments played at the same time. Everybody who hears that music naturally conceives the thought to invoke the Buddha, to invoke the Dharma, and to invoke the Sangha. Shariputra, that Buddha-land is arrayed with these good qualities and adornments.

"Shariputra, what do you think: Why is that Buddha is called Amida? Shariputra, the light of that Buddha is boundless; he shines without impediments all over the countries of the ten quarters. Therefore he is called Amida.

"Again, Shariputra, the life of that Buddha and of his people is endless and boundless in Asamkhya-kalpas, so he is named Amida. Shariputra, since Buddha Amida attained Buddhahood, ten kalpas[27] have now passed.

"Again, Shariputra, that Buddha has numerous disciples, who are all Arhats and whose number cannot be known by ordinary calculation. The number of Bodhisattvas cannot be known either. Shariputra, that Buddha-land is arrayed with such good qualities and adornments.

"Again, Shariputra, the beings born in the land Joyous Land are all in the stage of nonregression.[28] Among them is a multitude of beings bound to one birth only; and their number, being extremely large, cannot be known by ordinary calculation. Only can it be mentioned in boundless kalpas. Shariputra, the sentient beings who hear this account ought to pray that they may be born into that country; for they will be able to be in the same place together with those noble persons. Shariputra, by means of small good works or virtues no one can be born in that country.

"Shariputra, if there be a good man or a good woman, who, on hearing of Buddha Amida, keeps his name in mind with thoughts undisturbed for one day, two days, three days, four days, five days, six days, or seven days, that person, when about to die, will see Amida Buddha accompanied by his holy host appear before him; and immediately after his death, he with his mind undisturbed can be born into the Joyous Land of Buddha Amida. Shariputra, as I witness this benefit, I say these words; every being who listens to this preaching ought to offer up prayer with the desire to be born into that country.

[10] "Shariputra, as I now glorify the inconceivable excellences of Amida Buddha, there are also in the Eastern quarters Buddha Akshobhya, Buddha Merudhvaja, Buddha Mahameru, Buddha Meruprabhasa, Buddha Manjughosha, and Buddhas as many as the sands of the Ganges River, each of whom, in his own country stretching out his long broad tongue that covers three thousand greater worlds completely, proclaims these truthful words: 'All you sentient beings should believe in this sutra, which is approved and protected by all the Buddhas, and which glorifies the inconceivable excellences of Buddha Amida.'

"Shariputra, in the Southern worlds there are Buddha Candrasuryapradipa, Buddha Yacahprabha, Buddha Maharciskandha, Buddha Merupradipa, Buddha Anantavirya, and Buddhas as many as the sands of the Ganges River, each of whom, in his own country stretching out his long broad tongue that covers three thousand greater worlds completely, proclaims these truthful words: 'All you sentient beings should believe in this sutra, which is approved and protected by all the Buddhas, and which glorifies the inconceivable excellences of Buddha Amida.'

---

[27] *kalpas:* A kalpa is a period of 430 million years. It is the traditional period of time that one universe exists before it ends and another is re-created.

[28] *stage of nonregression:* Someone who reaches this stage never backslides and always advances toward the goal of becoming a Buddha.

"Shariputra, in the Western worlds there are Buddha Amidayus, Buddha Amida-lakshana, Buddha Amida-dhvaja, Buddha Mahaprabha, Buddha Mahanirbhasa, Buddha Ratnalakshana, Buddha Shuddharashmiprabha, and Buddhas as many as the sands of the Ganges River, each of whom, in his own country stretching out his long broad tongue that covers three thousand greater worlds completely, proclaims these truthful words: 'All you sentient beings should believe in this sutra, which is approved and protected by all the Buddhas, and which glorifies the inconceivable excellences of Buddha Amida.'

"Shariputra, in the Northern worlds there are Buddha Arciskandha, Buddha Vaishvanaranirghosha, Buddha Dushpradharsha, Buddha Adityasambhava, Buddha Jaliniprabha, and Buddhas as many as the sands of the Ganges River, each of whom, in his own country stretching out his long broad tongue that covers three thousand greater worlds completely, proclaims these truthful words: 'All you sentient beings should believe in this sutra, which is approved and protected by all the Buddhas, and which glorifies the inconceivable excellences of Buddha Amida.'

"Shariputra, in the lower worlds there are Buddha Simha, Buddha Yacas, Buddha Yashaprabhava, Buddha Dharma, Buddha Dharmadhvaja, Buddha Dharmadhara, and Buddhas as many as the sands of the Ganges River, each of whom, in his own country stretching out his long broad tongue that covers three thousand greater worlds completely, proclaims these truthful words: 'All you sentient beings should believe in this sutra, which is approved and protected by all the Buddhas, and which glorifies the inconceivable excellences of Buddha Amida.'

[15] "Shariputra, in the upper words there are Buddha Brahmaghosha, Buddha Nakshatraraja, Buddha Gandhottama, Buddha Gandhaprabhasa, Buddha Maharciskandha, Buddha Ratnakusumasampushpitagatra, Buddha Salendraraja, Buddha Ratnotpalashri, Buddha Sarvarthadarsha, Buddha Sumerukalpa, and Buddhas as many as the sands of the Ganges River, each of whom, in his own country stretching out

his long broad tongue that covers three thousand greater worlds completely, proclaims these truthful words: 'All you sentient beings should believe in this sutra, which is approved and protected by all the Buddhas, and which glorifies the inconceivable excellences of Buddha Amida.'

"Shariputra, what do you think: Why it is called the Sutra approved and protected by all the Buddhas? Shariputra, if there be a good man or a good woman who listens to those Buddhas' invocation of the name of Buddha Amida and the name of this Sutra, that good man or woman will be protected by all the Buddhas and never fail to attain supreme perfect enlightenment. For this reason, Shariputra, all of you should believe in my words and in what all the Buddhas proclaim. Shariputra, if there are men who have already made, are now making, or shall make prayer with the desire to be born in the land of Buddha Amida, they never fail to attain supreme perfect enlightenment; they have been born, are now being born, or shall be born in that country. Therefore, Shariputra, a good man or good woman who has the faith ought to offer up prayers to be born in that land.

"Shariputra, even as I am now praising the inconceivable excellences of those Buddhas, so all those Buddhas are magnifying the inconceivable excellences of myself, saying these words: Shakyamuni, the Buddha, has successfully achieved a rare thing of extreme difficulty; he has attained supreme perfect enlightenment in this world in the evil period of five corruptions: corruption of the kalpa, corruption of belief, corruption of passions, corruption of living beings, and corruption of life. For the sake of all the sentient beings he is preaching the Dharma which is not easy to accept. Shariputra, you must see that in the midst of this evil world of five corruptions I have achieved this difficult thing of attaining supreme perfect enlightenment, and for the benefit of all the beings I am preaching the Dharma which is difficult to be accepted. This is how it is esteemed as a thing of extreme difficulty."

After the Buddha preached this Sutra, Shariputra and the other monks, and the deities, men, and indeed everyone in all the worlds who listened to the Buddha's preaching, believed and accepted with joy. The worshipped the Buddha, and went away.

ETHICS

Conduct of the Monk*

The Dhammapada *(Verses on Teaching) is one of the fifteen books in the* Khuddaka-nikaya *of the* Sutta Pitaka. *A first-century* B.C.E. *collection of wise sayings, it summarizes Buddhist moral wisdom. Monks and nuns often memorize it at the beginning of their training, and it is studied as well by the laity.*[29]

Restraint in the eye is good, restraint in the ear is good, restraint in the nose is good, restraint in the tongue is good. In the body restraint is good, in speech restraint is good, in thought restraint is good. Restraint is good in all things. A monk restrained in all things is freed from all pain.

People call a monk one who controls his hand, who controls his feet, who controls his speech, who is well controlled, who delights inwardly, who is collected, who is solitary and content. The monk who controls his mouth, who speaks wisely and calmly, who teaches the meaning and the law, his word is sweet.

He who dwells in the law, delights in the law, meditates on the law, follows the law, that monk will never fall away from the true law.

[365] Let him not despise what he has received, nor ever envy others; a mendicant who envies others does not obtain peace of mind. Even the gods will praise a monk who, though he receives little, does not despise what he has received, if his life is pure and if he is not lazy.

He who never identifies himself with his name and form, and does not grieve over what he has left behind, he indeed is called a monk.

The monk who acts with kindness, who is calm in the doctrine of Buddha, will reach the quiet place [Nirvana], cessation of natural desires, and happiness. O monk, empty this boat! If emptied, it will go quickly. When you have cut off passion and hatred, you will go to Nirvana.

[370] Cut off the five senses, leave the five, rise above the five. A monk who has escaped from the five fetters is called Oghatinna, "saved from the flood."

Meditate, O monk, and do be not careless! Do not direct your thought to what gives pleasure. Then you may not have to swallow the iron ball (in hell) and cry out when burning, "This is pain." Without knowledge there is no meditation, without meditation there is no knowledge. He who has knowledge and meditation is near to Nirvana.

A monk who has entered his empty house, whose mind is tranquil, feels a super-human delight when he sees the law clearly. When he has considered the origin and destruction of the elements (skandhas) of the body, he finds happiness and joy that belong to those who know the immortal (Nirvana).

[375] This is the beginning here for a wise monk: watchfulness over the senses, contentedness, restraint under the law; keeping noble friends whose life is pure and who are not lazy. Let him live in charity, let him be perfect in his duties. Then in the fullness of delight he will put an end to his suffering.

---

*Dhammapada 25, 360–382.
[29] Taken, with editing, from F. Max Müller, *The Dhammapada, Sacred Books of the East,* vol. 10 (Oxford: Oxford University Press, 1881), pp. 85–88.

As the Vassika plant sheds its withered flowers, men should shed passion and hatred, O monks! The monk whose body and tongue and mind are quieted, who is collected, and has rejected the baits of the world, he is called quiet.

Rouse yourself by yourself, examine yourself by yourself, thus self-protected and attentive you will live happily, O monk!

[380] The self is the lord of self, self is the refuge of self. Therefore curb yourself as the merchant curbs a good horse.

The monk full of delight, who is calm in the doctrine of Buddha, will reach the quiet place (Nirvana), cessation of natural desires, and happiness.

Even a young monk who applies himself to the doctrine of Buddha will brighten up this world like the moon when free from clouds.

Admonition to Laity*

At the end of a discussion of monastic morality, the Buddha lays down instructions for householders (laity). Notice that the rules given are modeled on those given to monks.

I will also tell you about the householder's work. . . .

Let him not kill, nor cause to be killed any living being, nor let him approve of others killing. Let him refrain from hurting all creatures, both those that are strong and those that tremble.

[20] Then let [him] abstain from taking anything in any place that has not been given to him, knowing it to belong to another. Let him not cause anyone to take, nor approve of those that take. Let him avoid all theft.

Let the wise man avoid an unchaste life as a burning heap of coals. If he is not able to live a life of chastity, let him not transgress with another man's wife.

Let no one speak falsely to another in the hall of justice or in the hall of the assembly. Let him not cause anyone to speak falsely, nor approve of those that speak falsely. Let him avoid all sort of untruth.

Let the householder who approves of the Dhamma not give himself to intoxicating drinks. Let him not cause others to drink, nor approve of those who drink, knowing it to end in madness. For through intoxication stupid

people commit sins and make other people intoxicated. Let him avoid this seat of sin, this madness, this folly, which is delightful to the stupid.

[25] Let him not kill any living being, let him not take what has not been given [to him], let him not speak falsely, and let him not drink intoxicating drinks, let him refrain from unchaste sexual intercourse, and let him not eat untimely food at night. Let him not wear wreaths nor use perfumes, let him lie on a couch spread on the earth. They call this the eightfold abstinence (*uposatha*), proclaimed by Buddha, who has overcome pain.

Having with a believing mind kept abstinence (*uposatha*) on the fourteenth, fifteenth, and the eighth days of the half-month, and having kept the complete Patiharakapakkha[30] consisting of eight parts, then in the morning, after having kept abstinence, let a wise man with a believing mind make distributions according to his ability. Thus he will gladden the assembly of monks with food and drink.

Let him dutifully maintain his parents, and practice an honorable trade. The householder who observes this strenuously goes to the gods called Sayampabhas.

Cullavagga, Dammikasutta 18–29.
[30] *Patiharakapakkha*: further rules for continual abstinence and self-control.

The Wisdom of the Buddha*

This passage, often called "Twin Verses," is a general treatment of Buddhist morality. Each paragraph has two verses, usually opposites. A second section, from the chapter "On the Self," urges the virtue of self-reliance and self-dedication in the path to enlightenment.[31]

All that we are is the result of what we have thought: It is founded on our thoughts; it is made up of our thoughts. If a man speaks or acts with an evil thought, pain follows him, as the wheel follows the foot of the ox that draws the carriage. All that we are is the result of what we have thought. It is founded on our thoughts; it is made up of our thoughts. If a man speaks or acts with a pure thought, happiness follows him like a shadow that never leaves him.

"He abused me, he beat me, he defeated me, he robbed me"—in those who harbor such thoughts hatred will never cease. "He abused me, he beat me, he defeated me, he robbed me"—in those who do not harbor such thoughts hatred will cease.

[5] For hatred does not cease by hatred at any time. Hatred ceases by love; this is an old rule. The world does not know that we must all come to an end here. But for those who know it, their quarrels cease at once.

He who lives looking for pleasures only, his senses uncontrolled, immoderate in his food, idle, and weak, Mara [the tempter] will certainly overthrow him as the wind throws down a weak tree. He who lives without looking for pleasures, his senses well controlled, moderate in his food, faithful and strong, him Mara will certainly not overthrow, any more than the wind throws down a rocky mountain.

He who wishes to put on the yellow clothing[32] without having cleansed himself from sin, who disregards also temperance and truth, is unworthy of the yellow clothing. [10] But he who has cleansed himself from sin is well grounded in all virtues, and also keeps temperance and truth, he is worthy of the yellow clothing.

They who imagine truth in untruth, and see untruth in truth, never arrive at truth, but follow empty desires. They who know truth in truth, and untruth in untruth, arrive at truth, and follow true desires.

As rain breaks through a poorly thatched house, passion will break through an unreflecting mind. As rain does not break through a well-thatched house, passion will not break through a well-reflecting mind.

[15] The evildoer mourns in this world, and he mourns in the next; he mourns in both. He mourns and suffers when he sees the evil of his own work. The virtuous man delights in this world, and he delights in the next; he delights in both. He delights and rejoices when he sees the purity of his own work.

The evildoer suffers in this world, and he suffers in the next; he suffers in both. He suffers when he thinks of the evil he has done. He suffers more when going on the evil path. The virtuous man is happy in this world, and he is happy in the next; he is happy in both. He is happy when he thinks of the good he has done. He is still more happy when going on the good path.

The thoughtless man, even if he can recite a large portion [of the law], but is not a doer of it, has no share in the priesthood. He is like a cowherd counting the cows of others. [20] The follower of the law, even if he can recite only a small portion [of the law], but, having forsaken passion and hatred and foolishness, possesses true knowledge and serenity of mind, he, caring

---

*Dhammapada 1–20, 157–166.
[31] Taken, with editing, from Müller, *The Dhammapada,* pp. 1–8, 45–46.
[32] *the yellow clothing:* the saffron gown of the monk.

for nothing in this world or that to come, has a share in the order of monks.

[157, On the Self] If a man hold himself dear, let him watch himself carefully. During at least one out of the three watches [of the night] a wise man should be watchful.

Let each man direct himself first to what is proper, then let him teach others. Thus a wise man will not suffer.

If a man make himself as he teaches others to be, being himself well subdued, he may subdue [others]. One's own self is indeed difficult to subdue.

[160] The self is the lord of self; who else could be the lord? With self well subdued, a man finds a lord such as few can find. The evil done by oneself, self-begotten, self-bred, crushes the foolish, as a diamond breaks a precious stone.

He whose wickedness is very great brings himself down to that state where his enemy wishes him to be, as a creeping vine does with the tree that it surrounds. Bad deeds and deeds hurtful to ourselves are easy to do. What is beneficial and good is very difficult to do.

The foolish man who scorns the rule of the venerable [Arhat], of the elect [Ariya], of the virtuous, and follows false doctrine, bears fruit to his own destruction, like the fruits of the Katthaka reed.

[165] By oneself evil is done, by oneself one suffers. By oneself evil is left undone, by oneself one is purified. Purity and impurity belong to oneself; no one can purify another.

Let no one forget his own duty for the sake of another's, however great. Let a man, after he has discerned his own duty, always be attentive to his duty.

The Bodhisattva Ideal*

This simple and eloquent passage describes all the moral qualities of the bodhisattva. It comes from a text, the "Great Story" of the Buddha, which is a transition from Theravada to Mahayana.[33]

They are Bodhisattvas who live on from life to life in the possession of manifold good qualities. They are Bodhisattvas who have won the mastery over karma, and made their deeds renowned through their accumulation of merit. They are resolute and valiant, intent on endurance, trustworthy, upright and sincere. They are generous, firm, gentle, tender, patient, whole and tranquil of heart, difficult to overcome and defeat, intent on what is real, charitable, and faithful to their promises. They are intelligent, brilliantly intelligent, gifted with insight, and not given to gratification of sensual desires. They are devoted to the highest good. They win converts by the means of sympathetic appeal.

They are pure in conduct and clean of heart, full of exceeding great veneration, full of civility to elder and noble. They are resourceful, in all matters using conciliatory and agreeable methods, and in affairs of government they are adept in persuasive speech. They are men whose voice is not checked in the assembly, men who pour forth their eloquence in a mighty stream. With knowledge as their banner they are skilled in drawing the multitude to them. They are endowed with equanimity, and their means of living is beyond reproach. They are men of successful achievements, and are ready to come to the assistance of others and help those in distress. They do not become enervated by prosperity, and do not lose composure in adversity. They are skilled in uprooting the vices of mean men. They are

---

Mahavastu.

[33] Taken, with editing, from Davids and Oldenberg, *Vinaya Texts,* pp. 17–22.

unswerving in clothing the nakedness of others. They are anxious not to blight the maturing of their karma, and they acquire the roots of virtue by keeping themselves aloof from passion, hatred and folly. They are skilled in bringing solace to those in trouble and misfortune. They do not hesitate to render all kinds of service.

In all matters they are untiring in their purpose. They are endowed here in this world with the profound attributes of a Buddha. In their progress toward their goal they are undefiled in acts of body, speech and thought. Through the uprightness of their lives in former existences they are untarnished and pure in conduct. Possessing perfect knowledge they are men of undimmed understanding. They are eager to win the sphere of power of a Buddha—

so far are they from refusing it. With knowledge as their banner they are untiring in speech and skilled in teaching.

Being of irreproachable character, they are immune from disaster. They are free from sin. They shun the threefold distractions. Leaving vain babblers alone, they love their enemies. They do not indulge in sexual pleasures. They know how to win the affection of all creatures. When they enter the world they have become endowed with powers that are in accordance with the vow they have made. In all matters they are skilled in the knowledge of correct and faulty conclusions. They are rich in goodness and blessed with good qualities. Eminent, wise in their illimitable virtue, they are serene among their fellows.

ORGANIZATION

Founding of the Order*

After his enlightenment, the Buddha converts the five Hindu ascetics who had left him when he gave up their practice of extreme asceticism. This Vinaya Pitaka *selection offers a succinct view of general Buddhist teaching. Just as important, it offers a good view of the founding of the Buddhist order of monks and therefore of the Buddhist tradition itself.*[34]

The Blessed One, wandering from place to place, came to Benares, to the deer park Isipatana, to the place where the five monks were. The five monks saw the Blessed One coming from a distance. When they saw him, they agreed with each other, saying, "Friends, there comes Gotama. He lives in abundance, has given up his exertions, and has turned to an abundant life. Let us not salute him, nor rise from our seats when he approaches, nor take his bowl and his robe from his hands. But let us put there a seat; if he likes, let him sit down. . . ."

When they spoke to him, the Blessed One said to the five monks, "Monks, do not address the Tathagata by his name or with 'Friend.' The Tathagata is the holy, absolute Sambuddha.[35] Give ear, O monks! Immortality has been won by me. I will teach you; I will preach the doctrine to you. If you walk in the way I show you, you will, before long, have penetrated to the truth. You yourselves will know it and see it face to face. You will live with the highest goal of the holy life, for which noble youths give up the world completely and go forth into the houseless state."

Mahavagga 1.6.10, 11–16, 27–30, 32, 34, 37.
[34] Taken, with editing, from T. W. Rhys Davids and Hermann Oldenberg, trans., *Vinaya Texts,* part 1, *Sacred Books of the East,* vol. 13 (Oxford: Oxford University Press, 1881), pp. 91–102.
[35] *Sambuddha:* one who has reached the insight essential to the higher stages of arhatship.

When he had spoken, the five monks said to the Blessed One, "Friend Gotama, by those observances, by those practices, and by those austerities you have not been able to obtain power surpassing that of other men. You have not obtained the superiority of full and holy knowledge and insight. Now that you are living in abundance, have given up your exertions, and have turned to an abundant life, how will you be able to obtain power surpassing that of men? How will you obtain the superiority of full and holy knowledge and insight? . . ."

[15] The five monks spoke to the Blessed One a second time as before. And the Blessed One replied to the five monks a second time as before. And the five monks spoke to the Blessed One a third time as before. When they had spoken thus, the Blessed One said to the five monks, "Do you admit, O monks, that I have never spoken to you in this way before this day?"

"You have never spoken so, Lord."

"The Tathagata, O monks, is the holy, absolute Sambuddha. Give ear, O monks. . . ."

The Blessed One was able to convince the five monks. The five monks listened willingly to the Blessed One. They gave ear, and fixed their mind on the knowledge which Buddha imparted to them. . . . [There follows a statement of the Four Noble Truths and the Eightfold Path.]

[27] "O monks, as long as I did not possess with perfect purity this true knowledge and insight into these four Noble Truths . . . I knew that I had not yet obtained the highest, absolute Sambodhi in the world of men and gods, in Mara's and Brahma's world, among all beings, Samanas and Brahmanas, gods and men. But when I possessed with perfect purity this true knowledge and insight into these four Noble Truths . . . then I knew that I had obtained the highest, universal Sambodhi in the world of men and gods. . . . This knowledge and insight arose in my mind; this emancipation of my mind cannot be lost. This is my last birth; I shall not be born again!"

Thus the Blessed One spoke. The five monks were delighted, and they rejoiced at the words

of the Blessed One. When this exposition was given, the venerable Kondanna obtained the pure and spotless Eye of this truth: "Whatever is subject to the condition of origination, is subject also to the condition of cessation."

[30] And when the Blessed One had founded the Kingdom of Truth by propounding the Four Noble Truths, the earth-inhabiting gods shouted, "Truly the Blessed One has founded at Benares, in the deer park Isipatana, the highest kingdom of Truth, which may be opposed neither by a Samana nor by a Brahmana, neither by a deva, nor by Mara, nor by Brahma, nor by any being in the world." . . .

[32] The venerable Kondanna . . . overcame uncertainty, dispelled all doubts, and gained full knowledge. He was dependent on nobody else for knowledge of the doctrine of the teacher. He said to the Blessed One, "Lord, let me receive the pabbajja and upasampada ordinations from the Blessed One."

"Come, monk," said the Blessed One, "for the doctrine is well taught. Lead a holy life for the sake of the complete extinction of suffering." Then this venerable person received the ordination. . . .

[34] Then [the other monks] spoke to the Blessed One: "Lord, let us receive the pabbajja and upasampada ordinations from the Blessed One."

"Come, monks," said the Blessed One, "for the doctrine is well taught. Lead a holy life for the sake of the complete extinction of suffering." Thus these venerable persons received ordination. . . .

[47] Thus the Blessed One spoke. The five monks were delighted, and rejoiced at the words of the Blessed One. When this exposition had been given, the minds of the five monks became free from attachment to the world, and were released from the Asavas.[36] Then there were six arhants in the world.

---

[36] *Asavas:* mental defilement; the four Asavas are sensuality, lust for life, false views, and ignorance.

The Rules of Defeat for Monks and Nuns*

In this scripture from the Vinaya Pitaka, *the "rules of defeat" for monks are given and explained. "Defeat" means expulsion with no possibility of return. These rules govern the life of nuns as well as monks. Notice at the end of the passage the ritual for confession of these faults in the monastery, the basic method of which is similar for confession of all other faults. The four prohibitions here—against sexual intercourse, theft, killing, and lying—form the basis of Buddhist morality for the laity. The only qualification is that the prohibition of sexual intercourse is modified to a prohibition of intercourse outside marriage.*[37]

[Rules for Monks] The four Rules concerning those acts that cause Defeat now come into recitation.

If any monk who has taken upon himself the monks' system of self-training and rule of life and has not after that withdrawn from the training, or declared his weakness, shall have sexual intercourse with anyone, down even to an animal, he has fallen into defeat; he is no longer in communion.

If any monk shall take, from village or from forest, anything not given—what men call "theft"—he, too, has fallen into defeat; he is no longer in communion.

If any monk shall knowingly deprive a human being of life, or shall seek out an assassin against a human being, or shall utter the praises of death, or incite another to self-destruction, saying, "Ho, my friend! What good do you get from this sinful, wretched life? Death is better to you than life!"—he, too, is fallen into defeat; he is no longer in communion.

A monk, without being clearly conscious of possessing extraordinary qualities, may perhaps pretend that he has gained insight into the knowledge of the noble ones, saying, "Thus I know, thus I perceive." At some subsequent time, whether on being pressed or without being pressed, he may feel guilty and may want to be cleansed from his fault. He shall say, "Brothers, when I did not know, I said that I knew; when I did not see, I said that I saw—telling a fruitless falsehood." Then, unless he spoke through undue confidence, he has fallen into defeat; he is no longer in communion.

Venerable Sirs, the four Conditions of Defeat have been recited. When a monk has fallen into one or other, he is no longer allowed to reside with the monks. As before, so afterwards, he is defeated; he is not in communion.

Concerning them I ask the venerable ones, "Are you pure in this matter?" A second time I ask, "Are you pure in this matter?" A third time I ask, "Are you pure in this matter?" The venerable ones are pure. Therefore they keep silence. Thus I understand.

[Rules for Nuns] 1.   Should any nun willingly engage in the sexual act, even with a male animal, she is defeated and no longer in communion.

2.   Should any nun, in the manner of stealing, take what is not given from an inhabited area or from the wilderness . . . she is defeated and no longer in communion.

3.   Should any nun intentionally deprive a human being of life, or search for an assassin for her, or praise the advantages of death, or incite her to die: "My good man, what use is this wretched, miserable life to you? Death would be better for you than life," or with such an idea in mind, such a purpose in mind, should in various ways praise the advantages of death or incite her to die, she also is defeated and no longer in communion.

Patimokkha, Parajika Dhamma 1–4.
[37] Taken, with editing, from Davids and Oldenberg, *Vinaya Texts,* part 1, pp. 3–6.

4.   Should any nun, without direct knowledge, boast of a superior human state, a truly noble knowledge and vision as present in herself, saying, "Thus do I know; thus do I see," such that regardless of whether or not she is cross-examined on a later occasion, she—being remorseful and desirous of purification— might say, "Fellow nuns, not knowing, I said I know; not seeing, I said I see—vainly, falsely, idly," unless it was from over-estimation, she also is defeated and no longer in communion.

5.   Should any nun, lusting, consent to a lusting man's rubbing, rubbing up against, taking hold of, touching, or fondling (her) below the collar-bone and above the circle of the knees, she also is defeated and no longer in communion for being "above the circle of the knees."

6.   Should any nun, knowing that (another) nun has fallen into an act (entailing) defeat, neither accuse her herself nor inform the group, and then—whether she (the other nun) is still alive or has died, has been expelled or gone over to another sect—she (this nun) should say, "Even before, ladies, I knew of this nun that 'This sister is of such-and-such a sort,' and I didn't accuse her myself nor did I inform the group," then she also is defeated and no longer in communion for being "one who concealed a fault."

7.   Should any nun follow a monk suspended by a Community (of monks) acting in harmony, in line with the Dhamma, in line with the Vinaya, in line with the teacher's instructions, and he is disrespectful, has not made amends, has broken off his friendship (with the monks), the nuns should admonish her thus: "Lady, that monk has been suspended by a community acting harmony in line with the Dhamma, in line with the Vinaya, in line with the teacher's instructions. He is disrespectful, he has not made amends, he has broken off his friendship. Do not follow him, lady."

And should that nun, admonished thus by the nuns, persist as before, the nuns are to rebuke her up to three times so as to desist. If while being rebuked up to three times she desists, that is good. If she does not desist, then she also is defeated and no longer in communion for being "a follower of a suspended monk."

8.   Should any nun, lusting, consent to a lusting man's taking hold of her hand or touching the edge of her outer robe, or should she stand with him or talk with him or go to a rendezvous with him, or should she consent to his approaching her, or should she enter a hidden place with him, or should she give her body to him for the purpose of that unrighteous act, then she also is defeated and no longer in communion.

Rules Requiring Formal Meetings of Monks*

The next set of monastic rules covers thirteen matters for which a formal meeting of the order (samghadisesa) is required. The precise punishment, to be decided at a meeting of the whole monastic assembly, amounts to something less than permanent expulsion, often suspension for one month. All the rules are given here.[38]

The thirteen things which in their earlier and in their later stages require formal meetings of the Order now come into recitation.

1.   If a monk intentionally emits his semen, except while sleeping.

2.   If a monk, being degraded with perverted mind, comes into bodily contact with a woman by taking hold of her hand or her hair, or by touching any part of her body.

Patimokkha, Samghadisesa Dhamma 1–13.
[38] Taken, with editing, from Davids and Oldenberg, *Vinaya Texts*, part 1, pp. 7–14.

3. If a monk, being degraded with perverted mind, addresses a woman with wicked words, exciting her to passion as young men do to young women.

4. If a monk, being degraded with perverted mind, magnifies service to himself in the hearing of a woman, saying, "This, sister, would be the noblest of services, that to so righteous and exalted a religious person as myself you should serve by that act," meaning sexual intercourse.

5. If a monk acts as a go-between for a woman to a man, or for a man to a woman, or for a wife, or for a mistress, or even for a prostitute.

6. If a monk, at his own request, has a hut put up on a dangerous site, without the open space around it, or does not bring the monks to approve the site, or exceeds the due measure.

7. If a monk has a large house made on a dangerous site, without the open space around it, or does not bring the monks to the place to approve the site.

8. If a monk, in harshness, malice, or anger, harasses another monk by a groundless charge of having committed a Parajika offense, thinking to himself, "Perhaps I may get him to fall from this religious life"—and then later, either when he is pressed, or without his being pressed, the case turns out to be groundless, and the monk confesses his malice.

9. If a monk, in harshness, malice, or anger, harasses another monk by a groundless charge of having committed a Parajika offense, supporting himself by some point or other of no importance in a case that really rests on something of a different kind; thinking to himself, "Perhaps I may get him to fall from this religious life"—and then later, either when he is pressed, or without his being pressed, the case turns out to rest on something of a different kind, and that monk confesses his malice.

10. If a monk causes division in a community that is at union, or persists in calling attention to some matter calculated to cause division,

that monk should be addressed by the monks, "Sir, do not go around causing division in a community that is unified." If that monk, when he has thus been spoken to by the monks, should persist as before, then let that monk be [formally] admonished about it by the monks as a body, even to the third time, to the intent that he abandon that course. If, while being so admonished up to the third time, he abandons that course, it is well. If he does not abandon it, it is a Samghadisesa.

11. Now other monks, one, two, or three, may become adherents of that monk, and may raise their voices on his side: "Do not say, sirs, anything against that monk! That monk speaks according to the Dhamma, and he speaks according to the *Vinaya*." Then let those monks be addressed by the other monks in this way, "Do not say this, sirs! That monk does not speak according to the Dhamma, neither does he speak according to the *Vinaya*. Do not let division in the community be pleasing to you!" If those monks, when they have thus been spoken to by the monks, should persist as before, those monks should be formally judged by the monks, as a body, even to the third time, so that they abandon that course. If . . . they abandon that course, it is well. If they do not abandon it, it is a Samghadisesa.

12. A monk may refuse to listen to what is said to him. . . . He may allow nothing to be said to him, objecting, "Say nothing to me, Sirs, either good or bad; and I will say nothing, either good or bad, to you. Be good enough, sirs, to refrain from speaking to me!" Then let that monk be addressed by the monks, "Do not, sir, make yourself a person who cannot be spoken to. Make yourself a person to whom we can speak. Speak to the monks, sir, according to the Dhamma; and the monks, sir, will speak to you according to the Dhamma. For the society of the Blessed One grows large by mutual discussion and by mutual help." If that monk, when he has thus been spoken to by the monks, should persist as before, then let that monk be formally

judged by the monks as a body as many as three times, so that he may abandon that course. If he abandons that course, it is well. If he does not abandon it, it is a Samghadisesa.

13.   If a monk dwells near a certain village or town, leading a life hurtful to the laity and devoted to evil, so that his evil deeds are seen and heard, and the families led astray by him are seen and heard, let that monk be spoken to by the monks. The monks must say, "Your life, sir, is hurtful to the laity, and evil. Your evil deeds, sir, are seen and heard. You are leading families astray. Be so good, sir, as to depart from this residence; you have lived here long enough." If that monk, when thus spoken to by the monks, should persist as before, that monk should be formally judged by the monks as a body as many as three times, so that he abandon that course. If he abandons that course, it is well. If he does not abandon it, it is a Samghadisesa.

The Order of Nuns*

This selection narrates the story about how women were admitted into the monastic order as nuns. The Buddha was at first very reluctant to admit them, but he relented, giving special rules for an order of nuns. Nuns have historically played a much smaller role in Buddhism than the order of monks. Nuns and other Buddhist women struggling for a greater degree of liberation still must contend with patriarchal interpretation of this passage.[39]

Now at that time the Blessed Buddha was staying among the Sakyas in Kapilavatthu, in the Nigrodharama. And Maha-pajapati the Gotami[40] went to the place where the Blessed One was. When she arrived there, she bowed down before the Blessed One, and remained standing to one side. She said to the Blessed One, "It would be well, Lord, if women should be allowed to renounce their homes and enter the homeless state under the doctrine and discipline proclaimed by the Tathagata."

The Buddha replied, "Enough, O Gotami! Let it not please you that women should be allowed to do so." A second and a third time Maha-pajapati made the same request in the same words, and received the same reply. Then Maha-pajapati, sad and sorrowful that the Blessed One would not allow women to enter the homeless state, bowed down before the Blessed One. Keeping him on her right hand as she passed him, she departed weeping and in tears.

Now when the Blessed One had remained at Kapilavatthu as long as he thought fit, he set out on his journey toward Vesali. Traveling straight on, in due course he arrived there. The Blessed One stayed there in the Mahavana, in the Kutagara Hall.

Maha-pajapati cut off her hair and put on orange-colored robes. She set out, with several women of the Sakya clan, toward Vesali. In due course she arrived at Vesali, at the Mahavana, at the Kutagara Hall. And Maha-pajapati, with swollen feet and covered with dust, sad and sorrowful, weeping and in tears, took her stand outside under the entrance porch.

The venerable Ananda saw her standing there, and on seeing her so, he said to her, "Why do you stand there, outside the porch, with

---

Cullavagga 10.1.1–6.

[39] Taken, with editing, from T. W. Rhys Davids and Hermann Oldenberg, trans., *Vinaya Texts,* part 3, *Sacred Books of the East,* vol. 20 (Oxford: Oxford University Press, 1885), pp. 320–326.

[40] *the Gotami:* a relative of Gotama, and his nurse when he was an infant.

swollen feet and covered with dust, sad and sorrowful, weeping and in tears?"

"Because, Ananda, the Lord and Blessed One does not allow women to renounce their homes and enter the homeless state under the doctrine and discipline proclaimed by the Tathagata."

Then the venerable Ananda went up to the place where the Blessed One was. Bowing down before the Blessed One, he took his seat on one side. And, so sitting, the venerable Ananda said to the Blessed One: "Lord, Maha-pajapati is standing outside under the entrance porch. She has swollen feet and is covered with dust. She is sad and sorrowful, weeping and in tears, because the Blessed One does not allow women to renounce their homes and enter the homeless state under the doctrine and discipline proclaimed by the Blessed One. It would be well, Lord, if women were to have permission granted to them to do as she desires."

The Buddha replied, "Enough, Ananda! Let it not please you that women should be allowed to do so." A second and a third time Ananda made the same request, in the same words, and received the same reply.

Then the venerable Ananda thought, "The Blessed One does not give his permission. I will now ask the Blessed One on another ground." And the venerable Ananda said to the Blessed One, "Lord, can women—when they have gone forth from the household life and entered the homeless state, under the doctrine and discipline proclaimed by the Blessed One—can they gain the fruit of conversion, or of the second Path, or of the third Path, or of Arhatship?"

"They are capable (of all these), Ananda."

"Lord, Maha-pajapati has proved herself of great service to the Blessed One, when as aunt and nurse she nourished him and gave him milk, and on the death of his mother she nursed the Blessed One at her own breast. It would be well, Lord, that women should have permission to go forth from the household life and enter the homeless state, under the doctrine and discipline proclaimed by the Tathagata."

"Ananda, if Maha-pajapati takes upon herself the Eight Chief Rules, let that be reckoned as her initiation.

(1) Even if a woman has been a nun for a hundred years, she shall make salutation to, shall rise in the presence of, shall bow down before, and shall perform all proper duties toward a monk, even if he is only just initiated.

(2) A nun is not to spend the rainy season in a district in which there is no monk.

(3) Every half month a nun is to await from the monks two things: the request about the date of the Uposatha ceremony and the time when the monk will come to give the Exhortation.

(4) After keeping the rainy season, the nun is to inquire whether any fault can be laid to her charge before both Samghas—of monks and of nuns—with respect to three matters: what has been seen, what has been heard, and what has been suspected.

(5) A nun who has been guilty of a serious offense is to undergo the discipline of penance toward both the Samghas.

(6) When a nun, as novice, has been trained for two years in the Six Rules, she is to ask permission for the upasampada initiation from both Samghas.

(7) A nun is never to revile or abuse a monk.

(8) From this time on, nuns are forbidden to admonish monks, but the official admonition of nuns by monks is not forbidden. . . .

Then the venerable Ananda, when he had learned from the Blessed One these Eight Chief Rules, went to Maha-pajapati and told her all that the Blessed One had said. She replied, "A man or a woman, when young and of tender years, accustomed to adorn himself, would bathe his head and receive with both hands a garland of lotus or jasmine or atimuttaka flowers, and place it on the top of his head. In the same way, I take upon myself these Eight Chief Rules, never to be transgressed my life long."

Then the venerable Ananda returned to the Blessed One, and bowed down before him, and took his seat on one side. So sitting, the venerable Ananda said to the Blessed One, "Lord, Maha-pajapati has taken upon herself the Eight Chief Rules; the aunt of the Blessed One has received the upasampada initiation."

Then the Buddha said, "Ananda, if women had not received permission to go out from the household life and enter the homeless state under the doctrine and discipline proclaimed by the Tathagata, then the pure religion would have lasted long; the good law would have stood fast for a thousand years. But since women have now received that permission, the pure religion will not now last so long, and the good law will now stand fast for only five hundred years. Houses in which there are many women but only a few men are easily violated by robber burglars. In the same way, Ananda, under whatever doctrine and discipline women are allowed to go out from the household life into the homeless state, that religion will not last long. So, Ananda, in anticipation I have laid down these Eight Chief Rules for the nuns, never to be transgressed for their whole life."

RITUAL AND MEDITATION

The Relics of the Buddha*

One of the most important features of Buddhist worship has been veneration of the relics (physical remains, mostly bones) of the Buddha. To a Buddhist, these are the holiest physical objects in the world. This selection from the Death of the Buddha Sutra *tells the story of how the followers of the Buddha settled many arguments about how the relics of the cremated body of the Buddha should be distributed.*[41]

When they heard these things, the Mallas of Kusinara spoke to the assembled brothers. "The Blessed One died in our village domain. We will not give away any part of the remains of the Blessed One!"

When they had thus spoken, Dona the Brahmin addressed the assembled brothers. He said, "Hear, reverend sirs, one word from me. Our Buddha was accustomed to teach moderation. It is unseemly that strife should arise, and wounds, and war, over the distribution of the remains of him who was the best of beings! Let us all, sirs, unite in friendly harmony to make eight portions. Let thupas[42] arise widespread in every land, that humanity may trust in the Enlightened One! Brahmin, divide the remains of the Blessed One equally into eight parts, with fair division."

"Let it be so, sir!" Dona said in assent to the assembled brothers. He divided the remains of the Blessed One equally into eight parts, with fair division. He said to them, "Give me, sirs, this vessel, and I will set up over it a sacred memorial mound, and in its honor I will establish a feast." And they gave the vessel to Dona the Brahmin.

Mahaparinibbana Sutta 6.58–60.

[41] Taken, with editing, from Davids, *Buddhist Suttas,* pp. 133–134.

[42] *thupas (or stupas):* a house of worship enshrining relics of the Buddha.

Mindfulness in Meditation*

Buddhist monks must have a powerful concentration to fix their minds on the abstract processes and products of meditation. This passage from an influential Theravada meditation scripture discusses the way to full mindfulness.[43]

Monks, there is one road, one path for beings to purify themselves, to transcend sorrow and grief, to overcome suffering and melancholy, to attain the right way, to realize Nirvana: that is the fourfold establishment of mindfulness. What are the four mindfulnesses? They are the mindful contemplation of the body, the mindful contemplation of the feelings, the mindful contemplation of thoughts, and the mindful contemplation of the elements of reality.

How does a monk practice the mindful contemplation of the body? In this way: He goes to the forest, or to the foot of a tree, or to an empty room, and he sits down, cross-legged, keeps his back straight, and directs his mindfulness in front of him. Mindfully, he breathes in, mindfully, he breathes out; breathing in a long breath, he knows "I am breathing in a long breath"; breathing out a long breath, he knows "I am breathing out a long breath"; breathing in a short breath, he knows "I am breathing in a short breath"; breathing out a short breath, he knows "I am breathing out a short breath." He should be like a lathe operator who knows that "I am making a long turn" when he is making a long turn and that "I am making a short turn" when he is making a short turn. Thus a monk practices mindfully contemplating his body.

Furthermore, when a monk is walking, he knows "I am walking," and when he is standing, knows "I am standing," and when he is sitting, knows "I am sitting," and when he is lying down, knows "I am lying down." Whatever posture his body may take, he knows that he is taking it. Thus a monk practices mindfully contemplating his body.

And also, a monk is fully mindful of what he is doing, both going and coming, looking straight ahead and looking away, holding out his bowl or retracting it, putting on his robes, carrying his bowl, eating, drinking, chewing, tasting, defecating, urinating, moving, standing, sitting, sleeping, waking, talking, being quiet. Thus a monk practices mindfully contemplating his body.

And also, a monk considers his body itself, from the soles of his feet upward and from the top of his head downward, wrapped as it is in skin and filled with all sorts of impurities. He reflects, "In this body, there is hair, body-hair, nails, teeth, skin, flesh, sinews, bones, marrow, kidneys, heart, liver, pleura, spleen, lungs, colon, intestines, stomach, feces, bile, phlegm, pus, blood, sweat, fat, tears, lymph, saliva, snot, synovia, and urine." Thus a monk practices mindfully contemplating his body.

And also, a monk considers his body with regard to the elements that compose it. He reflects, "In this body, there is earth, water, fire, and air." He should think of these elements that make up the body as though they were pieces of the carcass of a cow that a butcher had slaughtered and displayed in a market. Thus a monk practices mindfully contemplating his body. And also, if a monk should see a corpse abandoned in a cemetery, dead one day or two or three, swollen, turning blue, and beginning to fester, he should concentrate on his own body and think, "This body of mine is just like that one; it has the same nature, and it will not escape this fate." And should he see a corpse abandoned in a cemetery, being eaten by crows, hawks, vultures, dogs, jackals, or various kinds of vermin, he should concentrate on his own body

*Majjhima-nikaya, Satipatthanasutta 10.1–9.
[43] Taken, with editing, from V. Trenckner, *The Majjhima-nikaya*, vol. 1 (London: Pali Text Society, 1888), pp. 55–63.

and think, "This body of mine is just like that one; it has the same nature, and it will not escape this fate." And should he see a corpse abandoned in a cemetery, a skeleton still covered with some flesh and blood and held together by tendons, or without flesh but smeared with blood and still held together, or without flesh or blood but still held together, or just bones no longer held together but scattered in different directions—here the bones of a hand, there the bones of a foot, here a tibia, there a femur, here a hipbone, there a backbone, over there a skull—he should concentrate on his own body and think, "This body of mine is just like that; it has the same nature, and it will not escape this fate." And should he see a corpse abandoned in a cemetery, bones bleached white as shells, old bones in a heap, bones that have completely decayed and become dust—he should concentrate on his own body and think, "This body of mine is just like that; it has the same nature, and it will not escape this fate." Thus a monk keeps mindfully contemplating his body.

And how, monks, does a monk practice the mindful contemplation of feelings? In this way: Experiencing a pleasant feeling, he knows "I am experiencing a pleasant feeling"; experiencing an unpleasant feeling, he knows "I am experiencing an unpleasant feeling." Experiencing a feeling that is neither pleasant nor unpleasant, he knows "I am experiencing a feeling that is neither pleasant nor unpleasant." Experiencing a pleasant physical feeling, he knows "I am experiencing a pleasant physical feeling"; experiencing a pleasant spiritual feeling, he knows "I am experiencing a pleasant spiritual feeling"; experiencing an unpleasant physical feeling, an unpleasant spiritual feeling, a physical feeling that is neither pleasant nor unpleasant, a spiritual feeling that is neither pleasant nor unpleasant, he knows he is experiencing those feelings. Thus a monk practices mindfully contemplating his feelings.

And how, monks, does a monk practice the mindful contemplation of thoughts? In this way: He knows a passionate thought to be a passionate thought; he knows a passionless thought to be a passionless thought; he knows a hate-filled thought to be a hate-filled thought; he knows a hate-free thought to be a hate-free thought; he knows a deluded thought, an undeluded thought, an attentive thought, a distracted thought, a lofty thought, a lowly thought, a mediocre thought, a supreme thought, a concentrated thought, a diffused thought, a thought that is free, a thought that is still bound, to be such thoughts as they are. Thus a monk practices mindfully contemplating his thoughts.

And how, monks, does a monk practice the mindful contemplation of the elements of reality? In this way: He practices the mindful contemplation of the elements of reality with regard to the five hindrances. And how does he do that? In this way: When there is within him sensual excitement, he knows that "sensual excitement is occurring within me"; when there is within him no sensual excitement, he knows that "sensual excitement is not occurring within me." When there is within him some ill will, he knows that "ill will is occurring within me"; when there is within him no ill will, he knows that "ill will is not occurring within me." And similarly he knows the presence and the absence within himself of laziness and lethargy, agitation and worry, and doubt. Thus he practices mindfully contemplating elements of reality within himself, he practices mindfully contemplating elements of reality outside of himself, and he practices mindfully contemplating elements of reality as they arise and as they pass away. And thinking that "this is an element of reality," he is concerned with it only insofar as he needs to be for the sake of knowledge and recognition; so he abides free from attachment and does not cling to anything in this world.

A monk also practices the mindful contemplation of the elements of reality with regard to the five aggregates of attachment. And how does he do that? In this way: He reflects "Such is physical form, such is the origin of physical form, such is the passing away of physical form." "Such is feeling, such is the origin of feeling, such is the passing away of feeling." "Such is perception, such is the origin of perception, such is the passing away of perception." "Such are karmic constituents, such is the origin of karmic constituents, such is the passing away of karmic constituents." "Such is consciousness, such is the origin of consciousness, such is the passing away of consciousness."

A monk also practices the mindful contemplation of the elements of reality with regard to the six senses and sense-objects. How does he do this? In this way: He knows his eyes, he knows visible forms, and he knows the attachments that develop in connection with the two of them. Similarly he knows his ears, and he knows sounds. He knows his nose and he knows smells. He knows his tongue and he knows tastes. He knows his body and he knows tactile things. He knows his mind and he knows thoughts. And he knows the attachments that develop in connection with any of them.

A monk also practices the mindful contemplation of the elements of reality with regard to the seven factors of enlightenment. How does he do that? In this way: When the first factor of enlightenment, which is mindfulness, is within him, he knows it to be present; when it is not within him, he knows it to be absent. And similarly, he knows the presence and absence within himself of the other factors of enlightenment: the investigation of Dharma, energetic effort, enthusiasm, serenity, meditative concentration, and equanimity.

A monk also practices the mindful contemplation of the elements of reality with regard to the Four Noble Truths. How does he do that? In this way: He knows "suffering" the way it really is, and he knows "the origination of suffering" the way it really is, and he knows "the cessation of suffering" the way it really is, and he knows "the way leading to the cessation of suffering" the way it really is.

A Mahayana View of the Merit of Making Images*

Another prominent feature of Buddhist worship— much more widespread than relic veneration—is using statues of the Buddha to focus one's thoughts toward enlightenment. In this passage from the Mahayana canon, the Buddha is said to lavish great merit on those who make his images. The belief that the Buddha gives his gracious blessing to those who seek it is a prominent theme in Mahayana Buddhism.[44]

And the Blessed One sat upon his lotus throne, upon the terrace of enlightenment; and each person in the four assemblies thought to himself: "Truly we wish to hear the Blessed One teach us the meritorious virtue of making images of the Buddha. For what blessings could we gain if we made an image in the form of the Buddha, yet with our meager talent failed to capture his likeness?"

And the bodhisattva Maitreya knew their thoughts: he arose from his seat, placed his robe over his right shoulder, and knelt upon the ground. He joined his palms together, and said to the Blessed One: "King Udayana has made an image of the Buddha. Whether the Buddha is in the world or has passed away into nirvana,

*Taisho Shinshu Daizokyo 16, no. 694.
[44] From Stephan Beyer, The Buddhist Experience: Sources and Interpretations (Belmont, CA: Dickenson, 1974), pp. 47–50, 54–55. Copyright © 1974, Dickenson Publishing Company. Used by permission of Wadsworth Publishing Company, Inc.

how much merit does one gain who follows the dictates of a faithful heart and builds an image such as his? My one wish is that the Blessed One explain this thing to me."

And the Buddha said to the bodhisattva Maitreya: "Listen attentively! Listen attentively, and ever bear in mind what I shall explain to you.

"Let a son of good family or a daughter of good family but be pure and faithful, and fix his mind solely upon the virtues of the Buddha, and meditate unceasingly upon his awe-inspiring virtue and majesty. Let him think upon the ten powers of the Buddha, and upon his fourfold fearlessness; upon his eighteen special qualities, and upon his great love and compassion; upon his omniscience, and upon all his signs of greatness.

"Let him see how every single pore of the Buddha's body glows with measureless multi-colored brilliant light, with immensities of surpassing blessings and adornments and accomplishments, with measureless insight and perfect enlightenment, with measureless meditation and forbearance, with measureless magic and spiritual power.

"Let him meditate upon the infinitude of all the virtues of the Buddha, upon his far removal from all the hosts of error, and upon his splendor unequaled in all the world. And let him fix his mind in this manner, and awaken deep faith and joy, and make an image of the Buddha with all its signs. Then he gains merit which is vast, and great, and measureless, and limitless, and which can be neither weighed nor counted.

"Maitreya, should a man draw and adorn an image with a host of varied colors; or cast an image of silver, or bronze, or iron, or lead, or tin; or carve an image of fragrant sandalwood; or cover an image with pearls, or shell, or well-woven and embroidered silk; or cover a wooden image with red earth and white lime plaster; or build an image to the best of his ability, even if it be so small as the size of a finger, as long as those who see it can see that it is in the form of the Blessed One—I shall now tell you what his blessed reward will be, and how he will fare in his next life.

"For a man who does these things may be born again into this world, but he will not be born into a poor family, nor will he be born in a barbarian border kingdom, nor into a lowly clan, nor as an orphan; he will not be born stupid or fierce, nor as a merchant or peddler or butcher; truly he will not be born into any low craft or impure caste, into any heretical practices or heretical views.

"For by the power of his intention he has cast aside the cause for such rebirth, and he will not be born into such states; but rather he will always be born into the household of a universal emperor, having powerful clansmen, or perhaps into the household of a Brahmin of pure practices, rich and honorable, lordly and without error.

"And the place where he is born will always be where Buddhas are served and worshipped; and perhaps there he shall be a king, able to maintain and establish the Law, teaching the Law which converts those of evil practices; and perhaps he shall be a universal emperor, having the seven jewels, bringing forth a thousand sons, and mounting into the sky to convert the four corners of the world.

"And when his length of days has been exhausted, the lord will be abundantly joyful, perhaps to rule as the king of the gods, or as lord of the Heaven of Delights, or of the Heaven of Power; for there will be no joy either of gods or of men which he will not taste. And thus his blessed reward will continue in heaven and will not be cut off when he dies.

"And he will always be born as a man: he will not take on the body of a woman, or of a eunuch, or of a hermaphrodite.[45] The body which he takes will be without defect or deformity: neither one-eyed nor blind; his ears not deaf; his nose not bent or twisted; his mouth not large or crooked; his lips not hanging down or wrinkled or rough; his teeth not broken or missing, not black or yellow; his tongue not slow;

---

[45] *hermaphrodite:* a person with male and female sexual organs and characteristics.

the back of his neck without tumor or boil; his form not hunched; his color not splotched; his arms not weak; his feet not large; and he will be neither too thin nor too tall, neither too fat nor too thin. . . .

"Maitreya, if there is a man who, in the midst of this world, can awaken his faith and build an image of the Buddha, then between his having done so and his not having done so the difference is . . . great: for anywhere this man is born, he is purified and free of all his past sins, and by all his skill may gain liberation even without a teacher. . . ."

And then the bodhisattva Maitreya said to the Buddha: "Blessed One, you have always said that good or evil deeds are never lost. Any being who has done such grievous sins should be born in a mean, low class and household, be poor and sick and die a speedy death. But if he can awaken his faith and build an image of the Buddha, then will he still experience the retribution for his host of sins?"

And the Buddha said to the bodhisattva Maitreya: "Maitreya, listen attentively, and I shall explain it to you. Should this being, who has done all those sins, put forth his heart to build a Buddha image, seek to wail and repent, take himself strongly in hand and vow to transgress no more, then everything that he has done before is all annulled. . . .

"And why is that? It is because all Buddhas have the measureless limitless blessed virtues of their Buddhahood: measureless limitless great insight, measureless limitless meditation and freedom, and all manner of superlative qualities of meritorious virtue. . . . The virtue of the Blessed Buddha is without limit or measure, and it cannot even be thought or talked of. And that is why, if a man awakens his faith and builds a Buddha image, every single one of his evil deeds will be exhausted and annulled; and from the store of the Buddhas he gains meritorious virtue without limit or measure, until he himself gains Buddhahood, and himself saves beings from all their suffering and woe forever."

Tibetan Scripture to Guide the Soul after Death*

Probably the most famous Tibetan scripture is the Bardo Thodol *(or* Bar-do thos-grol*), popularly known as the "Tibetan Book of the Dead" but more accurately translated "Listen and Be Liberated from the Intermediate State." This book provides texts to be read at and after death to guide the soul of the deceased through the intermediate ("Bardo") state to a happy reincarnation. This key reading at the point of death first speaks of the "clear light" of pure Nirvana; the person cannot reach it, and guidance is given to lead the soul through demonic nightmares to shelter in the womb of a being who will later give birth to the dead person's reincarnation.*[46]

"Noble person, (his/her name), now the time has come for you to seek a path [through the Bardo]. After your breath has almost ceased, that which is called the Clear Light of the first phase of the Intermediary State will dawn upon you. Its meaning was explained to you by your lama. It is existence as such, empty and bare like the sky; it will appear to you as the stainless and bare mind, clear and empty, without limitations or a center. At this moment you should recognize this and remain therein. I shall guide you to this insight." Before the physical breath has

---

*Bardo Thodol 1.1–2.
[46] From H. Coward, E. Dargyay, and R. Neufeldt, *Readings in Eastern Religion* (Waterloo, Ontario: Wilfrid Laurier University Press, 1988). Copyright © 1988 Wilfrid Laurier University Press. Used by permission.

totally ceased one should repeat this close to the dying person's ear many times so that it is imprinted on the mind. . . .

"Noble son, (name), listen! The intrinsic light of true being will now become apparent to you. This you must recognize! Noble son, the innate being of your present cognition is this very naked voidness, which does not exist as a thing, phenomenon, or color; it is mere voidness. This is the absolute reality of the female Buddha Samantabhadra.[47] As your cognition consists in voidness, don't let this opportunity become meaningless. . . . The nature of your own mind is void of an inherent being and of any substance, but your intelligence is crystal clear. This nature of your mind is inseparable from your intelligence; together they are the true being, the Buddha. The nature of your mind, equally clear and void, consists in a mass of light, and because of being free of becoming and decaying, it is the Buddha of boundless light. This you must recognize! . . .

"Noble son, for three and a half days you will be unconscious. When you awake from the coma you will think: 'What happened to me?' For this reason, you have to recognize that you are now in the intermediate state. At this time, when you depart from the world, all things will appear to you as light, and as celestial beings. The entire sky will shine with bright blue. . . .

"You should yearn for the light blue light, which is so brilliant and clear; and full of devotion you should address Vairocana with this prayer which you should repeat after me: 'Alas! At this time I am wandering through the world because of my great ignorance. I beg you, Vairocana, to guide me on the bright path of the primordial wisdom of the sphere being-as-such, the right path. May the divine mother, Akashesvari (Protector of the heavens) protect me from behind. I beg you, rescue me from the abyss of the intermediate state and guide me to perfect buddhahood.'

"Noble son, (name), hear me! You have not understood me even though I have directed you toward the right insight according to the instructions of this text. Now when you can't close the womb, then the time has truly come when you have to acquire a new body. There is more than only one profound and authentic instruction for closing the door of the womb. Remember them, be not distracted; imprint them on your mind.

"Noble son, although you are reluctant to go, torturers—which are evil deeds—chase you. Powerless, you have to go where you don't want to. Torturers and executioners pull you and you feel as if you are running away from darkness, tornadoes, cries of war, snow, rain, hail, and blizzards. In your anxiety you are looking for a refuge, and you escape and hide—as I have said before—in mansions, rock crevasses, caves, thick undergrowth, or in lotus flowers which close over you. You ask yourself whether they will get you there. 'If they detect me here, then everything is lost,' and while questioning whether you have escaped you cling to this spot. If they take you from there you are afraid of being overcome by the anxieties and terrors of the intermediate state. Thus you feel fear and anxiety and you hide in the middle of these burrows. Therein you seize a bad body that did not exist before, and you will suffer from various ills. This is a sign that the devils and demons have prevented your escape.

"Listen and memorize this instruction suitable for such an occasion! When the torturers chase you into a state of helplessness, or when fear and anxiety threaten you, then you should visualize a wrathful deity who destroys all these forms of threat. Quickly perfect your vision of the deity with all his limbs. . . . Through their blessing and compassion you will rid yourself from the torturers and will have the strength to close the door of the womb. This profound and accurate instruction you should keep in mind!"

---

[47] *Samantabhadra:* As in Buddhist tantric texts, the feminine here represents perfect wisdom.

A Zen Koan, "What Is Extraordinary?"*

Zen (Chinese: Chan) Buddhism seeks immediate enlightenment beyond study, sense-perception, and rationality. As an aid to this, Zen masters developed the koan, a difficult question that cannot be rationally answered. Famous koans include such gems as these: "What is the sound of one hand clapping?" "What did your face look like before your parents were born?" "If I have nothing, what should I do with it?" The Blue Cliff Record, a famous Zen scripture, puts koans into a fuller context for use in the monasteries. Written in China during the Song dynasty (960–1276 C.E.), each of the one hundred chapters deals with one koan, giving an introduction telling the impact of the koan; the story, taken from classical Zen lore, interspersed with parenthetical remarks by Zen master Yuanwu Keqin (1063–1135); a commentary on the story by Yuanwu; a poetic verse by the Zen poet Zuedou, illustrating the impact of the story, also with parenthetical comments by Yuanwu; and a commentary by Yuanwu on the verse. The story is intended to illuminate the koan, but on the whole the story also has a riddling quality.[48]

[Story] A monk asked [the ninth-century Zen master] Baizhang, "What is extraordinary?" (There's an echo in the words. He demonstrates his ability in a phrase. He flabbergasts people. Though he has eyes, he's never seen.) Baizhang said, "Sitting alone on the mountain." (His awesome majestic air extends over the whole land. The one standing and the one sitting are both defeated.) The monk bowed: (A clever monk. There still is such a person who wants to see such a thing.) Baizhang then hit him. (A competent Chan teacher, why does he not speak much? The imperative is not carried out vainly.)

[Commentary] He has the eye to face situations unconcerned with danger or death. So it is said, "How can you catch tiger cubs without entering a tiger's lair?" Baizhang was like a tiger with wings. Nor does this monk avoid life and death: he dares to grab the tiger's whiskers and ask what is extraordinary. This monk too has eyes. Baizhang immediately took up the burden with him and said, "Sitting alone on the mountain." The monk bowed. Chan practitioners must be able to discern the meaning before the question. This monk's bow was not the same as an ordinary bow; he had to have eyes to do it. He didn't spill his guts. Though they knew each other, they acted like they didn't.

When the monk asked what was special and Baizhang told him sitting alone on the mountain, the monk bowed and Baizhang hit him; see how when they let both do so at once, and when they gather back they wipe away the tracks and obliterate the traces. But what did the monk mean by bowing? If it was good, why did Baizhang hit him? If it was not good, what was wrong? Here you must be able to tell right from wrong, distinguish initiate from outsider, and stand on the summits of the summits of a thousand peaks, to begin to understand.

The monk's bow was like grabbing the tiger's whiskers; he was just contending for a pivotal position. Luckily Baizhang is perceptive; thus he hit the monk. Anyone else wouldn't have been able to handle the monk. The monk met mind with mind, conveyed intention with intention— that is why he bowed.

Nanquan said, "Last night at midnight Manjushri and Samantabhadra came up with

---

*The Blue Cliff Record 26.
[48] From Thomas Cleary, translator, The Blue Cliff Record, BDK English Tripitaka, vol. 75. Berkeley, CA: Numata Center for Buddhist Translation and Research, 1998. Copyright © 1998 Bukkyo Dendo Kyokai and Numata Center for Buddhist Translation and Research. Used by permission.

views of the Buddha and the Dharma. I gave them each a beating and sentenced them to be hemmed in by twin iron mountains." Then Zhaozhou said, "Who should take your beating?" Nanquan said, "Where was my fault?" Zhaozhou bowed.

Chan masters do not idly observe how the other takes action. The moment they are in charge of the situation, they bring it into play. They are naturally lively.

Wuzu would often say, "It's like coming to grips on the front lines." I'm always telling you simply to cut off subject and object all at once—then you'll be able to hold fast and act with mastery. Only then will you see Baizhang. But tell me, what about when letting go? Look at Xuedon's verse.

[Verse]
In the realm of the patriarchs gallops the heavenly colt.
(Such a one is born once in five hundred years. Among myriad people there's one or a half. The son takes up the father's work.)
Among expedients rolling out and rolling up are not the same path—
(Already so before the words. Baizhang is independent; it's a matter of his adept methodology.)
In a flash he retains the ability to change with circumstances.
(He came head on, turning left and right. Do you see where Baizhang helps people?)
How laughable—a man comes to grab the tiger's whiskers.
(He deserves a beating. Where there's a great reward, there must be a valiant man. He doesn't avoid losing his life. I leave this move to you.)

[Commentary on the verse] Xuedon can see all the way through, so he can come out with this verse. The heavenly colt runs a thousand miles a day, runs back and forth, up and down, gallops as if flying; so it is called a heavenly colt. Xuedou is praising Baizhang—in the territory of the patriarchs he runs from east to west, west to east, coming, going free in all direction, without any hindrance, just like the heavenly colt. He is well able to gallop; only thus can we see how free he is. This is because he attained Mazu's great ability and great function.

A monk asked Mazu, "What is the meaning of Buddhism?" Mazu hit him and said, "If I didn't hit you, everyone in the world would laugh at me." The monk asked, "What is the meaning of Buddhism?" Mazu said, "Come here and I'll tell you." The monk approached; Mazu boxed his ears, saying, "Six listeners don't draw the same conclusion." See how Mazu was so free; working with expedients, he sometimes rolled out, sometimes rolled up. Sometimes the rolling out isn't the rolling up, sometimes the rolling up isn't the rolling out. Sometimes rolling out and rolling up both aren't there. Hence the saying in praise of Baizhang's ability, "On the same path but not the same groove."

Xuedou says, "In a flash he retains the ability to change with circumstances." This refers to the monk's speed in changing with the situation. Yantou said, "Turning away from things is superior; pursuing things is inferior. In battle each occupies a pivotal position. Xuedou said, "The wheel of potential has never turned. If it turns, it must go both ways." And if it can't be turned, what's the use? Even great people must know something of changing with circumstances. People these days just offer their true feelings and play into the hands of another. What end will there be?

This monk was able to change in a flash, so he bowed. Xuedou says, "How laughable—a man came to grab the tiger's whiskers." Baizhang was like a tiger—how laughable that this monk went to grab the tiger's whiskers.

LATER DEVELOPMENTS OF SCRIPTURAL THEMES

Enlightenment according to Milarepa, a Founder of Tibetan Buddhism*

Milarepa was a leader in bringing Buddhism to Tibet in the twelfth century C.E. *This account has achieved near-scriptural status and is one of the most beloved stories among Tibetan Buddhists. In this reading, Milarepa renounces ordinary life and withdraws to meditate in the mountains and teach the essentials of enlightenment according to Tibetan Buddhism.*[49]

They [his friends] left, and I ate the good food they had brought. The sensation of pleasure and pain and the feelings of hunger increased so much that I could no longer meditate. I thought that there was no greater obstacle for me than this inability to meditate. Breaking the seal of the scroll that the lama had given me, I looked at it. It contained the essential instructions to overcome obstacles and improve practice, instructions for transforming vice into virtue, and more especially the advice to take good food at this time.

I understood that, through the force of my former perseverance in meditation, my nerves had absorbed creative energy. Due to my inferior food the energy remained inactive. The beer had stimulated my nerves to some extent and [my sister's] beer and food had completed the process.

Following the directions on the scroll, I worked hard on the vital exercises recommended for body, breathing, and meditation. As a result, the obstructions in the smaller nerves as well as those in the median nerves were cleared away. I attained an experience of joy, lucidity, and pure awareness similar to what I had known about in theory. In fact it was an extraordinary experience of illumination which was very powerful and stable. Having overcome the

obstacles, I realized imperfections as perfections; even through discriminating thought, I perceived the inherent simplicity of the Dharma.

I understood that in general all things related to samsara and nirvana are interdependent. Furthermore I perceived that the source consciousness is neutral. Samsara is the result of a wrong point of view. Nirvana is realized through perfect awareness. I perceived that the essence of both lay in an empty and luminous awareness. More particularly, this special experience of my illumination was the fruit of my previous meditations and the immediate effects of the food and the profound instructions of the lama. I also had a very special understanding that the methods of the Esoteric Path [Vajrayana, or Tibetan Buddhism] are for the transformation of all sensory experience into spiritual attainment. . . .

I thought that I should now work for the good of sentient beings. As I was reflecting on this a prophecy came to me: "Devote yourself wholly to meditation in this life, in accordance with the lama's instructions. There is nothing greater than serving the teachings of the Buddha and thereby saving sentient beings through meditation." Again I thought, "If I meditate as long as I live, I will be setting the best example for future disciples to renounce the world and meditate." And I was certain that both the tradition of the Dharma and sentient beings would derive much benefit from that.

Then I thought, "I have stayed in this place too long and have talked too much about my

---

The Life of Milarepa 2.7.
[49] Taken, with editing, from W. Y. Evans-Wentz, *The Life of Milarepa* (Oxford: Oxford University Press, 1925).

knowledge of the Dharma to those who visited me. People saw me flying after my experience of illumination. If I stay here any longer I will fall under the influence of the world. There exists a risk of encountering Mara's obstacles, and the Eight Worldly Reactions will disturb my meditation. I must go and meditate at Chuwar according to the prophecy of the lama." . . .

When I arrived at Dingri, by the Chuwar road going through Peykhu, I sat down by the side of the road and watched what was going on. Some pretty young girls wearing jewels passed me on their way to Nokme. Seeing my emaciated body, one of them said, "Look! What misery! May I never be reborn as such a creature." Another one said, "How pitiful! A sight like that depresses me." I thought to myself, "I have compassion for these ignorant beings." And, feeling pity, I stood up and said to them, "Daughters, do not speak in this way. There is no reason for you to be so distressed. You could not be born like me, even if you wished. It is astonishing that you feel compassion, but your compassion comes from pride and a wrong understanding. . . ." Then Bodhi Raja of Ngandzong asked: "Lama Rimpoche, it seems to me that you are either the incarnation of Vajradhara Buddha and that you engage in all these actions for the benefit of sentient beings, or you are a great Bodhisattva who has attained the state of 'Non-returning' and who has accumulated immense merit for many eons. In you, I see all the characteristics of a true yogin who sacrifices his life for the Dharma practice.

"We human individuals cannot even conceive the extent of your asceticism and your devotion to your lama, let alone practice it ourselves. If we dared to practice in this way, our bodies could not bear such an ordeal. That is why it is certain that you were a Buddha or Bodhisattva from the very beginning. And so, although I am incapable of religion, I believe that we sentient beings will be led toward liberation from samsara through seeing your face and hearing your words. Revered Master, I beg you to tell us if you are the incarnation of a Buddha or a Bodhisattva."

The master replied: "I never heard whose incarnation I am. Maybe I am the incarnation of a being from the three lower realms, but if you see me as Buddha you will receive his blessing by virtue of your faith. Although this belief that I am an incarnation springs from your devotion to me, actually there is no greater impediment to your practice. It is a distortion of the true Dharma. The fault lies in not recognizing the true nature of the achievement of great sinner like myself. I have reached a stage not far from Enlightenment due to my belief in karma, my subsequent renunciation of the aims of worldly life, and due especially to my single-minded devotion to meditation.

"More particularly, if you receive initiation and the secret instruction which brings spontaneous awakening unclouded by conceptualizations, and if you then meditate under the guidance of an enlightened lama, you will undoubtedly attain Enlightenment.

"If you commit the ten harmful deeds and the five deadly sins, without doubt you will be reborn into the torments of the lowest realms. This is because there is no belief in karma and but little devotion to the Dharma. Whoever wholeheartedly believes in karma and dreads the suffering of the lower realms, a great longing for illumination will arise in him. This will lead him to devote himself to a lama, to meditation, and to maintaining a deeper insight. It is possible for every ordinary man to persevere as I have done. To consider a man of such perseverance as the reincarnation of a Buddha or as a Bodhisattva is a sign of not believing in the short path. Put your faith in the great law of cause and effect. Contemplate the lives of enlightened teachers; reflect upon karma, the misery of the cycle of existence, the true value of human life, and not knowing the hour of death. Devote yourselves to the practice of the Vajrayana!"

The Main Characteristics of Falun Gong*

Falun Gong ("Practice of the Wheel of Law"), more often called by its practitioners Falun Dafa ("Great Teaching of the Wheel of Law"), is a new religious movement based on Chinese spiritual practice. It traces most of its roots to Buddhism but also shares some with Taoism. The ruling Communist party of China has persecuted it as an evil cult that poses a threat to the state because it is a religious movement outside of government control. The zeal of its followers and the appeal of its teachings continue to attract millions of followers in China and worldwide. Its main text, Zhuan Falun, "Turning the Wheel of Law," has already gained scriptural status in the movement.[50]

Our Falun Dafa is one of the eighty-four thousand cultivation ways in the Buddha School. During the historical period of this human civilization, it has never been made public. In a prehistoric period, however, it was once widely used to provide salvation to humankind. In this final period, I am making it public again. Therefore, it is extremely precious. . . .

Falun Dafa is a cultivation practice of mind and body, and it requires exercises. On the one hand, the exercises are used to strengthen supernormal abilities. What is "strengthening"? It is the reinforcement of your supernormal abilities by your powerful gong potency,[51] thus making them progressively stronger. On the other hand, many living beings need to be developed in your body. In high-level cultivation practice, the Tao School requires the birth of the Immortal Infant (yuan ying), while the Buddha School requires the Vajra's indestructible body.[52] Furthermore, many supernatural abilities must be developed. These things need to be developed through the physical exercises, and they are what our exercises cultivate. A complete cultivation practice of mind and body requires both cultivation and practice. . . .

Ours is a genuine cultivation practice of both mind and body. The gong that we cultivate is stored in every cell of the body, and the gong of high-energy matter is even stored in the original minuscule particles of matter at an extremely microscopic level. As your gong potency becomes greater, the density and power of gong will also increase. Such high-energy matter has intelligence. Because it is stored in each cell of the human body all the way to the origin of life, it will gradually become the same form as the cells in your body, assuming the same molecular combinations and form of nuclei. Its essence has changed, however, for this body is no longer composed of original physical cells. . . . Therefore, on the surface you still appear to be an ordinary person. The only difference is that you look younger than those of your age. Certainly, the bad things in your body, including illnesses, must be removed first, but we do not treat illness here. We are purifying your body, and the term is not "healing illness," either. We just call it "purifying the body," and we clean out the bodies of true practitioners. . . .

After a period of cultivation practice, our Falun Dafa practitioners look quite different in appearance. Their skin becomes delicate and reddish-white. For the elderly, wrinkles become fewer or even extremely few, which is a common phenomenon. . . . In addition, elderly women will regain their menstrual period since a cultivation practice of mind and body requires menses to cultivate the body. One's period will come, but the menstrual flow will not be much. At present,

---

*Li Hongzhi, Zhuan Falun, Lecture 1, Conclusion.

[50] Taken from Li Hongzhi, Zhuan Falun (New Delhi: B. Jain, 2000), pp. 38–47. Copyright © 2000, Li Hongzhi. Used by permission of the publisher. www.bjain.com.

[51] gong potency: spiritual and physical power.

[52] Vajra's indestructible body: diamond-like being, from the Tibetan term for its form of Buddhism, "Vajrayana."

that little bit will suffice. This is also a common phenomenon. Otherwise, how can they cultivate their bodies without it? The same is true for men: The elderly and the young will all feel that the entire body is light. As for true practitioners, they will experience this transformation.

This practice of ours cultivates something very immense, as opposed to the many practices that imitate animals in their exercises. This practice cultivates something simply quite enormous. All of the principles that Sakyamuni [Buddha] and Lao Zi [Lao Tzu, the founder of Taoism] discussed in their time were confined to principles within our Milky Way. What does our Falun Dafa cultivate? Our cultivation practice is based upon the principles of the universe's evolution, and it is guided by the standard of the universe's highest characteristic. We cultivate something so enormous that it equates to cultivating the universe.

Our Falun Dafa has another extremely unique, most distinctive feature that is unlike any other practice. . . . Our practice cultivates a Falun in the lower abdomen. I personally install it for practitioners in the class. While I am teaching Falun Dafa, we install it for everyone in succession. Some people can feel it while others cannot; the majority of people can feel it. This is because people have different physical conditions. . . . Falun is a miniature of the universe that possesses all of the universe's capabilities, and it can operate and rotate automatically. It will forever rotate in your lower abdominal area. Once it is installed in your body, year-in and year-out it will not stop and will forever rotate like this. While rotating clockwise, it can automatically absorb energy from the universe. Additionally, it can itself transform energy to supply the energy required for transforming every part of your body. Also, it emits energy while rotating counter-clockwise, releasing undesirable elements that will disperse around your body. When it emits energy, the energy can be released to quite a distance, and then it will bring in new energy again.

The emitted energy can benefit the people around you. The Buddha School teaches self-salvation and salvation of all sentient beings. One does not only cultivate oneself, but also offers salvation to all sentient beings. Others can benefit as well, and you can unintentionally rectify other people's bodies, heal their illnesses, and so on. Of course, the energy is not lost. When Falun rotates clockwise, it can collect the energy back since it rotates continuously. . . . If there is a phone call or someone knocks at the door, you may go ahead and take care of it right away without having to finish the practice. When you stop to do something, Falun will immediately rotate clockwise and take back the emitted energy from around your body. . . .

If you are a true practitioner, our Falun will safeguard you. I am rooted in the universe. If anyone can harm you, he or she would be able to harm me. Put simply, that person would be able to harm this universe. What I have said may sound quite inconceivable. You will understand it later as you study further. There are also other things that are too profound for me to make known. We will systematically expound the Fa[53] of high levels, from the simple to the profound. It will not work if your own xinxing[54] is not righteous. If you pursue something, you may get into trouble. I have found that many veteran practitioners' Falun have become deformed. Why? You have intermingled other things with your practice, and you have accepted other people's things. Why didn't Falun protect you, then? If it is given to you, it is yours, and it is dictated by your mind. It is a principle of this universe that nobody should interfere with what you pursue. If you do not want to practice cultivation, no one can force you—that would be the same as doing a wrong deed. Who can force you to change your heart? You must discipline yourself on your own. . . . If you follow a practice,

---

[53] *Fa:* Buddhist principles and practices.
[54] *Xinxing:* inner moral character.

you must give your heart to it until completely enlightened in that school. Only then can you practice cultivation in another school, and that will be a different system. Because a system of genuine teachings is passed down from a very remote age, it will have gone through quite a complex process of transformation. Some people go by how they feel in practicing something. What does your feeling account for? It is nothing. The actual transformation process takes place in other dimensions and is extremely complex and intricate. . . .

I am not saying that everyone has to study Falun Dafa. If you do not study Falun Dafa and have received true teachings from other qigong[55] practices, I will approve of it as well. Let me tell you, however, that to truly practice cultivation toward high levels, one must be single-minded with one practice. There is

one thing that I must also point out: At present, no other person is truly teaching people toward high levels like me. In the future you will realize what I have done for you. Thus, I hope that you do not have very poor enlightenment quality. A lot of people want to practice cultivation toward high levels. This is now provided right before you, and you may still be unaware of it. You have been everywhere looking for a teacher and spent a fortune, yet you have found nothing. Today, it is offered to you at your doorstep, and maybe you have not realized it! This is an issue of whether you can become enlightened to it and whether you can be saved.

---

[55] *qigong:* traditional Chinese exercise that cultivates qi (chi), vital energy.

A Contemporary Statement of Buddhist Essentials*

Thich Nhat Hanh [tick naught han] *is second only to the Dalai Lama as a leading teacher of Buddhism. In his native Vietnam, he championed a movement known as "Engaged Buddhism," which combines monastic meditative practices and nonviolent civil disobedience. He set up relief organizations to rebuild destroyed Vietnamese villages, instituted a Peace Corps of sorts for Buddhist peace workers, founded a peace magazine, and urged world leaders to use nonviolence as a tool. Although his struggle meant that he had to leave Vietnam, it won him a worldwide following. He established the Plum Village Meditation Center in southern France as his main headquarters. The* Fourteen Mindfulness Trainings *reflects his main thinking and is a leading contemporary restatement of the essentials of Buddhist scriptures.*[56]

1.   Openness
Aware of the suffering created by fanaticism

and intolerance, I am determined not to be idolatrous about or bound to any doctrine, theory or ideology, even Buddhist ones. Buddhist teachings are guiding means to help me learn to look deeply and to develop my understanding and compassion. They are not doctrines to fight, kill or die for.

2.   Nonattachment to Views
Aware of suffering created by attachment to views and wrong perceptions, I am determined to avoid being narrow-minded and bound to present views. I will learn and practice nonattachment from views in order to be open to others' insights and experiences. I am aware that the knowledge I presently possess is not changeless, absolute truth. Truth is found in life and I will observe life within and around

---

*Thich Nhat Hanh, *Fourteen Mindfulness Trainings.*
[56] Taken from www.plumvillage.org, with permission.

me in every moment, ready to learn throughout my life.

3.   Freedom of Thought
Aware of the suffering brought about when
I impose my views on others, I am committed
not to force others, even my children, by any
means whatsoever—such as authority, threat,
money, propaganda or indoctrination—to
adopt my views. I will respect the right of
others to be different and to choose what to
believe and how to decide. I will, however, help
others renounce fanaticism and narrowness
through compassionate dialogue.

4.   Awareness of Suffering
Aware that looking deeply at the nature of
suffering can help me develop compassion and
find ways out of suffering, I am determined not
to avoid or close my eyes before suffering. I am
committed to finding ways, including personal
contact, images and sounds, to be with those
who suffer, so I can understand their situation
deeply and help them transform their suffering
into compassion, peace and joy.

5.   Simple, Healthy Living
Aware that true happiness is rooted in peace,
solidity, freedom and compassion, and not in
wealth or fame, I am determined not to take as
the aim of my life fame, profit, wealth or
sensual pleasure, nor to accumulate wealth
while millions are hungry and dying. I am
committed to living simply and sharing my
time, energy and material resources with those
in real need. I will practice mindful consuming,
not using alcohol, drugs or any other products
that bring toxins into my own body and the
collective body and consciousness.

6.   Dealing with Anger
Aware that anger blocks communication and
creates suffering, I am determined to take care
of the energy of anger when it arises and to
recognize and transform the seeds of anger that
lie deep in my consciousness. When anger
comes up, I am determined not to do or say
anything, but to practice mindful breathing or
mindful walking and acknowledge, embrace

and look deeply into my anger. I will learn to
look with the eyes of compassion on those
I think are the cause of my anger.

7.   Dwelling Happily in the Present Moment
Aware that life is available only in the present
moment and that it is possible to live happily in
the here and now, I am committed to training
myself to live deeply each moment of daily life.
I will try not to lose myself in dispersion or be
carried away by regrets about the past, worries
about the future, or craving, anger or jealousy
in the present. I will practice mindful breathing
to come back to what is happening in the
present moment. I am determined to learn the
art of mindful living by touching the wondrous,
refreshing and healing elements that are inside
and around me, and by nourishing seeds of joy,
peace, love and understanding in myself, thus
facilitating the work of transformation and
healing in my consciousness.

8.   Community and Communication
Aware that lack of communication always brings
separation and suffering, I am committed to
training myself in the practice of compassionate
listening and loving speech. I will learn to listen
deeply without judging or reacting and refrain
from uttering words that can create discord or
cause the community to break. I will make every
effort to keep communications open and to
reconcile and resolve all conflicts, however small.

9.   Truthful and Loving Speech
Aware that words can create suffering or happiness, I am committed to learning to speak
truthfully and constructively, using only words
that inspire hope and confidence. I am determined not to say untruthful things for the sake
of personal interest or to impress people, nor to
utter words that might cause division or hatred.
I will not spread news that I do not know to be
certain nor criticize or condemn things of
which I am not sure. I will do my best to speak
out about situations of injustice, even when
doing so may threaten my safety.

10.   Protecting the Sangha
Aware that the essence and aim of a Sangha is

the practice of understanding and compassion, I am determined not to use the Buddhist community for personal gain or profit or transform our community into a political instrument. A spiritual community should, however, take a clear stand against oppression and injustice and should strive to change the situation without engaging in partisan conflicts.

11. Right Livelihood

Aware that great violence and injustice have been done to the environment and society, I am committed not to live with a vocation that is harmful to humans and nature. I will do my best to select a livelihood that helps realize my ideal of understanding and compassion. Aware of global economic, political and social realities, I will behave responsibly as a consumer and as a citizen, not investing in companies that deprive others of their chance to live.

12. Reverence for Life

Aware that much suffering is caused by war and conflict, I am determined to cultivate nonviolence, understanding and compassion in my daily life, to promote peace education, mindful mediation and reconciliation, within families, communities, nations and in the world. I am determined not to kill and not to let others kill. I will diligently practice deep looking with my Sangha to discover better ways to protect life and prevent war.

13. Generosity

Aware of the suffering caused by exploitation, social injustice, stealing and oppression, I am committed to cultivating loving kindness and

learning ways to work for the well-being of people, animals, plants and minerals. I will practice generosity by sharing my time, energy and material resources with those who are in need. I am determined not to steal and not to possess anything that should belong to others. I will respect the property of others, but will try to prevent others from profiting from human suffering or the suffering of other beings.

14. Right Sexual Conduct (for lay members[57])

Aware that sexual relations motivated by craving cannot dissipate the feeling of loneliness but will create more suffering, frustration and isolation, I am determined not to engage in sexual relations without mutual understanding, love and a long-term commitment. In sexual relations, I must be aware of future suffering that may be caused. I know that to preserve the happiness of myself and others, I must respect the rights and commitments of myself and others. I will do everything in my power to protect children from sexual abuse and to protect couples and families from being broken by sexual misconduct. I will treat my body with respect and preserve my vital energies (sexual, breath, spirit) for the realization of my bodhisattva ideal. I will be fully aware of the responsibility for bringing new lives in the world, and will meditate on the world into which we are bringing new beings.

---

[57] *for lay members:* What follows here is a statement of sexual morality for lay members; monks are to be celibate. The thirteen other sections apply to monks as well as laity.

GLOSSARY

Abhidhamma [ahb-hee-DAHM-muh] ***Pitaka*** "Special Teaching Basket"; the third basket of the Theravadin canon; it contains seven treatises based on the teachings of Buddha (Sanskrit: *Abhidharma*).

Arhat [AHR-haht] "Worthy One"; a title given to a person who achieves enlightenment (Sanskrit: *Arhant*).

bodhisattva [bohd-hee-SAHT-vuh] a person who comes very close to achieving Buddha nature [enlightenment] but postpones it for the sake of helping others to achieve it.

Buddha [BUHD-ah, rhymes with "could-a"] a person who has reached enlightenment; although Gotama is the Buddha par excellence, the term applies to all individuals who attain this state.

dhamma [DAH-muh] teaching, path, way (Sanskrit: *dharma*).

Jatakas [JAH-tah-kuhs] "Lives"; the book of tales of Gotama Buddha's previous lives.

sutta [SUH-tuh] a writing, a scripture (Sanskrit: *Sutra*).

Sutta Pitaka "Discourse Basket"; the second basket of the Theravadin canon; it features the basic teachings of Buddhism (Sanskrit: *Sutra Pitaka*).

Tathagata [tah-THAH-gah-tuh] "One who has come [or "gone"] thus"; a person who has achieved enlightenment.

Tipitaka [tih-pee-TAH-kuh] "Three Baskets"; the main internal divisions of the Theravadin canon (Sanskrit: *Tripitaka*).

Vinaya [vih-NIGH-yuh] *Pitaka* "Discipline Basket"; the first basket of the Theravadin canon; it deals with the rules of monastic life.

QUESTIONS FOR STUDY AND DISCUSSION

1. What are the main features of the Theravadin scripture canon?

2. How is the life of Gotama Buddha an example for all Buddhists? Is it true to say that most of Buddhism is founded on the life of Gotama?

3. In what sense are the Four Noble Truths the essence of Buddhism?

4. What are the characteristics of monasticism as described in Buddhist scripture?

5. To what degree is Buddhism a religion made for monastics?

6. How is the role of women in Buddhism described in its scripture? Consider especially the role of nuns.

7. In what ways do the scriptures reflect the basic differences and similarities between southern (Theravada) and northern (Mahayana) Buddhism? Consider both canon and content.

8. Based on your understanding of Buddhist scripture, how would you describe Nirvana?

9. What are some basic similarities and differences between Hinduism and Buddhism?

SCRIPTURES IN FILM

Although the life of Gotama Buddha has great meaning as a narrative for Buddhists and for many other people, no feature film has been made of his life. Martin Meissonier's 2001 film *Life of Buddha* is a blend of documentary and drama. For a film that tells the story of Buddha in tandem with a search for a new Tibetan leader that leads to the United States, see *Little Buddha* (1993, rated PG), directed by Bernardo Bertolucci and starring Keanu Reeves. Two films made in 1997 and rated PG-13 tell the story of the current Dalai Lama. The better one is *Kundun,* directed by Martin Scorsese; the other is *Seven Years in Tibet,* directed by Jean-Jacque Annaud and starring Brad Pitt.

SUGGESTIONS FOR FURTHER READING

Primary Readings

Wisdom Publications (www.wisdompubs.org) is a source for many important Theravada and Tibetan texts. See also the new, "BDK English Tripitaka" series of key texts from the Chinese/Japanese canon published by the Numata Center for Buddhist Translation and Research. The fullest and most accessible collection of Buddhist scripture in English translation is the *Sacred Books of the East* series. Its vol. 10 contains the *Dhammapada,* trans. F. Max Müller, and the *Sutta-Nipata,* trans. V. Fausboll; vol. 11, various suttas, trans. T. W. Rhys Davids; vols. 13, 17, and 20, the most important *Vinaya* texts, trans. T. W. Rhys Davids and H. Oldenberg; vol. 19, a translation of the Chinese version of the *Acts of the Buddha;* vol. 21, the *Lotus Sutra,* trans. H. Kern; vols. 35 and 36, the *Questions of King Milinda;* and vol. 49, various Mahayana texts, prominently the *Acts of the Buddha,* trans. E. B. Cowell, F. Max Müller, and J. Takakusu.

E. Conze, *Buddhist Scriptures.* London: Penguin, 1959. An excellent anthology by a leading expert on Buddhism.

W. T. de Bary, *The Buddhist Tradition in India, China and Japan.* New York: Vantage Books, 1972. The finest of all the anthologies of the three major traditions of Buddhism.

J. Strong, *The Experience of Buddhism: Sources and Interpretations.* Belmont, CA: Wadsworth, 1995. A comprehensive anthology of Buddhist scripture and other literature.

Secondary Readings

N. S. Barnes, "[Women in] Buddhism." In A. Sharma, ed., *Women in World Religions.* Albany: State University of New York Press, 1987. Gives good attention to the historical witness of Buddhist scriptures to the role of women.

M. Levering, "Scripture and Its Reception: A Buddhist Case." In Levering, ed., *Rethinking Scripture: Essays from a Comparative Perspective.* Albany: State University of New York Press, 1989, pp. 58–101. A fascinating glimpse of the use of scripture in a Buddhist nunnery.

D. S. Lopez Jr., *Elaborations on Emptiness: Uses of the Heart Sutra.* Princeton: Princeton University Press, 1996. Explores the philosophical and ritual uses of this most important text.

R. A. Ray, "Buddhism: Sacred Text Written and Realized." In F. M. Denny and R. L. Taylor, eds., *The Holy Book in Comparative Perspective.* Columbia: University of South Carolina Press, 1985. Gives very good attention to orality.

K. A. Tsai, *Lives of the Nuns: Biographies of Chinese Buddhist Nuns from the Fourth to Sixth Centuries.* Honolulu: University Press of Hawaii, 1995. A translation of and commentary on a Chinese book written to demonstrate the power of Buddhist scripture in the lives of female monastics.

Illustrated Folio from a Jaina **Kalpa Sutra** *Palm-Leaf Manuscript*
This thirteenth-century manuscript shows a Shvetambara monk sitting cross-legged and preaching to a prince, who raises his hands in reverence; the scriptures are open before them on a reading stand. Note the hole for threading the binding string at the center of the folio. *Credit:* Edwin Binney 3d Collection, copyright © 2005, San Diego Museum of Art.

CHAPTER FOUR

Jainism

❖ A Jaina man makes his way into a temple in Calcutta. He stands reverently before a life-sized statue of a naked man who in ancient times attained Nirvana. As other worshippers walk respectfully around the statue several times, he stands still at its base and reads from the Jaina scriptures.

❖ A group of Jaina nuns walks slowly and carefully down a dirt road in northern India. Dressed in white, they have muslin cloths over their mouths to keep out flying insects. They use small brooms to gently sweep the ground in front of them as they walk, looking for even the smallest visible creatures. They are practicing one of the most important of their vows, noninjury to any living thing.

❖ In the streets of Bombay, two men come along carrying between them a light cot alive with bedbugs. They stop before the door of a Jaina household and cry, "Who will feed the bugs?" Someone tosses a coin from a window, and one of the men places himself carefully on the bed, offering himself as a living grazing ground to his fellow beings. The donor of the coin gains credit, and the man on the cot gains the coin.

INTRODUCTION

Jainism was founded by Mahavira (Great Hero) in the sixth century B.C.E. Mahavira taught a stricter version of the Hindu Upanishadic way, giving special emphasis to **ahimsa** [ah-HIM-suh], "noninjury" to all living beings. Rejecting belief in a supreme god, Jains seek release from endless reincarnation through a life of strict self-denial. Four million Jains in India have had an influence all out of proportion to their comparatively small numbers. Gandhi, for example, drew inspiration from their teaching of nonviolence. The Jaina scriptures afford an excellent glimpse into this tenacious religion, especially its main teachings and monastic life.

Overview of Structure

Jaina scripture is known in religious scholarship as the *Agama* [ah-GAH-muh], "Tradition." Most Jains call it the *Siddhanta* [sid-DAHN-tuh], "Doctrine." The two main branches of Jainism, the Shvetambaras and the Digambaras, share a few books but for the most part have different canons. Shvetambara ("white-clad" monks) is the larger group. It teaches that a woman can achieve Nirvana without having to be reborn as a man; thus this group has an order of nuns. Digambara ("sky-clad" or naked monks) teaches that women cannot achieve Nirvana.

The Shvetambara canon is commonly said by Western scholars to have forty-five books in six sections: *Angas* [AHN-guhs] (Limbs), *Upangas* (sub-*Angas*), *Prakirnakas* (mixed texts), *Chedasutras* (on authority and discipline), *Culikasutras* (Appendices), and *Mulasutras* ("basic texts"). The *Angas* are the oldest part of the canon. The first *Anga* is the *Acaranga Sutra,* containing the most reliable Jaina story of Mahavira and laws for monks and nuns. The second *Anga* is the *Sutrakritanga,* which contains the main Jaina teachings. The best-known *Mulasutra* is the *Uttaradhyayana Sutra,* which contains teachings Jains believe to be the last words of Mahavira. Besides these books, Jains also say that their original and pure teachings were contained in fourteen *Purvas* (Foundations), now all lost. The difficulties among the two sects and within each sect's canon are traced to the loss of these books. (The smallest of the Jaina sects, the Sthanakavasis, denies the existence of any scripture.)

The Digambaras accept as canonical the ancient *Purvas* that survive. They also accept the **Prakaranas** [prah-KAR-ah-nuhs], which form the main part of their canon: the *Mulacara* (on conduct), the *Samayasara* (on doctrine), the *Pravancanasara* (teaching), and the *Aradhana* (Accomplishment). They also treat as scripture many scholastic commentaries on the scriptures (*anuyoga*), which range from the first to the ninth centuries C.E. Both Jaina groups accept the important *Tattvarthadhigama Sutra* (Book for Attaining the Meaning of Principles) by Umasvamin, the first work on Jaina philosophy to be written in Sanskrit. The fixing of the number of Shvetambara texts at forty-five, and their subdivision into six groups, was largely the work of the nineteenth-century German scholar Georg Buhler. Since the 1970s, this partition has been called into question as simplistic and not reflecting actual Jaina usage. Kendall Folkert, for example, states, "When one asks contemporary Jains what their scriptures are, one receives widely varying answers, responses that vary not because of ignorance, but because there does not appear to be a wholly accepted body of scripture that is of equal value to the entire community." Folkert also notes that Digambaras sometimes accept Shvetambara texts.[1]

The *Agama* discusses a vast number of subjects in books written by many Jaina leaders over a long period. Some of it is in prose, some in verse, and some in mixed prose and verse. Its content, though frequently repetitious and diffuse, at times is succinct and systematic.

Origin, Development, and Use

Jains believe that when Mahavira achieved Nirvana, he emitted a "sacred sound" that his followers translated into words. Thus the authority for the most ancient scriptures of both Jaina sects is Mahavira himself, but (in typical Indian fashion) he is not thought to have written these scriptures. Some of them claim to be speeches given by Mahavira to Gautama Indrabhuti, whose disciple Sudharman gave them in turn to his pupil Gambusvamin. The types of literature mentioned earlier developed over time, all of them handed on orally in the monastic community until about 500 C.E., when they were edited and written down.

---

[1] K. W. Folkert, "The 'Canons' of 'Scripture,'" in M. Levering, ed. *Rethinking Scripture: Essays from a Comparative Perspective* (Albany: State University of New York Press, 1989), p. 175.

Like Theravada Buddhism, which it resembles, Jainism has put monks in control of the development and use of its scriptures. Mahavira gave the holy teaching as an ascetic. He gave it to his monk followers, who passed it down for a thousand years until other monks wrote it down. Thus the content of Jaina scripture is dominated by monastic teachings, ideals, and rules. The *Agama* was always intended not for a popular audience but for monks and, to a much lesser degree, nuns. These monks and nuns have the time to study it, learn it, and teach it to one another. Typically, a monk studies the four *Mulasutras* at the beginning of his career. If he masters them, he goes on to other more difficult texts and can perhaps become one of the highly respected monks who is a teacher of scripture in the monastery. Study of scripture is commanded in the rules for monks, and knowledge derived from the sacred books is typically the first step to release. This monastic orientation of the scriptures explains to a large extent their repetition and the numerous lists of various items that make them especially difficult for the layperson to comprehend.

Nevertheless, the Jaina laity uses the scriptures extensively. Jains tend to be better educated than the average Indian, and their high literacy rates have made their scriptures accessible to believers, who read and reflect upon them in houses of worship. Usage at festivals is also striking. For example, the *Kalpa Sutra* is formally read aloud at Paryusana, the end-of-the-year festival of confession and rededication.

HISTORY

The Life of Mahavira*

This passage tells the story of Mahavira as an example for believers, and especially for monks and nuns, of one who has achieved Nirvana. Mahavira renounced the world, gave away his property, pulled out his hair, and finally starved himself to death. The gods who see and admire these feats are not supreme gods, and Mahavira shows himself superior to them as a jina [JEE-nuh], a "conqueror" who has achieved Nirvana. The Kalpa Sutra *contains a story of Mahavira with more legendary touches than this.*[2]

In that period, in that age, once upon a time, after the lapse of nine complete months and seven and a half days, in the first month of summer . . . on its thirteenth day . . . the Kshatriya woman Trisala, perfectly healthy herself, gave birth to a perfectly healthy boy, the Venerable Ascetic Mahavira.

In that night when the Kshatriya woman Trisala gave birth to the Venerable Ascetic Mahavira, there was a great divine, godly luster originated by descending and ascending gods and goddesses. They were of the four orders of Bhavanapatis, Vyantaras, Gyotishkas, and Vimanavasins. In the meeting of the gods their bustle amounted to confusion. In that night . . . the gods and goddesses rained down a great shower of nectar, sandal powder, flowers, gold, and pearls. In that night the gods and goddesses performed the customary ceremonies of auspiciousness and

Acaranga Sutra 2.15.6–9, 14, 16–20, 22–25, 27.

[2] All scripture selections in this chapter are taken, with editing, from Hermann Jacobi, *Jaina Sutras, Sacred Books of the East,* vols. 22, 45 (Oxford: Oxford University Press, 1884, 1895).

honor, and anointed Mahavira as a **Tirthankara** [tihr-TAHN-kah-ruh].[3] . . .

[14] Then the Venerable Ascetic Mahavira, after his intellect had developed and his childhood had gone, lived in the enjoyment of the allowed, noble fivefold joys and pleasures: sound, touch, taste, color, and smell. . . .

[16] The Venerable Ascetic Mahavira's parents were worshippers of Parsva and followers of the Sramanas.[4] For many years they were followers of the Sramanas, and for the sake of protecting the six classes of lives they observed, repented, confessed, and did penance for their sins. On a bed of Kusa-grass they rejected all food. Their bodies were dried up by their last mortification of the flesh, which is to end in death. Thus they died in the proper month and, leaving their bodies, were born as gods in Adbhuta Kalpa. Descending after the end of their allotted length of life, with their departing breath they will reach absolute perfection. They will reach wisdom, liberation, final Nirvana, and the end of all misery.[5]

In that period, in that age the Venerable Ascetic Mahavira . . . lived thirty years among the householders under the name of Videha. After his parents had gone to the worlds of the gods . . . he gave up his gold and silver, his troops and chariots. He distributed, portioned out, and gave away his valuable treasures consisting of riches, plants, gold, pearls, etc. He gave them to those who wanted to make presents to others. Thus he gave away his possessions for a whole year. In the first month of winter, in the first fortnight, in the dark fortnight of Margasiras, on its tenth day, while the moon was in conjunction with Uttaraphalguni, he decided to retire from the world. . . .

Then the four orders of gods awakened the best of Jinas, the Venerable Mahavira, saying, "**Arhat** [AHR-haht]![6] Propagate the religion which is a blessing to all creatures in the world!" When the gods and goddesses . . . had become aware of the Venerable Ascetic Mahavira's intention to retire from the world, they assumed their proper form, dress, and banners. They ascended their own vehicles and chariots with their proper pomp and splendor, together with their whole retinue. Rejecting all large matter, they retained only tiny matter.[7] Then they rose up, and with that excellent, quick, swift, rapid, divine motion of the gods, they came down again. They crossed numberless continents and oceans till they arrived in Gambudvipa at the northern Kshatriya part of the place called Kundapura. In the northeastern quarter of it they suddenly halted. . . .

At that period, in that age, in the first month of winter . . . on its tenth day . . . fasting three days without taking water, having put on one garment, the Venerable Ascetic Mahavira with a train of gods, men, and Asuras[8] left the northern Kshatriya part of the place Kundapura by the high road for the park Gnatri Shanda. There, just at the beginning of night, he caused his palanquin to stop quietly on a slightly raised untouched ground. He quietly descended from it, sat quietly on a throne with the face toward the east, and took off all his ornaments and finery.[9] . . .

When the Venerable Ascetic Mahavira had adopted the holy conduct which produced that state of soul in which the reward of former actions is temporarily counteracted, he reached the knowledge called Manahparyaya, by which he knew the thoughts of all thinking beings. . . .

---

[3] *Tirthankara:* "Ford-finder"; a person who goes across the river of the world's misery to Nirvana. Jains believe that Mahavira was the last of twenty-four Tirthankaras.

[4] *Sramanas:* ascetic renunciants.

[5] *Descending . . . misery:* They will achieve Nirvana in their next incarnation and be reborn no more.

[6] *Arhat:* "Worthy One," another name for a person who has reached Nirvana.

[7] *large matter . . . tiny matter:* The gods change their form to a more spiritual and less physical state.

[8] *Asuras:* spirits.

[9] *took off . . . finery:* He is not naked, for he wears a cloth underneath. This reflects the Shvetambara orientation of this book.

Then he formed the following resolution: "I shall for twelve years neglect my body and abandon the care of it. I shall with a right disposition bear, undergo, and suffer all calamities arising from divine powers, men or animals."

The Venerable Ascetic Mahavira formed this resolution. Neglecting his body, he arrived in the village Kummara when only one division of the day remained. Neglecting his body, the Venerable Ascetic Mahavira meditated on his Self in blameless lodgings, in blameless wandering, in restraint, in kindness, in avoidance of sinful influence, in a chaste life, in patience, in freedom from passion, in contentment, in control, and in correctness. All the while he practiced religious postures and acts. He walked the path of Nirvana and liberation, which is the fruit of good conduct. With right disposition he endured, sustained, and suffered all calamities arising from divine powers, men, and animals. With undisturbed and unaffected mind, he was careful in body, speech, and mind.

The Venerable Ascetic Mahavira spent twelve years in this way of life. During the thirteenth year in the second month of summer . . . on its tenth day, on the northern bank of the river Rigupalika, in the field of the householder Samaga, in a north-eastern direction from an old temple, not far from a Sal tree, in a squatting position with joined heels exposing himself to the heat of the sun, with the knees high and the head low, in deep meditation, in the midst of abstract meditation, he reached Nirvana. He reached the full, unobstructed, unimpeded, infinite, and supreme knowledge and intuition called Kevala.[10]

[25] When the Venerable One had become an Arhat and Jina, he was a Kevalin, omniscient and comprehending all objects. He knew all conditions of the world, of gods, men, and demons. He knew from where they come, where they go, whether they are born as men or animals, or become gods or demons. He knew their food, drink, doings, desires, open and secret deeds, their conversation and gossip, and the thoughts of their minds. He saw and knew all conditions in the whole world of all living beings. . . . [27] On the day when the Venerable Ascetic Mahavira had reached the highest knowledge and intuition, he reflected on himself and the world. First he taught the Law to the gods, and then to men.

---

[10] *Kevala:* knowledge that frees a person from the cycle of rebirth.

TEACHING

The World Is Uncreated*

This passage considers some of the Hindu arguments for the existence of personal creators of the universe, and it rejects them in favor of classic Jaina atheism. Therefore, all persons are "on their own" in their search for liberation.

Foolish people say that a Creator made the world. The teaching that the world was created is wrong, and should be rejected. If God created the world, where was he before creation? If you say he was transcendent then, and needed no support, where is he now?

No single being had the skill to make this world. Besides, how can a spiritual god create that which is material? How could God have made the world without any raw material? . . .

Mahapurana 4.16–31, 38–40.

If you say that this raw material arose naturally you fall into another error. For the whole universe might thus have been its own creator and have arisen naturally in the same way.

If God created the world by an act of his own will, without any raw material, then the world is just his will and nothing else—and who will believe this nonsense? If he is ever perfect and complete, how could the will to create have arisen in him? If, on the other hand, he is not perfect, he could no more create the universe than a potter could. If he is formless, actionless, and all-embracing, how could he have created the world? Such a soul, devoid of all modality, would have no desire to create anything.

If he is perfect, he does not strive for the three goals of humanity, so what advantage would be gained by creating the universe? If you say that he created for no purpose, because it was his nature to do so, then God is pointless. If he created in some kind of sport, it was the sport of a foolish child, leading to trouble. . . .

If God made the world out of love for living things and need of them, why did he not make creation wholly blissful, free from misfortune?

If he were transcendent he would not create, for he would be free. Nor would he create if involved in transmigration, for then he would not be almighty.

So the doctrine that the world was created by God makes no sense at all. God commits great sin in killing the children that he himself created. If you say that he kills only to destroy evil beings, why did he create such beings in the first place? . . . Good men should combat the believer in divine creation, who is maddened by an evil doctrine. Know that the world is uncreated, as time itself is, without beginning and end. . . . It is uncreated and indestructible, it endures through the compulsion of its own nature.

The Causes of Sin*

This reading teaches the understanding of all that hurts other beings and renunciation of it. The first section deals with reincarnation, the second with ahimsa as the path out of it.

O long-lived Gambusvamin! I Sudharman[11] have heard the following discourse from the venerable Mahavira:

Many do not remember whether they have descended in an eastern direction when they were born in this world, or in a southern, or in a western, or in a northern direction. . . . Similarly, some do not know whether their soul is born repeatedly or not. They do not know what they were before, or what they will become after they die and leave this world. Now this is what one should know, either by one's own knowledge or through the instruction of the highest [i.e., a Tirthankara], or having heard it from others: what direction he descended. Similarly, some know that their soul is born repeatedly, that it arrives in this or that direction, whatever direction that may be. [5] He believes in soul, believes in the world, believes in reward, and believes in action (acknowledged to be our own doing in such judgments as these): "I did it"; "I shall cause another to do it"; "I shall allow another to do it." In the world, these are all the causes of sin, which must be comprehended and renounced. A man who does not comprehend and renounce the causes of sin is born repeatedly in many births, experiencing all painful feelings.... He who understands and renounces these causes of sin is called a karma-knowing sage. Thus I say.

Acaranga Sutra 1.1–2.
[11] *Gambusvamin:* the pupil of Sudharman.

[21] The living world is afflicted, miserable, difficult to instruct, and without insight. In this world full of pain, with beings suffering by their different acts, benighted people cause great pain. See! There are beings individually embodied.[12] See! Some men control themselves, while others only pretend to be houseless.[13] One destroys this earth-body[14] by bad and injurious acts. He hurts many other beings besides, through his doing acts relating to earth. About this the Revered One has taught the truth. For the sake of the splendor, honor, and glory of this life, for the sake of birth, death, and final liberation, for the removal of pain, man acts sinfully toward earth. He causes others to act so, and allows others to act so. This deprives him of happiness and perfect wisdom. He is informed about this when he has understood or heard, either from the Revered One or from the monks, the true faith. Some truly know this injuring to be bondage, delusion, death, and hell. A man is longing for this when he destroys this earth-body by bad, injurious acts. He destroys many other beings as well, through his deeds relating to earth. Thus I say.

---

[12] *beings individually embodied:* Individual souls exist as absolute realities, not as a part of one world-soul.
[13] *pretend to be houseless:* unfaithful monks.
[14] *earth-body:* all lives composed of the elements of the earth.

Can Women Achieve Liberation?*

The two main groups of Jains disagree on whether women are able to achieve liberation from continued reincarnation. The first section outlines the Shvetambara affirmation of this possibility; the second states the fuller Digambara denial. Notice how the argument turns on the issue of monastic clothing that separates the two groups.

[*Strinirvana-pariccheda* 2, 4] Women can be liberated, because women possess all the causes necessary for it. The cause of liberation is fulfillment of the three jewels [correct view, correct knowledge, and correct conduct], and this is not incompatible with being a woman. So, nuns are able to understand the Jina's words, have faith in them, and practice them faultlessly. Therefore, they can attain liberations as women. Someone might say that women cannot attain release because they wear clothes. . . . The Lord Arhats, our guides for the path to nirvana, taught that women must wear clothes and prohibited them from renouncing clothes. Therefore it follows that clothes are necessary for release, like a whisk broom is necessary to protect small creatures from violence.

[*Sutraprabrita* 1.22–26] The [Shvetambara] nun eats food only once a day, but wears a piece of clothing; the novice nun wears two pieces of clothing. In the teaching of the Jina, no person who wears clothing attains liberation, even if that person is a Tirthankara. The path to liberation is that of nakedness, and all other paths are wrong. The sutras teach that the genital organs of women, the area between their breasts, their navels and armpits have very small living beings, so how can women be ordained [since the care of their bodies would harm these beings]? If a woman is pure because of correct views, they become associated with the path. But even if she practices correct, ascetic conduct, nowhere in the teaching is it said that women can be ordained. Women do not have purity of mind, and their minds are slack. Since they get their period each month, they have no meditation free from anxiety.

---

* *Strinirvana-pariccheda* 2, 4; *Sutraprabrita* 1.22–26.

The World Is Full of Suffering*

This eloquent passage is spoken by Prince Mrigaputra to his parents. Seeking by a series of striking metaphors to persuade them to become monks, he impresses them with the horrors of constant suffering born of constant reincarnation.

From clubs and knives, stakes and maces, breaking my limbs, an infinite number of times I
  have suffered without hope.
By sharp-edged razors, by knives and shears,
  many times I have been drawn and quartered, torn apart and skinned.
Helpless in snares and traps, like a deer, I have
  been caught and bound and fastened, and
  often I have been killed.
A helpless fish, I have been caught with hooks
  and nets; An infinite number of times I have
  been killed and scraped, split and gutted.
A bird, I have been caught by hawks or trapped
  in nets,
Or trapped by birdlime, and I have been killed
  an infinite number of times.
A tree, with axes and saws by the carpenters an
  infinite number of times I have been felled,
  stripped of my bark, cut up, and sawn into
  planks.
As iron, with hammer and tongs by blacksmiths, an infinite number of times I have
  been struck and beaten, split and filed. . . .
Ever afraid, trembling, in pain and suffering,
  I have felt the greatest sorrow and agony.
In every kind of existence I have suffered pains
  that have known no reprieve for a moment.

---

* *Uttaradhyayana Sutra* 19.61–67, 71, 74.

The Road to Final Deliverance**

This passage presents a summary of the way to salvation. The four main steps are by knowledge, faith, conduct, and ascetic practice ("austerities"). Notice the Indian penchant to number things, useful in monastic teaching.

Learn the true road leading to final deliverance, which the Jinas have taught. It depends on four causes and is characterized by right knowledge and faith. Right knowledge, faith, conduct, and austerities—this is the road taught by the Jinas who possess the best knowledge. . . . Beings who follow this road will obtain blessedness.

Knowledge is fivefold: (1) knowledge derived from the sacred books; (2) perception; (3) supernatural knowledge; (4) knowledge of the thoughts of other people; (5) the highest, unlimited knowledge. [5] This is the fivefold knowledge. The wise ones have taught the knowledge of substances, qualities, and all developments. . . .

Dharma, Adharma,[15] space, time, matter, and souls are the six kinds of substances. They make up this world, as has been taught by the Jinas who possess the best knowledge. Dharma, Adharma, and space are each one substance only; but time, matter, and souls are an infinite number of substances. The characteristic of Dharma is motion, that of Adharma

---

** *Uttaradhyayana Sutra* 28.
[15] *Dharma, Adharma:* good and evil, respectively.

immobility, and that of space, which contains all other substances, is to make room (for everything).

[10] The characteristic of time is duration, that of soul the realization of knowledge, faith, happiness, and misery. The characteristic of Soul is knowledge, faith, conduct, austerities, energy, and realization of its developments. The characteristic of matter is sound, darkness, luster, light, shade, sunshine, color, taste, smell, and touch. The characteristic of development is singleness, separateness, number, form, conjunction, and disjunction.

The nine truths are (1) soul; (2) the inanimate things; (3) the binding of the soul by karma;[16] (4) merit; (5) demerit; (6) that which causes the soul to be affected by sins; (7) the prevention of asrava by watchfulness; (8) the annihilation of karma; (9) final deliverance. He who truly believes the true teaching of the fundamental truths possesses righteousness.

Faith is produced by (1) nature; (2) instruction; (3) command; (4) study of the Sutras; (5) suggestion; (6) comprehension of the meaning of the sacred lore; (7) complete course of study; (8) religious exercise; (9) brief exposition; (10) the Law.

He who believes by nature truly comprehends, by a spontaneous effort of his mind, the nature of the soul, inanimate things, merit, and demerit. He puts an end to sinful influences. He who spontaneously believes the four truths (explicitly mentioned in the last verse), which the Jinas have taught, thinking they are of this and not of a different nature, believes by nature. But he who believes these truths, having learned them from somebody else, either a Khadmastha[17] or a Jina, believes by instruction. [20] He who has gotten rid of love, hate, delusion, and ignorance, and believes because he is told to do so, believes by command. He who obtains righteousness by the study of the Sutras, either *Angas* or other works, believes by the study of Sutras. He who by correctly comprehending one truth arrives at the comprehension of more—just as a drop of oil expands on the surface of water—believes by suggestion. He who truly knows the sacred lore,

namely the eleven *Angas,* the *Prakaranas,* and the *Drishtivada,* believes by the comprehension of the sacred lore. He who understands the true nature of all substances by means of all proofs and nayas,[18] believes by a complete course of study.

[25] He who sincerely performs all duties implied by right knowledge, faith, and conduct, by asceticism and discipline, and by all Samitis and Guptis,[19] believes by religious exercise. He who holds no wrong doctrines though he is not versed in the sacred doctrines nor acquainted with other systems, believes by brief exposition. He who believes in the truth of the realities, the Sutras, and conduct, as it has been explained by the Jinas, believes by the Law.

Right belief depends on the acquaintance with truth, on the devotion to those who know the truth, and on the avoiding of schismatic and heretical tenets. There is no right conduct without right belief, and it must be cultivated for obtaining right faith. Righteousness and conduct originate together, or righteousness precedes conduct. [30] Without faith there is no knowledge, without knowledge there is no virtuous conduct, without virtues there is no deliverance, and without deliverance there is no perfection.

The excellence of faith depends on the following eight points: (1) that one has no doubts (about the truth of the tenets); (2) that one has no preference (for heretical tenets); (3) that one does not doubt its saving qualities; (4) that one is not shaken

---

[16] *karma:* fruit of evil deeds, a physical accretion on the soul.
[17] *Khadmastha:* a person who is advanced in knowledge but not to the full knowledge of Nirvana.
[18] *nayas:* literally, "leadings," probably referring to logical arguments.
[19] The five *Samitis,* rules for monks, are how to walk in a way noninjurious to other beings; how to speak; how to beg for food; how to excrete bodily wastes in a noninjurious manner; and how to use the few possessions allowed a monk. The three *Guptis* regulate thought, speech, and the body.

in the right belief (because heretical sects are more prosperous); (5) that one praises the pious; (6) that one encourages weak brethren; (7) that one supports or loves the confessors of the Law; (8) that one tries to exalt it.

Conduct that produces the destruction of all karma is (1) the avoidance of everything sinful; (2) the initiation of a novice; (3) purity produced by peculiar austerities; (4) reduction of desire; (5) annihilation of sinfulness according to the precepts of the Arhats, as well in the case of a Khadmastha as of a Jina.

Austerities are twofold, external and internal. Both external and internal austerities are sixfold. By knowledge one knows things, by faith one believes in them, by conduct one gets freedom from karma, and by austerities one reaches purity. Having by control and austerities destroyed their karma, great sages go to perfection and get rid of all misery. Thus I say.

ETHICS

Ahimsa*

This selection details the duty of noninjury, the first vow of monks. Noninjury is one of the leading duties of the laity as well. For example, observant Jains do not eat after sunset because they are less able to see any insects then.

These classes of living beings have been declared by the Jinas: earth, water, fire, wind; grass, trees, and plants; and the moving beings, both the egg-bearing and those that bear live offspring, those generated from dirt and those generated in fluids. Know and understand that they all desire happiness. By hurting these beings, people do harm to their own souls and will repeatedly be born as one of them.

Every being born high or low in the scale of the living creation, among movable and immovable beings, will meet with its death. Whatever sins the evildoer commits in every birth, for them he must die. In this world or in the next the sinners suffer themselves what they have inflicted on other beings, a hundred times, or suffer other punishment. Living in the Samsara[20] they always acquire new karma and suffer for their misdeeds.

[5] Some leave their mother and father to live as Sramanas, but they use fire. The prophet [Mahavira] says, "People who kill beings for their own pleasure are wicked." He who lights a fire kills living beings; he who extinguishes it kills the fire. Therefore a wise man who well considers the Law should light no fire. Earth contains life, and water contains life; jumping or flying insects fall in the fire; dirt-born vermin and beings live in wood. All these beings are burned by lighting a fire.

Plants are beings that have a natural development. Their bodies require nourishment, and they all have their individual life. Reckless men who cut them down for their own pleasure destroy many living beings. By destroying plants, when young or grown up, a careless man does harm to his own soul. The prophet says, "People who destroy plants for their own pleasure are wicked."

---

*Sutrakritanga 1.7.1–9.
[20] *Samsara:* the wheel of rebirth.

Rules for Monastic Life*

Rules for both conduct and thought govern the life of a monk or a nun. Although the passage speaks of "compassion for living things" as a motivation for noninjury, the main motivation is less altruistic—to avoid as much as possible one's collection of karma.

Learn from me, with attentive minds, the road shown by the wise ones. This road leads a monk who follows it to the end of all misery.

Giving up the life in a house, and taking the vow to wander, a sage should know and renounce those attachments that take hold of men. A restrained monk should abstain from killing, lying, stealing, and sexual intercourse, from desire, love, and greed.

Even in his thoughts, a monk should not long for a pleasant painted house filled with the fragrance of garlands and frankincense, secured by doors, and decorated with a white ceiling-cloth. [5] For in such a dwelling a monk will find it difficult to prevent his senses from increased desire and passion. He should be content to live on a burial-place, in a deserted house, below a tree, in solitude, or in a place that had been prepared for the sake of somebody else. A well-controlled monk should live in a pure place that is not too crowded, and where no women live. He should not build a house, nor cause others to build one. Many living beings both movable and immovable, both tiny and large, are killed when a house is being built. Therefore, a monk should abstain from building a house.

[10] The same holds good with the cooking of food and drink, or with one's causing them to be cooked. Out of compassion for living beings one should not cook or cause another to cook. Beings which live in water, in plants, or in earth and wood are destroyed in food and drink.

Therefore, a monk should cause nobody to cook. Nothing is so dangerous as fire, for it spreads in all directions and is able to destroy many beings. One should not light a fire.

Even in his thoughts a monk should not long for gold and silver. Indifferent alike to dirt and gold, he abstains from buying and selling. If he buys, he becomes a buyer; if he sells, he becomes a merchant. A monk is not to engage in buying and selling. [15] A monk who is to live on alms should beg and not buy. Buying and selling is a great sin; but to live on alms is befitting. He should collect his alms in small parts according to the Sutras and to avoid faults. A monk should contentedly go on his begging-tour, whether he gets alms or not.

A great sage should eat not for the sake of the pleasant taste of the food but only for the sustenance of life. He should not be dainty or eager for good food; he should restrain his tongue and be without desire. Even in his thoughts he should not desire to be presented with flowers, to be offered a seat, to be eloquently greeted, to be offered presents, or to get a magnificent welcome and treatment.[21] He should meditate on true things only, committing no sins and having no property.

He should walk about with no care for his body until his end draws near. [20] Rejecting food when the time of his death is near, and leaving the human body, he becomes his own master and is liberated from misery. Without property, without egoism, free from passions . . . he obtains absolute knowledge and reaches eternal blessedness. Thus I say.

---

*Uttaradhyayana Sutra 35.
[21] *presented . . . treatment:* These usually come when a monk visits layfolk in public or in their homes.

The True Monk*

This passage repeats many of the rules mentioned previously, but in a more positive and winsome way. It receives its title from the repeated refrain "he is a true monk."

He who adopts the Law in the intention to live as a monk should live in company with other monks, upright, and free from desire. He should abandon his former connections, and not long for pleasures; he should wander about as an unknown beggar. Then he is a true monk.

He should live free from love, a model of righteousness, abstaining from sins, versed in the sacred lore, protecting his soul, wise, hardy, and observing everything. He who is attached to nothing is a true monk.

Ignorant of abuse and injury, a steadfast monk should be a model of righteousness, always protecting his soul, neither rash nor passionate. When he endures everything, then he is a true monk. He who is content with lowly beds and lodgings, bears heat and cold, flies and gnats, is neither rash nor passionate, and endures everything, he is a true monk.

[5] He does not expect respectful treatment, nor hospitality, nor reverence, nor praises. He controls himself, keeps the vows, practices austerities, lives together with other monks, and meditates on his soul; this is a true monk. If he does not care for his life, or abandons every delusion, if he avoids men and women, always practices austerities, and does not betray any curiosity, then he is a true monk.

He who does not profess and live on divination from cuts and shreds, from sounds on the earth or in the air, from dreams, from diagrams, sticks, and properties of buildings, from changes in the body, from the meaning of the cries of animals, he is a true monk. He who does not praise or pay attention to the warriors, Ugras, princes, Brahmins, Bhogas, and artists of all sorts, who abstains from this, he is a true monk.

[10] He who does not, for earthly gain, improve his acquaintance with householders, with whom he fell in as a monk, or was in friendly relation before that time, he is a true monk. A Nirgrantha is forbidden to take a bed, lodging, drink, food, or any dainties and spices from householders, if they do not give it themselves. He who is not angry at such occasions is a true monk.

If a monk gets any food and drink, or dainties and spices, and does not feel compassion on a sick fellow-monk in thoughts, words, and deeds, then he is not a true monk. But if he has his thoughts, words, and acts under strict discipline, then he is a true monk. Dishwater, barley mush, cold sour gruel, water in which barley has been washed—such loathsome food and drink he should not despise, but call at the lowliest houses for alms; then he is a true monk. . . .

[15] He who understands all religious disputations, who lives with fellow-monks, who practices self-discipline, who meditates on his soul, who is wise, hardy, and observes everything, who is calm, and does not hurt anybody, he is a true monk.

He who, not living by any craft, without house, without friends, subduing his senses, free from all ties, sinless, and eating only a little, leaves the house and lives single, he is a true monk.

Thus I say.

---

* *Uttaradhyayana Sutra* 15.1–16.

ORGANIZATION

The Five Great Vows*

A monk or nun entering the life of renunciation takes these solemn, final vows. Notice that the vow of ahimsa comes first. The ideals of these vows are also influential among the laity, and they take "Lesser Vows" modeled on the full monastic vows but not as strict. Because of faithfulness to their vows, Jains have a strong reputation in India for truthfulness (vow 2 below) and honesty (vow 3).

The Venerable Ascetic Mahavira, endowed with the highest knowledge and intuition, taught the five great vows, with their clauses . . . to the Sramanas and Nirgranthas,[22] to Gautama, etc.

The first great vow, Sir, is this. I renounce all killing of living beings, whether tiny or large, whether movable or immovable. I myself shall not kill living beings nor cause others to do it, nor consent to it. . . .

The second great vow is this. I renounce all vices of lying speech arising from anger or greed or fear or mirth. I shall neither myself speak lies, nor cause others to speak lies, nor consent to the speaking of lies by others. . . .

The third great vow is this. I renounce all taking of anything not given, either in a village or a town or a wood, either of little or much, of small or great, of living or lifeless things. I shall neither take myself what is not given, nor cause others to take it, nor consent to their taking it. . . .

The fourth great vow is this. I renounce all sexual pleasures, either with gods or men or animals. I shall not give way to sensuality, nor cause others to give way to it, nor consent to their giving way. . . .

The fifth great vow is this. I renounce all attachments, whether little or much, small or great, living or lifeless. I myself shall not form such attachments, nor cause others to do so, nor consent to their doing so. As long as I live, I confess and blame, repent and remove myself [of these].

---

* *Acaranga Sutra* 2.15.i–v.

[22] *Sramanas and Nirgranthas:* Jaina monks.

LATER DEVELOPMENTS OF SCRIPTURAL THEMES

Stories from Jaina Commentaries**

The Shvetambara Jain stories illustrate in a popular way the basic teachings of the faith. The first passage illustrates the importance of renunciation. The second story comes from around the eleventh century C.E. and illustrates overcoming difficulties and attachments to become a monk.[23]

[The story of the Brahmin and his wife] After hearing the Law from an authentic elder, a

Brahmin and his wives gave up worldly life. They led a very rigorous religious life, but their love for each other did not leave them. One of the ladies still had some pride: she was a

---

** *Avasyaka* 1.484.11–485.13; *Mulasuddhiprakarana*, 179–180.

[23] From Phyllis Granoff, ed., *The Clever Adulteress and Other Stories* (Ontario: Mosaic Press, 1990). Translated by Nalini Balbir and Phyllis Granoff. Used by permission.

Brahmin indeed! After death they went to the world of the gods and enjoyed life for the life-time they had.

There was, on the other hand, the city of Ilavardhana which had Laa as its patron deity. The wife of a caravan-leader who had no child worshiped her. The former Brahmin fell from the world of the gods and was born as this lady's son. He was therefore given the name of Ilaputra. He studied the arts. As for the Brahmin's former wife, she was born in an acrobat's family.

Both the boy and the girl had now reached marriageable age. One day the boy fell in love with the girl's beauty. Though he asked for her, he did not get her. Her parents said, "We shall give you the equivalent of her weight in gold. She is our imperishable treasure. But if you set off on tour with us and learn our art, we shall give her to you." So Ilaputra set off on tour with them and learned their art. Then he was asked to give a show in front of the king on the occasion of a wedding-ceremony. The company went to Bernatada. The king attended the show together with his harem. Ilaputra was on the stage, but the king had eyes only for the girl. The king did not give any money. There was loud applause: "Acrobat," people said to Ilaputra, "Do a falling stunt."

On top of a bamboo there is a piece of wood. Two nails are fixed on it. The acrobat wears shoes which are pierced at the bottom. Then, holding a sword and a shield in his hands, he jumps into the sky. The nails should be fitted into the holes of the shoes by seven jumps forwards and backwards. If the acrobat fails, he falls down and is broken into pieces.

That was the feat Ilaputra did. The king went on gazing at the young girl. People created an uproar. Nobody gave any money since the king did not give anything. The king thought, "If this acrobat dies, the girl will be mine." So he said to Ilaputra, "I did not see. Do it again." The boy did it again, but again the king did not see. He did it a third time, a fourth time he was asked to do it again. The audience was disgusted. Standing on the top of the bamboo, Ilaputra

thought, "Enough of worldly pleasures! This king is not even satisfied with so many wives. He wants to attach himself to this actress, and in order to fulfill his desire he wants to kill me." He was ready to give up worldly life.

One day in a merchant's house he saw some monks who were receiving alms from fully adorned ladies. He noticed that the monks looked very peaceful, and said, "Happy are those who have no more desire for sexual enjoyments. I was a merchant's son. See what condition I have reached after having left my family!" In that very place, having achieved unconcern for worldly objects, he got Omniscience. The unconcern of the girl too should be fully described, and also that of the chief queen. The king, too, felt remorse. All four became Omniscient and Emancipated.

[The Story of the Merchant Abhinava] There is in our own continent of Jambudvipa, in the very center of the area known as Southern Bharata, an ancient city named Vesali, which was exceedingly famous. There once reigned King Cedaa, who like some mythical beast that slays the proud lion of the jungle, had slain his proud and mighty enemies. He was lord over eighteen vassal kings. And there dwelt in that city two merchants. One was named Junnasetthi, "The Old Merchant," and the other was called Ahinavasetthi, "The Young Merchant." The first was as poor as poor can be, while the other was as rich as rich can be.

Now one day the lord of the triple world, the lord of heaven, earth and the nether world, the Jina Mahavira, came into that city in the course of his monastic wanderings. This was in the time before he had reached his state of perfect enlightenment. And one night the rains began. Mahavira took refuge in some shelter there and assumed a posture of meditation that he would keep for the four months of the rainy season.

The old merchant saw him there and his heart was filled with feelings of awe and reverence. Waves of joy flowed over his whole body and he proclaimed, "Today truly my whole life's purpose is fulfilled. Today my life indeed seems worth living. For today I can bow down to the feet of the Blessed One, which are like pure water to cleanse the dirt of sin." And with feelings like this every day he went to bow down to the feet of the Blessed One. He would stay a few moments each day, with his hands joined together and held over his head in a gesture of reverence, and worship the Blessed One. And he thought, "Now I come here every day and it seems that the Blessed One never moves from this place. He is every day engaged in meditating, his body unmoving, as he observes the fast for four months of the rainy season. If only the Blessed One would break his fast at my house when the time comes, then truly I would consider myself to be the most fortunate man in the world."

And while he occupied himself with pious thoughts like these, in no time at all the four months of the rainy season passed and there came the day for the Blessed One to break his fast. Bowing down to the Blessed One the old merchant said, "Friend to all the world! Lord of Ascetics! Blessed One, bless me today by breaking your fast at my house." And with these words he returned home. There he made everything ready and he waited expectantly looking at the door. He kept thinking to himself all the while, "The Blessed One is coming, the Blessed One is coming, and I shall fulfill my every desire by giving him food to break his fast. If the Lord of the Inas comes to my house, then I shall have crossed this ocean of rebirths, whose waves are our sufferings, and in whose depths lurk countless misfortunes like so many sharks."

As his desire for the highest bliss grew and grew and waves of joy coursed through his body while he waited there, the Jina passed him by and went into the house of the young merchant. And the young merchant, recalling the teaching that a gift given to the proper recipient leads to fruits right in that very same lifetime, fed the Blessed One. And at the very moment that he did so the five marvelous signs appeared on account of the power of that gift that was given to such a worthy person as Mahavira. A rain of jewels fell from the sky, while the Gods waved

the ends of their robes in congratulations. The Gods beat their heavenly drums and a fragrant perfumed rain fell from the sky. Heavenly voices could be heard, praising the gift.

Now when the old merchant heard the sound of the heavenly drums beating he wondered what had happened. Someone then told him, "The Blessed One has been given food to break his fast." His earlier religious resolve was thus broken. In the meantime the Blessed One continued on his wanderings, leaving that city.

Now it chanced that the Jina Parsvanatha came there. All of the townspeople reverently rushed out to greet the Jina. And that Blessed One discoursed on the Jain religion, which is like a boat for fortunate souls, ferrying them across the ocean of rebirths. "Listen, all of you fortunate souls who are destined to achieve final release! The Jain faith alone is your refuge in this cycle of rebirths. All of the rest is mere delusion. All material prosperity, every worldly joy comes from this religion if it is well practiced. Indeed it leads even to heaven and final release. And its duties are said by the Jinas to be fourfold, giving to others, observing a moral life, practicing austerities, and engaging in right meditation. And so you should practice these things, particularly giving, so that you may obtain the bliss of true peace."

Now at that time, all the townspeople, who had been amazed by the great merit that the young merchant obviously had, seeing their chance, humbly asked the Blessed One: "Blessed One! Right now, here in this city, who is the person who has the most merit?" And at that the Blessed One pronounced the old merchant to have the greatest merit.

The people all quickly replied, "Blessed One! But he was not the one to give the Jina food to break his fast. The other one did, and the five divine signs appeared in his house." But the Blessed One told them, "If the old merchant had not heard that the Jina had already been given food to break his fast, for sure he would have obtained omniscience just one second later. Now it is true that the young merchant experienced the divine signs in his house, and it is true that he achieved merit that will give rise to its fruit right here in this very lifetime, but he did not acquire any merit that will carry over into a future rebirth, for he lacked the proper mental attitude for that when he gave his gift."

And when they heard that answer all the townspeople felt great respect for the old merchant.

GLOSSARY

Agama [AH-gah-muh] "Tradition"; the Western name for the Jaina canon.

ahimsa [ah-HIM-suh] "noninjury" to any living being.

Angas [AHN-guhs] "Limbs"; the first and main section of the Shvetambara canon.

Arhat [AHR-haht] "Worthy One"; a person who has reached Nirvana.

jina [JEE-nuh] "conqueror"; a person who has reached Nirvana.

Prakaranas [prah-KAR-ah-nuhs] The main section of the Digambara canon.

Siddhanta [sid-DAHN-tuh] "Doctrine" or "Teaching"; the name that Jains use for their scripture.

Tirthankara [tihr-TAHN-kah-ruh] "Ford-finder"; a person who has traveled from the misery of this world across the river of existence to liberation, and who enables others to do so by teaching and example.

QUESTIONS FOR STUDY AND DISCUSSION

1. Compare the lives of Mahavira and Siddhartha Gotama (the Buddha). How are they remarkably alike, and what might their dissimilarities be?

2. One scholar has called Jainism the "unhappy face of Buddhism." Judging from the Jaina scriptures, would you agree or disagree? Why?

3. Discuss the division between the Shvetambara and Digambara sects on the place of women as monastics. To what degree may this issue be reflected in arguments over the role of women in the monastic orders or clergy of other faiths?

4. Discuss the basic idea of ahimsa in Jainism. Why has it been influential in the wider Indian tradition? How might it be applicable to the peoples of other, non-Indian faiths?

SUGGESTIONS FOR FURTHER READING

Primary Readings

L. Basham, "Jainism and Buddhism." In W. T. de Bary, ed., *Sources of Indian Tradition.* New York: Columbia University Press, 1958, pp. 39–92. Excellent translations with introductions of about twenty short but important passages in Jaina religion and philosophy.

H. Jacobi, trans., *Gaina Sutras.* In F. M Müller, gen. ed., *Sacred Books of the East,* vols. 22 and 45. Oxford: Oxford University Press, 1884, 1895; reprinted, New Delhi: Motilal Banarsidass, 1964. Contains selections of two *Angas,* a *Mulasutra,* and a *Chedasutra;* still the fullest English translation.

Secondary Readings

P. Dundas, *The Jains*. London: Routledge, 1993. The best and most recent introduction to Jainism, with an excellent examination of Jaina attitudes to scripture.

K. W. Folkert, "The 'Canons' of 'Scripture.'" In M. Levering, ed., *Rethinking Scripture: Essays from a Comparative Perspective:* Albany: State University of New York Press, 1989, pp. 170–179. A thought-provoking analysis of the present reception of Jaina scriptures in light of the comparative study of world scriptures.

K. W. Folkert, *Scripture and Community: Collected Essays on the Jains,* ed. J. E. Cort. Studies in World Religions Series. Cambridge, MA: Harvard University Center for the Study of World Religions, 1995. Treats the various aspects of Jaina tradition, with special attention to scriptures and monasticism.

P. S. Jaini, *The Jaina Path of Purification*. Berkeley: University of California Press, 1979. For the more advanced student; a nice complement to Dundas' book.

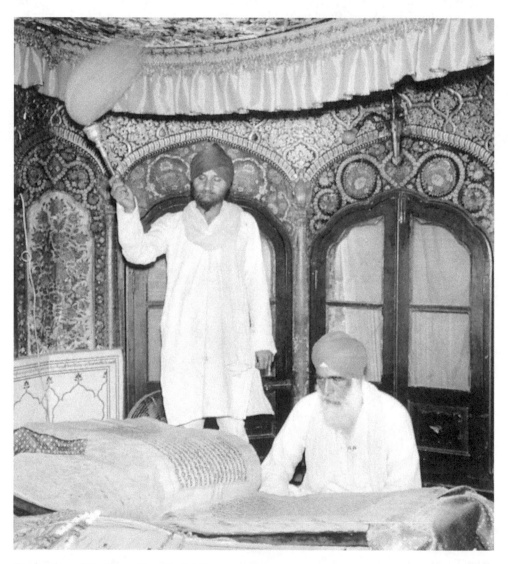

***Recitation of the* Guru Granth Sahib**
An official reader recites the Sikh holy book in the Golden Temple of Amritsar, India, while an attendant behind him waves a horse-hair fan to venerate the book. *Credit:* Gunter Reitz/Mary Evans Picture Library.

CHAPTER FIVE

Sikhism

❖ A turbaned man walks down a bridge to the gate of the Golden Temple of Amritsar, India. Once inside, he approaches the central and only object of veneration, the large scripture book called the *Adi Granth*. Placed on cushions on a raised platform under a richly ornamented canopy, the *Granth* is read by an official reader as an attendant waves a ceremonial whisk over it. The worshipper bows reverently before the book with folded hands, listening to the melodious reading.

❖ Worshippers at a Sikh temple see, in quick succession, three life-cycle ceremonies. First, a baby is brought in for naming; as the *Adi Granth* is opened at random, the first letter on the left-hand page becomes the first letter in the child's first name. Second, a young couple comes to be married; during the ceremony, the couple circles the *Granth* several times to the accompaniment of verses from its marriage hymns. Third, the relatives of a recently deceased Sikh come for the conclusion of funeral rites; a prominent feature is the continuous reading of the entire *Granth,* and the relatives are present for the solemn conclusion of the reading.

INTRODUCTION

The Sikh religion was founded about 1500 C.E. by Guru Nanak. Its home is the Punjab region of northern India, where today it numbers more than nine million believers. Sizable Sikh communities are also found in Canada and Great Britain. Designed to appeal to Hindus and Muslims, Sikhism contains elements of both faiths. With Hinduism, it shares mysticism and devotion; with Islam, a rigid monotheism. Yet it rejects elements of both these traditions, especially their leaders and rituals. Sikhism grew through a line of ten gurus until it reached its present form as expressed in its scripture, which believers consider the successor of the tenth guru. In the veneration of scripture, Sikhism is unsurpassed among world religions.

Overview of Structure

The *Adi Granth* ("the first/original book") has three main parts, arranged in order of their importance. First and most important is the *Japji* [JAHP-jee], a poem that the faithful consider a summary and capstone of Sikhism. Written by Guru Nanak, the *Japji* differs from the rest of the *Adi Granth* [AH-dee GRAHNTH] by having no hymn tune. Appended to the *Japji* are fourteen hymns, all of them appearing later in the *Adi Granth*. The second main part, by far the longest, is the collection of **ragas** [RAH-guhs], thirty-nine in all. Each raga ("tune") is divided by different poetic meters and lengths, which are subdivided by guru author, proceeding chronologically through the line of gurus. Each guru calls himself "Nanak," usually at the conclusion of the hymn, but the different guru authors are identified by the numbered use of the term **Mahala** [ma-HAH-luh]. Mahala 1 denotes the compositions of Guru Nanak, Mahala 2 of Guru Angad, and on, up to Mahala 5 for Guru Arjan. The third main part of the *Adi Granth* is a mixed collection of twenty-six small books, most elaborating on the ragas. It also features hymns of many Hindu saints and Sufi Muslim mystics, which early Sikhs found congenial. Sikhs have always seen this inclusiveness as proof of the universality of their tradition. As it now stands, the *Adi Granth*'s material ranges in time from the twelfth-century hymns of Jaidev to the hymns of the ninth guru, Tegh Bahadur, who died in 1675.

The *Adi Granth* states in hymnic form the main beliefs of the Sikhs. The *Adi Granth* rejects what it perceives as the ritualism and formalism of Islam and especially of Hinduism, arguing for moral purity as the chief basis of religion. Hindu caste structure is repeatedly rejected; all men are to live as equals. Karma and reincarnation are accepted, but the practice of the Sikh religion will release believers from rebirth and lead to blessedness in heaven. Above all, the *Adi Granth* promotes the strict doctrine of one God and mystical devotion to his name. This loving God offers salvation by his grace to those who meditate on him and live in his truth. The non-Sikh reader looks in vain for stories about the life of the founder or other gurus. These have been collected instead into the **janam-sakhis** [JAH-num SAH-kees], "birth stories," traditional narratives that are highly legendary and have semicanonical status among devout Sikhs.

The main language of the *Adi Granth* is Punjabi. The text also shows strong traces of influence from Hindi and from several other north Indian languages. The *Adi Granth* employs the Sadhukari (or Sant-Basha) dialect, which was used by religious poets in north India in the fifteenth and sixteenth centuries. Its language is complicated enough to require special training for **granthis** [GRAHN-thees], official readers, but most observant Sikhs can understand the scripture well enough to read it on their own.

Use

All Sikh usage of the *Adi Granth* is steeped in an attitude of profound respect. Devout Sikhs generally refer to the *Adi Granth* by a more venerable name, the *Sri Guru Granth Sahib* (*Guru Granth* for short), or "Revered Teacher Granth." This name is based on the origin of the Sikh scripture. Sikhs believe that each of their ten gurus had the same soul, the soul of Nanak, and that the last guru, Gobind Singh, bestowed this soul and its guru status on the *Granth,* which became the book embodiment of the soul of the gurus, the statement of the essence of Sikhism, and the final authority for the religion's continuing life.

Sikhs also call the *Adi Granth* the "living embodiment of the Guru." One of their leading theologians has claimed, "This is the only scripture of the world which was compiled by one of the founders of a religion himself and whose authenticity has never been questioned."[1] Moreover, the *Adi Granth* has served for almost three hundred years as a force for unity in Sikhism. Doctrinal disputes are traditionally ended by consulting it, at random if need be. Sikhs have a strong mystical feeling for the *Granth* and treat it as an icon. No doubt the musical nature of its recitation

---

[1] Gopal Singh, ed., *Sri Guru Granth Sahib* (Calcutta: M. P. Birla, 1989), p. 1.

contributes to its emotive power. Nevertheless, Sikhism also stresses the importance of meditating on and comprehending the meaning of its scripture.

The Sikh temple is in essence a shrine for the *Adi Granth*. Temple officials ceremoniously close the holy book and "put it to bed" at night. Before dawn they bring it out again, install it in its place, and open it. All this is done to the accompaniment of hymns from the *Adi Granth*'s pages. Despite its large size, Sikhs carry it above their heads, wearing gloves. When open, the *Granth* is draped in fine silk and placed on a special cot under a rich canopy at the focal point of the temple. Worshippers come to walk around it, bow to it, listen to its reading, and sometimes even pray to it. They must never turn their backs on it. Granthis (often mistaken for "priests" by outsiders) wear white scarves to cover their mouths as they read so that their breath does not touch the holy book. Sikh men take turns fanning it with a horse-hair, yak-hair, or peacock-feather whisk—the **chaur** [chowr], one of the symbols of Sikhism. This scripture-centered activity goes on every day at the temple; there is no weekly service. At special festivals, a nonstop oral reading by a team of granthis is held that lasts two days and nights. Every life-cycle celebration centers in some way around the *Adi Granth*. In sum, it is no exaggeration to say that all the worship of the Sikhs centers on and originates in the *Adi Granth*.

This usage also carries over into the Sikh home. A prosperous Sikh household has a special room solely for the prominent placement of the *Granth*. Almost every other Sikh household has a **gutka** [GUHT-kuh], an anthology of the most important passages from the *Adi Granth* and a few passages from the *Dasam Granth*. Daily readings are held in the home. Early-morning recitation by memory of the *Japji* and other long sections is common, often lasting for more than an hour. Devout Sikhs commit large portions of the *Adi Granth* to memory, and it is constantly on their lips during the day and night, especially in the five required daily prayers.

A memorable feature of Sikh scripture usage is **vak lao** [vahk low], "taking [God's] word." In the home or in the temple, the scripture is always opened at random, and the reading begins from the top of the left-hand page. This reading is thought to hold special significance for the occasion; it is God's word for the moment, which must be "taken" into the believer's life.

Origin and Development

The overall structure of the *Adi Granth* suggests its origins and growth. Guru Nanak (1469–1539), in a typical Hindu attitude, rejected the authority of the written word, stressing instead interior meditation on the "holy [oral] word." The *Japji* and the various hymns he composed were passed along orally. Guru Angad, whom Nanak made his successor, devised a Punjabi alphabet for the Gurmukhi language, and the *Adi Granth* was later written in this script. Guru Amar Das, third in the line, compiled a hymnal of his own poems, the poems of his two predecessors, and poems from pre-Sikh mystics. The fifth guru, Arjan, revised this hymnal and compiled the oral and written work of all his predecessors into the *Adi Granth* in 1603–1604. Tradition says that Arjan's opponents were writing and circulating books falsely attributed to Nanak in an effort to corrupt Sikhism and turn it away from Arjan's leadership. In response, Arjan compiled the *Adi Granth*.

The sixth guru, Arjan's son Har Gobind, altered the Sikh movement's original pacifism to militancy. The tenth and final guru, Gobind Singh, is considered by Sikhs to be, after Nanak, their most important leader. Before his death in 1708, he declared that the line of gurus was complete. From this time on, the only guru of the community was to be the *Adi Granth* itself, which Gobind edited into its final, present form. (He himself wrote portions of the *Dasam Granth*.) Thus, the *Adi Granth* serves as the teacher and authority for Sikhs, quite literally as the book containing the soul of the gurus.

The **Dasam Granth** (Tenth Book), a secondary scripture work for Sikhs, consists mostly of legendary narratives not found in the *Adi Granth*. Certain parts of the *Dasam Granth* [DAH-sum GRAHNTH] are well known and much used among Sikhs, especially the teachings of the tenth and final guru, Gobind Singh. Often quoted is his famous statement: "The temple and the mosque are one; so too are puja [Hindu worship] and [Muslim] prostration. All men are one though they seem to be many." Coupled with these more ecumenical sayings are statements of the rising militancy of the Sikhs.

TEACHING

Selections from the *Japji**

Practicing Sikhs repeat this entire poem from memory every morning during prayers—no small feat, because the Japji *is almost twice as long as the excerpts given here. They consider it the essence and epitome of their faith. The* Japji *moves back and forth among several topics: (1) God's name, greatness, and power; (2) God's creation of the world; (3) the way of salvation by meditating on God's name; (4) good and evil; (5) relations with Hinduism and Islam. The rich sonority of the* Japji *comes through in this translation. It begins with the* **Mul** *("root")* **Mantar** *[mool MAHN-tahr], a confession of faith considered the capstone of the whole composition.[2] In the tradition of Indian devotional poetry, the author's name is mentioned in most stanzas.*

There is only one God whose name is true, the
    Creator, devoid of fear and enmity, immor-
    tal, unborn, self-existent; by the favor of the
    Guru.[3] Repeat His Name!

The True One was in the beginning; the True
    One was in the primal age.
The True One is now also, O Nanak; the True
    One also (forever) shall be.
[1] By thinking I cannot obtain a conception
    of Him, even though I think hundreds of
    thousands of times.
Though I be silent and keep my attention
    firmly fixed on Him, I cannot preserve
    silence.
The hunger of the hungry for God does not
    subside, though they obtain the load of the
    worlds.

---

*Japji 1–3, 5–6, 9, 12–13, 15, 17–18, 20–22, Epilogue.
[2] All selections from the Sikh scriptures are taken, with editing, from Max A. Macauliffe, *The Sikh Religion: Its Gurus, Sacred Writings and Authors* (Oxford: Oxford University Press, 1909).
[3] *by the favor of the Guru:* known through the Guru.

If man should have thousands and hundreds of thousands of devices, even one would not assist him in obtaining God.

How shall man become true before God? How shall the veil of falsehood be torn?

By walking, O Nanak, according to the will of the Commander as preordained.

By His order bodies are produced; His order cannot be described.

By His order souls are infused into them; by His order greatness is obtained.

By His order men are high or low; by His order they obtained preordained pain or pleasure.

By His order some obtained their reward; by His order others must ever wander in transmigration.

All are subject to His order; none is exempt from it.

He who understands God's order, O Nanak, is never guilty of egoism. . . .

Millions of men give millions upon millions of descriptions of Him, but they fail to describe Him.

The Giver gives; the receiver grows weary of receiving.

In every age man subsists by His bounty.

The Commander by His order has laid out the way of the world.

Nanak, God who is free from care is happy. . . .

[5] He is not established, nor is He created.

The Pure One exists by Himself.

They who worshipped Him have obtained honor.

Nanak, sing His praises who is the Treasury of excellences.

Sing and hear and put His love into your hearts.

Thus shall your sorrows be removed, and you shall be absorbed in Him who is the abode of happiness.

Under the Guru's instruction God's word is heard;

Under the Guru's instruction its knowledge is acquired;

Under the Guru's instruction man learns that God is everywhere contained. . . .

[9] By hearing the Name man becomes as Shiva, Brahma, and Indra.

By hearing the Name even the low become highly lauded.

By hearing the Name the way of Yoga and the secrets of the body are obtained.

By hearing the Name man understands the real nature of the *Shastras,* the *Smritis,* and the *Vedas.*

Nanak, the saints are ever happy.

By hearing the Name sorrow and sin are no more. . . .

[12] The condition of him who obeys God cannot be described.

Whoever tries to describe it shall afterward repent.

There is no paper, or pen, or writer

To describe the condition of him who obeys God.

So pure is His name—

Whoever obeys God knows the pleasure of it in his own heart.

By obeying Him wisdom and understanding enter the mind;

By obeying Him man knows all worlds;

By obeying Him man suffers no punishment;

By obeying Him man shall not depart with Jam[4]—

So pure is God's name—

Whoever obeys God knows the pleasure of it in his own heart. . . .

[15] By obeying Him man attains the gate of salvation;

By obeying Him man is saved with his family;

By obeying Him the Guru is saved, and saves his disciples;

By obeying Him, O Nanak, man wanders not in quest of alms—

So pure is God's name—

Whoever obeys God knows the pleasure of it in his own heart. . . .

---

[4] *Jam:* death. By obeying God, a person will not be reborn to die again.

[17] Numberless Your worshippers, and numberless Your lovers;

Numberless adorers, and numberless they who perform austerities for You;

Numberless the reciters of sacred books and *Vedas;*

Numberless Your Yogins whose hearts are indifferent to the world;

Numberless the saints who ponder on attributes and divine knowledge;

Numberless Your true men; numberless almsgivers;

Numberless Your heroes who face the steel of their enemies;

Numberless Your silent worshippers who lovingly fix their thoughts upon You.

What power have I to describe You?

So lowly am I, I cannot even once be a sacrifice to You.

Whatever pleases You is good.

O formless One, You are always secure.

Numberless are the fools appallingly blind;

Numberless are the thieves and devourers of others' property;

Numberless those who establish their sovereignty by force;

Numberless the cut-throats and murderers;

Numberless the sinners who pride themselves on committing sin;

Numberless the liars who roam about lying;

Numberless the filthy who enjoy filthy gain;

Numberless the slanderers who carry loads of calumny on their heads;

Nanak thus describes the degraded.

So lowly am I, I cannot even once be a sacrifice to You.

Whatever pleases You is good.

O Formless One, You are always secure. . . .

[21] Pilgrimage, austerities, mercy, and almsgiving on general and special occasions

Whoever performs, may obtain some little honor;

But he who hears and obeys and loves God in his heart

Shall wash off his impurity in the place of pilgrimage within him.

All virtues are Yours, O Lord; none are mine.

There is no devotion without virtue.

From the Self-existent proceeded Maya,[5]

Whence issued a word which produced Brahma and the rest—

"You are true, You are beautiful, pleasure is ever in Your heart!"

What the time, what the epoch, what the lunar day, and what the week-day,

What the season, and what the month when the world was created,

The Pandits[6] did not discover; had they done so, they would have recorded it in the *Puranas.*

Nor did the Qazis[7] discover it; had they done so, they would have recorded it in the *Qur'an.*

Neither the Yogi nor any other mortal knows the lunar day, or the week-day, or the season, or the month.

Only the Creator who fashioned the world knows when He did so.

How shall I address You, O God? How shall I praise You? How shall I describe You? And how shall I know You?

Says Nanak, everybody speaks of You, one wiser than another. . . .

Men have grown weary at last of searching for God's limits; they say one thing, that God has no limit.

The thousands of *Puranas* and Muslim books tell that in reality there is but one principle.

If God can be described by writing, then describe Him; but such description is impossible.

O Nanak, call Him great; only He Himself knows how great He is. . . .

[Epilogue] The air is the guru, water our father, and the great earth our mother;

---

[5] *Maya:* "deceit, illusion," God's mystical power by which God created matter.

[6] *Pandits:* highly learned Brahmins.

[7] *Qazis:* Islamic judges.

Day and night are our two nurses, male and
female, who set the whole world playing.
Merits and demerits shall be read out in the
presence of the Judge.
According to men's acts, some shall be near,
and others distant from God.

Remembering God*

*In Sikhism, the way of salvation is by profound
reflection on, and commitment to, God's name.
"Remembering" is not the opposite of "forgetting"
but a way to this reflection and commitment.
These are the words of Guru Arjan, often repeated
after the* Japji *in the morning prayer service.*

I bow to the primal Guru;
I bow to the Guru of the primal age;
I bow to the true Guru;
I bow to the holy divine Guru.

Remember, remember God;
By remembering Him you shall obtain
happiness,
And erase from your hearts trouble and afflic-
tion.
Remember the praises of the one all-supporting
God.

Numberless persons utter God's various names.
Investigating the *Vedas,* the *Puranas,* and the
Smritis,
Men have made out the one word that is God's
name.
His praises cannot be recounted.

Says Nanak, save me, O Lord, with those who
are desirous of one glance of You.
In this *Sukhmani* is the name of God which like
ambrosia bestows happiness,
And gives peace to the hearts of the saints.

By remembering God man does not again enter
the womb;
By remembering God the tortures of Death
disappear;
By remembering God death is removed;

They who have pondered on the Name and
departed after the completion of their
toil,
Shall have their countenances made bright,
O Nanak; how many shall be emancipated
in company with them!

By remembering God enemies retreat;
By remembering God no obstacles are met;
By remembering God we are watchful night
and day;
By remembering God fear is not felt;
By remembering God sorrow troubles not:
Men remember God in the company of the
saints.
Nanak, by the love of God all wealth is
obtained.

By remembering God we obtain wealth,
supernatural power, and the nine treasures;
By remembering God we obtain divine
knowledge, meditation, and the essence of
wisdom;
Remembrance of God is the real devotion,
penance, and worship;
By remembering God the conception of duality
is dispelled;
By remembering God we obtain the advantages
of bathing at places of pilgrimage;
By remembering God we are honored at His
court;
By remembering God we become reconciled to
His will;
By remembering God men's lives are very
profitable;
They whom He has caused to do so remember
Him.
Nanak, touch the feet of such persons.[8]

---

* *Gauri Sukhmani,* Mahala 5.
[8] *touch the feet of such persons:* show them respect because
you approve of them.

Creation of the World*

The world was directly and purposefully created by God; it still reflects God's goodness. This composition by Guru Nanak extolling God's creation is sung in every Sikh temple in the morning.

Wonderful Your word, wonderful Your knowledge;
Wonderful Your creatures, wonderful their species;
Wonderful their forms, wonderful their colors;
Wonderful the animals which wander naked;
Wonderful Your wind; wonderful Your water;
Wonderful Your fire which sports wondrously;
Wonderful the earth, wonderful the sources of production.
Wonderful the pleasures to which mortals are attached;
Wonderful is meeting, wonderful parting from You;
Wonderful is hunger, wonderful repletion;
Wonderful Your praises, wonderful Your eulogies;
Wonderful the desert, wonderful the road;
Wonderful Your nearness, wonderful Your remoteness;
Wonderful to behold You present.
Beholding these wonderful things I remain wondering.
Nanak, they who understand them are supremely fortunate.

By Your power we see, by Your power we hear;
By Your power we fear, or enjoy the highest happiness;
By Your power were made the nether regions and the heavens; by Your power all creation;
By Your power were produced the *Vedas*, the *Puranas*, the Muslim books, and by Your power all compositions;
By Your power we eat, drink, and clothe ourselves;
By Your power springs all affection;
By Your power are the species, classes, and colors of creatures; by Your power are the animals of the world.
By Your power are virtues; by Your power are vices;
By Your power, honor and dishonor;
By Your power are wind, water, and fire; by Your power is the earth.
Everything exists by Your power; You are the omnipotent Creator; Your name is the holiest of the holy.
Says Nanak, You behold and pervade all things subject to Your command: You are altogether unrivalled.

---

*Asa Ki Var, Mahala 1.

Dancing for Krishna**

Sikhism developed out of devotional Hinduism. Here Guru Amar Das rejects the Krishnavites' idea that merit is earned by participation in the dancing for Krishna that occurs at his festivals. In typical Guru Granth *style,* Guru Amar Das *adapts the practices of other religions to Sikhism by reinterpreting them for the new faith.*

I dance, but it is my heart I cause to dance;
By the favor of the Guru I have effaced myself.

He who keeps his mind firmly fixed on God shall obtain deliverance and the object of his desires.

Dance, O man, before your Guru;
He who dances as it pleases the Guru shall obtain happiness, and at the last moment the fear of Death shall forsake him.

**Rag Gurji, Mahala 3.

He whom God causes to dance and whom He loves is a saint.

He himself sings, he himself instructs, and puts ignorant man on the right way.

He who banishes worldly love shall dance day and night in God's house and never sleep.

Every one who dances, leaps, and sings of other gods is lulled to sleep in the house of riches; such are the perverse who have no devotion.

Demigods and men who abandon the world dance in religious works; Munis and men dance in the contemplation of divine knowledge.

The Sidhs, Strivers, and holy men who have acquired wisdom to meditate on God dance in God's love.

The regions, worlds, beings endowed with the three qualities, and they who love You, O God, dance.

Men and the lower animals all dance, the four sources of life dance.

They who please You dance, the pious who love the Word. . . .

He to whom You are gracious shall obtain You by the favor of the Guru.

If I forget the True One even for a moment, that moment passes in vain.

Remember Him at every breath and He will pardon you from His own grace.

It is they who please You, O God, and who meditate on the Word, who really dance.

Nanak says, they to whom You are merciful shall easily obtain bliss.

The Hindu Thread*

This passage from Guru Nanak features a strong rejection of Hindu ritual practices. Singled out for criticism is the Hindu sacred string, worn on the body. As in the previous selection, Hindu practice is reinterpreted for Sikhs: "Make a sacred thread for the soul."

Make mercy your cotton, contentment your thread, continence its knot, truth its twist.

That would make a sacred thread for the soul; if you have it, O Brahmin, then put it on me.

It will not break, or become soiled, or be burned, or lost.

Blest is the man, O Nanak, who has such a thread on his neck.

You purchase a sacred thread for four damris, and seated in a square[9] you put it on;

You whisper instruction that the Brahmin is the guru—

Man dies, the sacred thread falls, and the soul departs without it.

Though men commit countless thefts, countless adulteries, utter countless falsehoods and countless words of abuse;

Though they commit countless robberies and villainies night and day against their fellow creatures;

Yet the cotton thread is spun, and the Brahmin comes to twist it.

For the ceremony they kill a goat and cook and eat it, and everybody then says, "Put on the sacred thread."

When it becomes old, it is thrown away and another is put on.

Nanak, the string does not break if it is strong.

By adoring and praising the Name honor and a true thread are obtained.

In this way a sacred thread shall be put on which will not break, and which will be fit for entrance into God's court.

There is no string for the sexual organs (to wear), no string for women;

*Asa Ki Var, Mahala 1.
[9] *seated in a square:* a square drawn on the ground in which the thread ceremony occurs.

There is no string for the impure acts which
    cause your beards to be daily spat upon.
There is no string for the feet, no string for the
    hands,
No string for the tongue, no string for the eyes.
Without such strings the Brahmin wanders astray,
Twists strings for the neck, and puts them on
    others.
He takes a fee for marrying;

He pulls out a paper, and shows the fate of the
    wedded pair.[10]
Hear and see, you people; it is strange
That man who is mentally blind is called wise.

---

[10] *He pulls . . . pair:* shows them an astrological prediction,
still an important part of Hindu marriage.

ETHICS

Truth Is the Basis of Conduct*

*This passage expresses the simplicity of Sikh ethics.
All good conduct comes from a love of the truth,
which in turn comes from being filled with God.*

He alone is truly truthful
In whose heart is the True One living,
Whose soul inside is rinsed of falsehood
And his body outside is cleansed by washing.

He alone is truly truthful
Who loves truth with passion,
Whose heart rejoices in the Name
And finds the door to salvation.

He alone is truly truthful
Who knows the art of living,
Who prepares his body like a bed
And plants the seed of the Lord therein.

He alone is truly truthful
Who accepts the true message,
Toward the living shows mercy
Gives something as alms and in charity.

He alone is truly truthful
Whose soul in pilgrimage resides,
Who consults the true Guru and by his counsel
    ever abides.

Truth is the cure for all ills.
It exorcises sin, and washes the body clean.
Those that have truth in their aprons,
Before them Nanak humbles himself.

---

*Hymns of Guru Nanak.

Prayer for Forgiveness**

*This lyrical prayer by Guru Arjan expresses the
moral structure of Sikhism. God is holy and
forgives those who confess their sin. The prayer ends
with the worshipper assured of forgiveness.*

Hear my supplication, O my Lord God,
Though I am full of millions of sins, nevertheless
    I am Your slave.
O You Dispeller of grief, merciful, fascinating,
Destroyer of trouble and anxiety,

I seek Your protection; protect my honor.
You are in all things, O spotless One;
You hear and behold us; You are with us all,
    O God;
You are the nearest of all to us.

O Lord, hear Nanak's prayer; save the slave of
    Your household.

**Rag Bihagra, Mahala 5.

You are ever omnipotent; we are poor and beggars.

O God, save us who are involved in the love of money.

Bound by covetousness and worldly love, we have committed various sins.

The Creator is distinct and free from entanglements; man obtains the fruit of his acts.

Show us kindness, You purifier of sinners; we are weary of wandering through many a womb.

Nanak represents—I am the slave of God who is the support of the soul and life.

You are great and omnipotent; my understanding is feeble.

You cherish even the ungrateful; You look equally on all.

Unfathomable is Your knowledge, O infinite Creator;

I am lowly and know nothing.

Having rejected the gem of Your name, I have amassed money;

I am a degraded and silly being.

By the commission of sin I have amassed what is very unstable and forsakes man.

Nanak has sought Your protection, O omnipotent Lord; preserve his honor.

When I sang God's praises in the association of the saints,

He united me, who had been separated from Him, with Himself.

By ever thoroughly singing God's praises, He who is happiness itself becomes manifest.

My couch, when God accepts me as His own, is adorned by Him.

Having dismissed anxiety I am no longer anxious, and suffer no further pain.

Nanak lives beholding God and singing the praises of the Ocean of excellences.

Against the Use of Wine*

Although the Sikh scriptures contain no formal listing of ethical commands, one of the firmest and most explicit moral commands of Sikhism is the prohibition of alcoholic beverages, which it shares with Islam. Notice once again the reinterpretation of an evil practice: "Make God's name your wine."

The barmaid is misery, wine is lust; man is the drinker.

The cup filled with worldly love is wrath, and it is served by pride.

The company is false and covetous, and is ruined by excess of drink.

Instead of such wine make good conduct your yeast, truth your molasses, God's name your wine;

Make merits your cakes, good conduct your clarified butter, and modesty your meat to eat.

Such things, O Nanak, are obtained by the Guru's favor; by partaking of them sins depart.

---

*Rag Bihagra, Mahala 1.

ORGANIZATION

The Guru**

This hymn by Guru Amar Das expresses the characteristic attitude of later Sikhs toward the line of the gurus. Though the Sri Guru Granth Sahib *is not explicitly mentioned, Sikhs hearing this hymn would think that everything said about the guru* *applies to their* Guru Granth, *in which the soul of the guru is incarnated.*

**Rag Gauri, Mahala 3.

Through the Guru a few obtain divine
  knowledge;
He who knows God through the Guru shall be
  acceptable.
Through the Guru there results divine
  knowledge and meditation on the True One;
Through the Guru the gate of deliverance is
  attained.
It is only by perfect good fortune the Guru
  comes in one's way.
The true become easily absorbed in the True One.
On meeting the Guru the fire of avarice is
  quenched.
Through the Guru peace dwells in the heart.
Through the Guru man becomes pure,
  spotless, and immaculate.

Through the Guru the Word which unites man
  with God is obtained.
Without the Guru every one wanders in
  doubt.
Without the Name great misery is suffered.
He who is pious meditates on the Name.
On beholding the True One, true honor is
  obtained.

Whom shall we call the giver? The One
  God.
If He be gracious, the Word by which we meet
  Him is obtained.
May Nanak meet the beloved Guru, sing the
  True One's praises,
And becoming true be absorbed in the True
  One!

God's Power in the Sikh Community*

The final shape of the Sikh community (panth)
was established by the tenth guru, Gobind Singh.
This hymn by Guru Arjan contains a line,
"Victory be ever to the society of the saints," very
reminiscent of the shout used to close many Sikh
services: "The Khalsa shall rule!"

There is none beside Him,
In whose power are lords and emperors;
In whose power is the whole world;
Who has created everything.
Address your supplication to the true Guru,
That he may arrange all your affairs.

His court is the most exalted of all;
His name is the support of all the saints.
The Lord whose glory shines in every heart
Is contained in everything, and fills creation.

By remembering Him the abode of sorrow is
  demolished;
By remembering Him Death molests us not;
By remembering Him what is withered
  becomes green;
By remembering Him the sinking stone floats.
Victory be ever to the society of the saints!
God's name is the support of the lives of His
  servants.
Says Nanak, hear, O God, my supplication—
By the favor of the saints, grant me to dwell in
  Your name.

---

*Rag Gauri, Mahala 5.

RITUAL AND MEDITATION

Hymn for the Installation of the *Guru Granth**

Although the content of this hymn seems to be unrelated to the Guru Granth, *Sikhs in the temple sing it as the holy book is brought out in the morning and put to rest at night.*

O God, this is the desire of my heart:
That You, the Treasure of mercy, the
    Compassionate, should make me the slave of
    Your saints;

That I should devote my body and soul to their
    service and sing God's praises with my tongue;
That I should ever abide with the saints and
    remember You at every breath I draw.
The Name is my sole support and wealth; from
    it Nanak obtains delight.

**Rag Devgandhari*, Mahala 5.

A Marriage Hymn**

Here is a hymn typically sung at Sikh weddings. Devotion to God and devotion to one's spouse are masterfully blended. The believer is represented as the bride, God as the groom.

The stars glitter on a clear night.
Holy men, the beloved of my Lord, are awake;
The beloved of my Lord are ever awake, and
    remember His name night and day.
They meditate in their hearts on His lotus feet,
    and forget Him not for a moment.
They renounce the mental sins of pride and
    worldly love, and efface the pain of wrong-
    doing.
Nanak represents, the servants of God, the dear
    saints are ever awake.

My couch has splendid trappings.
In my heart joy has sprung up since I heard
    that my Lord was approaching.
On meeting my Lord I have entered on
    happiness and am filled with the essence
    of joy and delight.
He embraced me; my sorrows fled; my soul,
    mind, and body all bloomed afresh.

I have obtained my heart's desires by meditating
    on God; the time of my union with Him
    I account auspicious.
Nanak testifies, when he met the Bearer of
    prosperity, the essence of all pleasure was
    prepared for him.

My companions meeting me asked me to
    describe my Spouse.
I was so filled with the sweets of love that
    I could not speak.
The attributes of the Creator are deep, mysteri-
    ous, and boundless; the *Vedas* have not
    found His limit.
She who meditates on the Lord with devotion
    and love, who ever sings His praises,
And is pleasing to her God, is full of all virtues
    and divine knowledge.
Nanak testifies, she who is dyed with the color of
    God's love shall be easily absorbed in Him.

***Rag Asa*, Mahala 5.

When I began to sing songs of joy to God,
My friends became glad, my troubles and my
  enemies fled away,
My happiness and comfort increased, I rejoiced
  in God's name, and He Himself bestowed
  mercy on me.

I clung to His feet, and being ever wakeful
  I met Him.
Happy days came, I obtained peace with all
  treasures and was blended with God.
Nanak testifies that the saints of God are ever
  steadfast in seeking His protection.

LATER DEVELOPMENTS OF SCRIPTURAL THEMES: THE *DASAM GRANTH*

Guru Gobind Singh's Story*

Guru Gobind tells not only his own story but the story of the one soul of the line of gurus.[11]

I shall now tell my own history,
How God brought me into the world as I was
  performing penance
On the mountain of Hem Kunt,
Where the seven peaks are conspicuous—
The place is called the Sapt Shring—
Where King Pandu practiced Yoga.
There I performed very great austerities
And worshipped Great Death.
I performed such penance
That I became blended with God.

My father and mother had also worshipped the
  Unseen One,
And strove in many ways to unite themselves
  with Him.
The Supreme Guru was pleased
With their devotion to Him.
When God gave me the order
I assumed birth in this age.
I did not desire to come,
As my attention was fixed on God's feet.

God remonstrated earnestly with me,
And sent me into this world with the following
  orders:
"When I created this world
I first made the demons, who became enemies
  and oppressors.

They became intoxicated with the strength of
  their arms,
And ceased to worship Me, the Supreme Being.
I became angry and at once destroyed them.
In their places I established the gods.
They also busied themselves receiving sacrifices
  and worship,
And called themselves supreme beings.
Shiva called himself the imperishable God.
Vishnu too declared himself to be God;
Brahma called himself the supreme Brahma,
And nobody thought Me to be God. . . .
Brahma made the four *Vedas*
And caused all to act according to them;
But they whose love was attached to My feet
Renounced the *Vedas*.
They who abandoned the tenets of the *Vedas*
  and other books
Became devoted to Me, the supreme God.
They who follow true religion
Shall have their sins of various kinds blotted
  out.
They who endure bodily suffering
And cease not to love Me,
Shall all to go paradise,

Dasam Granth, Vichitar Natak 6.
[11] This and the following reading are taken from Max A. Macauliffe, *The Sikh Religion,* vol. 5 (Oxford: Oxford University Press, 1909), pp. 286–287, 296–300.

And there shall be no difference between Me
and them.
They who shrink from suffering,
And, forsaking Me, adopt the way of the *Vedas*
and *Smritis* shall fall into the pit of hell,
And continually suffer transmigration. . . .

I then created Muhammad,
And made him king of Arabia.
He too established a religion of his own,
Cut off the foreskins of all his followers,
And made everyone repeat his name;[12]
But no one fixed the true Name in man's
heart. . . .

I have cherished you as My son,
And created you to extend My religion.
Go and spread My religion there,
And restrain the world from senseless acts."

I stood up, clasped my hands, bowed my head,
and replied:

"Your religion shall prevail in the world when
You assure me your assistance."

On this account God sent me;
I took birth and came into the world.
As He spoke to me so I speak unto men;
I bear no enmity to any one.
All who call me the Supreme Being
Shall fall into the pit of hell.
Recognize me as God's servant only:
Have no doubt whatever of this.
I am the slave of the Supreme Being,
Come to behold the wonders of the world.
I tell the world what God told me,
And will not remain silent through fear of
mortals.

[12] *repeat his name:* in the confession, "There is no God but God, and Muhammad is God's prophet."

God as the Holy Sword*

One of the most important developments in the early history of Sikhism was the shift from pacifism to militancy. This famous hymn expresses this militancy with its personification of the sword as God, and its promotion of what Sikhs call the "battle for righteousness." Today a Sikh child is baptized with water that has been stirred by a two-edged sword, and the dagger between two swords is a prominent symbol of modern Sikhism.

I bow with love and devotion to the Holy Sword.
Assist me that I may complete this book.
You are the Subduer of countries, the
Destroyer of the armies of the wicked, in the
battlefield You greatly adorn the brave.
Your arm is unbreakable, Your brightness
resplendent, Your radiance and splendor
dazzle like the sun.
You bestow happiness on the good, You terrify
the evil, You scatter sinners, I seek Your
protection.

Hail! hail to the Creator of the world, the
Savior of creation, my Cherisher, hail to You,
O Sword!
I bow to Him who holds the arrow in His
hand; I bow to the Fearless One;
I bow to the God of gods who is in the present
and the future.
I bow to the Scimitar, the two-edged Sword,
the broad-bladed sword, and the Dagger.
You, O God, always have one form; You are
always unchangeable.
I bow to the Holder of the mace,
Who diffused light through the fourteen
worlds.
I bow to the Arrow and the Musket,
I bow to the Sword, spotless, fearless, and
unbreakable;
I bow to the powerful Mace and Lance
To which nothing is equal.

Dasam Granth, Vichitar Natak 6.

I bow to Him who holds the discus,
Who is not made of the elements and is terrible.
I bow to Him with the strong teeth;
I bow to Him who is supremely powerful,
I bow to the Arrow and the Cannon
Which destroy the enemy.

I bow to the Sword and the Rapier
Which destroy the evil.
I bow to all weapons called Shastar, which may
  be held.
I bow to all weapons called Astar, which may
  be hurled or discharged.

GLOSSARY

Adi Granth [AH-dee GRAHNTH] "the first/original book"; the main scripture of Sikhism, consisting primarily of the words of the first five gurus; also known as the *Sri Guru Granth Sahib* and the *Guru Granth*.

chaur [chowr] a horse-hair, yak-hair or peacock-feather fan used to venerate the *Adi Granth;* it is waved over the scripture to cool the book and repel flies.

Dasam Granth [DAH-sum GRAHNTH] "Tenth Book"; secondary scripture consisting mostly of the words of the tenth guru, Gobind Singh.

gutka [GUHT-kuh] an anthology, for private use, of the most important passages from the *Adi Granth* and a few passages from the *Dasam Granth.*

granthi [GRAHN-thee] an official reader of the *Adi Granth.*

janam-sakhis [JAH-num SAH-kees] "birth stories"; traditional narratives about the lives of the gurus, especially Nanak.

Japji [JAHP-jee] a poem by Guru Nanak considered to express the essence of Sikhism; it is the first main section of the *Adi Granth.*

Mahala [ma-HAH-luh] a term in the *Adi Granth* used to differentiate the compositions of the first five gurus.

Mul Mantar [mool MAHN-tahr] "Root Formula"; the opening confession of faith of the *Japji.*

ragas [RAH-guhs] the thirty-nine basic "tunes" on which melodies used for singing the *Adi Granth* are based.

vak lao [vahk low] "taking [God's] word" by opening the *Adi Granth* at random and beginning the reading from the top of the left-hand page.

QUESTIONS FOR STUDY AND DISCUSSION

1. Describe the main teachings of the *Adi Granth.* Which do you see as most important, and why?

2. "Of all the religions of Asia, Sikhism has the best claim to be a 'religion of the book.'" Do you agree or disagree? Why?

3. Which attitudes, teachings, and practices of Sikhism seem to you to resemble Hinduism? Which seem to be distinct?

4. How does Sikh tradition, as expressed in its scriptures, vary between inclusiveness toward other faiths and exclusiveness?

5. Describe the shift from pacifism to militarism in Sikh tradition. What similar shifts can you think of in other religions?

SUGGESTIONS FOR FURTHER READING

Primary Readings

M. Dass, *Songs of the Saints from the Adi Granth*. Albany: State University of New York Press, 2000. A fresh, complete translation of the songs of the saints (*sants*), important for the prehistory of Sikhism and its links to devotional Hinduism.

M. A. Macauliffe, *The Sikh Religion: Its Gurus, Sacred Writings and Authors,* 6 vols. Oxford: Oxford University Press, 1909; reprinted, New Delhi: S. Chand, 1963. Provides full selections from the Sikh scriptures, with good, literal translations.

W. H. McLeod, *Textual Sources for the Study of Sikhism*. Totowa, NJ: Barnes & Noble, 1984. An excellent anthology of Sikh scriptures and more recent writings.

C. Shackle and A. Singh Mandair, *Teachings of the Sikh Gurus: Selections from the Sikh Scriptures*. London: Routledge, 2005. Key texts of the *Adi Granth* and the *Dasam Granth* in a fresh translation, arranged by themes.

T. Singh et al., eds., *Selections from the Sacred Writings of the Sikhs*. London: Allen & Unwin, 1960. Generous selections from the *Adi Granth* and the *Dasam Granth*.

Secondary Readings

M. Juergensmeyer and N. G. Barrier, eds., *Sikh Studies*. Berkeley, CA: Graduate Theological Union, 1979. Papers from the Berkeley Conference on Sikh Studies; see especially the essays on scripture by W. McLeod, S. Singh, and F. Staal.

T. N. Madan, "The Double-Edged Sword: Fundamentalism and the Sikh Religious Tradition." In M. E. Marty and R. S. Appleby, eds., *Fundamentalisms Observed*. Chicago: University of Chicago Press, 1991, pp. 594–627. A study of the "fundamentalist" dimensions of the movement led by J. S. Bhindranwale, with good attention to its approach to scripture.

G. S. Mann, *The Making of Sikh Scripture*. Oxford: Oxford University Press, 2001. This discussion of the origin and meaning of Sikh scripture challenges many traditional understandings.

H. McLeod, "The Sikh Scriptures." In H. McLeod, *Evolution of the Sikh Community*. Oxford: Clarendon Press, 1976, pp. 59–82. A succinct survey of the origin, development, and use of Sikh scriptures, with special emphasis on textual problems.

P. Singh, *The Guru Granth Sahib: Canon, Meaning and Authority*. New Delhi: Oxford University Press, 2000. Clear, comprehensive treatment of the origin, development, and use of the *Adi Granth*.

Reading by the Moon
Zu Luo, one of China's twenty-four paragons of filial piety and a disciple of the historical Confucius, studies by the light of the moon. Here he is shown in a print by Yoshitoshi Taiso (1839–1892) carrying rice to his parents while studying. Copyright © 2005 Asian Art & Archaeology, Inc./CORBIS.

CHAPTER SIX

Confucianism

❖ In a high school in Beijing, China, students read and consider the meaning of the main Confucian book, the *Analects*. They read aloud, listen to their teacher's lecture, and discuss its meaning for China today. This study of Confucian scripture is undertaken by many Chinese throughout the world, but its recent revival in communist China heralds the return of classic Chinese values and the waning, many hope, of communist ideology.

❖ In Hong Kong, a solitary sage studies ancient Chinese poems. He pauses to reflect on their meaning, especially on how they relate to his Confucian beliefs. After reflecting, he writes out the passage calligraphically. He is practicing self-cultivation toward becoming a "superior man," the highest goal of the Confucian tradition, and his study of the ancient classics is a key ingredient in bringing about this perfection.

❖ In Los Angeles, a sociologist researches the extraordinary success of Chinese American students in the University of California system. Her conclusion: The social and intellectual values of these students' Confucian tradition—family loyalty, love of learning, self-cultivation, all values of the Confucian scriptures—have produced a remarkable academic achievement.

INTRODUCTION

Confucianism is the system of religion and philosophy begun by the sage Kung Fu-tzu ("Master Kung"), known to the Western world as Confucius (551–479 B.C.E.). Although his teachings had little impact during his lifetime, they were kept alive by the efforts of his disciples. In the second century B.C.E., Confucianism became the official religion of China. Since then it has been closely identified with the essence of traditional Chinese culture, forming the basis of Chinese education, ethics, and state-craft and influencing some of the lands surrounding China, especially Korea and Japan. In Taiwan, study of the Confucian books is required in schools. No longer the state religion of China since the communist takeover in 1949, Confucianism has experienced a rebirth of sorts in other parts of Asia. It teaches a personal and social morality stressing the practice of key virtues such as filiality, humaneness, propriety, and faithfulness. Its full and well-defined scriptural canon, reflecting the Chinese love of books and learning, provides excellent insight into Confucianism.

Overview of Structure

Confucianists call their earliest scriptures Classics, or **Ching** [jing]. In Chinese as in English, the word *classic* suggests a literary work that embodies principles accepted as authoritative over a long time up through the present. The Confucian canon is divided into two parts: the *Five Classics* (*Wu Ching*) and the later *Four Books* (*Ssu Shu*). The *Five Classics* form the foundation of the later works written by Confucius and his followers. Hundreds of years before the birth of Confucius, these early books were known, respected, and authoritative. According to some lists, they number as many as thirteen, but the best-known list has five books. Confucianists believe that Confucius edited all these works and wrote commentaries for some. Though this claim is doubtful as fact, most scholars do hold that the early Confucian tradition played a strong role in shaping and transmitting these books when it took them into its canon. Also, the traditional claim expresses the high value the Confucian tradition placed on the ancient classics. As Confucius himself once said, "It is by the *Poetry* that the mind is aroused; by the *Rites* that the character is established; by the *Music* [now lost, but perhaps incorporated in part into the *Rites*] that the finish is received" (*Analects* 8.8).

The first and oldest of the *Five Classics* is the **I Ching** [ee jing], the "Classic of Changes," a diviner's manual that developed over several hundred years, beginning in the early part of the Chou dynasty (1120–221 B.C.E.). The book contains pairs of eight basic trigrams (combinations of three horizontal lines) that believers have used to provide information about the future and recommend a course of action to meet it. The *I Ching* is built on the **yin-yang,** great interactive cosmic forces such as passivity and activity, darkness and light, and other opposing pairs. This cosmology has given the book great popularity among educated Chinese. In Confucian history it was also sometimes used philosophically, especially because of the "wings," or commentary appended to the hexagrams. Of all Chinese literature, the *I Ching* has been the most often translated into English and other modern European languages, because of its cosmological appeal rather than as a book of divination; currently more than twenty translations are in print. In China, however, the religio-magical use has tended to predominate. (This book is important for Taoists as well and is a prominent part of their canon.)

The second of the *Five Classics* is the *Shu Ching*, the "Classic of History/Documents." It consists of royal chronicles, narratives, decrees, and the like from the early Chou period, which Confucius looked on as an ideal age. Much of its content is later, forged additions.

The third of the *Five Classics* is the *Shih Ching* [shir jing], the "Classic of Poetry." It consists of **305** relatively short poems dating from the tenth to the seventh centuries B.C.E., all set to music. These songs, dealing with love, rituals, family relations, and government, were sung in worship services, especially in sacrifice to ancestors. By the time of Confucius, the *Poetry* had become the leading model of Chinese literary expression. The writings of Confucius are filled with allusions to it.

Fourth is the *Ch'un ch'iu,* the "Spring and Autumn Annals." The expression *spring and autumn* refers to the entire year, not just to those two seasons. The *Annals* is a sober and rather reliable chronological account of events in the state of Lu, Confucius' home state, from **720** to **480** B.C.E. Its ideas of respect for law and custom in government are only implicitly Confucian.

Fifth is the *Li Chi* [lee kee], the "Classic of Rites." This collection features rituals and ceremonies of ancient China, both public and private. The *Li Chi* was probably collected in the second century B.C.E. The word **li** can be variously translated "ritual," "propriety," or "manners," and all these ideas are important in the *Li Chi*.

The *Four Books* of the Confucian canon are built on what Confucius and his followers saw as the main teachings of the earlier *Five Classics*. First among them is the *Analects (Lun yu)* of Confucius. The *Analects* (collected sayings) is by far the most important text in the history of Confucianism and our most reliable source for knowledge of Confucius himself. It contains sayings of the Master and occasionally anecdotes about him as remembered by his disciples and recorded after his death. The *Analects* contains 12,700 characters (ideograms) in twenty short books. Like most other collections of sayings, the *Analects* is loosely organized and repetitive at times. Yet it treats well all the important concepts of the Confucian tradition: the cardinal virtues of humanity, propriety, respect for parents; becoming a superior man; and proper government.

The second of the *Four Books* is the *Mencius (Meng-tzu),* named for its author, who, after Confucius, was the most significant figure in Confucian tradition. Mencius (ca. 371–ca. 289 B.C.E.) died in the third century B.C.E., and his disciples compiled this book after his death. More than twice as long as the *Analects,* the *Mencius* has well-developed treatments of several important topics, especially proper government. Mencius saw filiality as the greatest of the virtues and held strongly to the teaching of innate human goodness.

Third is the *Great Learning (Ta hsueh)* a short book that is an excerpt on virtuous government from the *Li Chi*. Its first, short chapter is held to be the work of Confucius. The next ten chapters are a commentary on the first by Tseng-tzu, one of Confucius' disciples. The *Great Learning* teaches that rulers govern by example. If the ruler is morally good, so will be his government and his subjects. If the ruler is not good, his subjects will incline to evil and his rule, along with the Mandate of Heaven to govern, will collapse.

Fourth is the *Doctrine of the Mean (Chung yung)*. Like the *Great Learning,* it was originally a chapter in the *Li Chi*. "Mean" is a broad concept embracing many aspects of virtue: moderation, right conduct, decorum, sincerity. The good Confucianist is expected to "keep to the middle" between emotional and intellectual extremes. It is in the middle that the superior man is formed and comes into harmony with the **Tao** [dow], the cosmic "Way" of life. This book was important in the neo-Confucian movement that arose in the twelfth century.

Use

The official use of Confucian scriptures flows from their adoption as the state litera-ture of China. For more than two thousand years, all education was based either directly or indirectly on them. The first books boys studied and memorized in elementary school were the *Four Books,* especially the *Analects* and *Great Learning.* The rigorous civil service exams that allowed a young man to become a government official at the county, provincial, or national level were also based on the scriptures. Each county in China had a school where the scriptural lore was taught. Men who became unusually expert in the scriptures as applied to government were known as *mandarins;* the last known mandarin died in 1991. The imperial university in Beijing had five professorial posts in scripture that were designed to promote the excellence of the whole system. The personal intention of Confucius was thus fulfilled, not during his lifetime but after it, when the government of China came to be based on his leading ideas.

Confucius' ideal of providing education to all who desired and could master it fell by the wayside as this training for government became limited to the upper classes who could pay for it. Although only a small percentage of the population of China has been able to read, the influence of the Confucian scriptures through oral teaching and general cultural transmission has been so thorough that the social relationships and cultural attitudes of most Chinese have become essentially Confucian. It is often remarked that no matter the specific religion of the Chinese—Buddhist, Taoist, Muslim, Christian, whatever—they are also Confucian. Thus, largely through the influence of its scriptures, Confucianism has taken its place as the leading historic religion of China. Now that communist values are waning in the People's Republic of China, educators are returning to Confucian scriptures to provide a core moral education, especially the values of civility and obedience to law.

The Confucian approach to scripture is almost exclusively cognitive. Confucius and his followers rejected mysticism for the most part, and in subsequent centuries the sometimes bitter struggle with the more mystical Taoist tradition reinforced this cognitive orientation. Teacher and student discuss scriptural meaning in an orderly, rational way. The individual scholar often practices "quiet sitting," solitary study that involves recitation of the text, meditation on its meaning, and calligraphic reproduction of the text itself.

The literary style of the Confucian canon influences this use. Confucian scriptures share a basic literary style known as **wen-yen** (roughly translated as "formal-classical"). This style is known for brief, even compressed composition. Each Chinese ideogram character must be considered carefully to bring out the meaning. This style is one reason why Confucianists have generated a massive commentarial literature that seeks to shed more light on the canon itself. In the Confucian tradition, these commentaries have become accepted works in understanding the canon. Moreover, this formal-classical style means that translations of Confucian and Taoist scriptures often vary greatly among themselves, more so than translations of the scriptures of other religions. This compressed style invites the reader of both the Chinese original and the English translation to meditate carefully and deeply about its meaning. (For an example of differing contemporary translations of Chinese scripture, see pages 197–198.)

Origin and Development

The Confucian canon has not come down to us in an easily traceable chain of tradition. The *Analects* and the *Mencius* were probably first written down in the centuries following the deaths of their authors. The *Great Learning* and *Doctrine of the Mean* were separated from the *Classic of Rites* and made independent books. Then in 213 B.C.E., Emperor Shih Huang-ti, a radical innovator opposed to ancient traditions, ordered all Confucian books to be destroyed. This famous "Burning of the Books" resulted in the loss of several versions of the Confucian books, although most of them survived in some form. The Confucian canon was reedited and republished under the next dynasty, the Han (**206** B.C.E.–**220** C.E.). During this dynasty, Confucianism was made the official state religion, and the Confucian canon was officially adopted as the basis of thought and conduct—indeed, of all official Chinese culture. In the twelfth century, the *Four Books* were recognized as an independent collection, and they soon became more central to Confucian life than the older *Five Classics,* which came to be interpreted through the *Four Books.* State sanction for the Confucian scriptures lasted until 1905, when the government of China abolished the civil service system based on the canon.

HISTORY

The Character of Confucius*

The Analects *depicts Confucius as a model of the "superior man." By following his own teaching, he became an example to his followers. The first passage is Confucius' own summary of his progress in self-cultivation. The second describes key elements in his character. The third gives fascinating detail about some of his daily habits.*[1]

[2.4] The Master said, "At fifteen, I had my mind focused on learning. At thirty, I stood firm. At forty, I had no doubts. At fifty, I knew the decrees of Heaven.[2] At sixty, my ear was an obedient organ for the reception of truth. At seventy, I could follow what my heart desired, without transgressing what was right."

[7.1] The Master said, "I am a transmitter and not a maker. I believe in and love the ancients, and I venture to compare myself with our old P'eng."[3]

The Master said, "The silent treasuring up of knowledge; learning without tiring; and instructing others without being wearied—which one of these things belongs to me?"

The Master said, "Leaving virtue without proper cultivation; not thoroughly discussing what is learned; not being able to move toward righteousness of which a knowledge is gained; and not being able to change what is not good—these are the things which cause me much concern."

When the Master was unoccupied with business, his manner was easy, and he looked pleased.

[5] The Master said, "My decline is extreme. For a long time, I have not dreamed, as I used to do, that I saw the duke of Chou."[4]

The Master said, "Let the will be set on the path of duty. Let every attainment in what is good be firmly grasped. Let perfect virtue be followed. Let relaxation and enjoyment be found in the arts."

The Master said, "From the man bringing his bundle of dried meat for my teaching, or more than that, I have never refused instruction to any one."[5]

The Master said, "I do not open up the truth to one who is not eager to get knowledge. Nor do

---

*Analects 2.4; 7.1–9, 19–24; 10.1–3, 8–12.

[1] All selections from the *Analects* and the *Mencius* are taken, with editing, from James Legge, trans., *The Chinese Classics* (Oxford: Oxford University Press, 1893).

[2] *decrees* (or "mandates") *of Heaven:* understood today by most Confucianists as the working of Nature in people and events, not primarily as the working of God.

[3] *old P'eng:* a sage from ancient times.

[4] *duke of Chou:* in Confucius' view, one of the greatest of the early Chinese sage-kings.

[5] *dried meat:* the smallest possible payment for instruction. Confucianism has believed that learning and self-cultivation should be open to all men who desire it.

I help out any of those who are not anxious to explain themselves. When I have presented one corner of a subject to any one, and he cannot from it learn the other three, I do not repeat my lesson."

When the Master was eating by the side of a mourner, he never ate to the full. He did not sing on the same day in which he had been weeping. . . .

[19] The Master said, "I am not one who was born in the possession of knowledge. I am one who is fond of antiquity,[6] and earnest in seeking knowledge there."

[20] The subjects on which the Master did not talk were extraordinary things,[7] feats of strength, disorder, and spiritual beings.

The Master said, "When I walk along with two others, they may serve me as my teachers. I will select their good qualities and follow them, their bad qualities and avoid them."

The Master said, "Heaven produced the virtue that is in me. What can Hwan T'ui do to me?"[8]

The Master said, "Do you think, my disciples, that I have any secrets? I conceal nothing from you. Everything I do is shown to you, my disciples. That is my way."

There were four things that the Master taught—literature, ethics, devotion of soul, and truthfulness.

[10.1] Confucius, in his village, looked simple and sincere, and as if he were not able to speak. When he was in the prince's ancestral temple, or in the (governmental) court, he spoke minutely on every point, but cautiously.

When he was on duty at court, in speaking with the great officers of the lower grade he spoke freely, but in a straightforward manner. In speaking with those of the higher grade, he did so mildly, but precisely. When the ruler was present, his manner displayed respectful uneasiness; it was serious, but self-possessed.

When the prince called on him to receive a visitor, his appearance changed, and his legs seemed to move forward with difficulty. He inclined himself to the other officers among whom he stood, moving his left or right arm, as their position required, but he kept the skirts of his robe evenly adjusted. He hastened forward, with his arms like the wings of a bird. When the guest had left, he would report to the prince, "The visitor is not looking back anymore." . . .

[8] He liked to have his rice finely cleaned, and to have his minced meat cut quite small. He did not eat rice which had been injured by heat or damp and turned sour, nor fish or meat which was spoiled. He did not eat what was discolored, or what was of a bad flavor, nor anything which was badly cooked, or was not in season. He did not eat meat which was not cut properly, nor what was served without its proper sauce. Though there might be a large quantity of meat, he would not allow what he took to exceed the due proportion for the rice.

Only in wine did he have no limit for himself, but he did not allow himself to be confused by it. He did not partake of wine and dried meat bought in the market. He was never without ginger when he ate. He did not eat much. When he had been assisting at the prince's sacrifice, he did not keep overnight the meat that he received. He did not keep longer than three days the meat of his family sacrifice. When eating, he did not converse. When in bed, he did not speak. Although his food might be coarse rice and vegetable soup, he would offer a little of it in sacrifice with a serious, respectful air.

If his mat was not straight, he did not sit on it.

[10] When the villagers were drinking together, after those who carried walking staffs left, he went out immediately. When the

---

[6] *antiquity:* Confucianists emphasize the Chinese custom of seeking direction from the ancient writings.

[7] *extraordinary things:* strange, perhaps supernatural events in nature.

[8] *Hwan T'ui:* an army officer who had attempted to kill Confucius.

villagers were going through their ceremonies to drive away diseases, he put on his court robes and stood on the eastern steps.

When he was sending complimentary inquiries to anyone in another state, he bowed twice as he escorted the messenger away.

When Chi K'ang sent him a present of medicine, he bowed and received it, saying, "I do not know it. I dare not taste it."

The stable burned down when he was at court, and on his return he said, "Has any person been hurt?" He did not ask about the horses.

TEACHING

The Way*

The "Way" (Tao) is an ancient idea in Chinese tradition. In Confucianism, where it forms one of the basic teachings, it is understood as the moral way of Heaven, to which the emperor as the Son of Heaven should aspire. In this selection, the relationship of the Way and good government is brought out.

Confucius said, "When [the Way of] good government prevails in the empire, ceremonies, music, and punitive military expeditions proceed from the Son of Heaven. When bad government prevails in the empire, ceremonies, music, and punitive military expeditions proceed from the princes. When these things proceed from the princes, as a rule, they most often lose their power in ten generations. When they proceed from the great officers of the princes, as a rule, they lose their power in five generations. When the subsidiary ministers of the great officers hold in their grasp the orders of the state, as a rule, they lose their power in three generations. When the Way and right principles prevail in the kingdom, government will not be in the hands of the great officers. When right principles prevail in the kingdom, there will be no discussions among the common people."

*Analects 16.2.

The Goodness of Human Nature**

Although Confucius did not discuss the question of goodness and evil in the human personality, Mencius took up this topic. He argued the optimistic idea that all people are by nature good. Therefore, the ruler must only be good himself and bring out the innate goodness of his subjects in order to establish his rule. In this selection, the philosopher Kao Tzu serves as a foil for the thoughts of Mencius.

The philosopher Kao said, "Man's nature is like the willow tree, and righteousness is like a cup or a bowl. Fashioning benevolence and righteousness out of man's nature is like the making of cups and bowls from the willow."

**Mencius 6.1.1–4, 6.

Mencius replied, "Can you, leaving untouched the nature of the willow, make with it cups and bowls? You must do violence and injury to the willow before you can make cups and bowls with it. If you must do violence and injury to the willow in order to make cups and bowls with it, according to your principles you must in the same way do violence and injury to humanity in order to fashion from it benevolence and righteousness! Your words would certainly lead all men to reckon benevolence and righteousness to be calamities."

The philosopher Kao said, "Man's nature is like water whirling round in a corner. Open a passage for it to the east, and it will flow to the east; open a passage for it to the west, and it will flow to the west. Man's nature is indifferent to good and evil, just as the water is indifferent to the east and west."

Mencius replied, "Water indeed will flow indifferently to the east or west, but will it flow indifferently up or down? The tendency of man's nature to good is like the tendency of water to flow downwards. All people have this tendency to good, just as all water flows downwards. Now by striking water and causing it to go up, you may make it go over your forehead, and, by damming and leading it, you may force it up a hill, but are such movements according to the nature of water? It is the force applied which causes them. When men are made to do what is not good, their nature is dealt with in this way." . . .

The philosopher Kao said, "To enjoy food and delight in colors is natural. Benevolence is internal and not external; righteousness is external and not internal."

Mencius asked him, "On what grounds do you say that benevolence is internal and righteousness external?"

He replied, "There is a man older than I, and I give honor to his age. It is not that there is first in me a principle of such reverence to age. It is just as when there is a white (haired) man, and I consider him white—according as he is so externally to me. On this account, I pronounce of righteousness that it is external."

Mencius said, "There is no difference between our pronouncing of a white horse to be white and our pronouncing a white man to be white. But is there no difference between the regard with which we acknowledge the age of an old horse and that with which we acknowledge the age of an old man? And what is it which is called righteousness? The fact of a man's being old? Or the fact of our giving honor to his age?"

Kao said, "There is my younger brother—I love him. But the younger brother of a man of Ts'in I do not love. The feeling is determined by myself, and therefore I say that benevolence is internal. On the other hand, I give honor to an old man of Ts'oo, and I also give honor to an old man of my own people. The feeling is determined by the age, and therefore I say that righteousness is external."

Mencius answered him, "Our enjoyment of meat roasted by a man of Ts'in does not differ from our enjoyment of meat roasted by ourselves. Thus, what you insist on takes place also in the case of such things, and will you say likewise that our enjoyment of a roast is external?" . . .

Mencius said, "From the feelings proper to it, human nature is constituted for the practice of what is good. This is what I mean in saying that human nature is good. If men do what is not good, the blame cannot be imputed to their natural powers. The feeling of sympathy belongs to all men; so does that of shame and dislike, of reverence and respect, and of approving and disapproving. The feeling of sympathy implies the principle of benevolence; that of shame and dislike, the principle of righteousness; that of reverence and respect, the principle of propriety; and that of approving and disapproving, the principle of knowledge. Benevolence, righteousness, propriety, and knowledge are not infused into us from without. We are certainly furnished with them. And a different view is simply from want of reflection. Hence it is said: 'Seek and you will find them. Neglect and you will lose them.' Men differ from one another in regard to them . . ., and it is because they cannot carry out fully their natural powers. It is said in the *Book of Poetry:*

'Heaven, in producing mankind,
Gave them their various faculties and relations
    with their specific laws;
These are the invariable rules of nature for all
    to hold;
And all love this admirable virtue.'

"Confucius said, 'The maker of this ode knew indeed the principle of our nature!' We may thus see that every faculty and relation must have its law, and since there are invariable rules for all to hold, they consequently love this admirable virtue."

ETHICS

The Virtues of the Superior Man*

*Confucius taught self-cultivation in knowledge and virtue. When one reaches moral and intellectual maturity, he is a "superior man." The Chinese phrase for "superior man," **chun-tzu** [jun-tzoo], literally means "prince's son," but Confucius taught that by education even a common man could become superior. (The noninclusive language is intentional—women were not expected or encouraged to pursue this self-cultivation.) Neo-Confucianism applies these passages to the closely related goal of becoming a sage.*

[1.1] The Master said, "Is it not pleasant to learn with a constant perseverance? Is it not delightful to have friends coming from far away? Is he not a man of complete virtue who feels no discomposure though men may take no note of him?"

The philosopher Yu said, "Few are those who, being filial and fraternal, are fond of offending their superiors. There have been none who, not liking to offend their superiors, have been fond of stirring up confusion. The superior man pays attention to the foundation. That being established, all practical courses naturally grow up. Filiality and fraternal submission—are they not the root of all benevolent actions?"

The Master said, "Fine words and a sly appearance are seldom associated with true virtue."

The philosopher Tsang said, "I daily examine myself on three points: whether I have been faithful in transacting business for others; whether I have been sincere in dealing with friends; whether I have mastered and practiced the instructions of my teacher." . . .

[6] The Master said, "A youth, when at home, should be filial, and away from home he should be respectful to his elders. He should be earnest and truthful. He should overflow in love to all, and cultivate the friendship of good people. When he has time and opportunity, after the performance of these things, he should employ them in the arts."

Tsze-hsia said, "If a man withdraws his mind from the love of beauty, and applies it as sincerely to the love of the virtuous; if, in serving his parents, he can exert his utmost strength; if, in serving his prince, he can devote his life; if, in his dealings with his friends, his words are sincere—although men say that he has not learned, I will certainly say that he has."

The Master said, "If the scholar is not serious, he will not call forth any veneration, and his learning will not be solid. Hold faithfulness and sincerity as first principles. Have no friends not equal to yourself. When you have faults, do not fear to abandon them."

The philosopher Tsang said, "Let there be a careful attention to perform the funeral rites for parents, and let them be followed when parents are gone with the ceremonies of sacrifice. Then the virtue of the people will resume its proper excellence." . . .

Analects 1.1–4, 6–9, 14; 15.17–23.

[14] The Master said, "He who aims to be a man of complete virtue in his food does not seek to gratify his appetite, nor in his dwelling place does he seek ease. He is earnest in what he does, and careful in his speech. He frequents the company of men of principle so that he may be rectified. Such a person may indeed be said to love learning."

[15.17] The Master said, "The superior man considers righteousness to be essential in everything. He performs it according to the rules of propriety. He brings it forth in humility. He completes it with sincerity. This is indeed a superior man."

The Master said, "The superior man is distressed by his lack of ability. He is not distressed by his lack of fame."

The Master said, "The superior man dislikes the thought of his name not being mentioned after his death."

[20] The Master said, "What the superior man seeks is in himself. What the inferior man seeks is in others."

The Master said, "The superior man is dignified, but does not wrangle. He is sociable, but not a partisan."

The Master said, "The superior man does not promote a man simply on account of his words, nor does he put aside good words because of the man."

Tsze-kung asked, "Is there one word which may serve as a rule of practice for all one's life?" The Master said, "Is not reciprocity [*shu*] such a word? What you do not want done to yourself, do not do to others."

Benevolence*

*Benevolence (**jen** [**ren**]) is the chief of the Confucian virtues. It denotes humaneness, fellow feeling, even love; in this translation it is rendered as "virtue." Confucianists, especially those aspiring to sagehood, train themselves in benevolence by reflecting on their lives in the light of the scriptures.*

The Master said, "Virtuous manners make a neighborhood excellent. If a man in selecting a residence does not choose one where such manners prevail, how can he be wise?"

The Master said, "Those without virtue cannot remain long either in a condition of poverty and hardship, or in a condition of enjoyment. The virtuous rest in virtue; the wise desire virtue."

The Master said, "It is only the [truly] virtuous man who can love, or who can hate, others."

The Master said, "If the will is set on virtue, there will be no practice of wickedness."

[5] The Master said, "Men desire riches and honors. If they cannot be obtained in the proper way, they should not be held. Poverty and a low condition are what men dislike. If it cannot be obtained in the proper way, they should not be avoided. If a superior man abandons virtue, how can he fulfill the requirements of that name? The superior man does not, even for the space of a single meal, act contrary to virtue. In moments of haste, he clings to it. In times of danger, he clings to it."

The Master said, "I have not seen a person who loved virtue, or one who hated what was not virtuous. He who loved virtue would esteem nothing above it. He who hated what is not virtuous would practice virtue in such a way

---

*Analects 4.1–6.

that he would not allow anything that is not virtuous to approach his person. Is any one able for one day to apply his strength to virtue? I have not seen the case in which his strength would be sufficient. If there might be any such case, I have not seen it."

The Actions and Attitudes of Filiality*

Filiality (hsiao [syow]), translated as "filial piety" in the older literature, is reverence for one's living ancestors and extends to worship of one's dead ancestors. The Classic of Rites *passage goes into great detail in laying down rules for proper filial conduct. It stresses deference, obedience, and faithfulness to one's parents.[9] In the* Analects *passage, Confucius stresses not only the actions of filiality but much more the attitude with which these acts are carried out. This attitude must be one of piety, the genuine reverence implied by hsiao.*

[*Classic of Rites* 10.1] The sovereign king orders the chief minister to send down his lessons of virtue to the millions of the people. . . .

[4] After getting properly dressed [in the morning], sons and their wives should go to his parents.[10] When they arrive, with bated breath and gentle voice they should ask if their parents' clothes are too warm or too cold, whether their parents are ill or pained or uncomfortable in any part. If they are, the sons should proceed reverently to stroke and scratch the place. They should in the same way, going before or following after, help and support his parents in leaving or entering the apartment. In bringing in the basin for them to wash, the younger will carry the stand and the elder the water. They will ask to be allowed to pour out the water, and when the washing is concluded, they will hand the parents the towel. They will ask whether they want anything, and then respectfully bring it. All this they will do with an appearance of pleasure to make the parents feel at ease.

They should bring gruel, thick or thin, spirits or juice, soup with vegetables, beans, wheat, spinach, rice, millet, maize, and glutinous millet—whatever the parents wish, in fact. They should bring dates, chestnuts, sugar and honey to sweeten their dishes; the ordinary or the large-leaved violets, leaves of elm-trees, fresh or dry, and the most soothing rice-water to lubricate them; and fat and oil to enrich them. The parents will be sure to taste them, and when they have done so, the young people should withdraw. . . .

From the time that sons receive an official appointment [to government service], they and their father occupy different parts of their residence. But at dawn, the son will visit them, and express his affection by the offer of pleasant delicacies. At sunrise he will retire, and he and his father will attend to their different duties. At sundown, the son will pay his evening visit in the same way. . . .

[10] While his parents are both alive, at their regular meals, morning and evening, the eldest son and his wife will encourage them to eat everything. They themselves will eat what is left. When

---

Classic of Rites 10.1, 4, 7, 10–11, 13–15; *Analects* 2.5–7; 4.18–21; 13.18.

[9] Taken, with editing, from James Legge, trans., *The Sacred Books of China: The Texts of Confucianism,* part 3, *Sacred Books of the East,* vol. 27 (Oxford: Oxford University Press, 1885), pp. 449–457.

[10] The passage presupposes that one's parents have an apartment or room in one's house, typically the case in traditional China.

the father is dead, and the mother still alive, the eldest son should wait upon her at her meals. The wives of the other sons will do with what is left as in the former case. The children should have the sweet, soft, and oily things that are left.

When sons and their wives are ordered to do anything by his parents, they should immediately respond and reverently do it. When going forward or backward, or turning round, they should be careful and serious. While going out or coming in, while bowing or walking, they should not presume to belch, sneeze, cough, yawn or stretch, to stand on one foot, to lean against anything, or to look sideways. They should not dare to spit or sniffle, nor if it is cold to put on more clothes, nor if they itch anywhere to scratch themselves. Unless for reverent attention to something, they should not presume to bare their [parents'] shoulders or chest. Unless it is in wading, they should not hold up their clothes. They should not display the inside of their clothing. They should not allow the spittle or snivel of the parents to be seen. They should ask permission to rinse away any dirt on their caps or belts, to wash their clothes that are dirty with lye that has been prepared for the purpose, and to stitch together any tear. . . .

Sons and sons' wives who are filial and reverential should not refuse or delay carrying out any order from his parents. When the parents give them anything to eat or drink that they do not like, they will nevertheless taste it and wait for their further orders. When their parents give them clothes that are not to their liking, they will put them on and wait in the same way. If the parents give them something to do but then employ someone else to take their place, although they do not like the arrangement, they will let that other person do it.

When sons and their wives have not been filial and reverential, the parents should not be angry and resentful with them but should try to instruct them. If they will not receive instruction, parents should then be angry with them.

If that anger does no good, they can then drive out the son and send the wife away, but they must not publicly show why they have treated them so.

[15] If a parent has a fault, the son should admonish him with bated breath, a mild appearance, and a gentle voice. If the admonition does not take effect, the son will be more reverential and more filial; if the father seems pleased, the son will repeat the admonition. If the father should be displeased with this, rather than allow him to commit an offense against anyone in the neighborhood or countryside, the son should strongly protest. If the parent is angry and more displeased and beats him until his blood flows, the son should not presume to be angry and resentful; rather, he should be even more reverential and more filial.

[*Analects* 2.5] Mang asked what filiality was. The Master said, "It is not being disobedient." Soon after, as Fan Ch'ih was driving him, the Master told him, saying, "Mang-sun asked me what filiality was, and I answered him, 'Not being disobedient.'" Fan Ch'ih said, "What did you mean?" The Master replied, "That parents, when alive, should be served according to propriety; that, when dead, they should be buried according to propriety; and that they should be sacrificed to according to propriety."

Mang Wu asked what filiality was. The Master said, "Do not make your parents anxious about anything else than your being sick."

Tsze-yu asked what filiality was. The Master said, "Filial piety nowadays means the support of one's parents. But dogs and horses likewise are able to do something in the way of support. Without reverence, what is there to distinguish the one support given from the other?" . . .

[4.18] The Master said, "In serving his parents, a son may protest to them, but gently. If he sees that they do not incline to follow his advice, he shows an increased degree of reverence but does not abandon his purpose. Should they punish him, he does not allow himself to murmur."

The Master said, "While his parents are alive, the son should not leave his home area to live far away. If he does go away, he must have a fixed place to which he goes."[11]

[20] The Master said, "If the son for three years [after his father's death] does not alter from the way of his father, he may be called filial."

The Master said, "The age of one's parents should always be remembered, as a reason for joy and for fear." . . .

[13.18] The duke of Sheh informed Confucius, "Some among us here may be called upright in their conduct. If their father stole a sheep, they will witness to the fact." Confucius said, "Among us, in our part of the country, those who are upright are different. The father conceals the misconduct of the son, and the son conceals the misconduct of the father. Uprightness is to be found in this."

---

[11] *a fixed place:* so his parents know where he is.

Propriety*

Li, "propriety," can also be translated as "ritual correctness" or "good manners." This selection highlights the traditional Confucian connection between propriety in the rites and in everyday life. In typically Confucian style, the Classic of Poetry *is quoted to illustrate the point. Confucian rituals carried out in the temples of Korea, Taiwan, and other lands still keep to the meticulous care prescribed here. Just as important, emphasis on li has given Chinese peoples their highly developed sense of politeness.*

The Master said, "If a man lacks the virtues proper to humanity [*jen*], what has he to do with the rites of propriety? If a man is without the virtues proper to humanity, what has he to do with music?"

Lin Fang asked what was the first thing to be attended to in ceremonies. The Master said, "A great question indeed! In festive ceremonies, it is better to be sparing than extravagant. In the ceremonies of mourning, deep sorrow is better than a minute attention to observances." . . .

[8] Tsze-hsia asked, "What is the meaning of the passage, 'The pretty dimples of her artful smile! The well-defined black and white of her eye! The plain ground for the colors?'"[12] The Master said, "The business of laying on the colors follows [the preparation of] the plain ground." "Ceremonies then are a subsequent thing?" The Master said, "Shang, you can bring out my meaning. Now I can begin to talk about the *Poetry* with you." . . .

[12] He sacrificed to the dead as if they were present. He sacrificed to the spirits as if the spirits were present. The Master said, "I consider my not being present at the sacrifice as if I did not sacrifice."

Wang-sun Chia asked, "What is the meaning of the saying, 'It is better to pay court to the oven than to the southwest corner'?"[13] The Master said, "Not so. He who offends against Heaven has none to whom he can pray."

The Master said, "Chou had the advantage of viewing the two past dynasties. How complete and elegant are its regulations! I follow Chou." . . .

[17] Tzu-kung wished to do away with the sacrifice of a sheep connected with the first day

---

*Analects 3.3–4, 8, 12–14, 17–19.

[12] A poem from the *Classic of Poetry*.

[13] A traditional saying, meaning that it is better to serve the gods of food than the ancestral spirits (of the household shrine at the southwest corner of the Chinese house).

of each month. The Master said, "Tzu, you love the sheep; I love the ceremony."[14]

The Master said, "Full observance of the rules of propriety in serving one's prince is (wrongly) accounted by people to be flattery."

The duke Ting asked how a prince should employ his ministers and how ministers should serve their prince. Confucius replied, "A prince should employ his minister according to the rules of propriety. Ministers should serve their prince with faithfulness."

---

[14] Also translated, "Tzu, you love the sheep, but I love the sacrifice."

The Love of Learning*

Love of learning is a leading moral quality of anyone who aspires to moral and intellectual superiority. Here Confucius explains its relationship to other prominent virtues.

The Master said, "Yu, have you heard the six words to which are attached six faults?" Yu replied, "I have not." "Sit down, and I will tell them to you. There is the love of being benevolent without the love of learning; the fault here leads to a foolish simplicity. There is the love of knowing without the love of learning; the fault here leads to dissipation of mind. There is the love of being sincere without the love of learning; the fault here leads to an injurious disregard of consequences. There is the love of straightforwardness without the love of learning; the fault here leads to rudeness. There is the love of boldness without the love of learning; the fault here leads to insubordination. There is the love of firmness without the love of learning; the fault here leads to extravagant conduct."

The Master said, "My children, why do you not study the *Book of Poetry*? The poems stimulate the mind. They may be used for purposes of self-contemplation. They teach the art of sociability. They show how to regulate feelings of resentment. From them you learn the more immediate duty of serving one's father, and the remoter duty of serving one's prince. From them we become acquainted with the names of birds, beasts, and plants."

---

*Analects 17.8–9.

The Basis of Good Government**

The text of Confucius is given in sections 1–7; what follows is from the ninth chapter of the commentary by the philosopher Tsang, which is appended to the Great Learning. *This passage, originally a chapter in the* Classic of Rites, *was made a classic by itself in one of the* Four Books *and has had a great influence on the idea and practice of government in China and other lands influenced by it.*[15]

The *Great Learning* teaches to show illustrious virtue, to love people, and to rest in the highest excellence. . . .

The ancients, who wished to illustrate illustrious virtue throughout the kingdom, first ordered well their states. Wishing to order well their states, they first regulated their families. Wishing to regulate their families, they first cultivated their persons. Wishing to cultivate

---

**The Great Learning 1, 3–7; 9.1, 3–5.
[15] Taken, with editing, from James Legge, trans., *The Sacred Books of China: The Texts of Confucianism*, part 4, *Sacred Books of the East*, vol. 28 (Oxford: Oxford University Press, 1885), pp. 411–413, 417–419.

their persons, they first rectified their hearts. Wishing to rectify their hearts, they first sought to be sincere in their thoughts. Wishing to be sincere in their thoughts, they first extended their knowledge to the utmost.

The extension of knowledge is by the investigation of things. [5] When things were investigated, knowledge became complete. Their knowledge being complete, their thoughts were sincere. Their thoughts being sincere, their hearts were then rectified. Their hearts being rectified, their persons were cultivated. Their persons being cultivated, their families were regulated. Their families being regulated, their states were rightly governed. Their states being rightly governed, the whole kingdom was made tranquil and happy.

From the Son of Heaven down to the multitudes of the people, all considered the cultivation of the person to be the root of everything else. It cannot be, when the root is neglected, that what springs from it will be well ordered. What was of great importance has never been slightly cared for, and at the same time what was of slight importance has never been greatly cared for. . . .

[9.1, from the commentary] What is meant by "In order rightly to govern the state, it is necessary first to regulate the family"[16] is this.

One cannot teach others when he cannot teach his own family. Therefore, the ruler, without going beyond his family, completes the lessons for the state. There is filiality, with which the sovereign should be served. There is fraternal submission, with which elders and superiors should be served. There is kindness, with which the multitude should be treated. . . .

[3] From the loving example of one family a whole state becomes loving, and from its courtesies the whole state becomes courteous, while from the ambition and perverseness of the one man [the emperor], the whole state may be led to rebellious disorder. Such is the nature of the influence. . . . Therefore, the ruler must himself be possessed of good qualities, and then he may require them in the people. He must not have bad qualities in himself, and then he may require that they shall not be in the people. Never has there been a man who, not having reference to his own character and wishes in dealing with others, was able to instruct them effectively. [5] Thus we see how the government of the state depends on the regulation of the family.

---

[16] Not a quote from the text of Confucius given above, but a good statement of an idea that occurs there.

The Ruler as Example to the People*

The teaching of Confucius on government follows closely that of the Great Learning. *Here he stresses the personal quality of the ruler, the humane nature of his government, and the rectification of names, in which all people do the duties implied in their social titles (for example, "father," "mother," "son," "prince.")*

[2.18] Tsze-chang was learning with a view to employment as a government official. The Master said, "Hear much and put aside the points of which you stand in doubt, while you

speak cautiously at the same time of the others—then you will afford few occasions for blame. See much and put aside the things which seem perilous, while you are cautious at the same time in carrying the others into practice—then you will have few occasions for repentance. When one gives few occasions for blame in his words, and few occasions for repentance in his conduct, he is in the way to get good compensation for employment."

Analects 2.18–20; 12.11, 17, 19; 13.4–6.

The duke Ai asked, saying, "What should be done in order to secure the submission of the people?" Confucius replied, "Advance the upright and set aside the crooked; then the people will submit. Advance the crooked; and set aside the upright; then the people will not submit."

[20] Chi K'ang asked how to cause the people to reverence their ruler, to be faithful to him, and to go on to move themselves to virtue. The Master said, "Let him preside over them with gravity; then they will reverence him. Let him be filial and kind to all; then they will be faithful to him. Let him advance the good and teach the incompetent; then they will eagerly seek to be virtuous."

[12.11] The duke Ching, of Ch'i, asked Confucius about government. Confucius replied, "There is government when the prince is a prince, and the minister is a minister, when the father is a father, and the son is a son."[17] "Good!" said the duke. "If, indeed, the prince is not a prince, the minister not a minister, the father not a father, and the son not a son, although I may prosper, can I enjoy it?" . . .

[17] Chi K'ang asked Confucius about government. Confucius replied, "To govern means to rectify. If you lead the people with correctness, who will dare not to be correct?". . .

[19] Chi K'ang asked Confucius about government, saying, "What do you say to killing the unprincipled for the good of the principled?" Confucius replied, "Sir, in carrying on your government, why should you use killing at all? Let your obvious desires be for what is good, and the people will be good. The relation between superiors and inferiors is like that between the wind and the grass. The grass must bend, when the wind blows across it."

[13.5] The Master said, "Though a man may be able to recite the three hundred odes, yet if, when entrusted with a governmental charge, he knows not how to act, or if, when sent to any quarter on a mission, he cannot give his replies unassisted, notwithstanding the extent of his learning, of what practical use is it?" The Master said, "When a prince's personal conduct is correct, his government is effective without the issuing of orders. If his personal conduct is not correct, he may issue orders, but they will not be followed."

---

[17] *There is government . . . a son:* Notice the Confucian teaching of rectification of names.

Confidence and Prosperity in Government*

The Mencius *has much to say about good government. The first excerpt deals with the need of the rulers to keep the confidence of the people. The second deals with the need for some level of economic prosperity so that both ruler and people may flourish.*

[4.3] Mencius said, "By benevolence the three dynasties gained the empire, and by not being benevolent they lost it. By the same means are determined the decaying and flourishing, the preservation and perishing, of states. If the emperor is not benevolent, he cannot preserve the empire from passing from him. If the sovereign of a state is not benevolent, he cannot

preserve his kingdom. If a high noble or great officer is not benevolent, he cannot preserve his ancestral temple. If a scholar or common man is not benevolent, he cannot preserve his four limbs. Hating death and ruin yet delighting in being unbenevolent is like hating to be drunk yet loving to drink wine." . . .

Mencius said, "There is a way to get the empire: Get the people, and the empire is obtained. There is a way to get the people: Get their hearts, and the

---

Mencius 4.3, 9; 1.6.20–24.

people are obtained. There is a way to get their hearts: Collect for them what they like, and do not lay on them what they dislike. The people turn to a benevolent rule as water runs downward, and as wild animals run to the wilderness."

[1.6.20–24] Mencius said [to King Hsuan of Ch'i], . . . "Only men of education are able to maintain a fixed heart without a fixed means of livelihood. As to the people, if they do not have a certain livelihood, then they will not have a fixed heart. And if they do not have a fixed heart, there is nothing that they will not do. They will go the way of self-abandonment, of moral deflection, of depravity, and of wild license. When they have been involved in these crimes, to follow them up and punish them is to entrap the people. How can such a thing as entrapping the people be done under the rule of a benevolent man?

"Therefore an intelligent ruler will regulate the livelihood of the people, so as to make sure that they shall have enough to serve their parents, and enough to support their wives and children. He ensures that in good years they shall always be abundantly satisfied, and that in bad years they shall escape the danger of perishing. Then he may urge them to what is good, and they will do it, for in this case the people will follow after the good with ease. But now the livelihood of the people is so regulated that they do not have

enough to serve their parents and enough to support their wives and children. Even though they may have good years, their lives are continually embittered, and in bad years they do not escape perishing. In such circumstances they only try to save themselves from death, and they are afraid they will not succeed. What leisure do they have to cultivate propriety and righteousness?

"If Your Majesty wishes to govern humanely the livelihood of the people, why not turn to that which is the essential step to it? Let mulberry trees be planted about the homesteads with their five sections of land, and persons of fifty years may then be clothed with silk. In keeping fowls, pigs, and swine, let not their times of breeding be neglected, and persons of seventy years may eat meat. Let there not be taken away the time that is proper for the cultivation of the farm with its hundred sections of land, and the family of eight that is supported by it shall not suffer from hunger. Let careful attention be paid to education in schools, especially education in the filial and fraternal duties, and gray-haired men will not be seen upon the roads carrying burdens on their backs or on their heads. It never has been that the ruler of a state where such results were seen—the old wearing silk and eating meat, and the young people suffering neither from hunger nor cold—did not attain to the office of emperor."

RITUAL AND MEDITATION

Divination*

The Classic of Changes (I Ching) *has been used for philosophical meditation, but its main use has been in divination. The traditional ceremony with milfoil sticks is often used, but rolling dice or any other method of selecting numbers can be employed. When the hexagram that matches the numbers thrown is located, it is read and applied* *to the inquirer's situation, giving the inquirer insight and foresight into the future.*[18]

---

* *Classic of Changes* 1, 47, 54.
[18] Taken, with editing, from James Legge, trans., *The Sacred Books of China: The Texts of Confucianism,* part 2, *The Yi King, Sacred Books of the East,* vol. 16 (Oxford: Oxford University Press, 1882), pp. 57–58, 161–163, 180–182.

THE CH'IEN HEXAGRAM:

Ch'ien [represents] what is great and originating, penetrating, advantageous, correct, and firm.

In the first [or lowest] line, undivided, [we see] the dragon lying hidden in the deep. It is not the time for active doing.

In the second line, undivided, [we see] the dragon appearing in the field. It will be advantageous to meet with the morally great man.

In the third line, undivided, [we see] the superior man active and vigilant all day, and in the evening still careful and apprehensive. There is danger, but there will be no mistake.

In the fourth line, undivided, [we see the dragon looking] as if he were leaping up, but still in the deep. There will be no mistake.

In the fifth line, undivided, [we see] the dragon flying in the sky. It will be advantageous to meet with the great man.

In the sixth [or topmost] line, undivided, [we see] the dragon exceeding the proper limits. There will be occasion for repentance.

[The lines of this hexagram are all strong and undivided, as appears from] the use of the number nine. If the host of dragons thus appearing were to divest themselves of their heads, there would be good fortune.[19]

THE K'UN HEXAGRAM:

In [the condition denoted by] K'un there may [yet be] progress and success. For the firm and correct, the [really] great man, there will be good fortune. He will fall into no error. If he makes speeches, his words cannot be made good.

The first line, divided, shows its subject with bare buttocks in difficulty under the stump of a tree. He enters a dark valley and for three years has no prospect [of deliverance].

The second line, undivided, shows its subject in difficulty amid his wine and food. Then comes to him the red knee-covers [of the ruler]. It will be well for him [to maintain his sincerity] in sacrificing. Active operations [on his part] will lead to evil, but he will be free from blame.

The third line, divided, shows its subject in difficulty before a [frowning] rock. He lays hold of thorns. He enters his palace and does not see his wife. There will be evil.

The fourth line, undivided, shows its subject proceeding very slowly [to help the subject of the first line], who is in difficulty by the carriage adorned with metal in front of him. There will be occasion for regret, but the end will be good.

The fifth line, undivided, shows its subject with his nose and feet cut off. He is in difficulty by [his ministers in their] scarlet aprons. He is leisurely in his movements, however, and is satisfied. It will be well for him to be [sincere] in sacrificing [to spiritual beings].

The sixth line, divided, shows its subject in difficulty, as if bound with creepers, or in a high and dangerous position and saying [to himself], "If I move, I shall regret it." If he does repent of former errors, there will be good fortune in his going forward.[20]

THE KUEI MEI HEXAGRAM:

Kuei Mei indicates that [under the conditions which it denotes] action will be evil and in no way advantageous.

---

[19] The point of the Ch'ien hexagram is that mildness of action plus firmness of decision leads to good fortune.

[20] The point of the K'un hexagram is that the person beset by problems can move out of them with a grasp of the situation and a change of attitude.

The first line, undivided, shows the younger woman married off in a position secondary to the real wife.[21] It suggests the idea of a person lame in one leg who yet manages to tramp along. Going forward will be fortunate.

The second line, undivided, shows her blind in one eye yet able to see. There will be advantage in her maintaining the firm correctness of a solitary widow.

The third line, divided, shows the younger woman who was to be married off in an inferior position. She returns and accepts an ancillary position.

The fourth line, undivided, shows the younger woman who is to be married off protracting the time. She may be late in being married, but the time will come.

The fifth line, divided, reminds us of the marrying of a younger woman to [King] Ti-yi, when the sleeves of the princess were not equal to those of the [still] younger woman who accompanied her in an inferior capacity. [The case suggests the thought of] the moon almost full. There will be good fortune.

The sixth line, divided, shows the young lady bearing the basket of harvest offerings, but without anything in it, and the gentleman slaughtering the sheep, but without blood flowing from it. There will be no advantage in any way.[22]

---

[21] *younger woman . . . real wife:* The symbolism here draws on the ancient Chinese custom of a man taking a concubine.
[22] The point of the Kuei Mei hexagram is that new undertakings are not advantageous, especially for those who, like the young woman, have difficulty accepting a low social role.

Songs for Sacrifice*

These selections from the Classic of Poetry *show the deep connection of ritual and virtue in Confucianism. The first song is for an emperor's sacrifice to an ancestor. The second is a complaint to Heaven about an unjust king. The last song provides fascinating details about the sacrificial service in the temple to honor ancestors.*[23]

SACRIFICIAL ODES OF KAU, ODE 7
They come full of harmony;
They are here in all seriousness,
The princes assisting,
While the Son of Heaven[24] looks profound.

[He says], "O Great and august Father,
While I present this noble bull,
And they assist me in setting forth the sacrifice,
Comfort me, your filial son.

"You lived with penetrating wisdom,
A sovereign with the gifts both of peace and
    war.

You gave rest even to great Heaven,
And ensured prosperity to your descendants.

"You comfort me with the eyebrows of long
    life;
You make me great with many blessings.
I offer this sacrifice to my meritorious father,
And to my accomplished mother."

MINOR ODES OF THE KINGDOM, ODE 10.1, 3
Great and wide Heaven,
Why do you constrict your kindness,
Sending down death and famine,

---

*Classic of Poetry: Kau 7; Minor Odes 10.1, 3; Minor Odes 5.
[23] Taken, with editing, from James Legge, trans., *The Sacred Books of China: The Texts of Confucianism,* part 1, *Sacred Books of the East,* vol. 3 (Oxford: Oxford University Press, 1879), pp. 304–305, 325–326, 357–358, 365–368.
[24] *Son of Heaven:* the king or emperor.

Destroying everything in the kingdom?
Compassionate Heaven, arrayed in terrors,
Why do you exercise no forethought, no care?

Leave the criminals alone;
They have suffered for their guilt.
But those who have no crime
Are indiscriminately involved in ruin.

How is it, O great Heaven,
That the king will not listen to just words?
He is like a man going astray,
Who knows not where he is going.
All you officers,
Let each of you attend to his duties.
Why do you not stand in awe of one another?
Because you do not stand in awe of Heaven.

MINOR ODES OF THE KINGDOM, ODE 5

Thick grew the prickly plants on the ground,
But they cleared away its thorny parts.
Why did they do this in old times?
That we might plant our grain and sacrificial
    grain;
That our crops might be abundant,
Our sacrificial grain luxuriant.

When our barns are full,
And our stacks can be counted by tens of
    thousands,
We proceed to make drinks and prepare grain,
For offerings and sacrifice.
We seat the representatives of the dead, and
    urge them to eat,[25]
Seeking to increase our bright happiness.

With correct and reverent behavior,
The bulls and rams all pure,
We proceed to the winter and autumnal
    sacrifices.
Some arrange the meat; some adjust its
    pieces.[26]
The chief officiant sacrifices inside the temple
    gate,
And all the sacrificial service is complete and
    excellent.

Grandly come our ancestors;
Their spirits happily enjoy the offerings;

Their filial descendant receives blessing.
They will reward him with great happiness,
With ten thousand years, life without end.

They attend to the ovens with reverence;
They prepare the trays, which are very large—
Some for the roast meat, some for the broiled.
Wives presiding are still and reverent,
Preparing the numerous smaller dishes.
The guests and visitors
Present the cup all around.

Every form is according to rule,
Each smile and word as it should be.
The spirits quietly come,
And respond with great blessings—
Thousands of years as the [fitting] reward.

We are completely exhausted,
And have performed every ceremony without
    error.
The able officiant announces to the filial
    descendant,
"Your filial sacrifice has been fragrant,
And the spirits have enjoyed your drinks and
    food.
They confer on you a hundred blessings,
Each as it is desired, each as sure as law.
You have been exact and expeditious;
You have been correct and careful.
They will always confer on you the choicest
    favors,
In thousands and tens of thousands."

The ceremonies have been completed,
And the bells and drums have given their
    warning.
The filial descendant goes to his place,
And the able officiant makes his announce-
    ment,
"The spirits have drunk to the full."
The great representatives of the dead then rise,

---

[25] *We seat . . . eat:* People who, in the ceremony, represent the deceased ancestors are seated and feted.

[26] In Confucian sacrifice, the animals are killed and cooked before the ceremony, not as a part of it.

And the bells and drums escort their withdrawal,
On which the spirits tranquilly return.

All the servants, and the presiding wives,
Remove the trays and dishes without delay.
The [sacrificer's] uncles and cousins
All go to the private feast that follows.
The musicians all go in to perform,
And give their soothing aid at the second
  blessing.

Your foods are set forth;
There is no dissatisfaction, but all feel happy.
They drink to the full, and eat to the full.

Great and small, they bow their heads, [saying],
"The spirits enjoyed your drinks and foods.
They will cause you to live long.
Your sacrifices, all in their seasons,
Are completely discharged by you.
May your sons and your grandsons
Never fail to perpetuate these services!"

Music and Morality*

Music has played a large role in Chinese culture and religion. One of the ancient Classics dealt exclusively with music. Although that text has unfortunately been lost, some of it probably has survived in the Classic of Rites (Li Chi). *Notice here how music expresses the cosmic forces of the universe, and how its extensive use in sacrifice furthers the meaning of the ceremony.*[27]

In framing their music, the ancient kings laid its foundation in the feelings and nature of men. They examined the notes by the measures for the length and quality of each, and adapted each note to express the meaning of the ceremonies in which it was to be used. They brought it into harmony with the energy that produces life, and to give expression to the performance of the five regular constituents of moral worth. They made it indicate that energy in its Yang or phase of vigor, without any dissipation of its power, and also in its Yin or phase of remission, without the vanishing of its power. The strong phase showed no excess like that of anger, and the weak no shrinking like that of pusillanimity. These four characteristics blended harmoniously in the minds of men and were similarly manifested in their conduct. Each occupied quietly its proper place, and one did not interfere injuriously with another.

After this they established schools for teaching their music, and different grades for the learners. They marked fully the divisions of the pieces. They condensed the parts and variations, giving beauty and elegance, in order to regulate and increase the inward virtue of the learners. They gave laws for the great and small notes according to their names, and they harmonized the order of the beginning and the end to represent the doing of things. Thus they made the underlying principles of the relations between the near and distant relatives, the noble and inferior, the old and young, males and females, all to appear clearly in the music. Hence it is said, "In music we must endeavor to see its depths."

[15] Hence the superior man returns to the good affections in order to bring his will into harmony with them, and he compares the different qualities of actions in order to perfect his conduct. Notes that are evil and depraved, and sights leading to disorder and licentiousness, are not allowed to affect his ears or eyes. Immoral music and corrupted ceremonies are not admit-

---

Classic of Rites 17.2.10–11, 15–16, 18.
[27] Taken, with editing, from James Legge, trans., *The Sacred Books of China: The Texts of Confucianism*, part 4, *Sacred Books of the East*, vol. 28 (Oxford: Oxford University Press, 1885), pp. 108–112.

ted into the mind to affect its powers. The spirit of idleness, indifference, depravity, and perversity finds no exhibition in his person. Thus he makes his ears, eyes, nose, and mouth the apprehensions of his mind, and the movements of all the parts of his body follow the course that is correct and do that which is right.

After this there ensues the manifestation of the inward thoughts by the modulations of note and tone, the elegant accompaniments of the lutes, small and large, the dances with shields and battle-axes, the ornaments of the plumes and ox-tails,[28] concluding with the pipes and flutes. All this has the effect of exhibiting the brilliance of complete virtue, stirring up the harmonious action of the

four seasonal energies, and displaying the true natures and qualities of all things. . . .

[18] Therefore, when the music has full course . . . the perceptions of the ears and eyes become sharp and distinct; the action of the blood and physical energies is harmonious and calm, bad influences are removed and manners changed, and all under heaven there is complete calm.

---

[28] *movements . . . ox-tails:* Pantomime dancing often accompanies the important rituals; both military dances (with *shields and battle-axes*) and civilian dances (with *plumes and ox-tails*) are performed by the dancers.

LATER DEVELOPMENTS OF SCRIPTURAL THEMES

Attack on Buddhism*

Han Yu (768–824 C.E.) led a Confucian attack against Buddhism and Taoism, asking the emperor to suppress these religions. Han was a poet and philosopher, and an official at the court of the emperor. This passage from a letter written to the emperor asks him to rethink his decision to view a relic of the Buddha's body, a bone. Han warns the emperor that viewing the bone would indicate imperial support of the Buddhist practice of relic worship.[29]

Buddhism is no more than a cult of the barbarian peoples which spread to China in the time of the Latter Han. It did not exist here in ancient times. . . . When Emperor Kao-tsu received the throne from the House of Sui, he deliberated whether he should suppress Buddhism. But at that time the various officials, being of small worth and knowledge, were unable fully to comprehend the ways of the ancient kings, and so could not implement the wisdom of the emperor and rescue the age from corruption. . . .

Buddha was a man of the barbarians who did not speak the language of China and wore clothes of a different fashion. His sayings did not concern the ways of our ancient kings, nor did his manner of dress conform to their laws. He understood neither the duties that bind sovereign and subject, nor the affections of father and son. If he were still alive today and came to our court by order of his ruler, Your Majesty might condescend to receive him, but. . . . he would then be escorted to the borders of the nation, dismissed, and not allowed to delude the masses. How then, when he has long been dead, could his rotten bones, the foul and inauspicious remains of his body, be rightly admitted to the palace? Confucius said, "Respect ghosts and

---

*Ch'ang-li hsien-sheng wen-chi 39.2b–42.
[29] From W. T. de Bary, *Sources of Chinese Tradition* (New York: Columbia University Press, 1964), pp. 371–372. Copyright ©1964 by Columbia University Press. Used by permission.

spirits, but keep them at a distance." Now without reason Your Majesty has caused this loathsome thing to be brought in and would personally go to view it. . . .

Your servant is deeply shamed and begs that this bone be given to the proper authorities to be cast into fire and water, that this evil may be rooted out, the world freed from its error, and later generations spared this delusion. . . . If the Buddha does indeed have supernatural power to send down curses and calamities, may they fall only upon the person of your servant, who calls upon High Heaven to witness that he does not regret his words.

Advice for Reading Texts*

After Confucius and Mencius, Chu Hsi (1130–1200) is the single most influential figure in Confucianism and the Chinese cultural tradition. The entire educational and civil service exam structure of China from the fourteenth century until the early twentieth was based on his theoretical and practical teachings. Chu's central concern was how a person could become a sage— that is, learned and morally good. To promote this state of being, he developed for his disciples a systematic program of self-cultivation. Here is part of his advice on reading and learning; it contains good guidance for students of all times and cultures.[30]

In a response to a student, Wen-kung explained the way of learning, citing Hsun-tzu's four lines, "[The superior man] recites texts in order to penetrate the Way, ponders in order to understand it, associates with men who embody it in order to make it part of himself, and shuns those who impede it in order to sustain and nourish it." Hsun-tzu's explanation is pretty good. As for the term "recite a text," I believe that when the ancients recited a text they kept track of the number of times [they said it out loud]. . . . It also means, "to understand thoroughly." Only if we've read to the point of intimate familiarity are we able to understand thoroughly. And if we haven't read to the point of intimate familiarity, there is nothing we can possibly ponder.

In reading, to comprehend a passage, you should have a detailed understanding of it. If you don't understand it in detail, your reading of other passages will be muddled too. If you understand one passage in detail, others will be easy to understand. Shan-ku's note explains the method of reading extremely well. Students who are overzealous don't understand in detail the meaning of what they read. In reading, you have to be very careful; it's essential that you understand every sentence and every character with certainty. If your effort is lax and you're not given to reflection, you'll simply conclude that there's nothing in your understanding of it that need be doubted; it isn't really that there's nothing to be doubted, but since your understanding isn't complete you just don't realize it. In learning, there's generally a distinction between young and old. When we're young, we have excess energy; it's essential that we leave nothing unread and that we analyze fully the meaning of what we read. By contrast, as we approach old age, we must select out what's important and devote our efforts to it; in reading a particular book, we're aware that later on it will be difficult to summon up the effort

---

*Conversations of Master Chu 4.37–39, 41.

[30] From Daniel K. Gardner, *Learning to Be a Sage: Selections from the Conversations of Master Chu* (Berkeley: University of California Press, 1990), pp. 136–39. Copyright © 1990 University of California Press. Used by permission of University of California Press and Daniel K. Gardner.

to look at it again. We must ponder it deeply and analyze it to its limits, and we'll understand its meaning.

It would seem that in the moral principle of the universe there's nothing but right and wrong. Right is right, wrong is wrong, and once we're certain about which is which, though we may not reread a text, the principle in it will naturally infuse us. We'll see it once and never forget it. This may all be compared to eating and drinking. If we chew slowly, the flavor lasts. If we take big bites and big gulps, in the end we don't know the flavor. . . .

[4.41] The value of a book is in the recitation of it. By reciting it often, we naturally come to understand it. Now, even if we ponder over what's written on the paper, it's useless, for in the end it isn't really ours. There's value only in recitation, though I don't know how the mind so naturally becomes harmonious with the psycho-physical stuff, feels uplifted and energized, and remembers securely what it reads.

Even supposing we were to read through a text thoroughly, pondering it over and over in our minds, it wouldn't be as good as reciting it. If we recite it again and again, in no time the incomprehensible becomes comprehensible and the already comprehensible becomes even more meaningful. But if the recitation doesn't reach the point of intimate familiarity, it won't be so meaningful at all. At the moment I'm not even speaking about the recitation of commentaries; let's simply recite the classical texts to the point of intimate familiarity. Whether we are walking or at a standstill, sitting or lying down, if our minds are always on these texts, we'll naturally come to understand them. It has occurred to me that recitation is learning. The Master said: "Learning without thinking is a waste; thinking without learning is dangerous."[31] Learning is reciting. If we recite it then think it over, think

it over then recite it, naturally it'll become meaningful to us. If we recite it but don't think it over, we still won't appreciate its meaning. If we think it over but don't recite it, even though we might understand it, our understanding will be precarious.

It's just like hiring somebody else to guard our home: because he isn't one of the family, in the end he can't be used as we would use a family member. Should we recite a text to the point of intimate familiarity, and moreover think about it in detail, naturally our mind and principle will become one and never shall we forget what we've read. I used to find it hard to remember texts. Then I simply recited them aloud. What I remember now is the result of recitation. Old Su[32] simply took the *Book of Mencius,* the *Analects,* the *Han Fei-tzu,* and the writings of the various sages and for seven or eight years sat quietly reciting them. Afterward he wrote a number of things that were very good. To be sure, his natural abilities couldn't be matched, but still it was essential that he recite as he did. And yet, reciting the texts, he merely wanted to pattern his writing on what was written there. Now if we were to turn our minds and his sort of natural ability to the investigation of moral principle, we'd find it right there in the text. Thus we know that the value of a text is in the intimate recitation of it. There is no other way.

---

[31] This quote is from the *Analects* 2.15.
[32] *Old Su:* a Confucian sage who lived from 1009 to 1061.

Neo-Confucian Ethics*

Chang Tsai (1020–1077) was a leading neo-Confucianist. In the more developed doctrines of being that are a hallmark of neo-Confucianism, Chang taught that the universe is one but its manifestations are many. When applied to ethics, this teaching became the notions of Heaven and Earth as universal parents and humaneness toward all people. This is the leading idea of the Western Inscription *(so called because it was inscribed on the western wall of Chang's study), the most beloved text of neo-Confucian literature.*[33]

Heaven is my father and Earth is my mother, and even such a small creature as I finds an intimate place in their midst.

Therefore that which fills the universe I regard as my body and that which directs the universe I consider as my nature.

All people are my brothers and sisters, and all things are my companions.

The great ruler (the emperor) is the eldest son of my parents (Heaven and Earth), and the great ministers are his stewards. Respect the aged—this is the way to treat them as elders should be treated. Show deep love toward the orphaned and the weak—this is the way to treat them as the young should be treated. The sage identifies his character with that of Heaven and Earth, and the worthy is the most outstanding man.

Even those who are tired, infirm, crippled, or sick; those who have no brothers or children, wives or husbands, are all my brothers who are in distress and have no one to turn to.

When the time comes, to keep himself from harm—this is the care of a son. To rejoice in Heaven and to have no anxiety—this is filial piety at its purest.

He who disobeys [the Tao, or Principle of Nature] violates virtue. He who destroys humanity is a robber.

He who promotes evil lacks [moral] capacity, but he who puts his moral nature into practice and brings his physical existence into complete fulfillment can match [Heaven and Earth].

One who knows the principles of transformation will skillfully carry forward the undertakings [of Heaven and Earth], and one who penetrates spirit to the highest degree will skillfully carry out their will.

Do nothing shameful in the recesses of your own house and thus bring no dishonor to them.

Preserve your mind and nourish your nature and thus (serve them) with untiring effort. The Great Yu heated pleasant wine but attended to the protection and support of his parents.

Border Warden Ying brought up and educated the young and thus extended his love to his own kind. Shun's merit lay in delighting his parents with unceasing effort, and Shensheng's reverence was demonstrated when he awaited punishment without making an attempt to escape. . . .

Wealth, honor, blessing, and benefits are meant for the enrichment of my life, while poverty, humble station, and sorrow are meant to help me to fulfillment.

In life I follow and serve [Heaven and Earth]. In death I will be at peace.

---

* Chang Tsai, *The Western Inscription*.

[33] From Wing-tsit Chan, *A Source Book in Chinese Philosophy* (Princeton: Princeton University Press, 1963), pp. 497–498. Copyright © 1963 Princeton University Press. Used by permission of Princeton University Press.

GLOSSARY

Pinyin spelling, where it differs from Wade-Giles, is given in parentheses before the pronunciation.

Ching (Jing) [jing] "Classics"; books that make up part of the early Confucian canon.

chun-tzu (jun-zi) [jun-tzoo] "prince's son"; in the teaching of Confucius, a "superior man" made so by the study and practice of virtue.

hsiao (xiao) [syow] filiality; love for and service to one's parents and deceased ancestors.

I Ching (*Yi Jing*) [ee jing] "Classic of Changes"; a diviner's manual; earliest of the Confucian scriptures.

jen (ren) [ren] the virtue of benevolence or humaneness.

li [lee] propriety, or decorum, both in the rites and in everyday life.

Tao (Dao) [dow] the cosmic "Way" of life; in Confucian scripture, often related to Heaven (e.g., the "Way of Heaven").

wen-yen the formal-classical style in which the Confucian classics are written.

yin-yang [not ying-yang] cosmic forces such as passivity and activity, darkness and light, and other opposing pairs.

QUESTIONS FOR STUDY AND DISCUSSION

1.   Compare and contrast the earliest Confucian canon, the *Five Classics,* with the later canon, the *Four Books.* What are their commonalities and differences?

2.   How do the Confucian scriptures bear witness to the importance of three elements often held to be common to all traditional Chinese religion: heaven, earth, and ancestor worship?

3.   Reflect on the lively political issue of the personal character of candidates for public office in contemporary North America. To what degree does Confucius' counsel about a morally superior ruler apply in our society?

4.   To what degree may filiality be a prescription for social pressures on the modern Western family?

5.   What is the continuing significance of the Confucian scriptures in modern life outside China?

6.   Do you think, with Mencius, that human nature is innately good? Why or why not?

7.   Apply the standards in the "Music and Morality" reading (pages 185–186) to the kinds of popular music you listen to. Do you agree with the results?

8.   Having read these Confucian scriptures, what is your own conclusion about this often discussed issue: Is Confucianism a religion or a philosophy?

SCRIPTURES IN FILM

Confucian scriptures are illustrated but not directly treated in several highly praised feature films. (This is exactly what we would expect for a religion so deeply identified with Chinese culture.) *The Last Emperor* (1987, rated PG-13), directed by Bernardo Bertolucci, tells the story of Pu Yi, China's final monarch; it was filmed in part in the

Forbidden City in Beijing. See the "director's cut" DVD for a fuller story that carries the life of Pu Yi through communist "re-education" camps. *Farewell My Concubine* (1993, rated R), directed by Chen Kaige, tells the story of two singers in the Beijing (Peking) Opera. It gives a good sense of the importance of music and dance in Chinese culture. *Raise the Red Lantern* (1998, rated PG), directed by Zhang Yimou, deals with the life of a traditional Chinese family in 1920, particularly the difficulties posed by second and third marriages. *Eat Drink Man Woman* (1994, not submitted for ratings but probably in the PG-13 to R range) explores family relationships in Taiwan as the Taiwanese people deal with modern times. Its focus on the life of a restaurant operator also gives some insight into how Chinese cuisine fits into wider Chinese culture.

SUGGESTIONS FOR FURTHER READING

Primary Readings

The fullest English translation of the Confucian canon continues to be by James Legge and others in F. Max Müller, gen. ed., *Sacred Books of the East*. Vol. 3 is the *Shu Ching*, the religious portions of the *Shih Ching*, and the *Hsiao Ching*; vol. 16 is the *I Ching*; vols. 27 and 28 are the *Li Chi*.

R. M. Barnhart, *Li Kung-lin's Classic of Filial Piety*. New York: Metropolitan Museum of Art, 1993. Features the paintings of Li Kung-lin (1041–1106) illustrating the *Filial Piety;* Li's paintings are some of the most important works of art in Chinese cultural history.

Wing-tsit Chan, *A Source Book in Chinese Philosophy*. Princeton: Princeton University Press, 1963. Full selections from religious-philosophical Confucian books and older classics, from a leading interpreter of Chinese religious literature to the West.

D. C. Lau, trans., *The Analects*. London: Penguin, 1979. An excellent contemporary translation, with good notes.

D. C. Lau, trans., *The Mencius*. London: Penguin, 1983. The same standard and format as in Lau's translation of the *Analects*.

R. Wilhelm, trans., *The I Ching*. Bollingen Series, no. 19. New York: Pantheon, 1961. Perhaps the best current translation of the *Book of Changes*.

Secondary Readings

J. B. Henderson, *Scripture, Canon, Commentary: A Comparison of Confucian and Western Exegesis*. Princeton: Princeton University Press, 1991. An excellent treatment of the important question of the relationship and explanation of scripture and commentary, with valuable comparative analysis of Chinese commentary and the Western (mainly Christian) commentarial tradition.

T. Kelleher, "[Women in] Confucianism." In A. Sharma, ed., *Women in World Religions*. Albany: State University of New York Press, 1987, pp. 135–159. An insightful essay on the influence of Confucian scripture on the roles of women in China.

M. Nylan, *The Five "Confucian" Classics*. New Haven: Yale University Press, 2001. A fascinating review of the history and influence of these books that challenges several current conclusions.

R. L. Taylor, "Confucianism: Scripture and Sage." In F. M. Denney and R. L. Taylor, eds., *The Holy Book in Comparative Perspective*. Columbia: University of South Carolina Press, 1985, pp. 181–203. An excellent study of the use of scripture to achieve sage-hood.

R. L. Taylor, *The Way of Heaven: An Introduction to Confucian Religious Life*. Leiden: Brill, 1986. A fine introduction to Confucian scripture in the context of religious life; many photographic illustrations of Confucian iconography and rituals.

Scripture Recitation in a Chinese Funeral
A Taoist priest in the Sichwan province of China reads a funeral text, and the men sitting around respond, to enable the soul of the deceased to pass successive judgments on its way to final blessing. *Credit:* Stevan Harrell, from the Image Bank of the Center for the Study of World Religions, Harvard University. Used by permission of Stevan Harrell.

CHAPTER SEVEN

Taoism

❧ In a temple in Kaoshiung, Taiwan, a medium known as a "spirit writer" falls under the possession of the temple's god. As he speaks the words of the god, a scribe standing nearby writes down the words. These words will be published in the temple's magazine and may perhaps form the basis of new Taoist scripture.

❧ A young man visits a Taoist temple in Hong Kong. He is puzzled about the course of his life and consults with a priest. They talk about the great Way and how he relates to it. The priest reminds him of several passages in the Taoist scriptures and explains their meaning. After some minutes of conversation, the young man goes away smiling, now more certain about the future.

❧ At the Hsing T'ien Temple in Taipei, Taiwan, the temple courtyard is filled with blue-robed women carrying out the faith healing for which the temple has gained its reputation. They lay hands on the sick or on clothing brought by the families of those too sick to come in person. In this way they carry out an ancient tradition of Taoism as discussed in many of its scriptures, that of healing and longevity.[1]

INTRODUCTION

Taoism is, after Confucianism, the most influential religion among Chinese people. According to Taoists, their faith was founded by Lao Tzu in the sixth century B.C.E. Since ancient times, the Taoist tradition has had two interacting parts: philosophical Taoism, rich in cosmological meditation and speculation; and religious (sometimes called "esoteric") Taoism, with its emphasis on exorcism, astrology, and gaining long life or even immortality. Although Taoism has had an important influence through history, its future is cloudy. Some scholars hold it to be a dying tradition. Whether it is or not only time will tell, but the scriptures of Taoism—especially the ***Tao Te Ching*** [DOW duh jing], "Classic of the Way and Its Working," and the ***Chuang-tzu*** [jwahng tzoo]—have earned an undying place in the history of the world's cultures and remain influential.

Overview of Structure

Taoist canon as a whole is known as the ***Tao Tsang*** [dow tsahng]. Its last main printing, in 1926, consists of 1,120 volumes. The *Tao Tsang* has traditionally been grouped into the *Three Caverns (San-Tung)*, reflecting three historic traditions within Taoism:

---

[1] B. E. Reed, "[Women in] Taoism," in A. Sharma, ed., *Women in World Religions* (Albany: State University of New York Press, 1987), p. 180.

the Supreme Clarity school, the Numinous Treasure school, and the Three Sovereigns school. Each "cavern" is divided into twelve sections. Their names indicate the overall content of the Taoist scriptures. They are "Original Revelations"; divine talismans; interpretations; diagrams; chronologies and genealogies; moral codes; ceremonial decorum; rituals; esoteric techniques (alchemy, astrology, exorcism, etc.); lives of past Taoist worthies; hymns; and messages to the dead. To the basic three-part form was added the *Four Supplements,* itself as mixed in content as the caverns.

Origin, Development, and Use

Critical study of the history of the Taoist canon is in its beginning stages, and the massive size of the canon makes the task especially challenging. Nevertheless, scholars have reached certain conclusions.

Taoists trace the origins of their religion and scriptures to the claimed founder of their tradition, Lao Tzu (sixth century B.C.E.). They hold that his disciples wrote down the first and most important work of the canon, the *Tao Te Ching,* shortly after his death. Indeed, Taoists often refer to the *Tao Te Ching* as the *Lao-Tzu.* Recent critical scholarship, however, has concluded that even though this book may have been started at this time, it is a collection of material from different authors that was assembled in the third century B.C.E.

The *Tao Te Ching* is the fountainhead of most of the Taoist scripture that followed. Its reflections on the **Tao** [dow] ("Way") and its **te** [duh] ("power") in eighty-one brief sections are written in a highly compressed style. The Chinese original features much parallelism among the lines of poetry and also a good deal of rhyme, lost in most translations. It points to a Tao that is cosmic, the origin of heaven and earth. This Tao is part of each individual's existence, and it is a social ideal as well.

Probably because of its cryptic quality and mixed content, the *Tao Te Ching* is scripture that all Taoists have responded to. Indeed, it is one of the few scripture books to be extensively used in both philosophical Taoism and religious Taoism. Also, to judge from the frequency with which it has been translated into English (more than one hundred times) and other European languages, the *Tao Te Ching* has had a significant appeal to peoples of other religions and cultures. The appeal of this book in the United States, for example, is echoed in the titles of more than fifty books, such as *The Tao of . . . Parenting, Dialogue, Spycraft, Coaching, Sales, Golf,* and even *Jesus* and *Islam.* (For an example of how contemporary English translations of the *Tao Te Ching* differ, see Figure 7.1.)

The second most important text of Taoism is the *Chuang-tzu,* named for its author, a fourth-century B.C.E. Chinese philosopher and teacher. This book is far removed from the *Tao Te Ching.* Full of anecdote and allegory, it challenges the reader with its provocative style and content. It stresses the illusory nature of knowledge and the difficulty, if not impossibility, of separating right and wrong. Nevertheless, the *Chuang-tzu* does include specific moral guidelines that proceed from the "two great sanctions": the moral requirements visible in nature and the inner conviction of what is right and wrong. Both of these principles are grounded in the great Tao.

Other important Taoist texts can be mentioned here only in passing. The *T'ai-shang* deals with retribution for sin and reward for evil. According to this work, the life span of people who live a good life in harmony with the Tao will be lengthened,

(*Continues on page 198*)

Figure 7.1   Four Contemporary Translations of Tao Te Ching, *Chapter 1*

1. by Stephen Addiss and Stanley Lombardo (1993)

Tao k'o tao fei ch'ang tao.
TAO called TAO is not TAO.
Names can name no lasting name.

Nameless: the origin of heaven and earth.
Naming: the mother of the ten thousand things.

Empty of desire, perceive mystery.
Filled with desire, perceive manifestations.

These have the same source, but different names.
Call them both deep—Deep and again deep:
The gateway to all mystery.

Source: From *Lao Tzu: Tao Te Ching,* translated by Lombardo and Addis, 1993. Reprinted by permission of Hackett Publishing Co., Inc.

2. by Ursula LeGuin (1998)

The way you can go
isn't the real way.
The name you can say
isn't the real name.

Heaven and earth
begin in the unnamed:
name's the mother
of the ten thousand things.

So the unwanting soul
sees what's hidden,
and the ever-wanting soul
sees only what it wants.

Two things, one origin,
but different in name,
whose identity is mystery.
Mystery of all mysteries!
The door to the hidden.

Source: From Lao Tzu: *Tao Te Ching,* Copyright © 1997. Reprinted by arrangement with Shambhala Publications, Inc., Boston. www.shambhala.com.

Figure 7.1 continued

3. by Benjamin Hoff (1981)

The way that can be defined to death is not the Way to Life.
The road that can be measured is not the endless road.
From nothing, the infinite universe began.
　　From no number, the countless things appeared.
From no name, their limitless sources will be known.

Looking out, its effects are seen;
Looking in, their cause is discovered.
With words, these are considered separate;
With vision, they are recognized as one.

Source: Benjamin Hoff, *The Way to Life: The Heart of the Tao Te Ching.* New York: Weatherhill, 1981, p. 1. Used by permission.

4. by James Legge (1891)

The Tao that can be trodden is not the enduring and unchanging Tao.
The name that can be named is not the enduring and changing name.

Conceived of as having no name, it is the Originator of heaven and earth;
Conceived of as having a name, it is the Mother of all things.

Always without desire we must be found,
If its deep mystery we would sound;
But if desire always within us be,
Its outer fringe is all that we will see.

Under these two aspects, it is really the same; but as development takes place, it receives the different names. Together we call them the Mystery. Where the Mystery is the deepest is the gate of all that is subtle and wonderful.

(*Continued from page 196*)

but those who lead an evil life will die early or have their punishment passed on to their descendants. The *Tao-fa hui-yuan* (Group of Taoist Rites) is a book of ceremonies to control demonic forces, both in nature and in the individual, when they result in sickness. The *Shang-ching hou-shen tao-chun lieh-chi* (Annals of the Lord of the Tao, the Sage-to-Come of Shang-ching) contains information on how certain Taoist masters (often called "adepts") used respiration techniques, alchemy, and other esoteric techniques to feed on astral powers and become immortal or even divine. Many other texts of religious/esoteric Taoism are written in a special script taught only to initiates into special sects, and Taoists have been very secretive about sharing this literature.

TEACHING

The Nature of the Tao*

The leading themes in the Tao Te Ching *are the nature of the Tao and how one follows it. These passages present the Tao as unnameable (Chapter 1), female in quality (6), the "mother" of heaven and earth (25), and accomplishing great things by means of small things (34). In the* Chuang-tzu, *the sage discusses the Tao in a more philosophical way yet also in the playful and challenging manner typical of the* Chuang-tzu.[2]

[*Tao Te Ching* 1] Tao called Tao is not Tao.
Names can name no lasting name.

Nameless: the origin of heaven and earth.
Naming: the mother of the ten thousand things.
Empty of desire, perceive mystery.
Filled with desire, perceive manifestations.

These have the same source, but different
   names.
 Call them both deep—
 Deep and again deep:
The gateway to all mystery.

[6] The Valley Spirit never dies.
It is called the Mysterious Female.

The entrance to the Mysterious Female
Is called the root of Heaven and Earth,
Endless flow
Of inexhaustible energy.

[25] Something unformed and complete
Before heaven and earth were born,
Solitary and silent,
Stands alone and unchanging,
Pervading all things without limit.
It is like the mother of all under heaven,
But I don't know its name—
 Better call it Tao.
 Better call it great.

Great means passing on.
Passing on means going far.
Going far means returning.

Therefore,
   Tao is great,
   And heaven,
   And earth,
   And humans.
Four great things in the world.
Aren't humans one of them?

Humans follow earth
Earth follows heaven
Heaven follows Tao.
Tao follows its own nature.

[34] Great Tao overflows
To the left   To the right.
All beings owe their life to it
And do not depart from it.
It acts without a name.
It clothes and nourishes all beings
But does not become their master.

Enduring without desire,
It may be called slight.
All beings return to it,
But it does not become their master.

It may be called immense.
By not making itself great,
It can do great things.

[*Chuang-tzu* 29] Tung-kwo tze asked Chuang Tzu, "Where is what you call the Tao to be found?" Chuang Tzu replied, "Everywhere." The other said, "Specify an instance of it. That will be more satisfactory." "It is here in this ant."

Tao Te Ching 1, 6, 25, 34; *Chuang-tzu* 29.
[2] All readings from the *Tao Te Ching,* except where noted, are taken from Stephen Addiss and Stanley Lombardo, *Lao-Tzu, Tao Te Ching* (Cambridge, MA: Hackett, 1993). Copyright © 1993 Hackett Publishing Co., Inc. Used by permission. Selections from the *Chuang-tzu* are from James Legge, *The Texts of Taoism, Sacred Books of the East,* vols. 39 and 40 (Oxford: Oxford University Press, 1891).

"Give me a lower instance." "It is in this earthenware tile." "Is that really the lowest instance?" Chuang Tzu said, "It is in that excrement." To this Tung-kwo tze gave no reply.

Chuang Tzu said, "Your questions, my master, do not touch the fundamental point of the Tao. They remind me of the questions addressed by the superintendents of the market to the inspector about examining the value of a pig by stepping on it and testing its weight as the foot descends lower and lower on the body. You should not specify any particular thing. One single thing does not describe the Tao. So it is with the Perfect Tao. And if we call it the Great Tao, it is just the same. It has the three terms 'Complete,' 'All-embracing,' and 'the Whole.' These names are different, but the reality sought in them is the same. They all refer to the One thing.

"Suppose we were to try to roam about in the palace of Nowhere. When met there, we might discuss the subject without ever coming to an end. Or suppose we were to be together in the region of Non-action. Should we say that the Tao was simplicity and stillness? or indifference and purity? or harmony and ease? My will would be aimless. If it went nowhere, I would not know where it had gone; if it went and came back again, I wouldn't know where it had stopped; if it went on going and coming, I would not know when the process would end. In vague uncertainty, I would be in the vastest waste. Though I entered it with the greatest knowledge, I would not know how inexhaustible it was. That which makes things what they are [the Tao] does not have the limit that belongs to things. . . . The Tao is the limit of the unlimited and the boundlessness of the unbounded.

"We speak of fullness and emptiness, and of withering and decay. It produces fullness and emptiness but is neither fullness nor emptiness. It produces withering and decay but is neither withering nor decay. It produces the root and branches but is neither root nor branch. It produces growth and spreading but is itself neither grown nor spread."

The World*

The typical Chinese expression for the world is "Heaven and Earth." These passages present the world, composed of the "ten thousand things," as proceeding from the Tao and holding to the way of inactivity. Wise persons will pattern their lives on the Tao that has made Heaven and Earth.

[7] Heaven is long, Earth enduring.
Long and enduring
Because they do not exist for themselves.

Therefore the Sage
    Steps back, but is always in front,
    Stays outside, but is always within.

No self interest?
Self is fulfilled.

[42] Tao engenders One,
One engenders Two,

Two engenders Three,[3]
Three engenders the ten thousand things.

The ten thousand things carry shade
And embrace sunlight.
Shade and sunlight, yin and yang,[4]
Breath blending into harmony.[5]

Humans hate
To be alone, poor, and hungry.
Yet kings and princes

---

*Tao Te Ching 7, 42, 52.
[3] The *One* is *ch'i*, the primordial, cosmic breath; the *Two* are yin and yang; the *Three* are the waters under the earth, the earth, and heaven.
[4] *Yin* and *yang* are cosmic principles or dualities: passive and active, earth and heaven, dark and light.
[5] *breath: ch'i*, the cosmic breath/wind.

Use these words as titles.
  We gain by losing,
  Lose by gaining.

What others teach, I also teach:
A violent man does not die a natural death.
This is the basis of my teaching.

[52] The world has a source: the world's mother.
Once you have the mother,
  You know the children.
Once you know the children,
  Return to the mother.

Your body dies.
There is no danger.

Block the passage,
Bolt the gate:
  No strain
Until your life ends.

Open the passage,
Take charge of things:
  No relief
Until your life ends.

Seeing the small is called brightness.
Maintaining gentleness is called strength.
Use this brightness to return to brightness.

Don't cling to your body's woes.
Then you can learn endurance.

The Domain of Nothingness*

A central teaching in Taoism is emptiness. When one becomes harmonious with the Tao, the world is without particulars. This is reflected in the idea that a true sage will not have a name. This passage alludes to related Buddhist themes.

T'ien Ken was traveling to the south of Yin Mountain. He had reached the river Liao when he met a nameless sage, to whom he said, "I beg to ask about governing the world."

"Go away," said the nameless man, "you are a low fellow. How unpleasant is your question! I want to be in companionship with the Maker of things. When wearied, I want to mount on the bird of ease and emptiness, proceed beyond the world, wander in the land of nowhere, and live in that domain of nothingness. Why do you come to worry me with the problem of setting the world in order?"

T'ien Ken again asked his question and the nameless man replied: "Make excursion in purest simplicity. Identify yourself with nondistinction. Follow the nature of things and have no personal bias, and then the world will be in peace."

Chuang-tzu 7.

The Relationship of Taoism to Confucianism**

Taoism and Confucianism have long been the two major traditions of China. Here is a statement from the Taoist side on their relationship, with the better judgment going of course to Taoism. The text deals with the question, Of Confucianism and Taoism, which is easier?[6]

Confucianism is difficulty in the midst of facility [ease]; Taoism is facility in the midst of difficulties.

The difficulties of Taoism are these: abandonment of social intercourse and renouncing wife

**Pao-p'u Tzu 7.5a.
[6] From James R. Ware, *Alchemy, Medicine, Religion in the China of A.D. 320: The Nei P'ien of Ko Hung (Pao-p'u tzu)*. Cambridge, MA: Massachusetts Institute of Technology Press, 1966. Copyright © 1966 by the Massachusetts Institute of Technology. Used by permission.

and family; rejection of fame and loss of income; removal of brilliances from one's sight and suppression of the tinkling marks of office from one's ears; the silence and retirement where one's sole profession is preservation of one's own integrity; not to be depressed by criticism nor elated by praise; to look upon honors without desiring them and to dwell humbly without shame. But Taoism also has its attractive side: no visits of congratulation or condolence, and no critical glances and looks at one's abode; no troubling of the internal gods with the Seven Classics and never a concern for the calendar; no bother about the advancing of asterisms[7] and no enslavement to a craft or to letters; all annoyances lifted, and an inner harmony that grows of itself; perfect freedom of action and thought, no fear, no grief. Therefore, I describe Taoism as facility in the midst of difficulties.

Everything done in Confucianism is modeled upon precedents. Leaving and staying have their set rules; speech and silence depend upon the hour. If a teacher is desired, he can be found in practically any house; it is a matter of written material, there are plenty of commentaries to resolve the doubts. This is what is easy in Confucianism.

Its difficulties are these: grasping the profound and rendering present the distant, and also confronting and reconciling the regulations coming from the rulers of old; . . . and acquiring a wide knowledge of all those many things said by the various schools of philosophy; constantly accumulating good works among the people, and giving the last drop of loyalty to one's lord; being able to interpret any signs conferred by heaven, and giving thought to the meanings of winds and clouds; to be considered unsuccessful for not knowing some solitary matter and to have to face criticism for one word of imprecision; to have one's every step taken as a model by the world, and to have one's every utterance repeated by all.

This is what I mean by difficulties in the midst of facility. But to put it honestly, Confucianism is difficult because of its multiplicities, while Taoism is easy with its conciseness.

---

[7] *asterism:* a cluster of stars smaller than a constellation, thought to have a negative impact on human life.

ETHICS

Nonaction*

*The leading ethical ideal of Taoism is **wu-wei** [woo-WAY], a wonderfully ambiguous term that is variously translated "effortless action," "nonaction" (in this translation), "active nonstriving," or "action without intent." By wu-wei, the sage seeks to come into harmony with the great Tao, which itself accomplishes by nonaction.*

Nonaction makes the person who practices it the lord of all fame; nonaction serves him as the treasury of all plans; nonaction fits him for the burden of all offices; nonaction makes him the lord of all wisdom. The range of his action is inexhaustible, but there is nowhere any trace of his presence. He fulfills all that he has received from Heaven, but he does not see that he was the recipient of anything. A pure vacancy of all purpose is what characterizes him. When the perfect man employs his mind, it is a mirror. It conducts nothing and anticipates nothing. It responds to what is before it but does not retain it. Thus he is able to deal successfully with all things and injures nothing.

---

*Chuang-tzu 7.

Individual Life in Harmony with the Tao*

These selections emphasize the necessity of bringing individual life into accord with the Tao and give advice on how to accomplish this through non-action and indirection.

[16] Attain complete emptiness,
Hold fast to stillness.

The ten thousand things stir about;
I only watch for their going back.

Things grow and grow,
But each goes back to its root.
Going back to the root is stillness.
This means returning to what is.
Returning to what is
Means going back to the ordinary.

Understanding the ordinary:
   Enlightenment.
Not understanding the ordinary:
   Blindness creates evil.
Understanding the ordinary:
   Mind opens.

Mind opening leads to compassion,
Compassion to nobility,
Nobility to heavenliness,
Heavenliness to Tao.
   Tao endures.
    Your body dies.
There is no danger.

[22] Crippled becomes whole,
Crooked becomes straight,
Hollow becomes full,
Worn becomes new,
Little becomes more,
Much becomes delusion.

Therefore Sages cling to the One
   And take care of this world;
Do not display themselves
   And therefore shine;
Do not assert themselves
   And therefore stand out;

Do not praise themselves
   And therefore succeed;
Are not complacent
   And therefore endure;
Do not contend
   And therefore no one under heaven
      Can contend with them.

The old saying
Crippled becomes whole
Is not empty words.
It becomes whole and returns.

[33] Knowing others is intelligent.
Knowing yourself is enlightened.

Conquering others takes force.
Conquering yourself is true strength.

Knowing what is enough is wealth.
Forging ahead shows inner resolve.

Hold your ground and you will last long.
Die without perishing and your life will endure.

[44] Name or body: which is closer?
Body or possessions: which means more?
Gain or loss: which one hurts?

Extreme love exacts a great price.
Many possessions entail heavy loss.

Know what is enough—
   Abuse nothing.
Know when to stop—
   Harm nothing.

This is how to last a long time.[8]

Tao Te Ching 16, 22, 33, 44.
[8]*last a long time:* Lines like these in the *Tao Te Ching* encouraged later Taoist practices for gaining long life and even immortality.

The Superior Man*

Here is a characteristically Taoist presentation of the superior man, designed of course to provide an alternative to the Confucian idea of superiority. Taoist superiority comes not through self-cultivation in the virtues but by tapping through inactivity into the superiority of the Tao. The full descriptions of the Taoist superior man form a complete list of the type of person that Taoists, especially philosophically oriented ones, seek to become.

The Master said, "The Tao covers and sustains all things. How great is its overflowing influence! The superior man ought to remove from his mind all that is contrary to it. Acting without action is what is called Heaven-like. Speech coming forth of itself is what is called a mark of the true virtue. Loving men and benefiting things is what is called benevolence. Seeing wherein things that are different yet agree is what is called being great. Conduct free from the ambition of being distinguished above others is what is called being generous. The possession in himself of a myriad points of difference is what is called being rich. Therefore to hold fast the natural attributes is what is called the guiding line of government; the perfecting of those attributes is what is called its establishment; accordance with the Tao is what is called being complete; and not allowing anything external to affect the will is what is called being perfect.

"When the superior man understands these things, he keeps all matters sheathed in himself, showing the greatness of his mind. Through the outflow of his doings all things move and come to him. Being such, he lets the gold lie hid in the hill, and the pearls in the deep; he considers not property or money to be any gain. He keeps aloof from riches and honors; he rejoices not in long life, and grieves not for early death. He does not regard prosperity as a glorious thing, nor is ashamed of indigence. He would not grasp at the gain of the whole world to be held as his own private portion; he would not desire to rule over the whole world as his own private distinction. His distinction is in understanding that all things belong to the one treasury, and that death and life should be viewed in the same way."

The Master said, "How still and deep is the place where the Tao resides! How limpid is its purity! Metal and stone without it would give forth no sound. They have the power of sound in them, but if they are not struck, they do not emit it. Who can determine the qualities that are in all things?

"The man of kingly qualities holds on to his way unoccupied and is ashamed to busy himself with the conduct of affairs. He establishes himself in what is the root and source of his capacity, and his wisdom grows to be spiritual. In this way his attributes become more and more great, and when his mind goes forth, whatever things come in his way, it lays hold of them and deals with them. Thus, if there were not the Tao, the bodily form would not have life, and its life, without the attributes of the Tao, would not be manifested. He who preserves the body and gives the fullest development to the life, he who establishes the attributes of the Tao and clearly displays the Tao, is possessed of kingly qualities. How majestic is he in his sudden pronouncements, and in his unexpected movements, when all things follow him! We call him the man whose qualities fit him to rule.

"He sees where there is the deepest obscurity; he hears where there is no sound. In the midst of the deepest obscurity, he alone sees and can distinguish various objects. In the midst of a soundless abyss, he alone can hear a harmony of notes. . . . In this way in his dealings with all things, while he is farthest from having anything, he can yet give to them what they seek. Although he is always hurrying forth, he returns to his resting place; now large, now small; now long,

---

*Chuang-tzu 12.

Government*

The social ethic of Taoism is largely concerned with government. Here it presents a quietist approach, the opposite of the activist approach of Confucianism. By inactivity in following the Tao, one can bring about the best state. This social ethic has led to several political options for Taoists: withdrawal from public life, mild participation in it, and at times participation in anarchy.

[3] Don't glorify heroes,
And people will not contend.
Don't treasure rare objects,
And no one will steal.
Don't display what people desire,
And their hearts will not be disturbed.

Therefore, the Sage rules
  By emptying hearts and filling bellies,
  By weakening ambitions and strengthening bones;
Leads people
  Away from knowing and wanting;
Deters those who know too much
  From going too far:
Practices non-action
  And the natural order is not disrupted.

[18] Great Tao rejected:
  Benevolence and righteousness appear.
Learning and knowledge professed:
  Great hypocrites spring up.
Family relations forgotten:
  Filial piety and affection arise.
The nation disordered:
  Patriots come forth.

[57] Use the expected to govern the country,
Use surprise to wage war,
Use non-action to win the world
How do I know?
  Like this!

The more prohibitions and rules,
  The poorer people become.
The sharper people's weapons,
  The more they riot.
The more skilled their techniques,
  The more grotesque their works.
The more elaborate the laws,
  The more they commit crimes.

Therefore the Sage says:
 I do nothing
  And people transform themselves.
 I enjoy serenity
  And people govern themselves.
 I cultivate emptiness
  And people become prosperous.
 I have no desires
  And people simplify themselves.

[64] At rest is easy to hold.
Not yet impossible is easy to plan.
Brittle is easy to break.
Fine is easy to scatter.

Create before it exists.
Lead before it goes astray.

A tree too big to embrace
  Is born from a slender shoot.
A nine-storey tower
  Rises from a pile of earth.
A thousand-mile journey
  Begins with a single step.

Act and you ruin it.
Grasp and you lose it.
Therefore the Sage
 Does not act
  And so does not ruin
 Does not grasp
  And so does not lose.
People commonly ruin their work
  When they are near success.
Proceed at the end as at the beginning
  And your work won't be ruined.
Therefore the Sage

Tao Te Ching 3, 18, 57, 64.

Desires no desires
Prizes no prizes
Studies no studies
And returns

To what others pass by.
The Sage
Helps all beings find their nature,
But does not presume to act.

Great and the Small Rulers*

In this passage, the Chuang-tzu *offers a critique of rulers. It argues, in its characteristic style, that true greatness is much more than just the ability to do one's job in government. As the quail rightly laughs at the mythical bird, the wise laugh at those with pretensions to greatness.*

In the barren north . . . there is a bird named the p'eng, with a back like Mount T'ai, and wings like clouds across the sky. Upon a whirlwind it soars up to a height of ninety thousand leagues. Beyond the clouds and atmosphere, with the blue sky above it, it then directs its flight to the south, and thus proceeds to the ocean there.

A quail laughs at it, saying: "Where is that bird going? I spring up with a bound, and when I have reached no more than a few yards I come down again. I just fly about among the brushwood and the bushes. This is also the perfection of flying. Where is that bird going?" This is the difference between the great and the small.

There are some men whose knowledge is sufficient for the duties of some office. There are some men whose conduct will secure unity in some district. There are some men whose virtue befits them for a ruler. There are some men whose ability wins credit in the country. In their opinion of themselves, they are just like the above.

---

*Chuang-tzu 1.

On Death**

This often-quoted story is an excellent example of the striking literary features of the Chuang-tzu.

When Chuang Tzu went to Khu, he saw an empty skull, bleached but still retaining its shape. Tapping it with his horse-switch, he asked it, "Did you, Sir, in your greed of life, fail in the lessons of reason and come to this? Or did you do so, in the service of a perishing state, by the punishment of the axe? Or was it through your evil conduct, reflecting disgrace on your parents and on your wife and children? Or was

it through your hard endurance of cold and hunger? Or was it simply that you had completed your term of life?"

Then he took up the skull and made a pillow of it when he went to sleep. At midnight the skull appeared to him in a dream and said, "All your words were about the entanglements of men in their lifetime. None of those things are found after death. Would you like to hear me, Sir, tell you about death?"

**Chuang-tzu 18.

"I would," said Chuang Tzu, and the skull resumed: "In death there are not the distinctions of ruler above and minister below. There are none of the features of the four seasons. Tranquil and at ease, our years are those of heaven and earth. No king in his court has greater enjoyment than we have."

Chuang Tzu did not believe it and said, "If I could get the Ruler of our Destiny to restore your body to life with its bones and flesh and skin, and to give you back your father and mother, your wife and children, and all your village acquaintances, would you wish me to do so?"

The skull stared intently at him, knitted its brows, and said, "How should I cast away the enjoyment of my royal court and undertake again the toils of life among mankind?"

Reward and Retribution*

Although the Tao does not have a strongly moral character, the Taoist tradition nonetheless developed the doctrine of reward for virtue (long life) and punishment for evil (shortened life or punishment of descendants). This passage gives a lyrical list of good deeds and excerpts the beginning of an even longer section on evil deeds.

There are no special doors for calamity and happiness; they come as men themselves summon them. Their recompenses follow good and evil as the shadow follows the substance.

Accordingly, in heaven and earth there are spirits that take account of men's transgressions and, according to the lightness or gravity of their offences, take away from their term of life. When that term is curtailed, men become poor and reduced and meet with many sorrows and afflictions. All (other) men hate them; punishments and calamities attend them; good luck and occasions for felicitation shun them; evil stars send down misfortunes on them. When their term of life is exhausted, they die.

There also are the Spirit-rulers in the three pairs of the T'ai stars of the Northern Bushel constellation over men's heads, which record their acts of guilt and wickedness and take away (from their term of life) periods of twelve years or of a hundred days.

There also are the three Spirits of the recumbent body that reside within a man's person. As each appointed day of reporting comes, they ascend to the court of Heaven and report men's deeds of guilt and transgression. On the last day of the moon, the spirit of the Hearth does the same.

In the case of every man's transgressions, when they are great, twelve years are taken from his term of life; when they are small, a hundred days.

Transgressions, great and small, are seen in several hundred things. He who wishes to seek for long life must first avoid these.

If his way is right, he should go forward in it; if it is wrong, he should withdraw from it.

He will not tread in devious byways; he will not impose on himself in any secret apartment. He will amass virtue and accumulate deeds of merit. He will feel kindly toward all creatures. He will be loyal, filial, loving to his younger brothers, and submissive to his elder. He will make himself correct and so transform others. He will pity orphans and have compassion on widows; he will respect the old and cherish the young. Even the insects, grass, and trees he should not hurt.

He ought to pity the evil tendencies of others; to rejoice over their excellences; to help them in their difficulties; to rescue them from their perils; to regard their gains as if they were

---

*T'ai-Shang 1.

his own and their losses in the same way; not to publish their shortcomings; not to flaunt his own superiorities; to put a stop to what is evil and exalt and display what is good. He ought to yield much and take little for himself; to receive insult without resenting it and receive honor with an appearance of apprehension; to bestow favors without seeking for a return and give to others without any subsequent regret—this is what is called a good man. All other men respect him; Heaven in its course protects him; happiness and financial rewards follow him; all evil things keep far from him; the spiritual Intelligences defend him; what he does is sure to succeed; he may hope to become Immaterial and Immortal.

He who wants to become an Immortal of Heaven ought to give the proof of 1,300 good deeds; and he who wants to become an Immortal of Earth should give the proof of three hundred.

But if the movements of a man's heart are contrary to righteousness, and his conduct is in opposition to reason; if he regards his wickedness as a proof of his ability and can bear to do what is cruel and injurious; if he secretly harms the honest and good; if he treats with clandestine slight his ruler or parents; if he is disrespectful to his elders and teachers; if he disregards the authority of those whom he should serve; if he deceives the simple; if he calumniates his fellow-learners; if he vents baseless slanders, practices deception and hypocrisy, and attacks and exposes his kindred by blood or marriage; if he is hard, violent, and without humanity—in the case of crimes such as these, (the Spirits) presiding over the Life, according to their lightness or gravity, take away the culprit's periods of twelve years or of one hundred days. When his term of life is exhausted, death ensues. If at death there remains any unpunished guilt, judgment extends to his posterity.

RITUAL AND MEDITATION

Methods of Prolonging Life*

This text, considered one of the most important in religious Taoism, stresses esoteric methods of achieving immortality. The first selection discusses the general principles of achieving longevity or immortality; the second points out how scripture texts can aid in this process.[9]

[15.6b] If you are going to do everything possible to nurture your life, you will take the divine medicines. In addition, you will never weary of circulating your breaths; morning and night you will do calisthenics to circulate your blood and breaths and see that they do not stagnate. In addition to these things, you will practice sexual intercourse in the right fashion; you will eat and drink moderately; you will avoid drafts and dampness; you will not trouble about things

that are not within your competence. Do all these things, and you will not fall sick.

On the other hand, you are sure to become ill if you are afraid of not always having your own way in society and of instability in your affairs; also, if laxity and lack of diligence trouble you. If all you have is a heart faithful to God and yet do nothing for your own benefit—your predestined life span being defective and your body threatened with harm—the Three

---

*Pao-p'u Tzu 15.6b–7a; 19.6b–7a.
[9] From James R. Ware, *Alchemy, Medicine, Religion in the China of A.D. 320: The Nei P'ien of Ko Hung (Pao-p'u tzu)*. Cambridge, MA: Massachusetts Institute of Technology Press, 1966. Copyright © 1966 The Massachusetts Institute of Technology. Used by permission.

Corpses[10] will take advantage of your weak months and perilous days, the hours when your longevity could be interrupted or sickness incurred, to summon vicious breaths and bring in any demons they might be able to find to do you injury. . . . And when this situation intensifies, it produces the various illnesses. But all of this was set in motion by the anxiety that was present in the first place.

Accordingly, those who first did something about God in antiquity exercised all the medical arts at the same time to save themselves from misfortunes that are ever present, but this principle is unknown to ordinary processors who, not understanding what they have been taught, pay no attention to the prescriptions for treating illness. Further, being unable to break with worldly life and live as hermits, and using only personal remedies to drive away illness, they lack all means for combating it and curing themselves. They are by no means as well off as the people in general who use various infusions. . . .

[19.6b] I heard Cheng Yin say that no Taoist book surpasses *San huang nei wen* and *Wu yueh chen hsing t'u* in importance.[11] They were the honored secrets of the genies and superior men of antiquity and could be taught only by those bearing the title of genie. Those receiving them transmitted them once after forty years, and in doing so oaths were taken by smearing the lips with the blood of a sacrificed animal, and agreements were entered into by the giving of a present. Writings of this type are to be found in all the famous mountains and the five revered mountains, but they are stored in hidden spots in caves. In response to those who have secured the divine process and entered a mountain to give sincere thought to it, the god of the mountain will automatically open the mountain and let such persons see the texts, just as Po Ho got his in a mountain, and immediately set up an altar, made a present of silk, drew one ordinary copy, and then left with them.[12] A purified place is always prepared for such texts, and whenever anything is done about them one must first announce it to them, as though one were serving a sovereign or a father.

The classic itself states that if *San huang nei wen* is in a household, it will banish evil and hateful ghosts, soften the effects of epidemics, block calamities, and rout misfortunes. If anyone is suffering from illness or on the point of death, let someone believing in the process with all his heart give this text to the patient to hold, and he will be sure not to die. If a wife is having trouble in childbirth to the point of possible death, let her hold this text, and her son will be born immediately. If pilgrims wishing to seek Fullness of Life will hold this text when entering the mountains, it will rout tigers and wolves, and none of the mountain powers, poisons, or evils will dare approach. When crossing rivers and seas, the processors will be able to dispel crocodiles and dragons, and halt the wind and waves with this book.

With the method taught in this text it is possible to initiate undertakings positively or negatively without inquiring about the correct site or choosing the right day, and one's household will be free from calamities. If you wish to build a new house or tomb, write several dozen copies of the Earth Augustus text and spread them on the site. Look at them on the following day, and if a yellow color is seen adhering to them, one may begin the work there and the household will be sure to become rich and prosperous. When others are being interred, copy the Man Augustus text and include your own full name written on a folded sheet of paper. Insert this in that person's grave without letting others know what you are doing, and you will be free from sudden misfortune and robbers. Anyone plotting against you will be sure to have his harm turned against himself.

---

[10] *Three Corpses:* worms in the body causing illness and death.

[11] Po Ho wrote both these books, which deal with gaining immortality.

[12] *drew one ordinary copy:* made a copy by hand.

The Life and Ascension of Shen Xi*

The highest form of attaining immortality in Taoism is ascension to heaven, there to become an immortal. Here is an eyewitness account of the ascension of Shen Xi from a fourth-century scripture, the Biographies of Spirit Immortals.[13]

Shen Xi was a native of Wu district in Jiangsu. He studied the Tao in Sichuan, attaining the magical powers of dissipating calamity, curing disease, and bringing relief to the common people. However, he knew nothing of the drugs of immortality and their use. Still, his virtue found favor in the sight of heaven and was duly recorded in the registers above.

On one occasion, Xi and his wife, Lady Jia, were returning from a visit to the family of their daughter-in-law when they encountered three chariots. One was drawn by a white deer, another by a green dragon, and the third by a white tiger. There were thirty or forty mounted attendants in dark red livery, armed with lances and swords. They crowded the narrow road, filling it with pomp and glitter.

They inquired if he was Shen Xi. The latter, wondering what to make of this astounding apparition, replied, "Indeed, I am. But why do you ask?" "Mr. Shen, sir," one of them explained, "you have deserved well of the people. The Tao is forever present in your heart, and from your earliest childhood, your conduct has been free from blame. However, your allotted lifespan is short and your years are approaching their close. So the Yellow Venerable Lord has sent down three immortal officials with their chariots to escort you to heaven.

"The gentleman in the chariot with the white deer is Bo Yanzhi, a palace official.

"The gentleman in the chariot with the green dragon is Sima Sheng, a lord of transcendence.

"The gentleman in the chariot with the white tiger is Xu Fu, a master of ceremony." Presently the three immortals came forward in their feathery robes. They held their official tablets in their hands and bestowed on Shen a tablet of white jade, a green jade scepter, and a set of red jade characters that he could not read. After this formal ceremony, they took him to heaven.

His ascension was witnessed by a number of field laborers in the vicinity. They did not know what to make of it. After a little while there came a thick mist, and when it cleared away, the whole company had disappeared. All that remained were the oxen which had drawn Shen's carriage. They were peacefully grazing in the fields. Someone recognized the animals as belonging to the Shen household and informed his family that he and his wife had vanished. Fearing that they had been carried off to the deep mountains by evil spirits, family and servants searched in every direction for a hundred miles around. But they did not find them.

Over four hundred years later, Shen Xi unexpectedly revisited his native village. He sought out one of his descendants, a man called Shen Huaixi, who explained that he had heard his elders speak of a certain ancestor who had become immortal. But, he said, this ancestor had never come back.

Shen stayed with his descendant for about a month. During that time, he recounted his first experience of ascension. "Although I was not brought before the Emperor of Heaven himself," he said, "I did get to meet the Venerable Lord, who is his right-hand man. The attendants instructed me not to make any formal acknowledgments, but simply to take my seat in silence.

"The celestial palace seemed composed of an insubstantial, luminous haze, shot through with

---

Shenxian zhuan, Daozang jinghua 5.11.
[13]From Livia Kohn, ed., *The Taoist Experience: An Anthology* (Albany: State University of New York Press, 1993), pp. 326–28. Copyright © State University of New York Press. Used by permission.

an enormous variety of colors too fantastic to describe. There were hundreds of attendants, mostly female. In the gardens grew trees bearing pearls and jade; all sorts of immortality herbs and magic mushrooms sprouted in great profusion.

"Dragons and tigers," he continued, "assembled in groups and frolicked in their midst. I could hear a tinkling sound, like that of copper and iron ornaments, but I've never discovered where it came from. The walls on all sides shone with a bright glow; they were covered with talismanic inscriptions.

"The Venerable Lord himself was about ten feet in height. His hair hung loose, and he wore an embroidered robe. His entire person radiated light. After a while, several jade maidens brought in a golden table with jade goblets and set it before me. They told me that this was the divine cinnabar elixir. Whoever drinks it is exempt from death. Both my wife and I were given a cup and promised a long life of ten thousand years.

"Next we were told to make a formal obeisance to the Venerable Lord but offer no thanks. When we had finished the divine medicine, they brought us two dates as large as hens' eggs, and several five-inch slices of something that looked like dried meat. 'Return to the world of mortals for a time,' they told us, 'and there cure the manifold diseases of humanity. Whenever you wish to ascend again, just write out this talisman and hang it on the end of a pole. Then someone will come and get you.' So they said, and handed me the talisman and an immortal recipe. Soon afterward I fell into a drowse. Suddenly I seemed to wake as if from a long sleep and found that I was back on earth. Many times I have tried it on sick people. The recipe really works!"

Proper Sexual Methods for Men and Women*

As a part of attaining health and longevity, proper practices guiding sexual intercourse are important in Taoism. Men are to increase their yang energy, women their yin energy. Both men and women are instructed here to take as many sexual partners as practicable, partners who are young and unacquainted with the deeper meaning of sex, although the writer recognizes that such instruction runs counter to social norms. The Dynastic History of the Later Han *sums it up: "The arts of the bedroom constitute the climax of human emotions and encompass the totality of Tao. Therefore, the ancient sages regulated external pleasures in order to control inner passions, and they made detailed rules and terms governing sexual intercourse."* [14]

According to Pengsu the Long-Lived, if a man wishes to derive the greatest benefit [from proper sexual methods], it is best to find a woman who has no knowledge of them. He also had better choose young maidens for mounting, because then his complexion will become like a maiden's. . . . It is best to obtain those between fourteen or fifteen and eighteen or nineteen. In any event, they should never be older than thirty. Even those under thirty are of no benefit if they have given birth. My late master handed down these methods and himself used them to live for three thousand years. If combined with [proper] drugs, they will even lead to immortality.

In practicing the union of yin and yang to increase your energy and cultivate long life, do not limit yourself to just one woman. . . . The more the better! Absorb her secreted essence[15]

Yufang bijue 635–636.

[14] From Douglas Wile, *The Art of the Bedchamber.* Albany: State University of New York Press, 1992. Copyright © 1992 State University of New York Press. Used by permission.

[15] *secreted essence:* the "essence" of a woman or a man is the liquid matter and energy released with orgasm. The task of Taoist sexual practices is to achieve, by mental and physical power, orgasm that does not release this essence but instead reverts it inward to build strength.

by mounting the "vast spring"[16] and reverting its essence upward [into you]. Your skin will become glossy, your body light, your eyes bright, and your energy so strong that you will be able to overcome all your enemies. Old men will feel like twenty and young men will feel their strength increase a hundredfold.

[Instructions for women] The Master of Pure Harmony says: "It is not only yang that can be cultivated, but yin too." The Queen Mother of the West, for example, attained the Tao by cultivating her yin energy. As soon as she had intercourse with a man he would immediately take sick, while her complexion would be even more radiant without the use of rouge or powder. . . . The Queen Mother had no husband but was fond of intercourse with young boys. If this is not fit to be taught to the world, how is it that such an elevated personage as the Queen Mother herself practiced it?

When having intercourse with a man, first calm your heart and still your mind. If the man is not yet fully aroused, wait for his energy to arrive and slightly restrain your emotion to attune yourself to him. Do not move or become excited, lest your yin essence become exhausted first [in orgasm, and flow to the man]. If this happens, you will be left in a deficient state and susceptible to cold wind illnesses. . . . If a woman is able to master this Tao and has frequent intercourse with men, she can avoid all grain for nine days without getting hungry.

---

[16] *vast spring:* a traditional Chinese euphemistic term for the female genitalia.

The Origins of Feng Shui*

Feng shui ["fung shway"] is the ancient Chinese practice of positioning objects to maximize the good effects of yin and yang and promote the flow of life-giving chi ["chee"]. These objects include graves, altars, buildings, and, recently, furniture and decorative items. Feng shui originated in burial practices. Good positioning of the body in relation to the earth is believed to lead to a better life in the afterworld for the spirit of the person buried, and hence to more blessing on the dead person's living descendants. The Book of Burial (Zang Shu) *by Guo Pu (276–324 C.E.) laid down the basic principles of feng shui that endure today.*[17]

[The purpose of] burial is to gain accord with the generative qi.[18] The five qi move within the ground and develop, thus generating the ten thousand things.[19] Human beings receive their bodies from their parents; the original bones gain qi and the remaining bones receive the yin. The Book says that qi responds to what it senses, and the good fortune of ghosts extends to the living. . . .

[7] Overall, life is the condensation of qi. That which is coagulated becomes the bone, which remains after death. Therefore, to bury the dead is to obey the principle of returning qi to the bones, thus generating life out of yin.[20] Qi follows the bones of hilly ridges and the

---

Zang Shu 1.1–4, 7–25, 30–43.
[17] From Juwen Zhang, *A Translation of the Ancient Chinese* The Book of Burial (Zang Shu) *by Guo Pu (276–324)* (Lewiston, NY: Edwin Mellen Press, 2004), pp. 41–84. Copyright © 2004 Juwen Zhang. Used by permission.
[18] *qi:* the primordial, cosmic breath, the power and energy of life; also spelled *chi*.
[19] *the ten thousand things:* traditional Chinese expression for the world and everything in it.
[20] *generating life out of yin:* not that the bones come back to life, but rather that life-giving energy flows to the spirit of the dead person.

branches of hills and mounds. [10] The Book[21] says [that] when qi rides with the wind, it disperses; when it reaches water, it ends. The ancients were able to condense the qi and keep it from dispersion, to move it and to make it cease. Therefore, they called it feng shui (wind-water). The law of feng shui is: getting water is superior; hiding from wind is secondary. The Book says [that] when external qi is blocked, it thus takes forms; when internal qi is stopped, it thus generates life. This is what it refers to. Why is it said thus? When there is abundance of qi, it still remains even though it overflows everywhere; it still condenses in a deep place even though it disperses.

[15] Therefore, it is best to bury the dead deep in dry land, and shallow in smooth plains. The Book says [that] once the depth is properly achieved, feng shui will be complete itself. The qi of yin and yang flows out and thus becomes wind; it ascends and thus becomes cloud; it descends and thus becomes rain; and it moves through the ground and thus becomes the generative qi. . . . The Book says [that] earth takes forms and qi moves along them, and out of this all things are generated. [20] Qi moves through the ground. Its movement depends upon the earth's course; its condensation depends upon the cessation of these courses.

To bury the dead is to trace the beginning point of qi and to [come into] accord with its cessation. The aspect of the ground follows its pulse and the aspect of mountains follows their bones; they are meandering easily either in east-west or south-north directions. The length of a thousand feet is called "aspect"; a height of a hundred feet is called "form." Where the aspect arrives and the form ceases to be, there is what is called the total qi. [25] At the spot of total qi is where you stop and bury the dead. . . .

[30] The accumulated [emerging aspects] ceases and condenses, and the harmonious yang and yin mingle. Where there are high ground and deep water, there are thick grass and dense woods. Such a place has wealth equaling one thousand chariots and has riches equaling ten thousand gold pieces. The Book says, where form ends qi accumulates, transforming to become ten thousand things—that is the ultimate ground [in which to bury the dead]. It is most precious if ground is a flat plain; it is most precious if soil is that with secondary ridges. [35] The spot where the secondary ridges begin, qi consequently originates; where the secondary ridges end, qi consequently terminates. The method of detecting secondary ridges is finding the places where they are slightly hidden, and slightly rising like mounds, and where they are metaphysically and subtly connected; that is where good fortune lies. The Book says [that] when the ground contains auspicious qi, the soil rises in consequence; where the secondary ridge carries the ending qi, water flows to lift it up; the aspect goes smoothly with the form, [and] repeats endless cycles.

By obeying the principle for burying the dead in such a place, there will be perpetual auspiciousness and no misfortune. In mountains, there are those that have precipitous aspects. One should obey the principle to bury the dead at the conjoining spot. [It is also necessary] to accord with the location from which it emerges, [40] to examine the location for deficiencies, to choose from what is accommodating, [and] to avoid what is harmful. This is how the superior man accomplishes remarkable feats and heavenly advantages; thus the mandate[d] fate of heaven is changed.[22]

---

[21] *The Book:* an earlier volume on this topic, the exact identity of which is unknown. Zhang suggests that it is likely an earlier version of the *Book of Burial,* perhaps the one version preferred by Wu Cheng (1246–1331 C.E.), who edited the *Book of Burial* that we have today.

[22] Zhang remarks, "This may be one of the most important parts in the entire book, in that it shows the positive side of *fengshui* practice: it is a search for harmony, in which mankind has a positive role in the process of bringing nature into accordance with the natural *Dao*" (Zhang, *Translation of the* Book of Burial, p. 85).

A Complete Taoist Scripture*

The Great Emperor Who Protects Life is a local Taoist god in southeast China. This scripture about him was written in the fifteenth century C.E. A good example of a short Taoist text celebrating a god by retelling his legend and giving moral commands to his people, it also shows a Buddhist influence on Taoism. It is notable for its request that people hire Buddhist or Taoist priests to chant it, or form scripture-recitation societies to chant it themselves.[23]

Raising our heads we invoke the August Heavenly Great Emperor Wu. He lived in the Quanzhou Commandery but was born near Zhangzhou. His brave and valiant awesome spiritual powers arose from his merciful heart. Because he used ritual powers he became a Medicine King. To the masses of the people he brought most abundant advantages. His fulfilment of his merit moved the Jade Sovereign. He was asked by Imperial decree what karmic path he had followed. [He replied that] upon obtaining correct knowledge and perception [he] expanded the Tao. [The Jade Emperor] commanded that the great lofty title of the numinous doctor be enhanced. Also, he sent [as subordinates] an Immortal Medical Official named Huang, the Awesome Martial Retainer Jiang Si shi, the Perfect Man of the Green Kerchief and two pages, the Six Ding Generals [who are] Strong Soldiers who Expel Evil, Maiden Qin, the Taiyi Female Physician, together with the Great Messenger who Flies to Heaven. [All of these] work together to support the weak and expel disease and misfortune.

I today with all my heart and with complete obedience, express my desire that you will be happy to let fall your mercy at my recitation [of your names].

CHANT FOR THE OPENING OF THE SCRIPTURE

Great Saint, Physician Spirit, Perfected Lord Wu
Wrote Talismans, let fall seal-script [revelations],
   and proclaimed scriptures

Swearing a vow that his Sacred Spell would
   have awesome power,
And bring auspiciousness, gather good fortune,
   and avoid disaster.

Formerly, the Perfected Lord of Merciful Salvation attended an audience in the Taiqing Palace within the Hall of the Three Origins. All the gods of the Stars were gathered round. The Heavenly Venerable said:

Now when I observe the 3,000 million worlds below, and the multitudes dwelling in Jambudvipa, [they are] all practicing the 10 evils and the 5 disobediences, disloyal and unfilial, unmannered and unrighteous, not revering the Three Treasures, ignorant of charity, unwilling to provide assistance, frequently carrying out evil deeds, killing living beings, behaving licentiously, stealing, coveting and getting angry, entangling themselves in a web of culpability, and disrupting the nation. [There] both kings and men are unjust; those above do not measure by the Tao, and those below do not uphold the Laws. The innocent are slaughtered, their spirits do not scatter, but instead turn into demonic flying zombies.

Therefore the foreign borderland peoples raised up weapons of war, and the people of South China, in cold and hot seasons, fell victim to malarial miasmas and yellow fever, became dumb and died horrible painful deaths. Then arose a mosquito borne plague of measles, with symptoms of red eyes and dysentery. Pigs, sheep, oxen, and horses became afflicted and died. Mountain demons and pythons, vipers, tigers, and elephants, birds, beasts,

---

*The True Scripture of the Great Emperor.

[23] From Kenneth Dean, *Taoist Ritual and Popular Cults of South-East China.* Princeton: Princeton University Press, 1993. Copyright © 1993 by Princeton University Press. Reprinted by permission of Princeton University Press.

and sea monsters [arose]. Wild winds drove the boats; dragons and demonic waves destroyed city walls and fords, and there were many floods and fires. And then there was trouble with [Imperial] Laws, for every year brought hunger and starvation, the five grains did not raise up.

As for those of you who performed charity, but for whom things did not work out as you wished, you should know that this is the [work of] demons. These demons are all martial fellows and stout soldiers, with brave and valiant divine energy. They [formerly] aided heavenly spirits to move clouds and spread vapors, so that winds and rain were seasonal, and the grains and rice grew ripe, and the Empire enjoyed Great Peace. Yet today they have all increased in number to a total of 84,000 and have suddenly raised up tornadoes and floods. The 404 diseases circulate through the seasons, bringing little good fortune to the world. The evil and rebellious masses encounter disasters and die. The Heavenly Venerable took pity on those people who had cultivated good fortune [by carrying out] the 10 good deeds. [He then] extended divine protection to them. Study the words of the prophecy:

A green dog barks,

A wooden pig squeals,

A rooster crows at the rabbit in the moon,

A round moon without luster.

Three disasters strike,

Nine rebellions arise.

In the jia and yi years there will be military ravages

In the bing and ding years fearful fires

In the wu and ji years locusts will spread plague

In the geng and ren years storms and flood,

Thus from jia year to the gui year,

The first five years will have barren harvests,

The last five years will have good harvests.

Alas we have come to the end of the world

The revolving [sun marked by the] gnomon[24] is about to stop

All the Buddhas will attain Nirvana

Saints and Sages will hide away

Common men and ignorant women are unaware and do not understand

Therefore I have transmitted this scripture

So that it may broadly save the world.

And pronounce this gatha:

The dog barks, the pig squeals

The bad will vanish, the good will survive

Take refuge in the Three Treasures

Uphold and recite this Scripture.

Revere it wherever you go

And it will always hold down demonic soldiers

Heavenly spirits will protect you

Family and nation will be at peace

Widely transmit the Way of the Scripture

Pass it all around . . .

The Most High Lord Lao said:

Whenever any good man or faithful woman worships the Three Treasures, and delights in charitable deeds, then on the gengshen, and jiazi days, and on the days of the Three Origins, the Seven [Dipper Stars], the Day of Destiny, and the winter sacrifice, they should fast and purify their hearts, recite this scripture, and revere these True Writings. Then spontaneously, heavenly spirits will protect them and they will not encounter any hardship.

I, [Lord Lao], will carry on this great work, and obtain for them good fortune and longevity. I [hereby] issue secret instructions and sacred talismans, altogether 120, and announce to the Perfected Lord of Merciful Salvation: Your Tao is complete and your Virtue prepared. Your good deeds are pure

---

[24] *gnomon:* the part of the sundial that casts a shadow and marks the time.

and resplendent. In heaven you [observe the] prohibitions, and have thereby established marvellous powers of wisdom. On earth you have mercy and compassion and the great mission of the salvation of [humankind]. Amongst men you have the honorable title of Perfected Lord of Trustworthy Benevolence. You can move between the Three Realms. You can subdue these demons and transmit the message of this Scripture. Save and deliver the masses, bring them all back together to the Great Tao.

When the Most High had finished speaking, the Heavenly Venerable rode away, the spirits of the stars all made their farewells and withdrew. Then the Perfected Lord of Merciful Salvation carried out the command from on high, swiftly ordering the miraculous realm. . . . He paced the Mainstays [of Heaven] and sprayed out vapor. An earthquake struck three times. Then he descended into a true medium, and pronounced this scripture and made this spell:

Transformation body of Guanyin
Gathered up the sprites on Bohai Island
My heart sinks in the six Harmonies
My chi revolves the five Elements
Compassionately I save the world
Saving from disease, I am a Physician Spirit
A glass of water with seven salts
My precious sword held straight out
I pace the Mainstays, breathing in and out
The masses of demons all collapse
A thousand disasters forever annihilated
A myriad blessing arrive
In the space opened up by the smoke of
  incense
The sacred form ascends
Recite my sacred spell
And I will descend in my true shape
Om, swiftly, swiftly, in accordance with the
  ordinances.

The True Medium spoke:
In my life I dwelt in Quanzhou commandery, and left traces [of my deeds] near Zhangzhou. From then until now through over 300 years I have piled up merit in labo-

rious deeds. Fine honors were commended and bestowed [upon me]. Formerly I shipped grain to save [people] in a drought. Also I led spirit soldiers and drove away pirate robbers. Recently I let flow a sweet spring to put an end to the sufferings of sickness. Now I transmit the Methods and Scriptures of the Spiritual Treasure in order to save the people of the world. If any man or woman obtain my true scripture with its marvellous seal, faithfully keep and worship them. Invite either Buddhist or Taoist priests to recite the scripture, or organize an association to read and recite it. Widely order its dissemination.

Then as for anything your heart desires there will be nothing that does not satisfy your wishes. Whenever anyone begins to build a well or a stove, or constructs a house or a tomb, or an enclosure for pigs, sheep, oxen, horses, chickens or ducks, and at that time there be vapors bearing sickness, then they may arrange incense, flowers, lamps, and tea, and offer up outstanding fruit, recite this scripture and repeat my spell seven times successively, and write with red vermillion the talismans and [recite] the incantations that I have revealed, placing them upon the door, then demons of disaster will spontaneously dissipate, and members of the family will be fine. That which I desire with all my heart is that you will all ascend to the banks of the Tao.

After the True Medium had finished speaking, he exhaled the soul and came to.

Perfected Lord, Perfected Lord
Regulate evil and behead plague [demons].
Employ your talisman, spells and [purify-
  ing] water
Broadly save the myriad peoples
Pace the Mainstays with correct chi
Forever cutting off the roots of misfortune
Awesome radiance shines brightly
Your illustrious sobriquet has been
  successively enhanced
With incense and temple sacrifices

Morning and night we earnestly worship you
The myriad spirits all pray
That they might all bathe in your divine merit
Recite my sacred spell
Sweep away the masses of evil
Swiftly, swiftly, in accordance with the ordinances.

[Spell for Commanding Water:]
Perfected   Lord   of   Trustworthy Benevolence
Transformation body of Guanyin
Compassionately you broadly save [people]
Your spirit descends once invoked
Moving clouds and spreading vapors
Curing illness and eliminating adversity
His fire vehicle removes poison
His water vehicle all strike home
His wind vehicle and chi vehicle
Penetrate to the mysterious obscurity
The green dragon guards wood
The white tiger protects metal
The red pheasant guards fire
The Dark Warrior is the spirit of Water
I am the Lord of Earth,
Chaotic Origin,
Ancestor of the Tao
Pacing the Mainstays with correct breaths
I protect the myriad beings

My merit is accomplished
Ascend with me
Swiftly, swiftly, in accordance with the ordinances
The Physician Spirit's honored name is proclaimed far and wide
Brightly shone his Spiritual Skill at his birth near Zhangzhou
Formerly the responsive transformation body of Guanyin
Removed by Ritual means the mass of demons and sprites from Bohai Island
Three shocks from the earthquake and the medium was possessed
Proclaimed the scripture and saves all beings
People of the world, burn incense and earnestly recite the scripture
A thousand disasters will be forever ended
And good fortune and longevity will come to you.

It is said that this scripture specifically cures periodic outbreaks of pestilence. Reciting it can liberate the masses from hardship. At the end of the original copy there was appended the "Marvelous Scripture of Immortal Maiden of Merciful Salvation Who Saves [Those in] Childbirth," which still awaits reprinting. ([This appendage is] Noted by Yang [Jun].)

GLOSSARY

Pinyin spelling, where it differs from Wade-Giles, is given in parentheses before the pronunciation.

Chuang-tzu (Zhuangzi) [jwahng tzoo]; the second most important book of the Taoist scriptures.

Feng shui [fung shway]; the ancient Chinese practice of positioning objects such as graves, buildings, and, recently, furniture, to maximize the good effects of yin and yang and the flow of chi.

Tao (Dao) [dow] the "Way" of the cosmos, which humans should discern and live by.

Tao Te Ching (Dao De Jing) [DOW duh jing] "Classic of the Way and Its Working"; the leading book of the Taoist scriptures.

Tao Tsang (Dao Zang) [dow tsahng] the Taoist canon.

te (de) [duh] virtue, power, working.

wu-wei [woo WAY] "nonaction," "active nonstriving," "effortless action"; the use of the natural power of the Tao in oneself.

QUESTIONS FOR STUDY AND DISCUSSION

1.   From your reading of these texts, how would you define or describe the Tao?

2.   In what ways is the *Tao Te Ching* the foundation of subsequent Taoist traditions?

3.   Compare and contrast the Taoist and Confucian ideas of the sage or superior man.

4.   Discuss the remarkable feminine imagery used, especially in the *Tao Te Ching,* to describe the Tao. Has this carried over into later Taoism in the form of a greater role for women in the religion? If not, why?

5.   Discuss the Taoist goal of longevity. How does the pursuit of this goal differ in religious and in philosophical Taoism?

6.   How might the perplexing style of the *Chuang-tzu* be particularly well designed to promote its goals?

7.   Compare and contrast the Taoist and Confucian ideas of government. How is it possible, as the *Tao Te Ching* claims, to govern by wu-wei?

8.   Contrast philosophical Taoism and religious Taoism. How are their differences and similarities reflected in their scriptures?

9.   One of the best-known Taoist sayings in North America is "A journey of a thousand miles begins with a single step" (see page 205). Given the context of this saying in the *Tao Te Ching* and the Taoist ideal of wu-wei, is this saying correctly interpreted by most people as a positive call to long-term action?

SUGGESTIONS FOR FURTHER READING

Primary Readings

S. Addiss and S. Lombardo, *Lao-Tzu, Tao Te Ching.* Cambridge, MA: Hackett, 1993. An excellent translation characterized by literary grace and terse poetic power.

R. G. Henricks, *Lao Tzu, Te-Tao Ching.* New York: Ballantine, 1989. A lively translation, with full introduction and commentary, of the recently discovered *Ma-wang-tui* texts. (The usual name of this book is reversed in these texts.)

L. Kohn, ed., *The Taoist Experience: An Anthology.* Albany: State University of New York Press, 1993. Presentation and explanation of sixty key texts in Taoism.

J. Legge, ed., *The Texts of Taoism.* New York: Julian, 1959; first published 1891 by Oxford University Press. A standard rendering of the *Tao Te Ching, Chuang-tzu,* and the *Thai Shang.*

J. R. Ware, *Alchemy, Medicine, Religion in the China of A.D. 320:* The *Nei P'ien* of *Ko Hung (Pao-p'u tzu).* Cambridge, MA: M.I.T. Press, 1966. A complete and accurate translation of the single most important text in the history of religious Taoism.

Secondary Readings

R. E. Allinson, *Chuang-Tzu for Spiritual Transformation: An Analysis of the Inner Chapters.* Albany: State University of New York Press, 1989. A challenging philosophical analysis of the heart of this classic.

Chih-chung Tsai (Zhirhong Cai), *Zhuangzi Speaks: The Music of Nature,* trans. Brian Bruya. Princeton: Princeton University Press, 1992. A best-selling book in its Chinese original, this volume features line drawings and cartoon interpretations of the *Chuang-tzu* by the Taiwanese cartoonist Chih-chung Tsai to express the ineffable Tao.

B. E. Reed, "[Women in] Taoism." In A. Sharma, ed., *Women in World Religions.* Albany: State University of New York Press, 1987, pp. 161–181. An insightful analysis of the role of the feminine in Taoist scripture, especially the *Tao Te Ching,* and women's less than prominent role in lived Taoist religion.

M. Saso, *Blue Dragon White Tiger: Taoist Rites of Passage.* Washington, DC: Taoist Center, 1990. A treatment of various life-cycle rituals.

K. Schipper and F. Verellen, *The Taoist Canon: A Historical Companion to the Daozang.* Chicago: University of Chicago Press, 2005. A three-volume handbook to the Taoist canon that sets out its contents chronologically, with a brief description of each book's contents and origin.

E. Slingerland, *Effortless Action: Wu-wei as a Conceptual Metaphor and Spiritual Ideal in Early China.* New York: Oxford University Press, 2003. Argues that wu-wei was an important concept not only in Taoism but in nearly all leading religions in early China.

Izanagi Creating the Japanese Islands
This hanging scroll painting by Kobayashi Eitaku (1843–1890) depicts a leading theme of the Shinto sacred writings, the creation of Japan as the first of all nations. *Credit:* Photograph copyright © 2004 Museum of Fine Arts, Boston. William Sturgis Bigelow Collection. Courtesy, Museum of Fine Arts, Boston.

Shinto

INTRODUCTION

Shinto, the ancient Japanese national religion, is unique among the religious traditions of Asia and the world. Of all the major faiths based in historically literate cultures, it is the only one that has no scripture as modern scholars understand that term. Shinto recognizes no book as officially authoritative. It has no canon and no formalized doctrines or ethical systems that could be shaped by a scripture. Therefore, our presentation of Shinto takes a format different from the other chapters.

Two books in particular do have a special standing in Shinto because of their antiquity and unique contents: the **Kojiki,** "Record of Ancient Matters," and the **Nihongi,** "Chronicles of Japan." Written by imperial decree in the eighth century C.E., these books have held a place of honor in Shinto. The Japanese have looked on them as the story of the foundation of Japan. For a thousand years schoolchildren were taught their stories as an education in patriotism. These books "are regarded as authoritative and provide [Shinto's] historical as well as its spiritual basis."[1]

Though not classified as scripture, the *Kojiki* [koh-JEE-kee] and *Nihongi* [nih-HAWN-gee] provide good evidence of the leading ideas of the Shinto tradition. First in importance is the existence of many **kami,** gods and spirits. Second, humanity is the offspring of the kami [KAH-mee] and is continually supported by their power. Third, the Japanese nation, especially the imperial family, is the center of humanity. Fourth, deep reverence is owed the emperor as the one through whom blessings flow to the nation.

Since the disestablishment of Shinto as the official state religion in 1945, the *Kojiki* and *Nihongi* have not been taught in Japanese schools. Moreover, as a part of the disestablishment, the emperor of Japan renounced his divinity, which these books were intended to buttress. Nevertheless, much of the traditional high regard for Shinto still lingers. For example, both pride and protests erupted in 1991 when Akihito, the new emperor, spent a night in a specially constructed Shinto shrine, a ritual once thought to bring about the emperor's rebirth as a child of the sun-god Amaterasu. So even though the imperial claims that the *Kojiki* and the *Nihongi* were written to support have been officially renounced, these sacred texts continue to provide valuable insight into the historical essence of Shinto and its traditional relationship to the Japanese national character.

The *Kojiki,* finished in 712 C.E., is the oldest surviving book in Japan. The only knowledge we have of its origin comes from the preface by its author Yasumaro (given in full in the first reading). This preface records that Emperor Temmu (r. 672–687 C.E.) decreed that a new book should correct the falsified genealogical records of the leading Japanese families. In this way the genealogical myths of the competing clans were incorporated

---

[1]Sokyo Ono, *Shinto, The Kami Way* (Rutland, VT: Charles Tuttle, 1962), p. 10.

into the genealogical myth of Temmu's clan. To do this, the *Kojiki* draws on two main works of the time: the *Teiki* (Imperial Sun-Lineage) and the *Honji* (Ancient Dicta of Former Ages). The first was a source of genealogies, the second a collection of myths, legends, and songs; both were probably oral collections. These two sources, when combined and reworked into the *Kojiki,* shape its characteristic emphasis on a reliable genealogy that extends back to the gods. Scholars discern in the *Kojiki* other revisions to older traditions. For example, it is likely that early indigenous Japanese ideas about the equality of men and women were modified by Confucian ideas of male superiority.

The *Kojiki* itself is divided into three books. The first book, a statement of early Japanese mythology, proclaims that the emperor's family is destined to rule Japan because it is the "offspring of the heavenly deities." The second and third books contain stories of the ancient emperors and their exploits, most of them legendary, up to the time of writing. Only a few of these stories have any obvious religious significance.

The *Nihongi* (also known as the *Nihonshoki*) was written shortly after the *Kojiki,* in 720 C.E. Shotoku Daishi, its traditional author, compiled the *Nihongi* in thirty books. It narrates a closely related version of the stories in the *Kojiki,* draws on the same sources, and is written in the same Chinese style. Its special concern is to show that the Teika reforms of 645 C.E., which brought Shinto under stricter government regulation, resulted in greater obedience to the way of the kami.

This chapter closes with excerpts from the **Norito,** a collection of Japanese ritual prayers. The chief priest recites these prayers on behalf of the faithful. It was believed that beautiful, correct words brought about good, and that inelegant, incorrect words caused evil. *Norito* includes words of praise for the gods, lists of offerings, words identifying the persons offering the prayer, and the subject of the prayer.

SELECTIONS FROM THE *KOJIKI* AND THE *NIHONGI*

Preface to the *Kojiki*

This preface is the author's dedicatory address to Gemmei, niece and daughter-in-law of Emperor Kamu-Yamato (Temmu), who commissioned the work but died before its completion. The preface is a summary of much of the contents of the entire Kojiki. *The narrator tells of the creation of the world, the birth of the early gods, and the creation of Japan. The middle sections deal with various emperors, from the first emperor, Jimmu, to Temmu, although the narrative seems to be speaking of Temmu continually through this section. His decision to sponsor the writing of the* Kojiki *is given special attention. The final sections tell the praises of the empress and provide the only infor-mation we have about the writing of this book. The significance of the* Kojiki *is given in this section: It is "the basis of the country, the grand foundation of the monarchy."*[2]

I, Yasumaro, say:

When chaos had begun to condense, but force and form were not yet manifest, and nothing was named, nothing done, who could

---

[2] Unless otherwise noted, all selections in this chapter are taken, with editing, from Basil Hall Chamberlain, trans., *Ko-ji-ki, Transactions of the Asiatic Society of Japan,* supplement to vol. 10 (Tokyo: Asiatic Society of Japan, 1906).

know its shape? Nevertheless Heaven and Earth first separated, and the Three Deities began creating.[3] The Passive and Active Essences[4] then developed, and the Two Spirits became the ancestors of all things.[5] Therefore he entered obscurity and emerged into light, and the washing of his eyes revealed the Sun and Moon. He floated on and plunged into the sea-water, and Heavenly and Earthly Deities appeared through the washings of his person. So in the dimness of the great commencement, we, by relying on the original teaching, learn the time of the conception of the earth and of the birth of islands. In the remoteness of the original beginning, we perceive the era of the genesis of Deities and of the establishment of humans by trusting the former sages. Truly, we know that a mirror was hung up,[6] that jewels were spat out, and that then a Hundred Kings succeeded each other. We know that a blade was bitten, and a serpent cut in pieces, so that ten thousand deities flourished. By deliberations in the Tranquil River the Empire was pacified; by discussions on the Little Shore the land was purified.

Then His Augustness Ho-no-ni-ni-gi first descended to the Peak of Takachi, and the Heavenly Sovereign Kamu-Yamato traversed the Island of the Dragon-Fly. A weird bear put forth its claws, and a heavenly saber was obtained at Takakura. Men with tails obstructed the path, and a great crow guided him to Yeshinu. Dancing in rows, they destroyed the criminals, and listening to a song they vanquished their foes. Being instructed in a dream, he was reverent to the Heavenly and Earthly Deities, and was therefore styled the Wise Monarch. Having gazed on the smoke, he was benevolent to the people, and is therefore remembered as the Emperor-Sage. . . .

In the august reign of the Heavenly Sovereign who governed the Eight Great Islands from the Great Palace of Kiyomihara at Asuka, the Hidden Dragon[7] put on perfection, the Reiterated Thunder came at the appointed moment. Having heard a song in a dream, he felt that he should continue the succession; having reached the water at night, he knew that he should receive the inheritance. Nevertheless Heaven's time was not yet, and he escaped like the cicada to the Southern Mountains.[8]

Then both men and matters were favorable, and he marched like the tiger to the Eastern Land.[9] Suddenly riding in the imperial chariot, he forced his way across mountains and rivers. The Six Divisions rolled like thunder, the Three Hosts sped like lightning. The erect spears lifted up their might, and the bold warriors arose like smoke. The crimson flags glistened among the weapons, and the ill-omened crew were shattered like tiles. Before a day had elapsed, the evil influences were purified. Then the cattle were let loose and the horses given repose, and with shouts of victory they returned to the Flowery Summer. The flags were rolled up and the javelins put away, and with dances and chants they came to rest in the capital city. The year was that of the Rooster, and it was the Second Moon. At the Great Palace of Kiyomihara, he ascended to the Heavenly seat. . . .

Then the Heavenly Sovereign commanded, "I hear that the chronicles of the emperors and likewise the original words in the possession of the various families deviate from exact truth, and are mostly amplified by empty falsehoods. If at the present time these imperfections be not amended, before many years shall have elapsed, the purport of this, the great basis of the country, the grand foundation of the monarchy,

---

[3] *Deities:* The Japanese *kami* is translated "Deities" throughout.

[4] *Passive and Active Essences:* yin and yang, respectively.

[5] The *Two Spirits* from which all creation came are Izanagi (the Male-Who-Invites) and Izanami (the Female-Who-Invites).

[6] *mirror:* In many Shinto shrines, a mirror is often the only visible symbol of the kami's presence.

[7] *the Hidden Dragon:* the emperor as the crown prince.

[8] *he escaped . . . Mountains:* He renounced ordinary life for a time.

[9] This paragraph tells how the emperor crushed an attempt by a rival to gain the imperial throne by force.

will be destroyed. So now I desire to have the chronicles of the emperors selected and recorded, and the old words examined and ascertained, falsehoods erased and truth determined, in order to transmit [the latter] to later ages."

At that time there was a retainer whose surname was Hiyeda; his personal name was Are. He was twenty-eight years old, and so intelligent that he could repeat with his mouth whatever met his eyes, and record in his heart whatever struck his ears. Then Are was commanded to learn by heart the genealogies of the emperors, and likewise the words of former ages. Nevertheless time elapsed and the age changed, and the thing was not yet carried out.

Lying face down in reverence, I consider how Her Majesty the Empress, having obtained the throne, illumines the empire. Being versed in the Triad [of heaven, humanity and earth], she nourishes the people. Ruling from the Purple Palace, her virtue reaches to the utmost limits of the horses' hoof-marks. Dwelling amid the Somber Retinue, her influence illumines the farthest distance attained to by vessels' prows. The sun rises, and the brightness is increased; the clouds disperse, neither is there smoke. The chroniclers never cease recording the good omens of connected stalks and double rice-ears. Never for a single moon is the treasury without the tribute of continuous beacon-fires and repeated interpretations. In fame she must be pronounced superior to Bum-Mei, in virtue more eminent than Ten-Itsu.[10]

She regretted the errors in the old words, and wished to correct the misstatements in the former chronicles. So on the eighteenth day of the ninth moon of the fourth year of Wa-do, she commanded me, Yasumaro, to select and record the old words learned by heart by Hiyeda No Are according to the Imperial Decree, and dutifully to lift them up to her.

In reverent obedience to the contents of the Decree, I have made a careful choice. But in high antiquity both speech and thought were so simple, that it would be difficult to arrange phrases and compose sentences in [Chinese] characters. . . . Moreover, where the meaning of the words was obscure, I have elucidated their meaning. But need it be said that I have nowhere commented on what was easy? Again, in such cases as calling the surname *Kusaka,* and the personal name written with the character *Tarashi,* I have followed usage without alteration. Altogether the things recorded commence with the separation of Heaven and Earth, and conclude with the august reign at Woharida.[11] . . . Altogether I have written three volumes, which I now reverently and respectfully present. I, Yasumaro, with true trembling and true reverence, bow my head, and bow my head again.

Reverently presented by the Court Noble Futo no Yasumaro, an Officer of the Upper Division of the Fifth Rank and of the Fifth Order of Merit, on the 28th day of the first moon of the fifth year of Wa-do.[12]

---

[10] *Bum-Mei . . . Ten-Itsu:* ancient Chinese rulers.
[11] *reign at Woharida:* the reign of the Empress Suiko, who died in 628 C.E.
[12] March 10, 712 C.E.

The Creation of Japan*

In Chapter 1 of the Kojiki, *the spontaneous birth of the first gods is described. Although the narration starts at the "beginning of heaven and earth," the myths of the* Kojiki *(and the* Nihongi *as well) are much more stories of the creation of Japan than full-fledged stories of the creation of the world. The reader notices, for example, no* mention of the making of humanity in general or of animals. At the end of Chapter 2, the key gods Izanagi (the Male-Who-Invites) and Izanami*

---

* Kojiki 1–5, 33.

(the Female-Who-Invites) come into being, and they begin to create islands. Chapters 4 and 5 tell the story of the births of their first children, and we can see a concern for proper male-female relationship. In Chapter 33, the culmination of these myths is reached when the grandson of Amaterasu descends from heaven to rule the land that was to become Japan.

[Chapter 1, "The Beginning of Heaven and Earth"] The names of the Deities that were born in the Plain of High Heaven when the Heaven and Earth began were the Deity Master-of-the-August-Center-of-Heaven, next the High-August-Producing-Wondrous-Deity, then the Divine-Producing-Wondrous-Deity. These three Deities were all Deities born alone, and hid their persons. The names of the Deities that were born next from a thing that sprouted up like a reed-shoot when the earth, young and like floating oil, drifted about medusa-like, were the Pleasant-Reed-Shoot-Prince-Elder-Deity and the Heavenly-Eternally-Standing-Deity. These two Deities were likewise born alone, and hid their persons. The five Deities in the above list are separate Heavenly Deities.

[Chapter 2, "The Seven Divine Generations"] The names of the Deities that were born next were the Earthly-Eternally-Standing-Deity, next the Luxuriant-Integrating-Master-Deity. These two Deities were likewise Deities born alone, and hid their persons. The names of the Deities that were born next were the Deity Mud-Earth-Lord, next his younger sister the Deity Mud-Earth-Lady; next the Germ-Integrating-Deity, next his younger sister the Life-Integrating-Deity; next the Deity Elder-of-the-Great-Place, next his younger sister the Deity Elder-Lady-of-the-Great-Place; next the Deity Perfect-Exterior, next his younger sister the Deity Oh-Awful-Lady; next the Deity the Male-Who-Invites, next his younger sister the Deity the Female-Who-Invites. From the Earthly-Eternally-Standing-Deity down to the Deity the Female-Who-Invites in the previous list are what are termed the Seven Divine Generations. (The two solitary Deities above [mentioned] are each called one generation.

Of the succeeding ten Deities each pair of deities is called a generation.)

[Chapter 3, "The Island of Onogoro"] Then all the Heavenly Deities commanded the two Deities His Augustness the Male-Who-Invites and Her Augustness the Female-Who-Invites, ordering them to "make, consolidate, and give birth to this drifting land." Granting to them a heavenly jeweled spear, they charged them thus. So the two Deities, standing upon the Floating Bridge of Heaven, pushed down the jeweled spear and stirred with it. When they had stirred the brine till it went curdle-curdle, and drew [the spear] up, the brine that dripped down from the end of the spear was piled up and became an island. This is the Island of Onogoro.

[Chapter 4, "Courtship of the Deities, the Male-Who-Invites and the Female-Who-Invites"] Having descended from Heaven onto this island, they saw to the erection of a heavenly august pillar, and they saw to the erection of a hall of eight fathoms. Then he asked the Female-Who-Invites, "In what form is your body made?" She responded, saying, "My body is formed with one part not fully formed." Then the Male-Who-Invites said, "My body is formed with one part more than fully formed. Therefore, would it not be good to take that part of my body which is more than fully formed and insert it into that part of your body which is less than fully formed, and procreate the land?" The Female-Who-Invites responded, "That would be good." Then the Male-Who-Invites said, "Let us walk in a circle about this heavenly pillar, meet, and have intercourse." Then she said, "You go around from the right, and I will go around from the left." Then they agreed and went around, and the Female-Who-Invites said first, "What a charming and lovable male!" Then the Male-Who-Invites said, "What a charming and lovable female!" When each had finished talking, he said to his wife, "It is not fitting that the woman speak first." But they still began procreating, and she gave birth to a leech-child. This child they placed in a boat of reeds, and let it float away. Next they gave birth to the Island of Aha. It also is not reckoned among their children.

[Chapter 5, "The Birth of the Eight Islands"] Then the two Deities took counsel, saying: "The children to whom we have now given birth are not good. It will be best to announce this in the august place of the Heavenly Deities." They ascended to Heaven and enquired of Their Augustnesses the Heavenly Deities. Then the Heavenly Deities commanded and found out by grand divination, and ordered them, saying: "They were not good because the woman spoke first. Descend back again and amend your words." So descending back, they again went round the heavenly august pillar as before. Then his Augustness the Male-Who-Invites spoke first: "Ah! What a charming and lovely maiden!" Afterward his younger sister Her Augustness the Female-Who-Invites spoke: "Ah! What a charming and lovely youth!" When these words were said, they had intercourse as before, and procreated the Island of Ahaji, Ho-no-sa-wake. Next they gave birth to the Island of Futa-na in Iyo. This island has one body and four faces, and each face has a name. So the Land of Iyo is called Lovely Princess; the Land of Sanuki is called Prince Good-Boiled-Rice; the Land of Aha is called the Princess-of-Great-Food; the Land of Tosa is called Brave-Good-Youth. . . .

[Chapter 33, "The August Descent from Heaven of His Augustness the August Grandchild"] Then the Heaven-Shining-Great-August-Deity and the High-Integrating-Deity commanded and charged the Heir Apparent His Augustness Truly-Conqueror-I-Conquer-Swift-Heavenly-Great-Great-Ears [saying: "The Brave-Awful-Possessing-Male-Deity] says that he has now finished pacifying the Central Land of Reed-Plains. In accordance with our gracious charge, descend to, dwell in, and rule over it." Then the Heir Apparent His Augustness Truly-Conqueror-I-Conquer-Swift-Heavenly-Great-Ears replied, saying: "While I have been getting ready to descend, there has been born [to me] a child whose name is His Augustness Heaven-Plenty-Earth-Plenty-Heaven's-Sun-Height-Prince-Rice-ear-Ruddy-Plenty. This child should be sent down. [As for this august child, he was augustly joined to Her Augustness Myriad-Looms-Luxuriant-Dragon-fly-Island-Princess, daughter of the High-Integrating-Deity, and begot children: His Augustness Heavenly-Rice-ear-Ruddy, and next His Augustness Prince Rice-ear-Ruddy-Plenty].

In accordance with these words, they laid their command on His Augustness Prince Rice-ear-Ruddy-Plenty, charging him with these words, "This Luxuriant Reed-Plain-Land-of-Fresh-Rice-Ears is the land over which you shall rule." So [he replied]: "I will descend from Heaven according to your commands." So when His Augustness Prince Rice-ear-Ruddy-Plenty was about to descend from Heaven, there was at the eight-forking road of Heaven a Deity whose refulgence reached upward to the Plain of High Heaven and downward to the Central Land of Reed-Plains. So then the Heaven-Shining-Great-August-Deity and the High-Integrating-Deity commanded and charged the Heavenly-Alarming-Female-Deity [saying]: "Though you are a delicate female, you are a Deity who conquers in facing Deities. So be the one to go and ask thus, 'This being the road by which our august child is about to descend from Heaven, who is it that is there?'" So to this gracious question he replied, saying, "I am an Earthly Deity named the Deity Prince of Saruta. The reason for my coming here is that, having heard of the [intended] descent of the august child of the Heavenly Deities, I have come humbly to meet him and respectfully offer myself as His Augustness's vanguard." Then joining to him His Augustness Heavenly-Beckoning-Ancestor-Lord, His Augustness Grand-Jewel, Her Augustness Heavenly-Alarming-Female, Her Augustness I-shi-ko-ri-do-me, and His Augustness Jewel-Ancestor, in all five chiefs of companies, they sent him down from Heaven. Thereupon they joined to him the eight-feet [long] curved jewels and mirror that had allured [the Heaven-Shining-Great-August-Deity from the Rock-Dwelling], and also the Herb-Quelling-Great-Sword, and likewise the Deity Thought-Includer, the Hand-Strength-Male-Deity, and the Deity Heavenly-Rock-Door-Opener of Eternal Night, and charged him, "Regard this mirror exactly as if it were our august spirit, and reverence it as if reverencing us." Next they said, "Let the Deity Thought-Includer take in hand our affairs, and carry on the government." These two Deities are worshipped at the temple of Isuzu. The next, the Deity of Luxuriant-Food, is the Deity dwelling in the outer temple of Watarahi. The next, the Deity Heavenly-Rock-Door-Opener, another name for whom is the Wondrous-Rock-True-Gate-Deity, and another name for whom is the Luxuriant-Rock-True-Gate-Deity—this Deity of the August Gate. The next, the Deity Hand-Strength-Male, dwells in Sanagata.

The Shrine at Ise*

The shrine at Ise is the most important Shinto shrine standing today. Here is a description of the initiation of the shrine and its connection between the emperor and Amaterasu, to whom the shrine is dedicated.

25th year, Spring, and month, 8th day. The Emperor commanded the five officers, Takenu Kaha-wake, ancestor of the Abe no Omi; Hiko-kuni-fuku, ancestor of the Imperial Chieftains; O-kashima, ancestor of the Nakatome Deity Chieftains; and Tochine, ancestor of the Mononobe Deity chieftains . . . saying: "The sagacity of Our predecessor on the throne, the Emperor Mimaki-iri-hiko-inie, was displayed in wisdom; he was reverential, intelligent, and capable. He was profoundly unassuming, and his disposition was to cherish self-abnegation. He adjusted the machinery of government, and did solemn worship to the Gods of Heaven and Earth. He practiced self-restraint and was watchful of his personal conduct. Every day he was heedful for that day. Thus the welfare of the people was sufficient, and the Empire was at peace. And now, under Our reign, will there be any remissness in the worship of the Gods of Heaven and Earth?"

3rd month, 10th day. The Great Goddess Amaterasu was taken from [the princess] Toyo-suki-iri-hime, and entrusted to [the princess] Yamato-hime no Mikoto. Now Yamato-hime sought for a place where she might enshrine the Great Goddess. So she proceeded to Sasahata in Uda. Then turning back from there, she entered the land of Omi, and went round eastwards to Mino, and so she arrived in the province of Ise.

Now the Great Goddess Amaterasu instructed Yamato-hime, saying: "The province of Ise, of the divine wind, is the land in which the waves from the eternal world reside, the successive waves. It is a secluded and pleasant land. In this land I wish to reside." In compliance, therefore, with the instruction of the Great Goddess, a shrine was erected to her in the province of Ise. Accordingly an Abstinence Palace was built at Kawakami in Isuzu. This was called the Palace of Ise. It was there that the Great Goddess Amaterasu first descended from Heaven.

---

*Nihongi 5.

The Story of Emperor Yuryaku and the Woman Akawi-ko**

Most of the Kojiki *is made up of legendary stories about the Japanese emperors told to extol their own greatness. This bittersweet story of the woman Akawi-ko and the emperor Yuryaku, with the*

poetic songs that conclude it, is indicative of Japanese literary style. In this chapter, the old

---

**Kojiki 154.

woman Akawi-ko comes before Emperor Yuryaku, the "Heavenly Sovereign," to prove her faithfulness to a command he had given her many years before.

Once when the Heavenly Sovereign, going out for amusement, reached the River Miwa, a very beautiful girl was washing clothes by the riverside. The Heavenly Sovereign asked the girl, "Whose child are you?" She replied, "My name is Akawi-ko of the Hiketa tribe." Then he said to her, "Do not marry a husband. I will send for you," and [with these words] he returned to the palace. Eighty years passed while she reverently awaited the Heavenly Sovereign's commands. Then Akawi-ko thought: "While looking for the [Imperial] commands, I have already passed many years. My face and form are lean and withered, so there is no longer any hope for me. Nevertheless, if I do not show [the Heavenly Sovereign] how truly I have waited, my disappointment will be unbearable." She caused merchandise to be carried on tables holding a hundred items, and came forth and presented [these gifts as] tribute. Then the Heavenly Sovereign, who had completely forgotten what he had formerly commanded, asked Akawi-ko, "What old woman are you, and why have you come here?" Then Akawi-ko replied, saying:

"Having in such and such a month of such and such a year received the Heavenly Sovereign's commands, I have been reverently awaiting the great command until this day, and eighty years have passed by. Now my appearance is quite decrepit, and there is no longer any hope for me. Nevertheless I have come forth in order to show and declare my faithfulness." Then the Heavenly Sovereign was greatly startled [and exclaimed], "I had quite forgotten the former event! Meanwhile, ever faithfully awaiting my commands, you have vainly let pass by the years of your prime. This is very pitiful." In his heart he wished to marry her, but he shrank from her extreme age, and could not make the marriage. However, he conferred on her an august song:

"The younger chestnut orchard plain of Hiketa: would I had slept with her in her youth! Oh! How old she has become!"

Then the tears that Akawi-ko wept drenched the red-dyed sleeve that she had on. In reply to the great august song, she sang this song,

"Left over from the piling up of the jewel-wall piled up round the august dwelling—to whom shall the person of the Deity's temple go?" . . .

Then the old woman was sent back plentifully endowed. So these songs are Quiet Songs.

SELECTIONS FROM THE *NORITO*

Festival of the Gates*

Here is a ritual prayer to specific kami to protect the emperor's palace from evil spirits.

I humbly speak your names: Kusi-iha-mato,
Toyo-iha-mato-no-mikoto,
Because you swell massively imbedded like
    sacred massed rocks
In the inner and outer gates of the four quarters.
Because if from the four quarters and the four
    corners

There should come the unfriendly and unruly
    deity called Ame-no-maga-tu-hi,
You are not bewitched and do not speak
    consent to his evil words—
If he goes from above you guard above.
If he goes from below, you guard below,

———————————

*Norito, Prayer 44.

And lie in wait to protect and to drive away
And to repulse him with words;
Because you open the gates in the morning and
    close the gates in the evening;
You inquire and know the names
Of those who go in and those who go out;
And if there be any fault or error,

In the manner of [the rectifying deities] Kamu-
    naho-bi and Oho-naho-bi
You behold it rectified and hear it rectified,
And cause [the court attendants] to serve
    tranquilly and peacefully.
Therefore [I speak] your names . . .
And fulfill your praises. Thus I humbly speak.

Ritual Prayer for Forgiveness and Purification of Governing Officials*

*Here is a prayer for the purification of the govern-
ment. The ritual actions accompanying the prayer
can often be seen in its text.*

He says [referring to the sovereign, in whose behalf
a priest of the Nakatomi clan or a diviner of the
Urabe clan recites]: Hear all of you assembled:
imperial and royal princes, nobles and officials.
Hear all of you assembled that on the occasion of
the great exorcism of the sixth month of the current
year, various offences and defilements incurred by
the functionaries of the government offices, including those attendants who wear the scarf, the sash,
the quiver and the sword, as well as those attendants
of the attendants, will be cleansed and purified.

Thus He speaks: "Hear all of you assembled!
The ancestral kami of the sovereign dwelling in
the Plain of High Heaven commanded the gathering of the 800 myriads of kami for consulta-
tion, and then declared, 'Our august grandchild
is commissioned to rule and pacify the country
of the Plentiful Reed Plains of the Fresh Ears of
Grain [Japan].' Following this commission, the
unruly kami [of the land of Japan] were either
pacified or expelled, and even the rocks, trees,
and leaves which had formerly spoken were
silenced, and thus enabling the august grandchild (Ninigi) to descend from the heavenly
rock-seat, dividing the myriad layers of heavenly
clouds, and reach the entrusted lands.

"Thus pacified, the land became the Great
Yamato or the country of the Sun-seen-on-high,
where the palace pillars were deeply grounded in

the rock below and the palace beams were built to
reach the Plain of High Heaven for the dwelling of
the august grandchild, who, living in the shadow
of heaven and sun, ruled the peaceful nation. With
the increase of the descendants of the heavenly
kami, however, various offences were committed
by them. Among them, the offences of destroying
the divisions of the rice fields, covering up the irrigation ditches, opening the irrigation sluices,
sowing the seeds over the seeds planted by others,
planting pointed rods in the rice fields, flaying
living animals or flaying them backwards, emptying
excrements in improper areas, and the like, are
called the 'offences to heaven.' The offences of
cutting the living or the dead skin, suffering from
white leprosy or skin excrescences, violating one's
own mother or daughter, step-daughter or
mother-in-law, cohabiting with animals, allowing
the defilements by creeping insects, the thunder or
the birds, killing the animals of others, invoking
evils on others by means of witchcraft, and the like,
are called the 'offences to earth,' and are differenti-
ated from the 'offences to heaven.'

"When these offences are committed, the chief
of the Nakatomi priestly clan is commanded, in
accordance with the ritual performed in the heavenly palace [of the Sun Goddess], to cut off the
bottom and the ends of a sacred tree and place
them in abundance as offerings on divine seats,

---

* *Norito, Prayer* 32.

and also to cut off the bottom and ends of sacred sedge reeds and slice them into thin pieces, and then to recite the potent words of the heavenly ritual prayers. When this ritual is performed properly, the heavenly kami will hear the words of petition by opening up the heavenly rock door and by dividing the myriad layers of heavenly clouds, while [at the same time] the earthly kami will hear the words of petition by climbing up to the peaks of high and low mountains and by pushing aside the mists of the high and the low mountains.

"When the heavenly and the earthly kami thus hear the ritual prayers, all the offences will be gone from the court of the august grandchild as well as from the four quarters of the land under the heaven, just as the winds of morning and evening blow away the morning and evening mists, as the anchored large ship is untied and is pushed out into the ocean, or as the dense bushes are cut off at the bottom by sharp sickles.

"Indeed, all offences and defilements will be purified and will be carried to the ocean from the peaks of the high and low mountains by the princess whose name is 'Descent into the Current,' the kami dwelling in the currents of the rapid stream which surges down the hillside.

"When the offences are thus taken to the ocean, the princess named 'Swift Opening,' the kami who lives in the meeting place of eight hundred currents of the brine, will swallow them up.

"When the offences are thus swallowed up, the kami who dwells at the breath-blowing-gate called the 'Lord Breath-blowing-gate' will blow them away into the netherworld.

"When the offences are thus blown away, the princess named 'Swift Wanderer,' the kami who dwells in the netherworld, will wander away with them and lose them. And when the offences are thus lost, it is announced that from this day onward there is no offence remaining among the officials of the sovereign's court and in the four quarters of the land under heaven, while the horses with their ears turned toward the Plain of High Heaven stand listening.

"Hear, all of you assembled! All the offences have been cleansed and purified on the great exorcism celebrated in the dusk on the last day of the sixth month of the current year.

"Oh, you diviners of the four provinces, leave here carrying the offences to the great rivers, and cast them away by the rite of purification." Thus he speaks.

GLOSSARY

kami [KAH-mee] gods or spirits, and their sacred power.

Kojiki [koh-JEE-kee] "Record of Ancient Matters."

Nihongi [nih-HAWN-gee] "Chronicles of Japan."

Norito [noh-REE-toh] Shinto book of prayers and rituals.

QUESTIONS FOR STUDY AND DISCUSSION

1. Describe the basic structure of Shinto polytheism as reflected in Shinto mythology.

2. Why, in your view, do the Japanese myths place so much emphasis on the creation of Japan instead of on the creation of the world?

3. Compare the status of the emperor in Confucianism and Shinto.

4. To what degree does the *Kojiki* reflect the traditional interpersonal customs of Japan?

5. How might the emperor's renunciation of divine standing have altered the reading of these texts and their influence in contemporary Japan?

SCRIPTURES IN FILM

The best recent film that portrays Japan's religion and culture is *The Last Samurai* (2003, rated R), directed by Edward Zwick. Tom Cruise plays an eighteenth-century American military adviser who, after he is captured in battle, embraces the samurai culture he was hired to destroy. The film begins with a brief retelling of the creation myth from the *Kojiki* and reflects its feeling for the land and peoples of Japan. The film also illustrates the Bushido code in action and the interplay between Buddhist tendencies to pacifism and traditional Shinto-samurai militancy.

SUGGESTIONS FOR FURTHER READING

W. G. Aston, *Nihongi: Chronicles of Japan from the Earliest Times to A.D. 697*. London: Kegan Paul, 1896.

B. H. Chamberlain, *Translation of Ko-ji-ki*. Tokyo: Asiatic Society of Japan, 1906; 2d ed., Kobe: Thompson, 1932. The standard translation of the *Kojiki*.

W. T. de Bary, *Sources of Japanese Tradition*. New York: Columbia University Press, 1958. Contains fresh translations of many important Shinto texts and a treatment of how early texts were used in Japanese history.

D. L. Philippi, *The Kojiki*. Princeton: Princeton University Press, 1969. Philippi's introduction and notes are full and helpful.

INDEX

(Note: boldface entries indicate pages where subjects are defined in a glossary section.)

CPSIA information can be obtained
at www.ICGtesting.com
Printed in the USA
FFHW01n1701120918
48333113-52154FF